RELIGIOUS IDENTITY IN LATE ANTIQUITY

Studies of religious interaction in the fourth century AD have often assumed that the categories of 'pagan', 'Christian' and 'Jew' can be straightforwardly applied, and that we can assess the extent of Christianization in the Graeco-Roman period. In contrast, Dr Sandwell tackles the fundamental question of attitudes to religious identity by exploring how the Christian preacher John Chrysostom and the Graeco-Roman orator Libanius wrote about and understood issues of religious allegiance. By comparing the approaches of these men, who were living and working in Antioch at approximately the same time, she strives to get inside the process of religious interaction in a way not normally possible due to the dominance of Christian sources. In so doing, she develops new approaches to the study of Libanius' religion, the impact of John Chrysostom's preaching on his audiences and the importance of religious identity to fourth-century individuals.

ISABELLA SANDWELL is Lecturer in Ancient History at the University of Bristol.

GREEK CULTURE IN THE ROMAN WORLD

Editors
SUSAN E. ALCOCK, University of Michigan
JAŚ ELSNER, Corpus Christi College, Oxford
SIMON GOLDHILL, University of Cambridge

The Greek culture of the Roman Empire offers a rich field of study. Extraordinary insights can be gained into processes of multicultural contact and exchange, political and ideological conflict, and the creativity of a changing, polyglot empire. During this period, many fundamental elements of Western society were being set in place: from the rise of Christianity, to an influential system of education, to long-lived artistic canons. This series is the first to focus on the response of Greek culture to its Roman imperial setting as a significant phenomenon in its own right. To this end, it will publish original and innovative research in the art, archaeology, epigraphy, history, philosophy, religion, and literature of the empire, with an emphasis on Greek material.

Titles in series:

Athletics and Literature in the Roman Empire
Jason König
Describing Greece: Landscape and Literature in the Periegesis *of Pausanias*
William Hutton
Reading the Self in the Ancient Greek Novel
Tim Whitmarsh
Image, Place and Power in the Roman Empire: Visual Replication and Urban Elites
Jennifer Trimble
The Making of Roman India
Grant Parker
Religious Identity in Late Antiquity: Greeks, Jews and Christians in Antioch
Isabella Sandwell

RELIGIOUS IDENTITY IN LATE ANTIQUITY

GREEKS, JEWS AND CHRISTIANS IN ANTIOCH

BY

ISABELLA SANDWELL

CAMBRIDGE UNIVERSITY PRESS
Cambridge, New York, Melbourne, Madrid, Cape Town,
Singapore, São Paulo, Delhi, Tokyo, Mexico City

Cambridge University Press
The Edinburgh Building, Cambridge CB2 8RU, UK

Published in the United States of America by Cambridge University Press, New York

www.cambridge.org
Information on this title: www.cambridge.org/9780521296915

© Isabella Sandwell 2007

This publication is in copyright. Subject to statutory exception
and to the provisions of relevant collective licensing agreements,
no reproduction of any part may take place without the written
permission of the copyright holder.

First published 2007
First paperback edition 2011

A catalogue record for this publication is available from the British Library

ISBN 978-0-521-87915-6 Hardback
ISBN 978-0-521-29691-5 Paperback

Cambridge University Press has no responsibility for the persistence or accuracy of URLs for external or third-party internet websites referred to in this publication, and does not guarantee that any content on such websites is, or will remain, accurate or appropriate.

But as for Christ you love him, you say, and adopt him as the guardian of your city instead of Zeus and the god of Daphne and Calliope.

(Julian, *Misopogon* 357c)

Contents

Preface	*page* ix
List of abbreviations	xi

PART I	INTRODUCTION	1
1	Understanding religious identity in fourth-century Antioch	3
2	Imperial society, religion and literary culture in fourth-century Antioch	34

PART II	CONSTRUCTED AND STRATEGIC RELIGIOUS IDENTITIES AND ALLEGIANCES	61
3	Chrysostom and the construction of religious identities	63
4	Libanius and the strategic use of religious allegiance	91

PART III	RELIGIOUS IDENTITIES AND OTHER FORMS OF SOCIAL IDENTIFICATION	121
5	Religious identity and other social identities in Chrysostom	125
6	Religious allegiance and other social identities in Libanius	154

PART IV	RELIGIOUS IDENTITY AND SOCIAL ORGANIZATION	181
7	Chrysostom and social structure among Christians in Antioch	185
8	Libanius, religious allegiance and social structure	213

PART V ASSESSING THE IMPACT OF CONSTRUCTIONS OF IDENTITY	241
9 Religious identity, religious practice and personal religious power	245
10 Conclusion	277
Bibliography	282
Index	308

Preface

This book started out as a PhD thesis completed at University College London in 2001. The original intention of that PhD was to produce a new approach to understanding religious interaction in the fourth century AD by exploring the writings of Libanius and Chrysostom alongside one another. I hoped to gain access to processes of religious interaction in a way that is not usually possible for the ancient world by taking advantage of the fact that these two authors, from different religious traditions, were working and writing in the city of Antioch almost contemporaneously. The original project did not get as close to achieving this goal as I would have liked. Four years of post-graduate study was barely enough time to get to grips with the massive body of material provided by Libanius and Chrysostom, let alone to develop a new theoretical model for understanding what their writings tell us about religious interaction. When I began to think about turning the PhD into a publishable book, it very quickly became clear that a lot more work was needed in order to make my study match the claims I was making for it. Over the last two years I have been engaged in this work and have tried to develop a strong theoretical grounding for ideas that previously had only embryonic form. The choice to alternate chapters on Libanius and John Chrysostom has remained, and chapters 5 and 6 in the current book bear quite a strong resemblance to chapters 1 and 2 in the original PhD. Otherwise, the current book is quite distinct from the PhD and has involved a complete reformulation of my arguments. In particular, my approach to how we use Libanius' writings on religion is now more sophisticated, as is my approach to issues of religious identity.

The completion of the book would not have been possible without the help of numerous individuals. Primarily, I am indebted to John North who has been with the project from the start as my PhD supervisor. Since the completion of the PhD he has continued to read drafts and offer invaluable advice and has been a constant source of encouragement. His approach to the study of ancient religion has had a massive impact on my thinking, often in ways that I do not even recognize at first, as has the example he has set that understanding the 'big picture' is always important. Another person who has been with the project from an early stage, and to whom I am greatly indebted, is Wendy Mayer. As a reader for an earlier, potential publisher, she read the original PhD. Since then, as a reader for Cambridge University Press, she has given detailed attention to numerous drafts and has played a crucial role in shaping the final form that it has taken. Her positive attitude towards my work as well as her expertise in the study of John Chrysostom have been invaluable. I must also thank Wendy Mayer for her less formal assistance in numerous email correspondences and for being a centre point around whom those interested in John Chrysostom have gathered. In the final months of completing this book Gillian Clark's comments and advice on drafts have also been invaluable. Her detailed corrections of my work and her breadth of knowledge of the late-antique world have been of the greatest assistance. I could not have asked for a better colleague during the final stages of writing this book. Two anonymous readers for Cambridge University Press have also read drafts. I must thank them for helping me to realize when I was not arguing the points that I thought I was arguing and for enabling me to see which aspects of my thinking were useful and important, and which confusing and superfluous. Without their comments and criticisms, this work would have taken much longer to reach its final state. Other people I must thank for practical help or general words of encouragement over the years of writing the PhD and the book are Richard Alston, Peter Brown, Peter Heather, Janet Huskinson, Wolf Liebeschuetz, Pierre-Louis Malosse, Stephen Mitchell, Charlotte Roueché and Charles Stewart. Elizabeth Burr, Jaclyn Maxwell, Alberto J. Quiroga Puertas and Silke Trzcionka have sent to me, or helped me to find, their unpublished works on John Chrysostom and Libanius. Thanks are also due to the Norman family for allowing me to see copies of A. F. Norman's unpublished translations of Libanius' orations and to Mary Whitby for helping me to obtain them. Friends and colleagues who have provided listening ears over coffees, lunches, drinks and emails include Céline Marquaille, Christy Constantakopoulou, Fiona Haarer, Riet van Bremen, Rebecca Flemming, Rachel Aucott and all my colleagues in the Department of Classics and Ancient History at the University of Bristol. Finally, I must thank Danny Penman and my family for putting up with the fact that I have devoted every spare minute of the last two years to completing this book.

Abbreviations

ACM	*Ancient Christian Magic, Coptic Texts of Ritual Power*, ed. M. Meyer, Princeton, 1999
CPG	*Clavis Patrum Graecorum*, vols. I–IV, by M. Geerard, Turnhout, 1974–83; (suppl.) M. Geerard and J. Noret, Turnhout, 1998
CTh	*Codex Theodosianus*
EEC	*Encyclopedia of Early Christianity*, ed. E. Ferguson *et al.*, New York, 1990
LRE	*The Later Roman Empire AD 284–602: a Social and Economic Survey*, by A. H. M. Jones, Oxford, 1964
PG	*Patrologia Graeca (Patrologiae cursus completus, series Graeca)*, ed. J.-P. Migne, Paris, 1860–94
PGM	*Papyri Graecae Magicae*, trans. K. Preisendanz *et al.*, Teubner edition, Leipzig, 1928–31
PL	*Patrologia Latina (Patrologiae cursus completus, series Latina)*, ed. J.-P. Migne, Paris, 1844–65
PLRE	*The Prosopography of the Later Roman Empire*, vol. I: AD 260–395, ed. A. H. M. Jones, J. R. Martindale and J. Morris, London, 1971
SC	*Sources chrétiennes*

Abbreviations of ancient texts are taken from the *Greek–English Lexicon* (LSJ), the *Oxford Latin Dictionary* and the *Greek Patristic Lexicon*. The exceptions to this are the abbreviations of the works of John Chrysostom which are listed below.

Ad Illum. Catech.	*Catecheses ad Illuminandos*
Adv. Eos.	*Adversus Eos qui apud se habent subintroductas virgines*
Adv. Jud.	*Adversus Judaeos*

Adv. Oppug.	Adversus Oppugnatores vitae monasticae
Contra Jud. et Gent.	Contra Judaeos et Gentiles, quod Christus sit deus
De Bapt. Christi	De Baptismo Christi
De Diab. Tent. Hom.	De Diabolo Tentatore
De Incomp. Dei Nat.	De Incomprehensibili Dei Natura
De Sac.	De Sacerdotio
De S. Bab. Contra Jul. et Gent.	De Sancto Babyla, Contra Julianum et Gentiles
Hom. in Act.	Homiliae in Acta Apostolorum
Hom. in Egyp. Mart.	In Martyres Aegyptios
Hom. in Gen.	Homiliae in Genesin
Hom. in Mart.	Homilia in Martyres
Hom. in Matt.	Homiliae in Matthaeum
Hom. de S. Bab.	De Sancto Hieromartyre Babyla
Hom. de S. Phil.	Homilia de Sancto Philogonio
Hom. de Stat.	Homiliae de Statuis ad populum Antiochenum habitae
In Cap. ad Galat. Comment.	Commentarius in Epistolam ad Galatas
In Ep. ad Coloss. Hom.	In Epistolam ad Colossenses
In Ep. ad 1 Cor. Hom.	In Epistolam Primam ad Corinthios
In Ep. ad 2 Cor. Hom.	In Epistolam Secundam ad Corinthios
In Ep. ad Ephes. Hom.	In Epistolam ad Ephesios
In Ep. ad Heb. Hom.	In Epistolam ad Hebraeos
In Ep. ad Philip. Hom.	In Epistolam ad Philippenses
In Ep. ad Rom. Hom.	In Epistolam ad Romanos
In Ep. ad 1 Thess. Hom.	In Epistolam Primam ad Thessalonicenses
In Ep. ad 2 Thess. Hom.	In Epistolam Secundam ad Thessalonicenses
In Ep. ad 1 Tim. Hom.	In Epistolam Primam ad Timotheum
In Ep. ad 2 Tim. Hom.	In Epistolam Secundam ad Timotheum
In Ep. ad Titus Hom.	In Epistolam ad Titum
In Kal.	In Kalendas
In Princ. Act.	In Principium Actorum
In S. Ignat. Mart.	In Sanctum Ignatium Martyrem
In S. Jul. Mart.	In Sanctum Julianum Martyrem
In S. Rom. Mart.	In Sanctum Romanum

PART I

Introduction

CHAPTER I

Understanding religious identity in fourth-century Antioch

IDENTITY AND RELIGIOUS INTERACTION IN ANTIOCH

I hate and I turn away from such a woman for this reason above all others, because she uses the name of God as an insult and because, while she says she is a Christian, she displays the actions of a Greek.
(John Chrysostom, *Ad Illum. Catech.* 2.5 (*PG* 49.240) = Harkins, *Baptismal Instruction* 12.59)[1]

By the gods, whom you have admired for a long time and now admit to, exceed Hyperchius' own father's goodwill towards him and imitate my own.
(Libanius, *Ep.* B.74.5 (F.804))[2]

The question of religious identity lies at the heart of understanding religious interaction. Talking about religious interaction means first saying something about the religious entities that we see to be taking part in that interaction. As Markus noted long ago, rather than try to assess how Christianized fourth-century society was, we need to 'set ourselves the task of tracing the shifting boundaries drawn by late antique people which determined how far their society measured up to what they saw as properly Christianised society'.[3] At the same time, because what it means to be the member of one religion can only be constructed in relation to what it means to be a member of another religion, religious interaction is always a

---

[1] Where possible I have used modern editions of the text of John Chrysostom's writings, usually in the Sources chrétiennes series. Otherwise, I have used the text reproduced in Migne's *Patrologia Graeca*.
[2] Throughout this work, I have used Foerster's text of Libanius' writings (F.). When I have mentioned a letter for which there is a translation into English by Norman or Bradbury I have marked it with N. or B. respectively. Both these translations and existing translations of Chrysostom's work have been very useful in making my own translations. In this current work, however, all translations of more than a few words are my own, except occasional examples where I adapt those found in the Nicene & Post-Nicene Fathers and the Fathers of the Church series.
[3] Markus 1990: 8.

prerequisite for the existence of religious identities.[4] Religious identities do not have an objective existence that naturally arises out of an essential and distinct package of religious traits. Rather, they result from boundaries that are constructed by human actors, who choose to identify themselves with some people and differentiate themselves from others.[5] Understanding religious interaction thus also means understanding the complex processes by which religious identities, religious boundaries and religious differences were constructed where they did not automatically exist. In fact, the assumption that everyone in late-antique society even thought in terms of religious identities must itself be scrutinized. Some late-antique people might not have chosen to see religious interaction as interaction between two mutually opposed and strongly bounded entities. Instead, they might have played up the similarities across religious boundaries, emphasized areas of compromise and allowed people to switch easily between religious allegiances. This means that we need to think about religious interaction in late antiquity not simply in terms of how people defined what it meant to be Christian or an adherent of Graeco-Roman religion. We also need to think of it in terms of how far late-antique individuals wanted to work with permanent religious identities in the first place. In exploring religious interaction in fourth-century Antioch I shall thus avoid a descriptive approach that seeks to measure how far Antioch was or was not Christianized, as scholars have usually done in the past, implicitly at least.[6] Instead, I shall seek to understand how people in the city might have defined religious identity and whether they even thought in terms of clear-cut religious identities. To do this I shall turn to the works of the Christian preacher John Chrysostom and the teacher and orator Libanius, who both lived and worked in Antioch in the mid to late fourth century.

John Chrysostom was a priest and preacher in the city of Antioch between 386 and 397. He used his many writings to outline what it meant to be truly Christian and to present an ideal image of strong Christian identity. In the passage quoted at the head of this chapter we see Chrysostom directly contrasting a woman's claim to be Christian with what he considered to be her 'Greek' behaviour in using amulets. Chrysostom's concern here was

---

[4] Throughout this work I shall be using the term 'identity' in the constructionist and relational model as used by social theorists following Frederick Barth.
[5] Barth 1969: 14 and Jenkins 2003: 4. On the construction of similarity within groups, see Jenkins 2003 80, 90 and 104–19 and Cohen 1985.
[6] See Soler 1999: 15–27. Soler's 1999 PhD dissertation was published as a book in the final stages of writing this current work so my references throughout this work are to the original dissertation. Even the original came into my hands only at a late stage and I was not able to incorporate it as fully as I would have liked.

primarily to clarify one aspect of Christian identity – Christians should not use amulets – but he could only do so by making a contrast with Greekness in his definition of the use of amulets as Greek. This is because constructions of identity must always be relational, in that they are constructed from the marking out of differences from others.[7] Neither Christian nor Greek nor Jewish identity existed essentially or objectively in Chrysostom's world. Rather, Chrysostom continually had to construct them out of a situation where many practices were shared by people whatever their religious allegiance. In this, Chrysostom was following a long Christian tradition of constructing Christian identity. As Lieu has shown, Christian writers constructed 'Christianity' from a direct contrast with 'Judaism' and 'paganism', despite the many similarities shared between the religions.[8] They sought, as Boyarin has pointed out, to 'eradicate the fuzziness of borders, semantic and social, between Jews and Christians and thus produce Judaism and Christianity as fully separate (and opposed) entities . . .'[9] Making strong assertions of religious identity was Christianity's way of bringing itself into existence, and Christians had to work at this continually. In the second century AD the North African Christian Tertullian was still struggling with this problem, as the earliest Christians had done. In his treatise *On Idolatry* we see him asserting appropriate Christian behaviour through comparison with what he defined as idolatry or the behaviour of Gentiles. He argues that the 'servants of the god' or the faithful (*fideles*) should not share in any of the 'dress', 'food', 'rejoicings', or any other aspect of life of the 'Gentiles (*nationes*)' (Tertullian, *De Idolatria* 13.1).[10] Christian authors after Tertullian continued to have to deal with these problems. Each Christian leader or writer might use different characteristics to define what it meant to be Christian or Jewish, but they were all concerned with this differentiation and consistently sought to maintain the boundary between Christianity and other religions over time.[11]

What was new in the fourth century was the scale on which these ideas about Christian self-definition could be propagated. The much larger audiences that filled the new basilica-style churches from the time of Constantine onwards opened the Christian message to a mass-market. This meant that questions about Christian identity, which before had been confined to smaller, more exclusive groups, were now becoming more and more central to social life. The increased centrality of Christianity to Roman society

---

[7] Barth 1969: 14. See also Jenkins 2003: 93 and Eriksen 1993: 38.   [8] Lieu 2004.
[9] Boyarin 2004: 2 and also 1–33. On early imperial Antioch, see Zetterholm 2003: 53–74.
[10] The whole work is full of comparisons between heathen and Christian behaviour.
[11] Lieu 2004: 62–146.

in turn made questions of religious identity more pertinent to Christian leaders than they had ever been.[12] Precisely because Christians were losing their position as a persecuted minority, excluded from mainstream society, they had to work harder to define what it meant to be Christian. It is in these terms that we must see Chrysostom's attempts to outline what it meant to be Christian in opposition to Greekness: he was attempting to construct a distinct Christian identity in a situation that challenged such a construction. Despite years of Christian attempts to assert such categories, Chrysostom had to continually define and reinforce his own particular versions of them. As external observers, *we* can see that Chrysostom had to construct Christian and Greek identities where they did not objectively exist. However, it is clear that *he* saw both being Christian and being Greek as fixed identities. It is also clear that he saw religious interaction as interaction between fixed and clear-cut identities. For Chrysostom, people had to choose whether they were a Christian or a Greek and there was to be no space for ambiguity between the two because religious identity had to be displayed visibly in every action at all times.

The Libanius quotation given at the head of this chapter reveals a very different approach to issues of religious identity and religious allegiance. Libanius was an orator and teacher in Antioch between 354 and the early 390s. He was clearly an adherent of traditional Graeco-Roman religion, but his approach to this religious allegiance and to religious issues generally was very different from that of John Chrysostom. References to religion and religious allegiance appear far less frequently in Libanius' writings than they do in Chrysostom's writings. When they do appear, they rarely have as their goal the construction of religious identities. In the letter quoted above, we see Libanius writing to his friend Modestus 2 soon after Modestus had been appointed prefect of Constantinople by the emperor Julian.[13] The main purpose of this letter was for Libanius to express his delight that Modestus was planning to help an ex-pupil of his, Hyperchius, become a senator in Constantinople (something in which Hyperchius eventually failed). It is only at the very end of the letter and almost in passing that we see any mention of Modestus' religion. We see Libanius referring to the change of religious allegiance that Modestus had undergone between the reigns of Constantius and Julian: once Julian had come to power, Modestus was able

---

[12] Markus 1990: 27–44.
[13] On their friendship, see *Ep.* B.61 (F.583 of 358). Where numbers appear after a name in this fashion, they refer first to Jones's numbering in *The Prosopography of the Later Roman Empire* and second to Petit's numbering in his *Les fonctionnaires dans L'œuvre de Libanius: analyse prosopographique*. Where there is only one number, this will refer to *PLRE*.

to 'admit to' or 'confess' the gods that he had only been able to 'admire' in private in the reign of Constantius. This brief reference shows that Libanius was concerned, to some degree at least, with the religious allegiance of individuals and that he saw it as something worth mentioning. Living in the fourth century, he could not help being aware that there were now different religious options open to people, and different gods that they could worship. The attempts by Christian leaders to impose distinct religious categories on social life had had some impact on society, and Libanius must have been aware that different emperors could hold different religious allegiances. The whole question of religious differentiation and categorization must thus have become relevant for Libanius in a way that it had not been for adherents of Graeco-Roman religion in earlier centuries.[14] But he refers to religious allegiance rather differently, much more obliquely than the Chrysostom passage: he does not say that Modestus had once been 'Christian' but under Julian had become 'pagan' or 'Greek', as Chrysostom might have done. Instead, he uses the more vague way of referring to the situation as a shift from admiring the gods in private to admitting them openly. Libanius also does not see the discrepancy between what Modestus truly felt religiously and his outward appearance under Constantius as evidence of his failure to live up to a distinct religious identity, as Chrysostom would do. The reason for these differences is that Libanius mentions religious allegiance not to construct an ideal religious identity but in order to make a specific point. To see this we have to understand the context of the letter to Modestus a little better.

Modestus had been 'count of the east' (*comes orientis*) under Constantius (358–62) but continued to be favoured by Julian and was made prefect of Constantinople by him when he became emperor. Libanius sent the letter under discussion to Modestus in Constantinople in the winter of 362/3, soon after he had taken up this position of prefect. In this context of the changeover from a Christian emperor to one who adhered to Graeco-Roman religion, we can see why it might suddenly become relevant to refer to Modestus' religious allegiance. Modestus' high position under Constantius and the fact that he had not been able to admit his admiration of the gods during this time might have put his loyalty to Julian and his religious policies into question, at least among some supporters of the new emperor. The reference to Modestus as someone who had always admired the gods, even under Constantius, could be used to counteract these doubts. It was a way to imply Modestus' credentials as a worshipper

---

[14] North 2005: 137.

of the gods and to recommend him to the supporters of Julian who were based in Constantinople. As it was common in antiquity for people to read letters aloud or to pass them on to others, Modestus could use this letter from Libanius as a way to silence doubts that people might have had about his religious loyalties. In referring to Modestus' religious allegiance in this way, Libanius was not trying to define what it meant to be a worshipper of the gods or to make a permanent statement about Modestus' religious identity. Rather, he was using the reference in a practical sense in order to achieve a specific purpose and to make a specific point about Modestus (and I paraphrase): 'Modestus may have looked like a Christian under Constantius but he is really one of us.' What is clear from this example is that Libanius himself was much less interested than Chrysostom in creating permanent religious identities. Instead, his use of references to religious allegiance to make a point is more akin to the modern ideas about identity as something that can be constructed. In such a model, individuals can choose or change social identities in order to gain the best material outcome for themselves.[15] Religious identity is something that can be suppressed or expressed, depending on whether it is stigmatized, useful, or meaningful to do so at a particular time.[16] What we can thus suggest is that Libanius, in comparison to Chrysostom, did not see religious interaction in terms of interaction between well-defined religious identities. Rather, he allowed people a more flexible approach to religious interaction in which they could play down their religious allegiance in certain circumstances in order to ease relations with others and then emphasize it again when it was useful or necessary to do so.

The very differences between Libanius' and Chrysostom's approaches to religious identity and religious allegiance are what make them so useful. If we look at Chrysostom's writings, we see a world in which issues of religious identity were of the greatest importance and in which he wanted religious interaction to be between a number of distinct and clearly defined religious identities. If we focus only on his writings, we would go away with a one-sided view of the religious situation. As Markus points out in his seminal 1990 work, *The End of Ancient Christianity*, 'the image of society neatly divided into "Christian" and "pagan" is the creation of late fourth-century Christians, and has been too readily taken at face-value by modern historians'.[17] In fact, constructions of identity rarely reflect the situation on the ground. As Erikson puts it, 'empirically, social identities

---

[15] Barth 1969: 24–6; S. Jones 1997: 72–4; Eriksen 1993: 45–6.
[16] S. Jones 1997: 76.   [17] Markus 1990: 28.

appear fluid, negotiable, situational and analogic (or gradualist)'.[18] In actual existence people could hold a religious identity to some degree, almost completely, or very little. They might lay claim to two or more social identities simultaneously and so hold multiple or overlapping identities.[19] We thus need to question how far Chrysostom's categorization of the world into clear-cut religious identities translated into the practice of individuals. Attempts at boundary construction are often found in situations where individuals continue to interact across those boundaries and we need to recognize the significance of this.[20] As Lieu says, 'the rhetoric of difference should not blind us to the threads of continuity . . . the challenges of the ambiguities of actual living'.[21] We need to be able to understand that Chrysostom's audiences may have been acting in very different ways to those outlined in his preaching. While calling themselves Christian they may not have defined this as strictly as Chrysostom did and may not have seen it as exclusive of the same behaviours as he did. It is for this reason that it is so important to look at Libanius' writings in conjunction with the preaching of Chrysostom.

Libanius shows us someone making use of notions of religious allegiance and labelling in a more practical and less ideal way. Studying Libanius' approach to religious allegiance alongside Chrysostom's approach will give us a more subtle picture of the religious situation of the fourth century, one that does not have to rely on a notion of clear-cut identities interacting with each other. It allows us to see the same religious situation from two very different points of view and to understand the different models of religious interaction that were circulating within fourth-century society. What might have been taking place was interaction between different approaches to religious identity and religious allegiance. On the one side were those who sought to construct religious identities as distinct and fixed. This included Christian preachers such as Chrysostom but also the emperor Julian who, during his brief reign, sought continually to make people decide on their religious identity. On the other side we see those who accepted the importance of religious allegiance in the fourth century, but used it in looser and more practical ways. This included men such as Libanius and Themistius but also, I would like to suggest, the majority of ordinary people in fourth-century society and even perhaps large sections of John Chrysostom's audiences. While the voice of the former group might appear stronger due to the number of surviving Christian texts, I shall argue that it

---

[18] Eriksen 1993: 158. [19] Eriksen 1993: 66–7, 154 and 156–8.
[20] Barth 1969; Eriksen 1993: 11–12 and 37–8; Jenkins 2003: 92–3. [21] Lieu 2004: 177.

is actually the voice of the latter that we should favour. This new approach allows us to revise how we think about processes of Christianization. Rather than measure how far the fourth century was becoming Christian, we can ask what impact Christian ideas about the importance of religious identities had on society. We can ask which approach to religious allegiance was more representative: that seen in Chrysostom's sermons or that exemplified by Libanius' writings. We can also assess how far we see religious interaction in the fourth century in terms of conflict between religious identities, as Chrysostom would have it, or in terms of coexistence between people who were very often willing to play down religious differences, as Libanius presents the situation.

There is just one last problem that I need to raise: the terminology to use to describe the different religious allegiances that we see in the fourth century. Historians have long been dissatisfied with simply adopting the term 'pagan', because it is a Christian category that flattens out the diversity of religious experience of those in the Graeco-Roman world.[22] However, they have also had to acknowledge that we do need terminology if we are to talk about the religious situation.[23] Some scholars have thus sought to develop alternatives to the term 'pagan', such as 'polytheist',[24] while others have continued to rely on 'pagan' because they feel we have no viable alternatives.[25] I myself do not find 'polytheist' a useful replacement as it implies a stark contrast with Christianity, namely that all Christians are monotheists while all non-Judaeo-Christians worship many gods, which is questionable.[26] I do have some sympathy with those who use the term 'pagan' and can see that on many occasions it is the best shorthand for all those who did not adhere to Judaism or Christianity in some form. However, in the context of the current work I shall avoid it because it does suggest a Christian view that the world is permanently drawn into distinct, all-defining religious identities. Because I am taking a constructionist approach to religious identity, I would also like to give some sense, at least, of how people at the time were talking about these issues, rather than simply to find terms that are convenient for me to use. Thus, when talking about Chrysostom's writings, I shall use his label of 'Greek' to describe those who were not Jews or Christians. When referring to Libanius' writings, the situation is not so easily resolved as he does not have a simple set of vocabulary for those who share his own religious allegiance, as we shall see in chapter 4. The

---

[22] North 2005: 127–8.
[23] Fowden 1991: 119 and 1993, 44 and 100; Trombley 1994: ix–x; and Ando 1996: 171–207.
[24] Fowden 1993: 44 and 100.   [25] Ando 1996: 175–6. See also North 2005: 127.
[26] North 2005: 135–6.

wide range of terminology that he uses to refer to those who worshipped the Graeco-Roman gods would make for some very unwieldy sentences. When discussing Libanius' writings I shall thus use the terms 'adherent of Graeco-Roman religion' or 'of traditional religion' (or similar phrases) as shorthand for his terminology. Although this is no more ideal than any other solution to the problem of terminology and will probably at times sound a little clumsy, it does at least constantly remind us that there is a problem and that it needs to be thought about.

Generally, problematization of the term 'Christian' is less common than that of the term 'pagan'. 'Christian' is easier to accept because Christians themselves used it as a self-referential term. I will use it in the chapters on Libanius, even though Libanius does not use it himself. However, I do need to acknowledge that it flattens the variety that can be seen in fourth-century Christianity and that in using it I will often only be referring to the branch of Nicene Christianity represented by Chrysostom. I shall also use the term 'Jew' throughout. This is probably the least problematic of the labels for religious allegiance, although again we need to be aware that there were many different kinds of Jews and that there are problems about whether the label is purely a religious one.

In order to understand the different approaches to religious allegiance exemplified in Chrysostom and Libanius we need to devote some time to exploring how they wrote about religion. *How* each wrote about religion and *what* each wrote were intimately connected and we need to gain a better understanding of this relationship. This will provide a stronger basis on which to decide whose approach to religious allegiance was more successful and more representative in the fourth century: that of John Chrysostom or that of Libanius.

CHRYSOSTOM AND PREACHING AS DISCOURSE AND IDEOLOGY

One of the primary purposes of Chrysostom's sermons was to construct and re-emphasize the defining features of Christian identity. Through his preaching he educated his audience about what it meant to be Christian and imposed on them Christian ways of thinking about the world. This was the case whether he was giving exegesis of the writings of Saint Paul or the Old Testament, trying to shape his audience's moral values or trying to convince them of theological points. When Chrysostom preached about the appropriate gender relations for Christians, or about proper attitudes to self-display and ostentation he was ultimately laying down guidelines for what it meant to be truly Christian, as he saw it.[27] Even the form of biblical exegesis used by Chrysostom can be seen as constitutive of Christian identity. It helped to determine how Christians should envisage God's action on earth and so the moral behaviour appropriate for them.[28] Chrysostom's concern with constructing Christian identity can also be seen more explicitly. He tells us that he wanted his preaching to be used by his audiences to help them to 'build a rampart . . . on every side' and carry around with them a perpetual 'armour' against the non-Christian world (*Catéchèse* 8.25 (SC 50.260) and *Hom. in Gen.* 4.4 (*PG* 53.40)).[29] His interest in boundaries inevitably led him to be concerned with those who lay outside Christianity. Just as Chrysostom was in the process of maintaining Christian identity and constructing his own version of it, so he also had to define what it meant to be a Greek and a Jew. He used his writings, and the constant rhetorical opposition of Christian with Jew and Greek, in order to make these categories real for his audiences. Speaking and writing were absolutely crucial to his goal of constructing a distinct Christian identity. Christianity had a special relationship with texts and writing and these media were central to the growth and spread of Christianity. From the time of Christianity's emergence as a sect within Judaism sacred texts were essential to its existence. Scripture was the word of God and the Apostles too were thought to be divinely inspired in their written records of the life of Jesus Christ, himself the Word made flesh.[30] In later years exegesis of the Gospels and of the writings of Paul proliferated, as did a whole host of writings defending the faith and representing its central message to both insiders and outsiders. This included treatises, letters, accounts of Christian martyrdoms and dialogues with non-Christians. All this literary output meant that Christianity was particularly good at representing its religious view to outsiders. It was constantly seeking to say 'this is what Christianity is' and 'this is why you should be Christian'. Religion and writing were thus inseparable for Christianity. As Lieu puts it: 'it was through her [Christianity's] remarkable literary creativity and productivity that a multi-faceted self-conscious identity was produced: in the words of Averil Cameron "But if ever there was a case of the construction of reality through text, such a case is provided by early Christianity."'[31]

The understanding of the ability of Christianity 'to construct reality through text' results from the constructive and creative power that is

---

[27] For example, Hartney 2004 and Leyerle 2001.   [28] Amirav 2003, especially 23–4.
[29] See also *In Ep. ad 1 Cor. Hom.* 16.1 (*PG* 61.129–30).
[30] Bowman and Wolff 1994: 12 and Cameron 1991: 6.
[31] Lieu 2004: 8, quoting Cameron 1991: 21. See also Perkins 1995: 1–14.

attributed to discourse in modern thought. In discourse theory, texts are no longer seen as simply descriptive or reflective of society. Collections of texts are said to constitute discourses which are able to create what could 'be seen, heard, spoken, thought, believed and valued – in other words what counts as the socially made reality'.[32] According to this view, Christian texts can be seen as discourse that, through its formulation of categories and ideas of selfhood, constructed the ways in which individuals 'came to understand themselves' and 'their roles in the world'.[33] Brown has shown how Christianity constructed the 'poor' as a significant category in late-antique society.[34] Perkins has argued that certain Christian (as well as non-Christian) texts constructed the category of the 'suffering self' as a useful and dominant means of self-understanding in the second and third centuries.[35] We can add to this the argument that Christian discourse also sought to construct the most important self-understanding of all: that of being Christian rather than Greek or Jew. These categories and ways of thinking about the self had not been prominent in the ancient world, so Christian texts had to make them so. Texts and discourse are particularly suited to constructing identities because of their use of clear-cut categories and contrasting oppositions to create meaning and give structure. Texts have an inherent drive to mark out the similarities and the differences that we saw to be so essential for the construction of social identity. This can be described as the 'textuality of identity'; 'the way texts construct identity through their poetics'.[36] By continually referring to the categories 'Christian', 'Jew' and 'Greek' in his writings Chrysostom was seeking to create for his audiences what could 'be seen, heard, spoken, thought, believed and valued'. Through these continual processes of education and exhortation he was trying to transform not only what his audiences knew about Christianity, but also how those in his audience saw themselves and how they related to others. Thus Chrysostom sought to change his audiences' *perception* of reality and so the way they lived in reality.

While it might be easy to accept that Christian texts sought to construct identities, assessing the impact of texts on how people actually lived is more difficult and is now the subject of some debate. For many scholars the creative power of Christian texts and Christian discourse meant that they played a central role in religious change and in the transformation of the behaviour of individuals. Averil Cameron argues that 'to deny the

---

[32] Hennessy 1993: 75.   [33] Perkins 1995: 3. See also Foucault 1984a: 11.
[34] Brown 1992 and Perkins 1995: 10–11.   [35] Perkins 1995.
[36] Lieu 2004: 27. See also Hall 2002: 19 and 23–4.

importance of Christian ideas altogether seems paradoxical' because otherwise we cannot account for the fact 'that [Christianity] did in fact establish itself in the hearts and minds of people'.[37] She states that it was through the written word that Christianity achieved this because it was through texts that people first became aware of the new religion and were attracted to its message.[38] Others have argued that it was reading Christian texts that led to the formation of the first Christian communities. Those following Stock's model of the 'textual community', originally developed to describe certain forms of medieval Christianity, see early Christian groups as arising 'somewhere in the interstices between the imposition of the written word and the articulation of a certain type of social organization'.[39] A 'process' of education from a text is said to have induced a permanent change in those being educated so that they develop an institutional structure that has the ability to perpetuate itself.[40] Philip Rousseau in *The Early Christian Centuries* exemplifies this approach; he focuses on the way that processes of reading, learning and education from specific texts among early Christians created 'textual' or 'learning' and 'reading communities'.[41] The same kinds of arguments have been played out in relation to the more specific question of the impact of Christian preaching on ancient society. Rousseau's views on the impact of preaching coincide with his views on the importance of textual and verbal processes in the transmission of the Christian message. The emphasis he places on teaching, learning and reading in processes of conversion means that he sees the impact of preaching in very positive terms. He argues that sermons would have been delivered in a fairly simple style and would have been understood by all, whatever their educational background.[42] Others have noted that ordinary people and not just the elite had a real taste for rhetorical display at the time and that it was precisely the skill of Christian preachers in using rhetoric that made their sermons so appealing to all.[43] In recent years this positive view has probably become dominant as people have sought to make sermons, especially those of John Chrysostom, accessible to historians and to see them as sources of information for the beliefs and practices of their audiences, as well as of those who wrote them.[44] The focus has been on how far people listened to sermons, what social background they were from and how far they understood

---

[37] Cameron 1991: 22 and 27.   [38] Cameron 1991: 39 and Perkins 1995: 9.
[39] Stock 1983 and 1990: 150.   [40] Stock 1990: 150.   [41] Rousseau 2002: 56. See also Lieu 2004: 28.
[42] Rousseau 2002: 391–400. See also Cunningham 1990; Wilken 1983: 105; Mayer and Allen 1993: 263–4; Kennedy 1983: 250; and Mayer 2000. In contrast, see E. G. Clark 2001 and 2004: 86–9.
[43] Auerbach 1965: 53, 56, 57 and 240; Gamble 1995: 8 and 18. See also, Roueché 1984: 182 and 188–90 and Liebeschuetz 1972: 21, referring to Seeck 1920: 84–101.
[44] Hartney has emphasized this positive view most recently (2004: 33–52, especially 33–7).

preaching. The assumption is that once sermons had been understood a straightforward process of education ensued that eventually changed the individual's behaviour and reorientated them socially.[45]

Others, in contrast, have questioned the role of Christian discourse in processes of Christianization and its success in changing the practice of individuals. MacMullen argues that Christianity did not have a great impact on the Roman world and did not change the lives of individuals very much.[46] He denies Christian discourse – and by this he means Christian theology, morality and cosmology as expressed in the spoken and written word – a formative role and argues that we need instead to look at 'Christians not just talking but doing'.[47] According to MacMullen, in contrast to Cameron, conversions to Christianity happened not because people heard and were impressed by Christian ideas but rather because they were impressed by Christian performances of power such as miracles and spiritual healing. As a result, for MacMullen, conversion to Christianity entailed only an acceptance of the minimum requirement that God and Jesus were the ultimate source of power and that not much really changed in the *practice* of the converts.[48] MacMullen has a negative view of the impact of preaching just as he argues more generally that Christian ideas had little impact on the practice of converts. He argues that sermons would have been rhetorical and literary in nature and not understood by the majority of ordinary listeners, so would have made little difference to their practice.[49] The extent of the impact that Christian preaching had on the world, as with any other aspect of Christian discourse, is thus still open to debate.

The assumption that understanding Chrysostom's preaching would automatically have led individuals to adopt the ways of thinking and behaving outlined in that message is rather mechanistic. In the first place, the regularity with which individuals attended Chrysostom's preaching is unclear.[50] What individuals then did with the teachings that they did attend is, in turn, not a simple question to answer. They may have understood and disagreed with what they heard, or understood and chosen to ignore it or they may have reacted in more complex ways. We can, for example, ask how far Chrysostom's audiences were attending sermons with the intention of learning at all. At various points in his sermons Chrysostom suggests that

---

[45] Maxwell has recently tried to push this approach further (Maxwell forthcoming: chapter 4 'Teaching to the converted').
[46] See MacMullen 1984: 20–1 and 1986: 322–43.
[47] MacMullen 1986: 324. It is views such as these that Averil Cameron was responding to when she reasserted the role of texts in Christianity's growth.
[48] MacMullen 1983: 174–92.   [49] MacMullen 1966: 108–12 and 1989: 503–11.
[50] This will be discussed further in chapter 7.

it was the rhetorical display, rather than the content of the sermon, or the religious occasion that his audience were interested in. On a number of occasions he has to berate groups in his audience for missing the ritual of the Eucharist because they left church immediately after the sermon (*In Ep. ad 1 Thess. Hom.* 4 (*PG* 62.422.19–21 and 25–8) and *In Ep. ad. 2 Thess. Hom.* 3 (*PG* 62.484.32–59)).[51] He also often complains that preachers feel the need to impress their public with their rhetorical display as much as to educate them (*De Prophetiarum Obscuritate* 1 (*PG* 56.165)) and *De Incomp. Dei Nat.* 1.334–8 (SC 28.130).[52] His own audience also treated him like a sophist and acted 'like spectators sitting in judgement' on his speaking (*De Sac.* 5.1 (SC 272.283)).[53] It is wrong simply to assume that Chrysostom's audiences would have been attending his sermons as if they were pupils ready to learn and to adjust their behaviour according to what he said. Their disposition towards the spoken word might have been quite different.

What we need is a more sophisticated model for understanding how text relates to practice than the 'discourse' model allows. We need to find a way to account for the tension between the desires of Christian leaders and the responses of their audiences. The suggestion that Christian texts created new ways of being for people freely and innocently ignores the role of power in such processes. When Christian leaders wrote and spoke they did not just offer new ways of being to their audiences; they sought to impose these new ways of being on people and to prohibit the old ways of living. They sought to reformulate the rules by which people lived by laying down new regulations and by dictating to people what they could and could not do. Much of this rule-giving was concerned with setting out what it meant to be a true Christian, while also giving guidance as to which practices were to be considered non-Christian. Before the fourth century Christian writers and teachers were in a position to impose their guidelines and regulations on only a relatively small group of people – those who chose to become converts or who had enough interest in Christianity to read its literature.[54] After the reign of Constantine this situation changed. Now Christianity was not only able to preach its messages and its new rules for living to much larger audiences but also empowered to do so to a much greater extent. The increase in numbers of converts to Christianity, in church building and in the output of Christian writing and preaching meant that much larger groups of people were suddenly gaining access to the Christian

---

[51] Allen 1997: 3–21 and 14–15 and Leyerle 2001: 60–7.
[52] On the performative aspects of Chrysostom's preaching, see Leyerle 2001: 10 and 60–7.
[53] See Cunningham 1990: 34 and Kennedy 1983: 145.
[54] On the access of Christians to books and written media, see Gamble 1995.

message.[55] The benefits and practical support that Christian emperors from Constantine onwards gave to the Church meant that Christian discourse and Christian forms of representation had new kinds of authority behind them. By the fourth century the Church was a wealthy institution that had a strong presence in all the cities of the empire. The Church in Antioch had its own courts (or at least the bishop often dealt with cases that might once have been dealt with by secular officials), its main building, the Great or Golden Church, stood next to the imperial palace, and zealous Christians could take violent measures in promoting Christianity. The fact that most fourth-century emperors made a point of adopting and showing public support for Christianity (whether Arian or Nicene) must also have had an impact. If the emperor chose to show his allegiance to the Christian God, then other people were likely to follow. In the fourth century the Christian Church, or at least whichever version of it was given imperial favour at the time, was in a much stronger position than before to assert its explicitly formulated rules and guidelines for living and its ideas about religious allegiance. It no longer had to confine itself to instilling these rules into small communities but could now claim to have a say in constructing rules that would be applicable to the whole of Graeco-Roman society. Our first step will thus be to conceptualize Christian texts as ideology and rule-making rather as discourse. We then need to ask how this ideology and rule-making related to the actual behaviour displayed by individuals in practice.

The sociologist Pierre Bourdieu (1931–2002) has argued that when societies function as they should, they rarely run according to explicitly formulated rules, but rather according to what he labels their 'habitus'.[56] The 'habitus', as defined by Bourdieu, is a set of deeply ingrained dispositions, traditional ways of being and socially shared ideas of what is appropriate. These are instilled in every individual from birth and go on to make up their unconscious sense of 'feeling right' in their social world. The most basic of these dispositions are bodily ones, which include an implicit understanding of the correct ways to sit, stand and carry oneself in public.[57] Others might include implicit assumptions about gender relations, morality, honour, the appropriate action to take when one is ill or, as in the present case, how to act religiously. The key point about these dispositions is that when

---

[55] The huge number of sermons surviving to us in modern times testify to the increased output of the Christian message in this period.
[56] The point has been made in the different circumstances of the discussion of Roman law.
[57] Bourdieu 1977a: 93–4 and 1990a: 10 and 316. In this Bourdieu followed Marcel Mauss's 'Les techniques du Corps', 1951.

they are working properly they are unconscious and unspoken rather than explicitly formulated in verbal categories. Bourdieu's notion of habitus thus has much in common with the work of cognitive anthropologists. This is exemplified in Bloch's notion of the importance of practical, non-linguistic forms of knowledge in the carrying out of many everyday tasks.[58] According to Bloch, as people go through their daily lives they do not walk around explaining every move and decision consciously to themselves; as he puts it, they do not go through some kind of linguistic checklist.[59] Rather, they act – 'by practice', that is, according to non-linguistic forms of knowledge that are stored in a bodily and non-conscious way (as, for example, the knowledge of how to drive). For Bourdieu the non-linguistic forms of knowledge that constitute people's inherited and unconscious sense of what is right and appropriate are continually reinforced by the tacit approval and disapproval of others. As Bourdieu puts it, 'This practical knowledge, based on the continuous decoding of the perceived – but not consciously noticed – indices of the welcome given to actions already accomplished, continuously carries out the checks and corrections intended to ensure the adjustment of practices and expressions to the reactions and expectations of the other agents.'[60] This does not involve people in obeying rules as 'execution of music' relates to 'the musical score'.[61] Rather it involves people in acting according to a much looser and less explicitly defined 'feel for the game', a natural sense of what is right and appropriate for any given situation.[62] As Bourdieu states, the precepts of custom [or habitus] have nothing in common with the transcendent rules of a juridical code: 'everyone is able not so much to cite and recite them from memory as to reproduce them (fairly accurately)' in practice.[63] It is the ability to reproduce the precepts of habitus that guides people in the variety of complex situations that face them in social life.

I want to argue that in the Roman imperial period a natural and habitual sense of how to deal with issues of religious difference and of religious allegiance would have developed. As Christian leaders began to create Christianity as a religion distinct from Judaism and Graeco-Roman religion in the first century AD, they had to lay down guidelines and definitions for what it meant to be a Christian rather than Jewish or Greek. As a result, during the imperial period Graeco-Roman society gradually became aware of Graeco-Roman religion as something that could be labelled and identified. People in that society also became increasingly aware that there were

---

[58] Bloch 1977 and 1991.   [59] Bloch 1991.   [60] Bourdieu 1977a: 10.   [61] Bourdieu 1977b: 118.
[62] Bourdieu 1977a: 95 and 1990b: 61–6.   [63] Bourdieu 1977: 17.

Understanding religious identity

now alternative religious groups to which people, including the Christians, could show allegiance.[64] This sense of the importance that could be placed on the gods or God one worshipped, and on the religion to which one adhered, would have been heightened by Constantine's adoption of the Christian God. By the early fourth century most people would have known that these were now issues of some importance. However, they also would have had a strong sense of the subtlety needed in dealing with these issues in a situation where people of different religious allegiances lived alongside each other. They would have ingrained in them unspoken dispositions and habits relating to tactful and appropriate ways of dealing with this sensitive situation. They would have acted out religious allegiance and religious difference as something that mattered at some times but not at others and that could be put aside when needed. How this might have worked can be seen in a comment that Ammianus Marcellinus makes on the emperor Julian's behaviour. In many ways Julian behaved like a Christian, at least in his attitude to religious allegiance. He wanted people to choose one religious identity or another and was not happy to accept the less confrontational approach to these issues that many people preferred. Ammianus clearly disapproved of this approach. When discussing Julian's behaviour as a judge he states that most of the time Julian was fair. Sometimes, however, he was 'untimely' or 'tactless' (*intempestivus*) because at inappropriate moments (*tempore alieno*) he would ask who the litigants worshipped (Amm. Marc. 22.10.2) (although Ammianus does go on to say that Julian never used a man's religion (*religio*) against him in court). Julian's act was tactless or untimely because he sought to make the religious identity of individuals relevant in a time and a place when it was not relevant (the law courts). As Bourdieu has shown, timing was a crucial factor in acting with good practical knowledge. Knowing on which occasions it was appropriate and useful to mention religious allegiance, and on which occasions it was not, was a 'question of style, which in this case means timing'.[65] By insisting on a strong sense of religious identity on inappropriate occasions, Julian was ignoring the subtle late-antique sense of what was appropriate religiously. It was this that upset Ammianus.

It was the rarely articulated sense of what was timely and appropriate in relation to religion in imperial society that Christian leaders were struggling with in their rule-making and ideology. By seeking to impose clear-cut categories of religious identity, Christian leaders were seeking to impose a rigid structure on a situation that was normally managed in a

---

[64] North 1992.   [65] Bourdieu 1977a: 6 and 1990a: 98–111.

more subtle way. Clearly, they objected to the fluid approach to religious allegiance and it was this that acted as a permanent trigger to their ideological and rule-bound impositions of religious identity. In Bourdieu's model an explicit formulation of rules and a greater emphasis on law codes only arises in abnormal situations or when there is a perceived problem. At such times 'partial and often fictitious explicit statements of the group's implicit axiomatics' will arise as those in authority seek 'to counter the failures or hesitations of habitus by stating the solutions appropriate to the case' in question.[66] At a time of religious change, when the Church was seeking to make the rules of what had once been a minority group those of the whole of imperial society, conflict inevitably arose. The attitude of rule-bound Christian leaders could never fit with the more subtle ways in which most people were using religious allegiance in the practice of their daily lives. However hard Christian leaders sought to impose their views on the world, the habitual sense of ordinary people as to what was appropriate would continue to resist this. No one would have wanted to be accused of being untimely in their approach to religious allegiance.

It is this struggle, and the unnaturalness of a rule-based approach, that must make us doubt the success that Chrysostom and other Christian leaders had in creating and maintaining religious categories for their audiences. We have to ask whether an explicit, linguistic, ideological, rule-based medium, such as Chrysostom's preaching, could change the habitual practice of his audience and of Graeco-Roman society as a whole. We have little direct access to how Chrysostom's audiences responded to his preaching. Libanius' writings, however, do give us access to how one, relatively ordinary representative of Graeco-Roman religion reacted to the new fourth-century religious context.

LIBANIUS AND THE PRACTICAL USE OF RELIGIOUS ALLEGIANCE

Libanius' representation of religion is very different from that seen in the above discussion of Chrysostom. In comparison, Libanius wrote about religion far less often and far less consistently; out of his sixty-four surviving orations only a few can be said to deal directly with religion. The most important are the Julianic orations (*Orations* 12–18 and 24), which were written either to or about the emperor Julian and often refer to his religious policy, and *Oration* 30 *To Emperor Theodosius in Defence of the Temples*,

---

[66] Bourdieu 1977a: 17 and also 1990a: 20.

which was written during the reign of Theodosius as a prolonged defence of the peasants and temples of the Antiochene countryside. Such explicit focus on the contemporary religious situation is, however, the exception rather than the rule in Libanius' writings. Other orations that deal directly with religion tend to be more literary in form. Included in this category are *Oration* 11 *In Praise of Antioch*, which includes many of the foundation myths of Antioch; *Oration* 9 *In Praise of the Kalends Festival*, which does include some description of the contemporary state of the festival; and *Oration* 5 *In Praise of Artemis*, which, while largely being a traditional hymn, makes some reference to Libanius' personal experiences with the goddess. Many of the other references to religion are made in passing during his discussion of other matters, so they tend to be very brief. Scholars usually see Libanius' writing about religion as distancing the reader from any 'true religion' that Libanius might have held. The textual and literary nature of his writings on religion is not seen to help the expression and promulgation of religion, as with Chrysostom, but rather to hinder them. As Liebeschuetz says of Libanius: 'Unlike Julian he does not display his soul in his writings and among the many references to gods and religious practices it is not at all obvious which represent his own feelings and which are literary reminiscences or rhetorical commonplaces'.[67] Scholars have dealt with this difficulty in studying Libanius' religion in a variety of ways. Early on in the academic study of Libanius, Misson, in a still useful work, attempted to outline a coherent religious system for Libanius by describing his depiction of the gods, divine intervention, prodigies, prayer and festivals.[68] Misson managed to do this only by drawing together and synthesizing all Libanius' diverse references to religion and by ignoring their literary context. He thus created a false unity, which simply does not exist in the writings. Scholars later in the twentieth century were much less open to the idea of Libanius' having a developed religious system of his own, or even to his having much interest in religion in the first place. They tended to talk about Libanius' religion as 'only literary' and so lacking any true grounding.[69] To do so they focused on the points where Libanius talks of the close link between Graeco-Roman religion, oratory and classical education and where he gives particular prominence to the literary gods: the Muses, Apollo and Hermes.[70] They then saw this close alignment between religion

---

[67] Liebeschuetz 1972: 11. [68] Misson 1914.
[69] P. Petit 1955: 191 and 193; Festugière 1959: 229; and Norman 2000: 171, note 5 on *Oration* 58: 'The profession of rhetoric embodies the real religion of Libanius.'
[70] *Or.* 62.8 (F.iv.350); *Or.* 1.129 and 274 (F.i.145–200); *Or.* 31.37, 40, 44 and 48 (F.iii.142, 143, 144 and 146); *Or.* 62.9 and 68 (F..351 and 381); *Or.* 63.4 and 14 (F.iv.183 and 187); and *Or.* 3.1 (F.i.268). See also the whole of *Oration* 58 and *Or.* 23.27 (F.ii.506) and *Or.* 9.187 (F.i.500).

and literature as something that needed explanation. They suggested that the reason for it was the attack on both spheres carried out by Christian powers, especially during the reign of Constantius.[71] At other times these writers describe Libanius as a religious traditionalist who supported Julian's religious 'revival' *in toto* and wanted a return to the classical civic religion of the past.[72] When Julian's 'revival' failed, Libanius is then seen as trapped in yearning for the past glories of classical civic religion and therefore unable to respond effectively to the realities of his own time. At times these views come together and Libanius' love of eloquence and literary expressions of religion are seen as all that is keeping loyalty to civic religion alive. Thus, Petit has described Libanius' *Oration* 11 *In Praise of Antioch* as a manifesto of the pagan 'faction', delivered at the Olympic games, that reasserted the pagan past and foundations of the city.[73] Others again have criticized this view, arguing that documents such as *Oration* 11 are purely literary artifacts.[74] What we see is a set of conflicting ideas of Libanius' religion in which his lack of interest in religion, the literary nature of his writings, the traditional and civic nature of his religion and his support for Julian's religious policy are all merged together without drawing out the problems and contradictions within these views.

Wöhrle has given a more nuanced account of the way Libanius wrote about religion; it is a short article that is the only recent work directly devoted to his religion. However, Wöhrle's basic argument is still that Libanius' religion can be characterized as nostalgic, classicizing and 'mehr eine literarische Geste als eine echte Religion'.[75] Wöhrle, like Festugière, sees the main function of religiosity for Libanius to be support of Hellenistic culture and civic life as a whole and explores the relationship between religion and *logoi* in Libanius' writings.[76] He also takes the common view that Libanius was indifferent to religion, so he emphasizes Libanius' ironic attitude to religious matters.[77] Other more recent works do not directly focus on religion, choosing instead to study Libanius' relationship with, or representation of, particular emperors.[78] Thus, for example, in one recent

---

[71] Festugière 1959: 25–39. [72] P. Petit 1955: 191–3. [73] P. Petit 1955: 206 and 192.
[74] Liebeschuetz 1995. [75] Wöhrle 1995: 71–3.
[76] For the former see Wöhrle 1995: 76–82. For the latter see Wöhrle 1995: 82–6.
[77] Wöhrle 1995: 73, 74 (on *Ep*. B.146 (F.727)) and 81, note 28 (on *Ep*. F.1074). This idea of Libanius' scepticism or irony goes back to Misson (Misson 1914: 18).
[78] On Libanius and Constantine, see Wiemer 1994 and Malosse 1997. On Libanius and Constantius, see Seiler 1998 and Malosse 2000/1. On Libanius and Julian, see Criscuolo 1994; Scholl 1994; Malosse 1995a and 1995b; P. Petit 1978; and Wiemer 1995a. See also Wiemer 1995b and Swain 2004.

work Swain allows Libanius to have strong religious feelings, but only if they were tied very closely to Julian's revival.[79]

The dominant picture of Libanius' religion in scholarship is that his ironic and sceptical approach precludes any personal religious feelings or any practical side to his religion. Because many of his references to religion have been couched in literary and traditional terms, he has been accused of being conservative and backward-looking and unable to respond successfully to the changed religious situation or to have any real engagement with contemporary religious life.[80] Accepting this idea would also entail accepting that Libanius offered little real competition to the model of religious interaction put forward in Chrysostom's preaching and that he was thus an ineffective spokesperson for the old Graeco-Roman religions. The problem with this view is that it relies on a misunderstanding of the nature of Graeco-Roman religion and its relationship to literature. The views that we have looked at all clearly considered the literary nature of Libanius' writings about religion to be a problem: either it needed to be explained or it detracted from the possibility of any true religious feeling on Libanius' part. What we should realize, however, is that literature and religion had a very different relationship in the ancient world from the one we are used to now.

Written texts had never played the same role in Graeco-Roman religions as they had in Christianity. Apart from certain philosophical discourses and the esoteric texts of Neoplatonic writers, adherents of Graeco-Roman religions tended to be little interested in constructing self-reflexive discourse that explained explicitly the nature of their religions.[81] At particular times in Graeco-Roman history there were momentary drives towards formulating religious knowledge, such as the works of Varro and Ovid's *Fasti* in the late Republic and the Augustan Age, but most of the time there was no one place where the essential features of Greek and Roman religion could be constantly defined and reinforced. Sacred laws or prophetic books (such as the Sibylline oracles in Rome) could supply some guidance, but these tended to relate only to specific local contexts rather than lay down general rules. Greek religion and, probably to a much lesser degree, Roman religion had myths about the Olympian gods which did to some extent shape the practice of cult – for example in the representation of divinities in statues and friezes in temples.[82] However, the texts containing these myths were

---

[79] Swain 2004: 396–9.
[80] See for example Downey 1961: 194–5; Festugière 1959; Liebeschuetz 1972: 15; Pack 1935: 41; and Downey 1961: 192.
[81] Beard, North and Price 1998: 284. See also Siegert 1997: 421.   [82] S. R. F. Price 1999: 13 and 15.

not determinative of religious practice and thought. Even such well-known works as those of Homer and Hesiod were not seen as definitive texts: alternative versions of the myths were given just as much credit, and cities and communities could always develop their own local myths.[83] In any case, it is not at all clear that myths were the most important aspect of Graeco-Roman religion.[84] Ritual rather than theology or textual elaboration on religion was the central aspect of Graeco-Roman cult.[85] This practical and ritual nature of Graeco-Roman religion entailed its being less concerned with explicitly formulated ideas about religion.

Dennis Feeney, in his *Literature and Religion at Rome*, has pointed out that modern preconceptions of religion and literature as distinct spheres of activity are inappropriate. He suggests that texts that we might normally see as literary products are valid forms of religious knowledge.[86] Poetic works, rhetorical speeches and historical writings can all be considered religious texts.[87] For the modern reader, the multiplicity of writings about religion in a variety of different genres that we see in the ancient world can be off-putting. The lack of concern with presenting any unified or consistent picture of religion and the subordination of discussion of religion to the literary conventions of the work in which they are found can lead us to deny their religious status.[88] We can, however, remove the problem if we no longer oppose literary descriptions of religion to some other level of 'real' religious experience or dismiss them as 'only literary'.[89] It is only possible to say that a representation of religion is 'only literary' or 'ironic' and 'sceptical' if we are comparing this with some notion of true, sincere and unmediated belief in religion.[90] Once we accept that belief is an irrelevant category with which to assess Graeco-Roman religion, we can move beyond this approach and begin to assess Graeco-Roman writings about religion in their own terms.[91] As Feeney suggests, we must accept that Graeco-Roman religion was made up of a multiplicity of different kinds of discourses that often appear contradictory: 'Educated Greeks and Romans of the post-classical era' could 'entertain different kinds of assent and criteria of judgment [about religion] in ways that strike the modern reader as mutually

---

[83] S. R. F. Price 1999: 13–15 and 19–25.   [84] Versnel 1990; Burkert 1983: 15–24 and Price 1999: 17.
[85] Bowman and Wolff 1994: 12–13 and Lane-Fox 1994: 126.
[86] Feeney 1988: 25 and 137. See also Swain 2004, who points out that Aristides had already made the link between literature and religion – and no one denies his religiosity
[87] See Feeney 1988 and also Davies 2004.   [88] Feeney 1988: 2.
[89] For similar points about the place of religion in Ammianus Marcellinus' *History*, see Rike 1987: 5, 7 and 8–9 on Momigliano 1977.
[90] Feeney 1988: 18–21.
[91] On the problem with the category of belief, see Feeney 1988: 12–14 and S. R. F. Price 1984: 9–11.

Understanding religious identity 25

contradictory'.⁹² Rather than try to single out the author's 'true' religious position, with Libanius' writings we must understand 'the particular system of rules appropriate to any given context' of his speech or writing.⁹³ From this point of view the literary and rhetorical nature of Libanius' writings about religion is no longer seen as a problem but instead becomes part of the solution. Exploring why Libanius said different things about religion at different times and understanding the impact of genre and context then become a fruitful and exciting exercise.

The period from the time of Constantius to the rule of Theodosius, during which Libanius was writing, saw a rapid changeover of emperors.⁹⁴ Upsetting an emperor or his powerful officials might lead at the very least to loss of favour and influence and at the worst to accusations of treason and magic.⁹⁵ The attitude of the current emperor could have a great impact on Libanius' writing. Libanius describes the problems he had in expressing certain opinions openly and how he sought to control the audiences of some of his letters and orations. In one letter he describes the recital of his funeral oration in honour of his uncle Phasganius. He says that he delivered the majority of the oration 'publicly' to good people but that the third part was delivered to a more select audience behind closed doors because in it he described his uncle's enemies, including the Caesar Gallus (*Ep.* N.64 (F.283)).⁹⁶ Gallus was now dead but he still had living supporters who might attack critics of the Caesar.⁹⁷ Libanius also expresses the same concern with the publication of his letters and sometimes chastises friends for 'publishing' letters when he had asked them not to do so (*Ep.* N.16 (F. 476)).⁹⁸ Elsewhere he talks of how it was dangerous to express certain opinions in written epistles and of how others too hid their true opinions in letters carried by those they did not trust (*Ep.* B.161.4 (F.1196) and *Ep.* B.10.2 (F. 630)). It is clear that the context in which Libanius was writing often determined what he was able to say. Long ago Paul Petit realized that exploring the rhetorical context of Libanius' works could help to understand the contradictions in what he wrote.⁹⁹ He shows, for example, that the manner in which Libanius represented a particular emperor varied greatly

---

⁹² Feeney 1988: 2, 14, 18 and 138. ⁹³ Feeney 1988: 14.
⁹⁴ Swain 2004: 362–3, 392 and 400. See also Eunapius, *VS* 496.
⁹⁵ On the ups and downs of Libanius' influence, see Norman 2000: xi–xviii and Bradbury 2004: 2–10.
⁹⁶ P. Petit 1956: 487–8. See also *Or.* 62.69 and 73 (F.iv.381 and 383) and *Ep.* N.37.2 (F.33).
⁹⁷ Possibly including his half-brother Julian who replaced him as Caesar. Norman 1992: vol. ii, 45 and 47, notes b and f.
⁹⁸ See also *Ep.* N.17 (F.477); *Ep.* N.40.1 (F.19); *Ep.* N.133.5 (F.1264); and *Ep.* N.168.4 (F.957).
⁹⁹ See P. Petit 1956.

depending on whether or not that emperor was alive.[100] This meant that very often the needs of the particular moment dominated the context of Libanius' speeches rather than any desire to put forward a consistent and coherent view on subject. This is particularly clear in his set-piece epideictic or panegyric orations, such as *Oration 11 In Praise of Antioch* or the orations delivered to the Emperors Constantius and Constans and the emperor Julian, but is also true, to greater or lesser degrees, for his other speeches. These factors also affected the way that Libanius wrote about religious matters. In the fast changing circumstances of the fourth century in which he had to deal with different emperors with different religious allegiances and with a complex and mixed religious situation, it is not surprising that Libanius expressed various different views of religion. Rhetoric and saying what was appropriate could act to smooth over differences and points of conflict. Just as Libanius was capable of defending the temples or the peasant farmers from around Antioch, he could also deliver a speech *In Praise of Constans and Constantius* that hid all his personal animosity to the emperors (*Oration* 59).[101] By taking the appropriate and timely position on each occasion Libanius could further his own goals and work to achieve the ends he desired.

We can thus argue that Libanius made references to religion according to his 'feel for the game' of what was acceptable in fourth-century imperial society. He did not treat statements about religion and religious allegiance as strictly defined rules that should be followed to the letter. Rather, he acted out ideas about religion in a practical way that was appropriate for his social context. As Bourdieu has noted, social rules and structures can never govern an individual's life totally at the expense of their own needs. Instead, the individual's 'feel for the game' allows them to 'play' the expectations and ideals placed on them in a practical way, in order to gain the most beneficial outcome.[102] As Jenkins says of Bourdieu's work on the manipulation of marriage rules in rural France, 'the official ideology of marriage preference is in fact a rhetorical resource to be drawn upon or not as circumstances require; it is emphatically not a prescription'.[103] The same can be said of ideals and expectations about religious allegiance. Many people in the fourth century would have had an awareness that religious allegiance could matter, particularly now that emperors were supporting worship of a

---

[100] P. Petit 1956: 483.
[101] See the translation by Dodgeon in Lieu and Montserrat 1996: 147–209.
[102] For Bourdieu's discussion of how individuals could strategically manipulate marriage laws and principles of inheritance see Bourdieu 1977b.
[103] Jenkins 2002: 39.

particular god or gods. However, they did not all see statements about religion and religious allegiance as prescriptive rules that defined their whole existence and had to be maintained constantly. In fact, the 'feel for the game' of fourth-century imperial society often demanded a *lack* of clarity in such statements. The use of statements about religion might thus have nothing to do with outlining ideals and constructing identities. It is precisely because Libanius did not put forward one explicitly formulated and coherent picture of religion, but rather showed religious allegiance in practice strategically that he is so useful to us. To put it in Jenkins's words, Libanius showed religious allegiance being used as a 'rhetorical resource to be drawn upon or not as the circumstances require it' not as a 'prescription'.[104] This is not to say that Libanius had no religion of his own, which is blatantly untrue. It is simply to say that we do not see Libanius' true religious feelings expressed consistently in his writings and that we should not expect to. His writings had entirely different and more practical goals and it is because of this that they will form such an important part of the present analysis.

COMPARING LIBANIUS' AND CHRYSOSTOM'S REPRESENTATION OF RELIGIOUS IDENTITY AND ALLEGIANCE

Reading Christian texts, of which there are so many for the fourth century, can make the ideals and rules of Christian leaders appear representative of social life as a whole. They can make it appear that their categories of Christian, Greek and Jew were all-pervasive and accepted by all people at all times. However, accepting the views put forward by such texts is problematic. As Bourdieu states of his study of French academic life, he would have gained a very misleading understanding if he had relied on the official literature of French universities as his only source.[105] He would only ever have been able to see French academia in the terms in which it wanted to be seen because 'when you are within the pre-constructed, reality offers itself to you. The given gives itself.'[106] In a similar way, it is clear that to study processes of Christianization from Christian discourses will always be problematic because these dominant ideologies will present themselves as the norm that cannot be questioned.[107] The power of ideology 'inheres precisely in this remarkable ability it has to set its agenda and mask

---

[104] Jenkins 2002: 39.   [105] Bourdieu 1992 on his *Homo Academicus* (1988).
[106] Bourdieu 1992.   [107] Comaroff and Comaroff 1992: 34 and 35.

the fact that its representation both has an agenda and that there could be other representations and agendas'.[108] Christian ideology provides only a one-sided account, as it does not reveal the points where individuals choose not to fit in with their constructions of religious identity or to treat them as only partial guidelines. As Lieu has pointed out, Christian texts are 'manipulative': they 'offer a set of dispositions as if they were determinative, when in fact they cannot have been so' and therefore 'seek to seduce us into a quasi essentialism'.[109] Accepting the views put forward by these Christian texts means taking the texts that are responsible for construction of identity and reality among Christians as evidence for the existence of those very things.

The problem is that such ideal official accounts of society can be very attractive to sociologists and historians. Bourdieu has argued that the position of the anthropologist or historian as an external observer of a society will always lead them to objectify and simplify that society.[110] Because they do not *implicitly* understand how that society works *in practice* and because they do not have a natural, habitual sense of what is appropriate (precisely because of their status as external observer), they seek to identify explanations, rules and structures that will give them an easy-to-read map of that society. They focus on these rules and structures because the mass of contradictory practices and behaviour that actually exist would be much harder to grasp. For this reason, they have a tendency to look out for, and to favour, accounts that reveal explicitly formulated rules, categorizations and distinctions and will assume that social behaviour will match those norms.[111] The direct questions of the anthropologists lead the native informant to give conscious, clear-cut and explicit explanations of their social behaviour,[112] explanations that will always lead to an overemphasis on ideals, norms and rules and so to the production of an 'official account' ('we usually do this . . .' and 'we ought to do that . . .'), rather than a description of how things are actually done.[113] This leads to a circular, self-perpetuating tendency. Anthropologists want to find rules and structures, so they turn to texts and local accounts that will provide evidence of these. While historians of the ancient world might seem less in danger of this tendency because we are unable to question ancient people, the texts on which choose to base our studies can be open to a similar critique. Our desire to see the fourth century as operating in a predictable way leads us to use distinct categories of 'Christian, 'pagan' and 'Jew'. We like to think that in every

[108] Perkins 1995: 2 and 13. See also Hennessy 1993: 9.   [109] Lieu 2004: 157.
[110] Bourdieu 1990a: 27 and 1977a: 1–2 and 19.   [111] Bourdieu 1990a: 27 and 1977a: 1.
[112] Bourdieu 1977a: 19. See also Bloch 1977 with Bourdillon 1978.   [113] Jenkins 2002: 48 and 53.

Understanding religious identity 29

situation individuals are following 'rules' of their religious allegiance: if we can define them as 'Christian' once, then they can always be said to be so and to act accordingly. This thinking lies behind our desire to find out the religious allegiance of ancient individuals, even when this is not made clear in the texts themselves.[114] Our interest in processes of Christianization and in the assignation of religious allegiance also leads us to choose to study precisely those texts that speak the most explicitly about these things. Chrysostom's sermons give us ideals, norms and explicitly formulated ideas of what society should be like or what Chrysostom would like it to be. We can imagine that the views and positions held in them might represent what his audience would tell us if we were to ask them directly 'what is your religion' or 'how do you view your relationship to Greeks' (they would answer 'I am a Christian and not a Greek'). They thus capture in a moment a person's religious identity and fix it forever when, in fact, over time and in practice the individual involved might move through a number of different states of religious identity and religious allegiance.

It is for this reason that Libanius' writings can be so important to us. They show us someone using ideas about religious identity and religious allegiance *in practice* and during the process of living and functioning in fourth-century imperial society. They show us how people used claims about religious allegiance and references to religiosity not just in an ideal sense, but also in a strategic sense, according to their habitual, implicit 'feel' for what was appropriate and useful for each occasion. For this reason, Libanius' writings allow us to see how religious allegiance need not dominate an individual's life but could be something that he or she emphasized at certain times and allowed to fade into the background at others. Because Libanius' writings often refer to religious allegiance only in passing and because they are one of the last places that scholars would look to describe the religious situation of the fourth century, they can offer a totally unexpected view of that religious situation – one that is much less predictable and more subtle but also more difficult to understand. Counterintuitively, Libanius, a worshipper of the gods who rarely wrote explicitly about religion, might be able to tell us more about the state of processes of Christianization in the fourth century than Chrysostom's preaching can.

Libanius' and Chrysostom's audiences shared the same social world of fourth-century Antioch. It is thus possible that Libanius can reveal at least something about how Chrysostom's audiences might have reacted to the

---

[114] As Paul Petit throughout his *Les fonctionnaires dans l'œuvre de Libanius: analyse prosopographique* (1994) and at P. Petit 1955: 201.

imposition of Christian rules. We can see that they might have adopted certain aspects of Chrysostom's ideology of religious identity but at the same time have brought them into line with their existing dispositions and 'habitual' ways of thinking and being. We can also see that they might have conformed to 'rules' about what it was to be 'Greek' or 'Christian' as and when it suited them, but at other times not have done so. As a result, we can say that the habitus and practical concerns of Chrysostom's audiences might have been just as determinative of their attitude to issues of religious identity as was Chrysostom's preaching. By reading the discourses of Libanius against the discourses of Chrysostom, we can find a new and oppositional way of reading Chrysostom's texts and of understanding the impact that they had on his audience. We can see that Christian discourse and Christian preaching do not have to be regarded as either determinative or as having no impact at all. Instead, we can see that individuals might have adopted Christian ideological constructs in different ways *in practice* depending on their previously held dispositions and ways of thinking.

By juxtaposing Chrysostom and Libanius in this way we can obtain a more balanced view and can decentre the constructions of boundaries and identity that we see in Chrysostom. It is this comparison between rules/ideology and practice/habitus and between Chrysostom and Libanius that will provide the structuring principle of this book. Chapter 2, will first provide some necessary background information on Antioch and its religious situation and on the writings of Libanius and Chrysostom. Part II will then carry out a more detailed study of representations of religious identity and religious allegiance in our two authors. Chapter 3 will look at Chrysostom's ideological and official account of how the Church wanted religious identities to be represented. It will explore Chrysostom's attempt to promote mutually exclusive and permanent forms of religious identities for his audiences, and in so doing, it will explore the particular way that Chrysostom, as opposed to any other Christian writer, defined and contrasted what it was to be 'Christian', 'Greek' or 'Jew'. We shall see that Chrysostom wanted his audiences to display their Christian identity visibly in all areas of their lives. To ensure that we do not accept Chrysostom's constructions of identity as the only way of viewing the fourth century, chapter 4 will turn to Libanius' representation of religious allegiance: how he wrote about Graeco-Roman religion and Christianity when he chose to do so. It will use the writings of Libanius to show how he and his circle of elite acquaintances used reference to religious allegiance in a practical way according to their sense of what was appropriate. We shall see these elite men shifting their religious allegiances to suit the moment, when it helped them to 'network' and to gain promotions and other benefits. We shall also see, however, that one of Libanius' responses to the strategic use of religious allegiance by others was to value the private and internal nature of true religious feeling.

Religious identity cannot be seen in isolation but must be seen to interact with, and sometimes even overlap, other kinds of social identity. Religious identity might also not always be the most important form of identification for people – at times political, civic and cultural identities might be more important.[115] Part III will thus turn to the relationship between religious identity and other kinds of social identity. In chapter 5 I shall investigate Chrysostom's attitudes to the relationship between religious identities and political, civic and ethnic/cultural identities. I shall argue that he tended to associate religious identity closely with these other ways of being, as he sought to erase any possibility of a neutral non-Christian or non-religious sphere that could be free from religious conflict. Here we shall see how having a strong sense of religious identity often goes hand in hand with a close association between religious identity and political, civic and cultural identity, and therefore with power. Rather than simply accept Chrysostom's view of the world I shall then compare it with Libanius' understanding of the relationship between religious allegiance and political, civic and ethnic identities. In chapter 6 I shall explore how Libanius was able to manipulate traditional understandings of the close relationship between religion, ethnicity and the political and civic spheres, *when it was useful for him to do so* in the fourth-century context. He had a tendency to present religion as a private matter and was able to envisage a neutral space where religious differences were not significant. So, in turn, we shall see that having a weaker sense of religious identity, or a lack of interest in marking out clear religious identities, often goes hand-in-hand with the separation of religious identity from other social identities.

It is easy to assume that there is a direct correlation between a religious identity and the social organization of that identity, when this might not always be the case.[116] As identity theorists have shown, there need not be any direct correlation between categorizations of social identity and social organization.[117] Where there is a correlation, this might be to much looser

---

[115] On these ideas, see S. Jones 1997: 156–7; Barth 1983: 81; and Jenkins 2003: 101.
[116] S. Jones 1997: 75 and Eriksen 1993: 156.
[117] Eriksen on Barth 1993: 41 and Handelman 1977: 187–200.

forms of social organization than the term 'group' suggests.[118] As Vincent has argued, we need to 'move further away from ... group to non-group, from a "cookie-cutter" concept of culture to a finer understanding of the ephemerality and inconsistency of social relations'.[119] Part IV will thus ask how far Chrysostom's and Libanius' ways of writing about religious identity and religious allegiance related to forms of social organization. Chapter 7 will explore the notion of the 'textual community' in relation to Chrysostom and the ways in which Chrysostom sought to construct a sense of community among his audience. At the same time, however, I shall question how far the 'Christian' label that Chrysostom sought to impose on his audiences can be seen to have correlated to a physical Christian community in Antioch. I shall argue that very often it cannot. Following on from this I shall, in chapter 8, see how far Libanius' writings support a picture of the world divided up into visible and distinct religious groups. I shall question the notion that there was a 'pagan faction' in the later years of Constantius' reign and the early years of Julian's rule and I shall argue that the traditional picture of Libanius as an avid supporter of Julian and his religion cannot easily be translated into assumptions about any kind of social organization among 'pagans'. I shall suggest, instead, that just as Libanius was less interested in defining religious identity than Chrysostom, so he also gives us a picture of much more fluid socio-religious relations.

Throughout parts II to IV Chrysostom's and Libanius' views and representations will be compared in order to decentre Chrysostom's depiction of the religious situation. In part V I shall seek to come to some conclusions about this and try to ascertain how far people in Antioch generally were adopting the guidelines for religious identity laid down by Chrysostom. Chapter 9 will investigate how far religious identities and religious allegiances were played out in religious practices and behaviours in Antioch. I shall consider the range of religious practices and behaviours available, from asceticism to the use of amulets, and study the attitudes of Chrysostom and Libanius to these practices, their popularity among Antiochenes and the extent to which they supported or undermined constructions of religious identities. We shall see that while Chrysostom wanted religious practice to be a marker of religious difference, Libanius strongly objected to such tactless displays of religious difference. We shall see that Libanius instead favoured more private and personal forms of religious worship that would

---

[118] Handelman 1977: 264 and Eriksen 1993: 41–2. [119] Vincent 1974: 376.

play down religious difference and religious conflict in the fourth century but also allow him personal access to the divine. Finally, I shall suggest that Chrysostom's audience probably also shared Libanius' understanding of religious practice and also favoured practices that gave them personal access to the divine. Chapter 10 will conclude by returning to what we have learnt about the relationship between Libanius' and Chrysostom's writings on religion and religious interaction.

CHAPTER 2

Imperial society, religion and literary culture in fourth-century Antioch

THE IMPERIAL CITY OF ANTIOCH

Seleucus I Nicator founded the city of Antioch on the banks of the river Orontes in 300 BC as part of his plan to Hellenize the region. The city came under Roman influence when Syria became a Roman province in 64 BC and continued to flourish throughout the imperial period. Despite some disruption in the 260s AD, when the city came under the control of the Palmyra, Antioch continued to be one of the largest and most important cities in the Roman empire after Rome and Alexandria. In the fourth century Antioch was a thriving city that confounds simplistic notions of civic decline in this period.[1] Throughout most of this century Antioch was the metropolis of the province of Syria, the base for emperors engaged in Persian campaigns and home to an imperial palace and the other buildings necessary for an imperial base. At the same time it continued to be a wealthy and politically active city, an important trading point and a centre for education and culture. In many ways Antioch was thus a typical Graeco-Roman city, if a particularly important one that was close to the centres of imperial power. We also need to remember, however, that Antioch was also a famously Christian city. It was supposedly at Antioch that the Christians were first given the name 'Christian' and where they were first seen as a group distinct from Judaism. Missionaries from the Church in Jerusalem, in particular Barnabas, Paul and Peter, went to Antioch soon after Jesus' death and are said to have started the gentile mission there.[2] By the fourth century, Christianity was well established in Antioch. From Constantine's reign onwards the city was one of the most important Christian cities in the empire: it was the site of several important churches as well as of a number of Church councils. Antioch was a city being pulled in two

---

[1] On Antioch in the fourth century, see Liebeschuetz 1972; Downey 1963 and 1962; Kondoleon 2000b; and Sandwell and Huskinson 2004.
[2] Acts 11.22–6. Downey 1963: 121 and see Acts 11.20.

different directions. As a Greek city under Roman rule it was subject to the influence of imperial power but as a Christian city it was also subject to the authority of the Church. To understand fully the structuring forces and material supports behind Libanius' and Chrysostom's writings about religion we need to understand in greater detail how the forces of imperial power, Graeco-Roman culture and the Christian Church played out in Antioch.

Antioch was an imperial city and as such had all the buildings and aggrandizement of other imperial cities. The island in the middle of the Orontes river to the north-west of the city was home to the imperial palace and to the main Hippodrome, where the emperor could display his magnificence to the people of the city. The island also contained numerous baths, theatres and forums as well as the impressive colonnade of the main street. It was a city that was attractive both to emperors wanting a base in the east and also to the entertainment-loving populace who made the most of all the forms of display in the city.[3] Antioch was also a city of great learning. The city's reputation for training in rhetoric and Greek literature rivalled that of Athens. Young men from around the eastern empire flooded into the city to attend the schools there, whether at the publicly funded and imperially appointed municipal school or at one of the many private schools that operated there.[4] The elite of the city would have imbibed classical culture just as their counterparts throughout the cities of the east did, and they continued to beautify their city with public and private buildings as such educated Greek men had always done. Antioch was also a city that continued to enjoy all that civic life could offer. In the ancient world it was renowned for one reason in particular: it was a city that enjoyed its luxury, entertainments and the cosmopolitan life.

As an imperial city in the increasingly centralized empire of the fourth century, Antioch could not help but be very aware of imperial power.[5] Proximity to the Mediterranean and to the Persian border made the city of crucial importance militarily and politically, and on a number of occasions it served as military headquarters for the emperor in the region. The re-emergence of the threat from Persia in the later years of Constantine's reign led to a build-up of troops in Antioch and finally to Constantine's sending his Caesar, his son Constantius, to the city.[6] Once Constantine had died and his son Constantius had taken over rule of the eastern empire, Antioch became Constantius' base for a number of years while he continued to

[3] Julian, *Mis.* 342B–364B. See also Maas 2000: 13–22 and Gonosová 2000: 115–44.
[4] Norman 2000: 66.   [5] See Cabouret 2004.
[6] Downey 1963: 146–7 and Malosse 2004.

prepare for war with Persia.⁷ During this time, in the early years of his reign, Constantius appears to have been particularly attached to the city and carried out a number of building works there.⁸ When Constantius had to travel to the western empire in AD 351 he appointed his nephew Gallus as Caesar, his representative in the east. Gallus too took Antioch as his headquarters. Constantius did not return to the city after this but instead favoured Constantinople, so allowing Gallus to continue his tyrannical rule in Antioch until AD 354 when he was murdered for his disloyalty to the emperor. Antioch came to favour again in the reign of Julian who spent many months of his short reign there. Julian arrived in the city in May 362 to prepare for a campaign against Persia. However, Julian also had great expectations for the city, hoping that the strong survival of Graeco-Roman culture there would make it a good base for his revival of traditional Graeco-Roman religion. He was soon disappointed as the population of the city did not react favourably to him and eventually, in March 363, he left the city for his Persian campaign, vowing never to return.⁹ Julian died in June 363 and his successor, Jovian, ruled for only nine months. The joint rule of Valens and Valentinan again saw Antioch coming to prominence as Valens chose Antioch to be the headquarters of his rule of the eastern empire. He spent most of his reign (364–78) in the city, only leaving in the spring of 378 to deal with a Gothic invasion in Thrace.¹⁰ Theodosius I, the last emperor of the period that concerns us, appears never to have visited the city.

What is clear from this brief summary is that Antioch was an important imperial city and had much direct contact with the emperors of the fourth century. For large parts of this period, Antioch was one of the main stages on which imperial affairs were played out. Each time an emperor stayed in the city he brought with him his family, court and army, and no one would have been able to be unaware of his presence. The influence of imperial power and of the concerns of court could thus never be too far away.¹¹ Even when the emperor himself was not staying in Antioch, as was the case for the years of Theodosius' reign, his presence could be felt through a number of other avenues. As one of the most important cities in the province of Syria and in the east of the empire, Antioch was often the base for imperial officials in the region. The praetorian prefect of the east was at times based in Antioch with all his staff, and the count of the east also had his base in Antioch, in

---

⁷ Downey 1963: 149. ⁸ Downey 1963: 149 and Julian, *Oration* 1.40d–41a.
⁹ For Julian's stay in Antioch see Downey 1963: 162–75. ¹⁰ Downey 1963: 178–9.
¹¹ Liebeschuetz 1972: 105–10.

the Temple of the Muses.[12] The governors of Syria (*consularis Syriae*) also took Antioch as their base, because it was the leading city of their province and dealt with all aspects of life in the city.[13] Finally, because of Antioch's importance as a military base, the city was usually home to a high-ranking general who would be keeping an eye on military affairs.[14] We also hear of many other officials passing through the city. As well as being the home of officials, Antioch regularly sent embassies to the imperial court and so again might interact with the emperor and his officials.[15] Finally, Antioch could be related to the central powers through the provincial assembly of Syria. This represented all the most important cities of the province and, under the aegis of the Syriarch, was responsible for the provincial games of Syria, which had important imperial associations.[16] The presence of the emperor and his officials in Antioch would have been felt in political, social and military terms. We know, for example, that the presence of their armies always had a great and not always positive impact on the city.[17] We also know that charges of magic and treason blighted the city when the emperor or his Caesar was present. Thus, it was during Valens' stay in the city that the treason trials following the Theodorus affair led to a persecution of the elite in the city.[18] Finally, survival of the civic council was one serious area of conflict between the city of Antioch and the Christian emperors in this period. Men such as Libanius constantly petitioned the emperors to stop councillors from fleeing their responsibilities by joining the army or the imperial bureaucracy. The emperors responded by issuing legislation but appear not to have taken steps that were more concrete or successful.[19]

Some of the greatest impact of the fourth-century emperors on Antioch was probably felt in the realm of religion. Throughout this period the Christian emperors were beginning to issue legislation against certain aspects of traditional Graeco-Roman religion. The exact nature, extent and intention of this legislation is much debated and it is not at all clear that any of the emperors of the fourth century intended an outright ban of Graeco-Roman religion before the last years of Theodosius' reign.[20] The biggest problem is to understand the impact this legislation had on Antioch itself. Each piece of imperial legislation was issued to deal with a specific

---

[12] On the former, see Liebeschuetz 1972: 59. On the latter, see Downey 1963: 148 and Liebeschuetz 1972: 110–11.
[13] Liebeschuetz 1972: 110–14.   [14] Liebeschuetz 1972: 114–18.   [15] Liebeschuetz 1972: 107–8.
[16] Liebeschuetz 1972: 108 and 136–44 and 1959.   [17] Downey 1963: 147 and 167.
[18] Amm. Marc. 19.1 and Liebeschuetz 1972: 178–9.   [19] Liebeschuetz 1972: 174–86.
[20] Barnes 1981, 210–12 and 246–8; Drake 1982; Barnes 1984; Errington 1988; Bradbury 1994; and Sandwell 2005: 93–7. See also Salzman 1987 and Hunt 1993.

problem in a specific place and was not intended to have general impact throughout the empire.[21] Only some of the legislation in the Theodosian Code would have been applicable in Antioch, and local officials would have enforced the legislation that *was* applicable to varying degrees.[22] The stay of Constantius' Caesar Gallus in the city saw a time of persecution of 'pagans' in Antioch, as did the time of Theodosius' praetorian prefect Cynegius 3.[23] Christian emperors also had an impact on Antioch through their support of Christian institutions. This started with Constantine who inaugurated the building of a large and impressive new church on the island region of Antioch, near the imperial palace. This structure was completed in the reign of Constantius and was known as the Great or Golden Church.[24] Certainly, the proximity of the Golden Church to the palace would have made a statement about the relationship of the Church to imperial power. Such ideas were reinforced by the role that Antioch played in the state-sponsored Church councils of the fourth century. It was at Antioch in 324 that the Arian controversy first came to a head and the synod of Antioch proposed the Council of Nicaea to solve the dispute. This was held in 325 and was presided over by Constantine, who used it to develop an anti-Arian formulation.[25] The first major council to be held at Antioch itself was that held in 341, on the occasion of the dedication of Constantine's Great Church. Constantius presided over this council and its search to find a credal formula that would solve the Arian crisis but this time in favour of the Arians (Constantius was close to a number of leading Arians, as was his Caesar Gallus when he came to the city).[26] The visible involvement that Christian emperors were willing to have in Church affairs in the city must have been noticed by people at the time and could only have increased the authority of the Church in the city. The Christian bishops now controlled the substantial wealth of the Church and used it to fund charitable organizations, and they could also act as a source of judicial authority, settling disputes.[27] At the same time, many representatives of the imperial government in Syria and Antioch and also of the local civic council of the city were now Christians.

What we can thus conclude is that there were a number of forces at work in Antioch in the fourth century. On the one hand, there were the traditions of Graeco-Roman civic and cultural life and the influence of

---

[21] Matthews 2000: 55.   [22] Sandwell 2005.   [23] Sandwell 2005: 105–8.
[24] Eusebius, *VC* 3.50 and Downey 1963: 143–4.   [25] Downey 1963: 145.
[26] Downey 1963: 150 and 152.
[27] Liebeschuetz 1972: 239–42 and Daley 1999: 431–61. See also *In Matt. Hom.* 66 (*PG* 58.658) and *In Ep. ad 1 Cor. Hom.* 15 (*PG* 61.179–80).

Roman imperial power in the presence of the emperors and their officials. On the other hand, there was the institution of the Church and the support that was being given to it by the now Christian emperors. To understand the impact of all these factors on Antioch's religious life we need to focus on the religious situation in the city.

THE RELIGIOUS CONTEXT OF FOURTH-CENTURY ANTIOCH

The major difficulty in the study of religious life in Antioch, however, has been the lack of material or archaeological evidence. As with the study of earlier periods in Antioch, there is a dearth of archaeological and epigraphic evidence for the religious situation of the fourth century. Extensive expeditions were carried out in the city in the 1930s by the Princeton team.[28] Little has been possible since then because the modern town of Antakya covers most of the ancient city. The most important find of these expeditions were the famous Antioch mosaics, depicting various mythological, dramatic and non-figurative designs as the decorations for the houses of the rich in the city.[29] In addition, survey work has recently revealed new material for the territory around Antioch and the outskirts of the city itself.[30] Only a small proportion of this archaeological evidence is, however, useful for the study of the religious situation, and archaeologists have found neither epigraphy nor burials from within the city itself. The Antioch mosaics can be related to debates about Christianization among the upper classes in Antioch and the extent to which their religion shows in their choice of decoration.[31] Some of the archaeological and epigraphic material from the territory of Antioch can also inform us about issues of Christianization.[32] There is, however, a real lack of information about the physical contexts of religion actually in Antioch.[33] Thus, we know of only four churches in the city, the Old Church, the Great Church, the Church of the Maccabees and the Church of Saint Babylas. Of these, we have physical remains of only the Church of Saint Babylas.[34] It is likely that our knowledge on this subject is greatly circumscribed. A city as large as Antioch would probably have had more churches than this, as well as numerous martyr shrines. No

---

[28] The five volumes entitled *Antioch-on-the-Orontes* 1932–72.
[29] For an introduction to the Antioch mosaics, see Huskinson 2004: 134–52.
[30] See Casana 2004: 102–25.
[31] For similar arguments in relation to sculpture found in Antioch, see Brinkerhoff 1970.
[32] Vorderstrasse 2004: 86–101; Trombley 2004: 59–85 and 1985: 327–52.
[33] Mayer 1998: 107 and 126–7.
[34] For the location of the churches, see J. Kelly 1995: 302–3. For the Church of Babylas, see Downey 1938: 45–8. For the Church of the Maccabees, see Vinson 1994.

archaeological remains of Graeco-Roman temples survive. We thus have to build up a picture of Antioch's position in fourth-century imperial and religious history largely from the literary material, which includes the writings of the historian Ammianus Marcellinus, who was born or lived in Antioch and referred to the city in his *History*.[35] It also includes the emperor Julian, who stayed in the city while emperor and composed his *Misopogon* there, a work that largely deals with the failure of his attempt to revive traditional paganism in the city. In addition, we have Theodoret of Cyrrhus, who was also born in Antioch, and the Church historians Sozomen and Socrates, who at times refer to Antioch in the broader accounts of religious developments in the eastern empire.[36] Later accounts of Antioch, including details of its religious life, are also given by Malalas and Evagrius Scholasticus.[37] What is missing from this plethora of textual material is any Jewish voice. For any account of the Jewish presence, as much else, we thus largely have to rely on the writings of Chrysostom and Libanius.

As befitted a Greek city founded by a Hellenistic king, Antioch had once had all the characteristics of traditional civic religion. Here, as in other Greek cities, a number of traditional Greek divinities were worshipped, often in combination with Syrian divinities.[38] Antioch had its own civic deities with their own myths – in particular Zeus, Apollo, the Muse Calliope and the Tyche of Antioch.[39] There was an oracular shrine of Apollo at Daphne, where Apollo had supposedly chased the nymph Daphne, and numerous temples to Zeus throughout the city. In the Roman period, Antioch also gained an Olympic games to be held in honour of Zeus, after successfully petitioning the emperor Claudius for permission to host the festival.[40] The Tyche of Antioch was the tutelary deity of the city and was present from the city's beginnings: Seleucus I commissioned a statue of the goddess and had it set up in the city in 296–293 BC.[41] She continued to represent the

---

[35] Matthews 1994; Fornara 1992; and Barnes 1998: 54–64.
[36] Theodoret, *Ecclesiastical History* and *A History of the Monks of Syria*, and Sozomen and Socrates' *Ecclesiatical Histories*.
[37] *The Chronicle of John Malalas* and *The Ecclesiastical History of Evagrius Scholasticus*. On Malalas' account of Antioch, see also Liebeschuetz 2004.
[38] Takács 2000: 197; Downey 1963: 120; and Norris 1990: 2341 and 2356.
[39] On the Tyche, see also Zetterholm 2003: 19 and Downey 1963: 35–7. On Calliope, see Downey 1963: 99 and 1961: 216–17. See also Libanius, *Or.* 1.102 (F.1.133). For descriptions of the foundation myths of the city, see Takács 2000: 198 and Libanius, *Or.* 11.44–52, 57, 59–67, 72–6, 85–6 and 94–100 (F.1.451–3, 454–5, 455–8, 460–1 and 464–9). See also *Or.* 11.65 and 76 (F.1.457 and 496) and Malalas 198.23–201.3. On these foundation myths in the mosaics of Antioch, see Norris 1996: 2334. For the various versions of the myth of Apollo at Daphne, see Pausanias 8.20.2–4; Libanius, *Or.* 11.94 (F.1.467); and Sozomen, *HE* 5.19. See also Norris 1990: 2335–6.
[40] Schouler and Million 1988: 71.
[41] As depicted on a Roman issue coin from the city (Takács 2000: 198).

city well into the fourth century as she is found in a set of four statues of Tyche representing the main cities of the Roman empire at this time.[42] The Muse Calliope had a statue erected to her in the theatre by Trajan and under Marcus Aurelius a *Mouseion*, a shrine to the Muses, was built.[43] A festival with horse races was also celebrated for this divinity. In this way Antioch had its own 'sacred identity' that was defined by particular divinities and their festivals and temples just as any other Greek city would have done.[44]

Civic religion is not, however, something static and unchanging. As early as the second to third centuries, other significant changes to civic life and civic religion also appear to have been taking place. Some scholars of this period see civic religion as having been threatened either by changes to Roman rule, or by the extension of Roman citizenship in the third century AD.[45] For others the increased pluralization of the religious situation or a turn towards more personal forms of religious authority in the second and third centuries AD are seen as detrimental to, or as providing an alternative to, the unity of civic life.[46] It is likely that Antioch was affected by these trends just as were other cities in the Greek parts of the Roman empire. We know that the period of Roman rule brought the normal range of 'mystery' religions such as the cult of Isis and Dionysus, which added some elements of choice to people's religious experience.[47] There is also evidence that Antioch faced even more disruption than other areas of the empire during the third century. Under Septimius Severus the city was punished for supporting a challenger to the throne, Pescennius Niger, by the loss of its status as metropolis of Syria and by the removal of the Olympic festival from the city. In 253 and 260 Persians sacked the city and burnt or destroyed many of its buildings. Valerian did attempt to rebuild the city but in the reign of Gallienus, Antioch fell under Palmyrian control, became part of the *de facto* Palmyrian empire and remained so until the reign of Aurelian in 272–3.[48] It seems unlikely that civic religion in Antioch would have remained unchanged through all these upheavals. We should thus be wary of talking of decline in the fourth century as if we can contrast this with some ideal state of civic religion in the century before. There is some

---

[42] In a collection of the British Museum, see Kondoleon 2000a: 118–20.
[43] Downey 1963: 99 and 1961: 216–17.   [44] For the 'sacred identity' of cities, see Rogers 1991
[45] Rives 1995: 171–2 and S. Mitchell 1990: 191–3. On the worship of emperors in Antioch, see Zetterholm 2003: 23 and Norris 1990: 2360–1.
[46] North 1992: 177–8; Rives 1995: 173 and 184–6; Lane-Fox 1986: 168–261; Robert 1968; S. Mitchell 1999; J. Z. Smith 1995: 20–7 and 1978: 186–7; and Veyne 1986: 259–83.
[47] Takács 2000: 199 and Norris 1990: 2362. See also Norris 1982: 189–207.
[48] See Downey 1963: 106–19 and Norris 1990: 2339.

evidence that the suburb of Daphne in Antioch (in particular the Oracle of Apollo, the Nymphaeum and the Temple of Hecate) had become the focus of Neoplatonic activity by the early fourth century.[49] By the mid to late fourth century, when Libanius was writing, there had already probably been many changes to civic religion.

If we turn to the fourth century, we know that many of the main temples in the city continued to stand for much of the period.[50] The only ones that we hear of being destroyed were the Shrine of Apollo, which burnt down in the reign of Julian, and Temple of Nemesis, which was demolished in 387.[51] Similarly, many of the traditional festivals appear to have survived in some form.[52] We hear of the New Year's festival; the festival of Poseidon held in early spring; the boxing matches in honour of Artemis (although Libanius complains of declining attendance even at these, the full festival was probably celebrated in the reign of Julian); the festival of Calliope (at least during the reign of Julian; after that only the horse races may have continued); the Maiumas in honour of Dionysus and Aphrodite all held in May; the festival of Adonis on 17 to 19 July and the festival of Dionysus held at the time of the wine harvest.[53] We can also add to this the Olympic festival that was celebrated for forty-five days every four years in honour of Olympian Zeus, which survived well into the 380s at least as can be seen by the many references in Libanius to attempts to obtain athletes and musicians for it.[54] We have no evidence at all for the cult of Isis in the city in the fourth century but there are some very brief references to the continued existence of some kind of Bacchic worship.[55] Although many temples of Antioch were still standing, this was often in a depleted form and it would have been difficult for people to use them for cult activities. Libanius describes how the Temple of Artemis needed restoration in the reign of Julian because statues and decorations had been taken from it

---

[49] Soler states that the Neoplatonic philosopher Iamblichus of Apamea had taught at Daphne before his death in AD 330 (Soler 1999: 86).

[50] See Soler 1999: 39–58.

[51] It is likely, though, that many smaller shrines were destroyed, especially during Caesar Gallus' stay in Antioch and in the years after Julian's death.

[52] See Soler 1999: 76–83 and 213–19.

[53] For the New Year's festival, see Libanius, *Or.* 9 (F.1.391–400) and Chrysostom, *In Kalends*. For Artemis, see Libanius, *Or.* 5 (F.i.301–20). For Calliope, see Libanius, *Ep.* N.100 (F.811) and *Ep.* F.1175. For the Maiumas, see Malalas 285.12–21, Theodoret, *HE* 3.14 and Libanius, *Or.* 41.16 (F.III.302) and *Or.* 50.11 (F.III.476). For Adonis, see Amm. Marc. 32.9.14 and 19.1.11. For Dionysus, see Libanius, *Ep.* B.153 (F.661); *Ep.* F.1480; *Ep.* F.1288; *Ep.* F.1212; and Theodoret, *HE* 4.24.3. See also Liebeschuetz 1972: 228–31 and Soler 1999: 189–223.

[54] For the Olympic festival, see Libanius, *Or.* 1.188 and 222 (F.1.168–9 and 181).

[55] Libanius, *Ep.* F.1480 and *Ep.* B.153 (F.661) and for a Bacchic revel in the forum of Antioch in the reign of Valens and Valentinian, see Theodoret, *HE* 4.24.

under Constantius (*Ep.* B.181 (F.712)).⁵⁶ The Temple of Tyche, or Fortune, was stripped in 359 and from then on was used only as a classroom and for other more general usage (Libanius, *Ep.* N.110 (F.1406) and *Ep.* N.45 (F.88)). When Julian came to power, he complained that it had become more like a theatre than a temple because it was used as a public meeting place by townsfolk who wanted to express their grievances (*Ep.* N.110 (F.1406).⁵⁷ Similarly, in AD 355 the first *comes orientis*, Felicianus, probably a Christian, was given the Temple of the Muses as headquarters (Malalas, 13.4 (319)) and in 386 the Temple of Dionysus, situated at the side of the Silipius, was used by Tisamenus, the Christian governor, as a Tribunal (Libanius, *Or.* 45.26 (F.III.371)). Thus, while many aspects of civic religion did survive into the fourth century, they often did not remain unchanged. In Antioch the Olympic festival and the festival of the province of Syria that was based in Antioch survived throughout the fourth century with great expenditure by the elites on athletes and wild animals.⁵⁸ The Kalends festival also continued to be celebrated regularly throughout the fourth century and we often hear of the gift giving that was one of the characteristic features of this festival.⁵⁹ Other festivals seem to have been celebrated in a less consistent fashion, with many only taking their full form under Julian, for example the festival of Calliope and Artemis. Artemis received some honours in May at the Maiumas, which was celebrated with nocturnal stage shows and water displays at Daphne, but only received the full honours of her own festival under Julian.⁶⁰ Similarly, while the racehorses in honour of Calliope survived throughout the fourth century, it was only during the reign of Julian that sacrifices in the theatre were also performed in her honour (Libanius, *Ep.* N.100 (F.811)). While in Antioch the entertainment aspects of civic festivals were still being funded, other aspects of these festivals were facing financial difficulties.

It is often stated that in the fourth century Antioch was a largely Christianized city. By the 380s, when he was preaching, John Chrysostom suggests

---

⁵⁶ See also the shrine of Asclaepius in Aegae, which was destroyed in the 350s but continued to be used in its ruined form (Libanius, *Ep.* B.146–8 (F.727, 695 and 1342)).

⁵⁷ Julian, *Ep.* 176. See also Libanius, *Ep.* F.847; *CTh* 16.10.3 of AD 346 and 380; and later *CTh* 16.10.19 of AD 408; and Downey 1966: 148.

⁵⁸ *Ep.* N.125 (F.1180); *Ep.* N.149 (F.843); *Ep.* F.1017; *Ep.* B.26 (F.440); *Ep.* B.44 (F.1399); *Ep.* B.49 (F.1148); *Ep.* F.1181; *Ep.* F.1182; and *Ep.* B.142 (F.1183). See also Liebeschuetz 1972: 136–44 and 1959: 113–26; and Downey 1939b: 428–38.

⁵⁹ *Ep.* N.123.3 (F.1128); *Ep.* N.140 (F.1473); *Or.* 1.243 (F.I.188–9); *Or.* 62.56 (F.IV.373–4).

⁶⁰ *Ep.* N.83 (F.710) and *Ep.* B.181 (F.712). This festival was outlawed for much of the later fourth century due to its immoral nature, but it continued to be performed in any case. The ban was repealed in 396 but was again reinforced in 399 (*CTh* 15.6.1 and 2). Libanius disapproved of the Maiumas too (Misson 1914: 146).

that Christians numbered 100,000 in the city, which would make up approximately half of the population (*Hom. in Matt.* 85/86 (*PG* 58.762–3)).[61] Chrysostom's figures should not be trusted as official statistics in any sense; he was just trying to convey a sense of the large numbers of Christians in Antioch. However, it is clear that a large proportion of the population were turning to Christianity in some form in the fourth century, and that increasingly this included the elite as well as the lower classes.[62] Not surprisingly, these changes to civic religion can to some degree be traced back to Constantine's adoption of Christianity. Constantine had requisitioned the wealth of Graeco-Roman temples to be given to Christianity, and Libanius speaks of the problems faced by worshippers of the gods on this front. They did not want to give offerings to the gods in the temples because they knew that the offerings would just be stolen by Christian monks or would be requisitioned by imperial authorities (Libanius, *Or*. 2.30–1 (F.I.248)).[63] Legal pressures might also be seen as responsible for the loss of certain elements of religious festivals, particularly animal sacrifice. Even if legislation did not decisively outlaw sacrifice, pressure from Christian officials and zealous Christian priests and monks clearly had an impact on the ability of adherents of Graeco-Roman religion to worship freely.[64] The reign of Constantius, especially Gallus' years as Caesar in the city, was a particularly difficult time for the public and civic aspects of Graeco-Roman religion in Antioch. We can couple all this with the evidence that has been taken to show the increased presence of Christianity in the city and the attempt of John Chrysostom to present the city of Antioch in Christian terms. All these trends make it clear that actual religious life in Antioch could no longer be described as civic, at least not simply or in the traditional sense. Gradually, 'Christianity was taking over the function of providing citizens with holidays and entertainment' with a calendar of feasts and martyr festivals.[65] The increasing number of martyr shrines, even if they were normally placed outside the city, for example in the cemetery on the road to Daphne, also contributed to this effect.[66] The increased importance of Christianity in the city can be seen through the number of churches that began to be built there in the fourth century. This included the Great or Golden Church of

---

[61] Elsewhere Chrysostom describes the total population of Antioch as numbering 200,000 (*In S. Ignat*.4 (*PG* 50.591)). See also Libanius, *Ep.* N.122 (F.1119), where Libanius gives a figure of 150,000 for the population of Antioch.
[62] Wilken 1983: 17 and 22. But in contrast, see P. Petit 1955: 200–3.
[63] See also *Or*. 18.286 (F.II.362); *Or*. 49.11 (F.III.458) and *Or*. 23.18 (F.II.502).
[64] See Sandwell 2005.
[65] Liebeschuetz 1972: 231. See also Leemans *et al.* 2003: 2–4 and Soler 1999: 445–75.
[66] Leemans *et al.* 2003: 5, and 113.

Constantine dedicated by Constantius in 341; a cruciform shrine for Saint Babylas at Kaoussie built by Bishop Meletius in 379–80; the Church of the Maccabees in the Jewish quarter; the ancient 'apostolic' church, which was in the old part of the city and is thought to date back to apostolic times.[67] There were also many other smaller churches and *martyria* that although not used for daily worship were the site for the many Christian festivals.[68] With Constantine's conversion, Christianity thus began to be increasingly at home in the civic context. Christianity, which had once defined itself in opposition to the world around, was now establishing a relationship with the powers of state and city.

Chrysostom represented just one Christian group in Antioch – those we call the Nicene Christians – and reading only his writings can give the impression that this Christian group was dominant in Antioch.[69] In fact, for large parts of the fourth century there were three active Churches or Christian groups in operation in the city with varying degrees of influence and official support. The interplay between these Christian groups, and the very way in which they labelled each other as heretical, was itself the result of complex processes of the construction of 'orthodoxy' at any one time and thus subject to the processes of identity construction described in the previous chapter. This construction of 'orthodox' Christian identity will only be touched on in this current work but it should be remembered that terms such as 'Nicene' and 'Arian' Christian are just as nebulous and constructed as the terms 'pagan' and 'Christian'. Despite these problems, it is worth summarizing the situation of these differing Christian groups in Antioch, even if it means oversimplifying and overobjectifying them. When Constantius came to power he became a supporter of what we call Arian Christianity, and, as a result, when a new bishop had to be chosen for Antioch in 357, the Arian Eudoxius was chosen. He was followed in 361 by another Arian bishop, Euzoius, who held his position until 378. During this time, the followers of the Council of Nicaea in Antioch were split into two groups: the Meletians, led by Bishop Meletius, and the Eustathians, who declared a priest called Paulinus bishop.[70] Under Constantius, the leaders of both of these groups of Nicene Christians were banished from Antioch but they returned once Julian came to power and issued his edict recalling all outlawed 'heretical' groups. The Arians, who still considered

---

[67] On the former, see Lassus 1938: 5–44. On the latter, see Schatkin 1988: 15 and Downey 1938: 45–8. See also Mayer and Allen 2000: 18 and Eltester 1937: 251–86.
[68] Liebeschuetz 1972: 176 and Mayer and Allen 2000: 17–20.
[69] On Chrysostom's account of the schisms in the Church at Antioch, see Guinot 2004.
[70] Socrates, *HE* 2.44. See also Wilken 1983: 11–12 and Downey 1963: 157 and 175–7.

themselves the officially endorsed religion, continued to worship from the Great or Golden Church near the palace, but now the Meletians occupied the apostolic church in the old part of the city and the Eustathians used one of the other small churches in the city.[71] Valens also favoured Arianism and under his rule the persecution of the Nicene groups in Antioch continued and even increased. Valens overturned Julian's measures, again expelled the Meletian Christians from the city and made Euzoius the official bishop. The Arians thus took over the major churches of Antioch while the Meletians were forced to worship in the open air outside the city, either on the slopes of the mountains or the banks of the river.[72] Paulinus was allowed to continue to practice in some of the smaller churches of the city. It was only under Theodosius I in the 380s that Nicene Christianity again gained a stronghold in Antioch. In a decree of 27 February 380 (*CTh* 16.1.2) Theodosius declared Nicene Christianity to be the religion of empire and condemned all heretics, in particular the Arians. As a result, the Arians of Antioch were expelled and Meletius was made leader of the Christian community there, being given the Great, or Golden, Church as his base. Flavian followed Meletius as bishop and it was under Flavian that John Chrysostom served as priest. During much of the time for which we have the sermons of Chrysostom, then, his Christian community was the official one in the city. However, the rival Christian groups did not disappear as quickly as the rulings of Theodosius might suggest. Later in the 380s those who were labelled Arians began to gain influence again and even challenged Chrysostom to defend his interpretation of Christianity against their own.[73]

Finally, we must not forget that there was still a strong community of those labelled Jews in Antioch in the fourth century. There had been those who thought of themselves as Jews present in Antioch since its foundation by Seleucus I in 300 BC. Many had fought in Seleucus' army and then settled there but Antioch's proximity to Jerusalem and Persia also made it a popular place for Jews to migrate to from there.[74] The Jews continued to have a strong presence in Antioch under Roman rule and by the fourth century there was not only a Jewish community in Antioch itself, in the east of the city, but also one in the suburb of Daphne and one in the countryside

---

[71] Theodoret, *HE* 11.31.11 and 3.4.3 and Socrates, *HE* 3.9.
[72] Theodoret, *HE* 5.24 and *H. R.* ed. 2. See also Downey 1963: 182–8 on the events under Valens and Theodosius I.
[73] Wilken 1983: 14–16. See John Chrysostom's sermons *De Incomp. Dei Nat.* (SC 28) and on these sermons Schatkin 1988.
[74] On the earliest Jewish community in Antioch, see Brooten 2000: 29–37; Wilken 1983: 35–8; Zetterholm 2003: 31–40; and Kraeling 1932: 130–60.

outside Antioch, probably to the north-east.[75] These Jewish communities appear to have had quite an impact on civic life: the former two at least had their own synagogue and they were made up of diverse social classes who interacted in social and political life.[76] At the same time, though, and again because of the proximity of Palestine, the Jewish community in Antioch maintained strong links with Jerusalem and the authorities there. In the fourth century Libanius and Chrysostom both refer to Jews and the Jewish community. For Chrysostom at least they were an unavoidable, if disliked, factor in the religious interaction of the time. We know from Chrysostom that many members of his Christian community also found Judaism very attractive and often took part in the rituals and activities of the Jewish community there.[77] Chrysostom talks of these Christians attending the Jewish synagogue in the city, so we know that this must still have been in existence. We also hear of the shrine of Matrona in the suburb of Daphne that still attracted Jews to celebrate the cult of the mother of the Maccabees.[78]

This is a bare outline of the state of Graeco-Roman religion in fourth-century Antioch. However, there is still a problem in how to interpret the religious continuities and changes outlined, in imposing our own characterizations onto them and in judging how far the city was Christianized. For this reason, most of this work will now be devoted to an exploration of how Chrysostom and Libanius understood and represented the religious situation in Antioch rather than to a straightforward description.

THE ORAL AND LITERARY WORLD OF LIBANIUS AND JOHN CHRYSOSTOM

Libanius was born in Antioch in AD 314 and after studying and working in various other cities, including Athens, Constantinople and Nicomedia, he returned there in 354 to work as a teacher and orator until he died, probably early in the 390s.[79] He was a member of the ruling class of the city and was exempt from curial duties only because of his status as official teacher in the city. There were a number of vicissitudes to his career as a teacher but he maintained this position into the 390s. Scholars agree that

---

[75] Wilken 1983: 36–7.
[76] Wilken 1983: 55–62. See also Zetterholm 2003: 38, who argued that at least until the second century AD eighteen synagogues would have been needed to accommodate the number of Jews in Antioch.
[77] Kondoleon 2000: 35 and Wilken 1983: 66–94. [78] Vinson 1994 and Soler 1999: 235–45.
[79] For a new and updated introduction to Libanius and his life, see Wintjes 2005. See also Liebeschuetz 1972: 1–16.

he was an ardent supporter of the traditional gods, but he had Christian as well as non-Christian friends. John Chrysostom was also born in Antioch, probably into a Christian family – his mother at least was Christian – in AD 349.[80] In 367, his eighteenth year, Chrysostom was baptized by Bishop Meletius and chose to work within the Church rather than follow a secular career.[81] He had received a traditional classical education under Libanius, but on becoming Christian began an education in the Christian teachings of Diodorus of Tarsus.[82] He was introduced to the teachings and modes of biblical interpretation of the 'Antiochene' school, which favoured more literal and historical interpretation of biblical texts than the allegorical approach of the Alexandrian school.[83] Chrysostom's mentor, Bishop Meletius, supported the Nicene 'orthodox' formulation of the relationship between God and Christ that was agreed upon at the Council of Nicaea in 325. As a result, he did not find favour when the Arian emperor Valens came to power in 371. Meletius was exiled and at the same time Chrysostom too left his clerical duties in the Church and went to live as a monk in the mountains outside Antioch. Six years later, when Bishop Meletius was allowed to return to his position in Antioch under the emperor Theodosius, Chrysostom followed him. Chrysostom then served there among the Nicene Christians first as a deacon and afterwards, from 386, as a priest with the duty of preaching in Antioch, until he was ordained bishop of Constantinople in 397. Libanius and Chrysostom were both born and writing in the city at approximately the same time and both have left us large amounts of written work.

We have surviving to us a huge body of Libanius' writings consisting of sixty-four orations, more than a thousand letters and a large number of declamations and other educational writings.[84] Libanius himself had a secretary who kept written copies of all his orations so that they could be preserved and sent to friends on request.[85] The letters that survive were those of which Libanius chose to keep copies in his files, hence there is a gap in the letters during the difficult years of the reign of Valens and Valentianian. After Libanius' death an unknown person published those letters that Libanius did keep on file.[86] Tackling the whole body of this literature would be an insurmountable task, but many of the writings are

---

[80] For an account of Chrysostom's life, see J. Kelly 1995. [81] Mayer and Allen 2000: 5.
[82] J. Kelly 1995: 18–20 and Wintjes 2005: 43–77.
[83] For the historical mode of exegesis at Antioch and in John Chrysostom, see Wallace-Hadrill 1982: 27–51; J. Kelly 1995: 95; and Garret 1992: 231. Some are now challenging the clear-cut opposition between the Antiochene and the Alexandrian schools.
[84] See Wintjes 2005: 17–28. [85] P. Petit 1956: 484.
[86] See Bradbury 2004: 21 and, more generally, 19–23.

less relevant to this study. While the declamations and educational writings are useful for understanding the state of classical education and rhetoric in the fourth century, they tend not to deal with subjects relating to actual social life in Antioch at the time and will not be used in this study.[87] Instead, I shall focus on the orations and letters. These are more directly concerned with everyday life and with social, religious and political situations that Libanius actually faced. The orations were written throughout Libanius' career and were addressed to a variety of addressees, from emperors to city councils to individuals, and were delivered in wide-ranging contexts: *Oration* 11 *In Praise of Antioch* was probably delivered publicly at an Olympic games in 356; *Oration* 12 *An Address to Julian* and *Oration* 13 *An Address to the Emperor Julian as Consul* were delivered in front of Julian; others found smaller and more personal audiences in the city of Antioch or were posted in written form.[88] The letters too are equally wide-ranging and we see Libanius writing to relatives, friends and officials in Antioch, throughout the east and even in Italy and North Africa.[89] They can be dated to two periods of Libanius' life. Firstly, to a period of ten years early in his return to his native city of Antioch – 355–65 – and, secondly, to a period of five years in the reign of Theodosius I up to his death – 388–93.[90] In both the letters and the orations Libanius wrote on a range of subjects relating to both civic life and life under the later Roman empire more generally. He covered topics from the treatment of prisoners in the city's jails to the decline of the city's councils, from the destruction of temples in the countryside around Antioch to orations in praise of Constantius and Julian. As the official sophist and teacher of Antioch, Libanius held the publicly funded teaching chair of the city, and as a member of one of the city's leading families he had a central role in many of the most important social and political events of the city in the fourth century. He was a well-connected man who knew everyone of importance and had the status to speak out on matters of public and personal interest. His orations and letters are thus crucial for understanding most aspects of social, civic and political life in the late-antique city of Antioch. When it comes to religious affairs, however, Libanius can be less informative than on other matters and his discussion makes up only a small proportion of the subject matter of his writings: often he refers to religion only in passing, when discussing other matters.

---

[87] On the declamations, see D. Russell 1996.
[88] On the dating of *Oration* 11 see Downey 1959: 652–86; Norman 2000: 3–4; and P. Petit 1983: 129–49. On the orations generally, see P. Petit 1956 and Liebeschuetz 1972: 23–39.
[89] On the letters, see Bradbury 2004: 1–2 and 19–23 and Liebeschuetz 1972: 17–22.
[90] See Norman 1992: vols. I and II and Bradbury 2004: 19.

Whole Orations on religious subjects such as *Oration 30 To Theodosius in Defence of the Temples* are the exception.

For Chrysostom too we have a voluminous amount of writing: approximately nine hundred of his sermons survive as well as a number of written treatises.[91] Scholars once thought that most of these came from Chrysostom's period in Antioch before he went on to become bishop of Constantinople.[92] However, recent work by Wendy Mayer has shown that we must be much more cautious about making such assumptions.[93] In an important new work Mayer has undertaken a comprehensive study of the way that provenance has been assigned to Chrysostom's sermons and has shown that the methodology for making these assignations is deeply flawed.[94] It is thus crucial to take care in the selection of homilies on which to carry out a study of the religious situation in Antioch. For this reason, and to provide a manageable body of relevant material for the present work, I have focused on specific series of sermons whose provenance was very likely to be Antioch. These series are the sixty-seven sermons *On Genesis* (*PG* 53.21–54.580) delivered in Lent in 385–8;[95] the seventy-four sermons *On 1 and 2 Corinthians* (*PG* 61.11–610) probably delivered in 392–3;[96] the twenty-one sermons *To the People of Antioch, On the Statues* (*PG* 49.15–222) delivered in Lent in 387;[97] and the twelve *Catechetical Sermons* (*PG* 49.223–40) probably delivered in two series, again in Lent, between 388 and 397, possibly in 391.[98] These provide a representative sample of Chrysostom's preaching, which is often repetitive in nature, returning again and again to the same themes. They are likely to have been delivered in the context of

---

[91] Mayer and Allen 2000: 7. The sermons survived because they were taken down by a stenographer as Chrysostom spoke and then written up. Some may thus have undergone some change from the form in which they were originally delivered but many of the remnants of oral delivery are still clear. On this problem, see Goodall 1979. The process of identifying the genuine and spurious sermons of Chrysostom is now also well underway, see *CPG* 4305–5190 (vol. II: 491–672) and the various works of Voicu (1996, 1997 and 2005).

[92] Mayer and Allen 2000: 7.

[93] Mayer 2001a: 83–105, 1998: 113, 1995b: 309–48 and 1995a: 27–89. See also Allen 1997: 3–21 and Mayer and Allen 1994: 21–39.

[94] Mayer 2005.

[95] For a recent translation see Hill 1986 and 1990. On the dating, see Hill 1986: 6 and Brändle and Jegher-Bucher 1995: 289.

[96] For the dating, see Brändle and Jegher-Bucher 1995: 292.   [97] Although see the next footnote.

[98] For the Greek text of the other baptismal sermons, see *Huit catéchèses baptismales inédites*, text and translation, Wenger 1957 and *Jean Chrysostome: Trois catéchèses baptismales*, text and translation, Piédagnel 1990; and for an English translation see Harkins 1963. For the dating, see van de Paverd 1991: 255–93, who proposes the year 391, and Harkins 1963: 15–18. Some scholars now argue that at least one of the sermons once considered a catechetical sermon (*Ad Illum. Catech.* 2 (*PG* 49.231–40) = Harkins, *Baptismal Instruction* 12)) was in fact part of the series on the statues (for example, van de Paverd 1991: 227–9; Piédagnel 1990: 20–32; and Valevicius 2000: 83–91). It would thus have been delivered in 387 along with the other sermons on the Riot of the Statues.

Antioch, although we should be aware that we can be completely certain about only a few of the homilies within each series.[99] As well as discussing these series of sermons, I shall give special attention to Chrysostom's works that directly relate to questions of religious interaction. These include his sermons *Against the Jews* (PG 48.843–942), delivered in 386/7; also his two apologetic treatises addressed to Greeks, *Discourse on Blessed Babylas and Against the Greeks* (PG 50.533–72) and *Demonstration against the Gentiles and Jews that Christ is God* (PG 48.813–38), written before he became deacon in 386 or in the early years of his preaching (possibly 378/9 for the former and 387 for the latter).[100] I shall then supplement this with other passages from the range of Chrysostom's sermons that are particularly relevant.[101] Religious issues are the *raison d'être* of Chrysostom's writings, which primarily consist of exegetical homilies on the Old and New Testament, baptismal instructions and occasional sermons to celebrate particular festivals and saints. However, Chrysostom does not exclude concern with the contemporary social context as this provides the lens through which he interprets the biblical and apostolic texts.[102]

We only have the works of Chrysostom and Libanius in the written form in which they were recorded and passed down. However, we must also remember that many of the works of both men also had some form of oral delivery in fourth-century Antioch. It is now believed that some at least of Chrysostom's sermons were delivered *ex tempore* without prior composition and were written down at the time of preaching by a stenographer.[103] This means that a close relation between the written versions that we have and the original orally delivered version can be posited.[104] It is, however, not always possible to distinguish clearly between texts that were originally delivered orally and then taken down by a stenographer and those that were originally recorded in written form and made to look as if they had

[99] See Mayer's tables for establishing the provenance of individual sermons 2005: 469–73 and 511–12.
[100] See translations by Schatkin and Harkins 1983 and by Harkins 1979. On the dating of the treatises against Greeks, see Mayer and Allen 2000: 7 and Brändle and Jegher-Bucher 1995: 278 and 283. On the dating of the sermons against the Judaizers, see Harkins 1979: l–lxii and Brändle and Jegher-Bucher 1995: 279.
[101] On these see Leemans *et al.* 2003.
[102] See Allen 1991 and 1994 and Mayer and Allen 1993: 260–80; and www.cecs.acu.edu.au/chrysostomresearch.htm 'A social lens: late antiquity in the sermons of John Chrysostom'. See also E. G. Clark 2001: 265–84.
[103] Goodall 1979: 62–7. Baur saw sermons as pre-composed literary works (Baur 1959–60: vol. 1, 206). For evidence of post-delivery revision of sermons, see Gignac 1998 and Boismard and Lamouille 1993.
[104] Amirav argues that there is little distinction between Chrysostom's preaching and his pre-formulated exegetical treatises, so playing down the context of oral delivery of sermons (Amirav 2003: 22–31 and 45–62).

been delivered orally. This is the case with Chrysostom's *Commentary on Isaiah* (SC 304), which contains features that suggest oral delivery. We do not know if these came about because the commentary was developed from a series of sermons, or if they were rhetorical devices only. We can make no firm distinction between oral and literary culture when we talk about how people learnt from these texts.[105] Libanius, on the other hand, did compose most of his speeches prior to delivery and they are thus often more polished works than Chrysostom's sermons. However, they were still usually intended to have some kind of listening audience and as such were part of the trend for public oratory that took off from the second century AD onwards in the Roman empire. Perhaps more surprisingly for modern audiences, Libanius' letters must be seen in this light too. Rather than being the more private documents that we are used to, letters in the ancient world were sent in the knowledge that they might well be read aloud to a number of other people by the recipient and then discussed.[106] Thus again, no clear distinction should be made between the written texts that we have left to us and the context of oral delivery that Libanius' orations and even sometimes his letters achieved in the fourth century. We thus need to understand the context of this oral delivery.

We know that Libanius taught and spoke in various public and private spaces in the city. In his *Autobiography*, Libanius recounted the first rhetorical performance that he gave on his arrival back in Antioch. He described this as taking place before a packed and appreciative audience in the city council house (*bouleuterion*) of Antioch (*Or*. 1.87 (F.1.126)). In the early days of his teaching career at Antioch Libanius had trouble in finding somewhere to teach. He was forced to use his own home until he managed to find a room on the 'fringe' of the market square vacated by a trader (*Or*. 1.101–2 (F.1.132)). On becoming the official sophist of the city, as a result of the illness of his predecessor, Zenobius, Libanius finally gained rooms in the *bouleuterion* as the permanent site for his teaching (*Or*. 1.105 (F.1.134) and *Ep*. N.29.4 (F.364) and *Ep*. N.45.2 (F.88)). When we turn to Libanius' non-pedagogical speaking, we know that his orations would have been delivered in a variety of contexts. Maxwell has shown that orators of the second sophistic as well as those of the fourth century, such as Themistius, could be concerned to deliver their speeches to as wide an

---

[105] On literacy among Christians and on the way that textuality could still be central without full literacy, see Stock 1983: 91; Cameron 1991: 109–11; and Gamble 1995.

[106] Trapp 2003: 17; Liebeschuetz 1972: 20; and Bradbury 2004: 19–20. For examples of people reading aloud, see *Ep*. N.12 (F.434); *Ep*. F.773.5; and *Ep*. B.107 (F.779).

audience as possible.¹⁰⁷ Some orations would have been delivered at festivals and in the public squares and would have been heard by large parts of the civic community of Antioch, such as Libanius' *Oration 11 The Oration in Praise of Antioch*. On one occasion Libanius himself implied that large audiences could come to listen to him as he described how he had to dampen down their over-enthusiastic applause (*Or.* 2.23–4 (F.11.246–7)). He delivered other orations to the civic council or before the emperor and his court.¹⁰⁸ Elsewhere, we hear of more intimate forms of delivery. Some of his non-classroom speeches were delivered to select audiences such as chosen and trusted groups of friends and officials in private houses – either his own or those of friends (*Ep.* N.64 (F.283)).

It is likely that Libanius' schoolrooms would have contained pupils from both Christian and non-Christian elites, whether the sons of the local Antiochene elite or of men from other eastern cities.¹⁰⁹ Some of Libanius' orations suggest an explicit concern with dealing with broader social issues in Antioch and with addressing the lower classes as well as the elite, for example speeches concerning the bakers, in *Orations* 29 and 27, the prisoners, in *Oration* 45, and the peasants around Antioch, in *Oration* 50. Libanius gives some suggestion that the people whom he was trying to help in these orations had heard what he had said in their defence as he can describe how they looked on him with gratitude when he walked through the workshops (*Or.* 2.6 (F.11.240–1)).¹¹⁰ There are also suggestions that Libanius' views might well have extended to larger audiences than those who directly heard his speaking. Libanius composed his orations before delivery and we hear of them being 'published' in the ancient sense that they were circulated among friends and associates.¹¹¹ In his *Oration 1 The Autobiography*, Libanius also describes how information about his career that he had only told his students was soon common knowledge in the city (*Or.*1.12 (F.1.86–7)). At another, in his *Oration 2 To Those Who Call Me Tiresome*, he expresses the hope that things that he had said to small audiences in certain orations might have 'been transmitted from person to person until it reached the ears of the emperor' (*Or.* 2.70 (F.11.261)).¹¹² This suggests that those who heard Libanius' orations might have passed on their content to others.

---

[107] Maxwell forthcoming: 15–19, 19–22 and 28. See her references to Themistius, *Or.* 24.302a–c, *Or.* 31.352 and *Or.* 26.313.
[108] Maxwell notes the public importance of such panegyric orations as a 'social act' (Maxwell forthcoming: 45). See also her references to Pernot 1993: 438.
[109] P. Petit 1957a: 196. [110] On this, see Maxwell forthcoming: 46 and Wiemer 1996.
[111] Norman 1960: 122–6. [112] See also P. Petit 1956: 507 on *Oration* 30.

We know more about the audiences of Chrysostom's sermons because he engaged more directly with those listening to him than Libanius appears to have done. By the time that Chrysostom became preacher, the Nicene faction of Christianity to which he belonged had imperial favour again. Thus, both Bishop Flavian and Chrysostom himself had use of the main churches in Antioch in which to preach (in contrast to earlier years when the previous Nicene bishop, Meletius, had had to preach on the hillside outside Antioch while the Arians had control of the churches). Chrysostom often preached to his own congregation in the Old Church in the old part of the city, although he also appears to have helped Flavian in the Great or Golden Church on the island in the Orontes on occasion and to have preached at various martyr shrines.[113] It is notoriously difficult to judge how far Chrysostom's references to the social status of his audiences represent reality.[114] He often made statements about the presence of the very rich and the treatment of the very poor but he probably exaggerated this stark contrast between rich and poor for rhetorical effect. It is now usually accepted that Chrysostom's audiences were made up of a wide cross-section of the community from the lower level of paid labourers through reasonably well-off traders to the wealthy upper classes.[115] Slaves might also have attended occasionally with their masters but the poorest members of society, beggars and the homeless probably did not attend in large numbers. Groups of people of different social status in fact probably attended church with different levels of regularity depending on their work commitments, as will be explored further in chapter 5. As well as different social groups attending church, it is clear that on occasion non-Christians (at least as Chrysostom considered them) did so too. This can be seen in the troubled times after the Riot of the Statues when Greeks and unbelievers appear to have come to church.[116] The fact that Chrysostom sometimes states 'now I am addressing the Greeks' does not mean that non-Christians were normally in his audience: this was just a turn of phrase to show what arguments should be used against the Greeks.[117] Chrysostom too, as we have seen, composed written treatises and it is quite likely that they would have been published in a similar manner to Libanius' orations. That Chrysostom's orally spoken sermons were taken down by a stenographer

---

[113] Mayer and Allen 2000: 17–18 and Eltester 1937: 251–86.
[114] Kyrtatas 1987: 102–7 and Mayer 1998: 123.
[115] For example Maxwell forthcoming: 65–87 and Mayer 1998. For a more cautious view, see E. G. Clark 2001.
[116] See J. Kelly 1995: 81–2 and also *Hom. de Stat.* 21.4 (*PG* 49.213) and *De Anna* 1.1 (*PG* 54.684).
[117] As at *In Ep. ad 1 Cor. Hom.* 6.5 (*PG* 61.51) and *Hom. in Gen.* 17.2 (*PG* 534.134).

as they were delivered means that they too could have been disseminated in written versions.[118]

One of the shared characteristics of the oral-literary works of Libanius and Chrysostom is that they were highly rhetorical by their very nature. As with most writings from this period, they were governed by the literary and rhetorical rules that so dominated late antiquity. As a Greek orator working under the Roman empire in the fourth century, Libanius fell at the tail end of the second-sophistic movement.[119] If anything, rhetoric can be seen to have had a higher status in the fourth century than it did in the second. It is likely that the fourth century saw a revival of deliberative political oratory and that there was a ready audience in Late Antiquity for rhetorical performances and the oratory of display.[120] As was the case with the authors of the second-sophistic movement, Libanius was writing and speaking as a Greek representing Greek cities under Roman rule. Also like these authors, Libanius had great ability in the rhetorical techniques of the schools and consciously emulated classical forms, styles and authors from the fifth century BC.[121] His writings are thus full of references to classical literature, use atticizing Greek and often make direct use of the stylistic techniques of men such as Demosthenes, Isocrates and Plato.[122] Libanius could also emulate the second-sophistic writers themselves. We see that on many occasions he refers to the second-century orator Aelius Aristides as someone he admires; occasionally he also directly imitates Aristides.[123] Libanius' *Oration 64 For the Dancers* directly engages with Aristides' speech against pantomimes. Elsewhere the imitation is less explicit but still clear: Libanius' *Oration 61 Monody for Nicomedia* is modelled on Aristides' *Monody for Smyrna*, and his *Oration 5 Hymn to Artemis* is modelled on the prose hymns of Aristides such as that to Athena. Similarities have also been posited between Libanius' *Oration 1 The Autobiography* and Aristides' *Sacred Tales*.[124] We see Libanius using topoi, models and ways of writing drawn from the rhetorical tradition and rhetorical handbooks. In every oration and even every letter Libanius is in part trying to display his skills in manipulating this tradition to other educated men who would have shared his joy in such an exercise.

This does lead to a feeling of artificiality in Libanius' writings. However, we should not be misled or allow ourselves to dismiss his writings as 'purely literary' as a result. In post-second-sophistic oratory, as with the oratory

---

[118] Kennedy 1983: 250. [119] Swain 2004: 355–400 (especially 362–73).
[120] Cameron 1991: 85–6 and chapter 4, and Maxwell forthcoming: 42–64.
[121] Kennedy 1983: 149–63. [122] Kennedy 1983: 149–63.
[123] *Ep.* N.143.1–2 (F.1534) and *Ep.* F.965. [124] Swain 2004: 371–3.

of classical Athens, rhetoric was the way in which elite men engaged with their social and political context. Members of the Greek elite used rhetoric and classical training generally to address and appeal to emperors and to take part in intercity rivalry.[125] Although these forms of public speaking had less political or public impact than those of the great classical orators Demosthenes and Isocrates, they still had a function in their own social context. Libanius' speeches and the rhetoric of the fourth century should be seen in this tradition of public speaking.[126] Libanius could use phrases and comparisons drawn from the mythical and classical past, use styles and forms copied from the second-sophistic movement and still say something about his own contemporary situation.[127] To see his use of rhetoric only in terms of how he engaged with reality is to miss some of its greatest importance. Much exciting work has been carried out in recent years on second-sophistic literature and writers. This has shown that to judge these authors in terms of how they represent reality is to miss the point that in their works they were engaged in complex forms of self-representation and constructions of self-image.[128] This thinking has, so far, been little applied to Libanius' writings, which clearly call out for such an approach. Libanius used rhetorical forms, topoi and genre not only to persuade people to his view, but also to portray a particular image of himself and to place himself in particular positions in fourth-century society.

As with many Christians, Chrysostom emphasized the simplicity of Christian forms of expression. In *On the Priesthood* he argued that for the 'defence of the right faith' 'the tricks . . . and ornaments of profane oratory' were not needed (*De Sac.* 4.6 (SC 272.268)).[129] However, despite these explicit denials, Chrysostom too wrote according to the rules of the classical schools. He had been a pupil of Libanius, and the written versions of his sermons betray constant use of rhetorical techniques.[130] He used techniques such as repetition, contrasts and hyberbole to emphasize the points he made and those such as metaphors and *ekphrasis* (descriptive digressions) to make his preaching more evocative and interesting.[131]

---

[125] On the context of the second sophistic, see Cameron 1991: 73–84 and also Maxwell forthcoming: 16–29.
[126] Swain 2004: 367–9 and 385.   [127] Schouler 1984: vol. II, 995. See also Doukellis 1995.
[128] Whitmarsh 2001.
[129] Kennedy 1983: 245–53. See also Chrysostom, *On Vainglory and the Right Way for Parents to Bring up their Children*, translated in Laistner 1951.
[130] J. Kelly 1995: 14–20; A. H. M. Jones 1953; Hubbell 1924; Ameringer 1921: 20–8 and 101–3; and Garret 1992: 240.
[131] Cunningham 1990: 35.

Similarly, he could use the rhetorical forms of invective and praise to condemn groups he wanted to discredit (such as the Jews and Judaizers) or to praise heroes of the Antiochene Church (saints and martyrs).[132] As was the case with other Christian literary forms of the fourth century, Chrysostom's sermons shared many features with written texts and literary culture generally.[133] However, rather than making them inaccessible, rhetoric was what gave sermons their popular appeal. J. Maxwell has recently shown in the case of Chrysostom how Christian preaching found its basis in popular, philosophic traditions of public speaking. Just as Cynics and Epicureans had addressed people publicly in the streets and marketplaces, so too did Christian preachers.[134] In this way, Maxwell has highlighted the importance of public delivery to many late-antique preachers.[135] The very fact that they used a rhetorical form of public display that was popular as well as common in the ancient world helped them to spread their Christian message rather than hindered them in any way.

Oral debate and the public presentation of one's views in rhetorical form were a normal part of social interaction and there are some examples of our two authors interacting in this way. In the period between October 362 and spring 363 Libanius wrote a monody, a poem of lamentation, on the Shrine of Apollo at Daphne after it had burned down that year – his *Oration 60 Monody on the Shrine at Daphne*. This monody was probably delivered orally soon after the fire. It then survived in written form into the 370s, probably as a pamphlet given public circulation, so was available for Chrysostom to answer in written form fifteen years later. Thus, in 378 Chrysostom wrote his treatise *Discourse on Blessed Babylas and Against the Greeks* (*PG* 50.533–72), including passages from Libanius' *Monody* in his argument that the Christian Saint Babylas was more powerful than the Greek God Apollo.[136] Another example can be seen in the way that Libanius and Chrysostom write about the Riot of the Statues of 387. At the time

---

[132] On his use of invective, see Wilken 1983: 95–127. On his use of the rhetoric of praise, see Leemans *et al.* 2003: 26–37.
[133] Laistner 1951; Jaeger 1961; Kennedy 1983; and Cameron 1991.
[134] Maxwell forthcoming: 16–41 and 62–3.
[135] Maxwell forthcoming: 15–19, 19–22 and 28. See her references to Themistius *Or.* 24.302a–c, *Or.* 31.352 and *Or.* 26.313.
[136] On this treatise, see Schatkin and Harkins 1983. On the dating of Libanius' monody and Chrysostom's discourse, see Schatkin, 1983: 31–2. On the diffusion of Libanius' *Oration 60*, see Naegele 1908: 117 and P. Petit 1956: 491. See also Chrysostom's *Comparison between a King and a Monk*, which took phrases that Libanius had used about Julian and turned them instead to the Christian monks (Hunter 1988: 525–31). See also both Chrysostom's sermon and Libanius' oration on the Kalends festival.

of the riot, as events were unfolding, Chrysostom turned his daily Lenten sermons to ease the anxiety of a population fearing imperial punishment and to record the role of the Christian bishops and monks in solving the crisis. A short time after the riot, and probably in direct reaction to Chrysostom, Libanius himself composed a series of orations on the riot (*Orations* 19–23 (F.II.372–507), two of which purported to have been written prior to the riot and to have been delivered as part of an embassy to the emperor Theodosius requesting leniency for the city.[137] What we can thus see is that both Chrysostom and Libanius put forward their view of the riot and who had resolved the situation with Theodosius. However, van der Paverd has now shown that neither writer was giving an accurate depiction of events: Chrysostom distorted the situation by suggesting that it was the speech of Bishop Flavian that had assuaged Theodosius' anger against Antioch while Libanius overemphasized his own role and that of Caesarius 6/7, the master of the offices.[138] Libanius simply did not want it to appear that the Christians had played an active role in representing the city to the emperor and had written and circulated his orations after the event in order to emphasize his own role and that of the secular officials.[139] In fact, it is likely that both Flavian and Caesarius played a role in gaining forgiveness for Antioch from Theodosius.[140] In both Chrysostom's treatise on Babylas and Libanius' *Oration* 21 and *Oration* 22 we can see a typical ancient practice of using a written text to present one's own final conclusions in an ongoing debate.[141]

What is more important, however, is to compare Libanius' broader approach to the relationship between rhetorical representation and religion. While Libanius did use rhetoric to engage with his present circumstances, he did so in a way that put rhetorical necessity before consistency. It is now being recognized that to expect consistency from rhetorical writers or to judge them for not showing it is unfair and misguided. What we see in Libanius is a range of views expressed in very different rhetorical contexts and in which he was acting on very different requirements. Chrysostom, however, used rhetorical tools and modes of expression not simply to decorate his text or to display his skill but also to get across his message in a way that was clear and interesting. While Chrysostom did make extensive

---

[137] On the Riot of the Statues, see French 1998: 469–84; van de Paverd 1991; and Browning 1952: 42, 13–20.
[138] Van de Paverd 1991: 131–49.
[139] Norman, Introduction to the Loeb translation, 1969–77: vol. I, 240.
[140] Van de Paverd 1991: 131–49.   [141] Lim 1995: 5 and 22.

use of rhetoric and was just as capable of adjusting his representation to suit the context there was a uniting theme underlying his use of rhetoric: for Chrysostom rhetoric and literary forms were put to the service of his Christian message and to his construction of Christian identity. It is by exploring Libanius' and Chrysostom's different uses of rhetoric and writing in relation to religion that we will best gain an understanding of religious interaction in fourth-century Antioch.

PART II

Constructed and strategic religious identities and allegiances

INTRODUCTION

It was suggested in part I that Libanius and Chrysostom had different ways of writing about religion and different approaches to issues of religious identity and religious allegiance. It was also suggested that there was a connection between the fact that they had different approaches to writing about religion and the fact that they conceived of religious allegiance in different ways. Part II will explore these ideas in more detail. Chapter 3 will study Chrysostom's construction of religious identity in his preaching. It will show that clear-cut religious identities and labels were central to his thinking. It will also show how Chrysostom used his oratorical powers to create these notions of identities as (new) ways of being for his audiences. I shall start by looking at Chrysostom's definition of the central features of Christianity in his *Catechetical Sermons* and elsewhere. I shall show that these definitions inevitably led him to construct a 'Greek' other at the same time. We shall then turn to Chrysostom's depiction of Greek religion in his sermons addressed to the Greeks and in other works. We shall see here that Chrysostom was working with a stereotype of Greek religion that functioned most easily as a direct contrast to Christianity. This will then be compared with the way that Chrysostom sought to draw clear-cut distinctions between Jews and Christians in his sermons on the Judaizers. It will be shown that Chrysostom sought to place being Greek, being Jewish or being an Arian Christian in direct opposition to his ideal model for being Christian. All the non-Christian religious identities could then, for Chrysostom, be associated with one another and dismissed as demonic. Chrysostom was far from being the only Christian writer to make such a contrast, but we shall be focusing on the particular ways in which Chrysostom chose to mark out these distinctions between Christian and non-Christian. These might be different from the ways chosen by other Christian writers but they could still function to maintain distinctions between the different groups. Throughout this discussion we shall see that while Chrysostom presented religious identities as essential and objective categories we can reveal their constructed nature and analyse them as such. This in itself will begin to decentre Chrysostom's categories and belie the notion that they have any universal significance.

In Chapter 4 we shall see Libanius' very different ways of writing about religious allegiance. We shall study the terminology that Libanius used to describe religious allegiance in order to show both that he used wider-ranging and less determinate language than Chrysostom did and that he did have some interest in using such religious labels. Libanius clearly had some sense of who shared his own religious allegiance and who did not and we shall explore the few occasions on which he did emphasize these differences between these two sets of people. However, these occasions will prove to be the exception rather than the rule because Libanius did not see religious allegiance as a category of analysis that was relevant in every situation, and defining the differences between Graeco-Roman religion and Christianity was not this central goal. We shall see that on the whole Libanius did not use references to religious allegiance to make ideal statements about fixed and permanent religious identities of individuals. Rather, he tended to use such references in a more strategic or practical way in order to make a specific point or to achieve a particular outcome. Making statements about religious allegiance was one of the rhetorical tools he used in his writings in order to promote his own interests and the interests of those he knew and it could be tailored to suit the context in which he was writing. Religious allegiance was something that could be adjusted as was suitable, brought to the fore when needed, or pushed to the background when this was more appropriate. I shall consider the impact that this had on how Libanius wrote about adherents of Graeco-Roman religion and then on how he wrote about Christians and Jews. Finally, I shall place the significance of this view of Libanius' attitude to religious allegiance in the broader context of fourth-century imperial society and in relation to questions of religious sincerity and political flattery. I thus hope to put to rest the notion that Libanius' strategic use of religious allegiance can be taken to imply anything about a lack of true religion on his part. The fact that he adjusted references to religious allegiance to suit the times does not mean that he had no true religious adherence of his own.

By contrasting Libanius' and Chrysostom's views of religious identity and religious allegiance in this way we shall decentre the Christian categories of 'Greek'/'pagan', 'Christian' and 'Jew'. We shall see that there was a way of representing the religious situation in the fourth century which was alternative to that seen in our Christian texts and which did not rely on constantly dividing the world into such strictly defined categories. This will force us to develop a more complex view of the religious situation of the fourth century.

CHAPTER 3

Chrysostom and the construction of religious identities

LABELLING AND THE CONSTRUCTION OF RELIGIOUS IDENTITIES

Labelling of the self and of others is an important part of the process of identity construction.[1] The fact that labels for religious allegiance permeate Chrysostom's writings is thus significant and should be seen as directly connected to his interest in identity construction. For adherents of his own religion he used the well-accepted label for the followers of Christ – *Christianoi*.[2] This was the name given to all Christians at baptism (*Catéchèse* 1.44 (SC 50.131)) but it also had special local significance because Antioch was believed to be the place where Christians were first called Christians (Acts 11.26) – something that Chrysostom often emphasized to his audiences (*Hom. in Matt.* 8 (*PG* 57.81)).[3] Chrysostom also spoke of Christians as believers (*pistoi*) and those within (*tous esō*) because they believed in Christ and the one God and belonged to the Christian community.[4] Those who followed the Graeco-Roman religions were at times labelled *Hellēnes*,[5] a usage that had become common in the fourth century.[6] Before the fourth century the most common terms used by Christians to describe those outside the Judaeo-Christian tradition had been *ethnē/ethnos*, and Chrysostom

---

[1] See Jenkins 2003: 5 and 87.   [2] The references are too many to list.
[3] See also *In Princ. Act.* 2 (*PG* 51.86); *Hom. de Stat.* 17 (*PG* 49.176); *In Ep. ad 1 Cor. Hom.* 21.9 (*PG* 61.178), and also J. Taylor 1994.
[4] The references to believers are too many to list. For 'those inside', see *In Ep. ad 1 Cor. Hom.* 16.2 (*PG* 61.130).
[5] *Hom. in Act.* 25 (*PG* 60.194); *In Ep. ad 1 Cor. Hom.* 33.7 (*PG* 61.284); *Hom. in Gen.* 6.12–21 (*PG* 534.58–61); 2.10 (*PG* 53.29–30); and *De S. Bab. Contra Jul. et Gent.* 1 (*PG* 50.533). See also *In Ep. ad 1 Cor. Hom.* 29.1 (*PG* 61.240); *In Ep. ad 1 Cor. Hom.* 4.5 and 9–11 (*PG* 61.33); 7.13–15 (*PG* 61.63–4) and 20.5 (*PG* 61.163); *Hom. in Gen.* 1.2 (*PG* 53.21) and 4.12–21 (*PG* 53.58–61); *De S. Bab. Contra Jul. et Gent.* 13 (*PG* 50.537); *Hom. de Stat.* 11.3 (*PG* 49.121) and 12.12 (*PG* 49.133); and *In Ep. ad Ephes. Hom.* 11 (*PG* 62.86).
[6] Bowersock 1990a: 10–11 and also Eusebius, *VC* 2.44 and Athanasius, *Ar.* 3.16 and 4.10.

sometimes still talked of *ta ethnē* in contrast to Jews.[7] Chrysostom also used the term 'unbelievers'[8] to describe those who did not believe in the Christian God and Jesus Christ,[9] and 'those outside' for those who were not 'subject to the doctrines and laws of Christ' and had not received the Gospel (*In Ep. ad 1 Cor. Hom.* 16.2 (*PG* 61.130)).[10] In this sense, these people were seen as the direct opposite of the believers and of those inside the Christian community, just as Christians could be contrasted with Greeks and the Jews. Finally, Chrysostom spoke often of Jews, the *Ioudaioi*, as another clearly defined religious group with a long-accepted label, who could be contrasted with Christians. At times he referred to Jews as outsiders and unbelievers alongside Greeks as they too did not believe in Christ and were outside the Christian community. Chrysostom also had a category for those whom he saw to be in between being Christian and being Jewish. He called these people Judaizers (*Ioudaizontes*) (*Adv. Jud.* 1.4.8 (*PG* 48.849) and 6.7.9 (*PG* 48.916)) or 'half-Christians (*christianos ōn ex ēmiseias*)' (*Adv. Jud.* 1.4.6 (*PG* 48.849)).[11] Chrysostom could then contrast these Judaizing Christians with 'sincere (*eilikrinēs*)' and 'genuine (*gnēsios*)' Christians (*Adv. Jud.* 1.3.4 (*PG* 48.847) and 5.12.12 (*PG* 48.904)). He used the term 'half-Christians' only to refer to Judaizing Christians; because he did not use it to describe Hellenizers we should not do so either, as some modern scholars have suggested.[12]

Through constant reference to Greeks, unbelievers, Christians and Jews, Chrysostom was trying to create these as categories of what could be 'seen, heard, spoken, thought, believed and valued' for his audiences.[13] Through constantly repeating the terms in his preaching, he hoped to formulate being Christian, Greek and Jewish as clear-cut identities and forms of selfhood to which his audience must subscribe because the distinctions were as natural as those between man and woman and human and animal. To instil this in his audience Chrysostom continually asserted the 'difference between the Christian and the unbeliever' in a variety of ways (*Hom. de*

---

[7] *Hom. in Gen.* 40.17 (*PG* 53.374) and 67.9 (*PG* 54.574); *In Ep. ad 1 Cor. Hom.* 24.5 (*PG* 61.201) and 29.2 (*PG* 61.241); *Ad Illum. Catech.* 9.23 (*PG* 49.227); and *Hom. de Stat.* 12.14 (*PG* 49.133–4).
[8] See Schatkin 1988: 28 and 129. As at *In Ep. ad 2 Cor. Hom.* 8.2 (*PG* 61.455–6) and Harkins, *Baptismal Instruction* 10.18; and *Catéchèse* 3.3 (SC 366.221–5) = Harkins, *Baptismal Instruction* 11.11–16. See also *Oratio adhortatoria ad Stagirium ascetam a Daemonio vexatum* 1.2 (*PG* 47.427).
[9] Schatkin and Harkins 1983: 178 on Baur 1959–60: vol. I, 340–52.
[10] *Ad Illum. Catech.* 2.1 (*PG* 49.231–2) = Harkins, *Baptismal Instruction* 12.5; *In Ep. ad 1 Cor. Hom.* 3.6 (*PG* 61.25), 4.11 (*PG* 61.38); and *Hom. de Stat.* 9.4 (*PG* 49.121) and 19.4 (*PG* 49.189).
[11] *Adv. Jud.* 1.4.3, 4.2.2 and 7.6.10 (*PG* 48.847, 876 and 927–8) and *Hom. in Gen.* 7.19 (*PG* 53.68). On half-Christians in Chrysostom, see Brottier 2004. The verb 'Judaize' can also be found in the *Apostolic Constitutions* 8.47.70.
[12] Brottier 2004: 439–57.   [13] Hennessy 1993: 75.

Gen. 4.20 (*PG* 53.47)).[14] He opposed Christians and Greeks by describing how they were at war with one another (*In Ep. ad 1 Cor. Hom.* 6.8 (*PG* 61.54)), contrasting the happiness or 'gladness' of Christians, or comparing the qualities of Christian courts to the situation of non-Christians (*Hom. de Stat.* 18.7 (*PG* 49.183) and (*In Ep. ad. 1 Cor. Hom.* 16.4–9 (*PG* 61.131–5)).[15] Throughout his preaching he used the categories of Jews and Greeks to make comparison with Christians, using the formula: 'Let the Greeks be ashamed and the Jews dismayed . . .' (*Hom. in Gen.* 1.2 (*PG* 53.21)).[16] The Greeks also became a marker of the outer limit of acceptable Christian behaviour as Chrysostom could always accuse his audiences of behaving exactly like Greeks.[17] Chrysostom could use examples of good behaviour among Greeks or Jews to chastise the failure of his audiences to live up to his high ideals of Christian behaviour: it was Christians who should 'put Greeks to shame' not the other way round (*In Ep. ad 1 Cor. Hom.* 6.1 and 7.12 (*PG* 61.47–9 and 61)).[18] Finally, Chrysostom could speak of Gentiles/Greeks in positive ways as people who should be cared for, addressed, or attracted to Christianity (*In Ep. ad 1 Cor. Hom.* 4.1–2 (*PG* 61.29–30)).[19] It should be clear by now that Chrysostom's statements about the religious allegiance of Christians often went hand in hand with statements about the religious allegiance of Greeks and Jews. Identities cannot be constructed in isolation but must always rely on contrast with another: Chrysostom could not construct a clear Christian identity for his audience without also making constant reference to what it was to be Greek or Jewish. In the next section of this chapter, we shall see that while Chrysostom's primary goal was to outline the defining, shared features of being Christian he often could not help also characterizing what made Greeks different. We shall then go on to see, in the third section of this chapter, that, vice versa, when characterizing what counted as Greek religion Chrysostom was really concerned with what it meant to be Christian.

---

[14] See also *Hom. de Stat.* 2.9, 16.7 and 18.7 (*PG* 49.37, 166 and 183).
[15] See also *In Ep. ad 1 Cor. Hom.* 3.9 (*PG* 61.28) and *Hom. de Stat.* 7.4 and 9.10 (*PG* 49.93 and 109–10).
[16] See also *Hom. de Stat.* 1.32 (*PG* 49.32), 21.4 and 13 (*PG* 49.213 and 217) and *In Ep. ad 2 Cor. Hom.* 8.4 (*PG* 61.458).
[17] See also *In Ep. ad 1 Cor. Hom.* 2.10 (*PG* 61.29–30) and *Hom. de Stat.* 1.16 (*PG* 49.24–5) – on weak believers in Corinth.
[18] See also *In Ep. ad 1 Cor. Hom.* 15.1 and 11, 23.1–2 and 29.9 (*PG* 61.121 and 127, 189–90 and 248); *Hom. in Gen.* 1.2 and 5.17 (*PG* 53.21 and 54); and *Hom. de Stat.* 16.1, 3 and 77 (*PG* 49.161, 163 and 166). For comparison with Jews in this way, see *In Ep. ad Rom. Hom* 12.20.3 (*PG* 51.176) and *Adv. Jud.* 4.3.8 (*PG* 48.875–6).
[19] See also *In Ep. ad 1 Cor. Hom.* 33.5 and 7 (*PG* 61.282 and 284); *In Ep. ad 2 Cor. Hom.* 8.1 (*PG* 61.454); and *Hom. de Stat.* 21.19 (*PG* 49.220).

THE CONSTRUCTION OF CHRISTIAN IDENTITY AND GREEKNESS

An essential aspect of Chrysostom's construction of Christian identity for his audiences lay in teaching them the defining features of Christianity. He outlined for them both the defining beliefs and doctrines of Nicaean Christianity and the central rules and guidelines for Christian behaviour and morality. Chrysostom's catechetical or baptismal sermons were the key texts in implementing this education of Christians just as they were becoming Christians. Chrysostom preached these sermons in Antioch in two separate series in two years at Lent between 388 and 390 to those who had chosen to undergo baptism and formal initiation into Christianity.[20] Some of these sermons formed part of the final preparation of the candidate for baptism while others provided some extra mystagogic instruction for the initiate after baptism had taken place.[21] More formal forms of instruction would also have been given to this group by Bishop Flavian. Chrysostom's sermons were simply supplementary to this episcopal instruction rather than being the sum of information the candidate would have received.[22]

The primary aim of Chrysostom's *Catechetical Sermons* was to teach catechumens the defining features of being Christian that they were to take on during baptism, the features that all baptized Christians, and no one else, shared. Chrysostom placed great emphasis on the need for the candidates for baptism to keep Christian dogma 'fixed in their minds' (*Catéchèse* 1.25 (SC 50.121)) and to understand the importance of good Christian conduct (*Catéchèse* 1.25–32 (SC 50.121–5)).[23] He taught them about God's nature and presented essential teachings from scripture such as the story of Adam's fall (*Catéchèse* 2.1–4 (SC 50.133–5)) or of Abraham (*Catéchèse* 8.7–9 (SC 50.251–3)). He also gave them some of their first official instruction into the meaning of the mysteries of the Church, both baptism itself and the Eucharist ceremony.[24] Chrysostom taught the candidates how they would become a 'new creature in Christ' and would 'put on Christ' themselves during baptism (*Catéchèse* 4.12 and 1.44 (SC 50.189 and 131)). While full

---

[20] Harkins 1963: 15–18 with van de Paverd 1991: 227–9.
[21] Although it is likely that often the more general congregation, at least those who had already been baptized, were present as well.
[22] *Catéchèse* 3.4 (SC 366.227) = Harkins, *Baptismal Instruction* 11.18. On these issues see Harkins 1963: 319, note 43.
[23] For the latter point see also *Catéchèse* 4.13, 23–6 and 32 (SC 50.190, 194–6 and 198–9), *Catéchèse* 5.1 and 9 (SC 50.200 and 204–5) and *Catéchèse* 6.11–12 (SC 50.221).
[24] On the former, see *Catéchèse* 2.11–26 (SC.139–48) and *Catéchèse* 1.7–15 (SC 366.125–44) = Harkins, *Baptismal Instruction* 9.11–20; and *Catéchèse* 2.1–7 (SC 366.169–95) = Harkins, *Baptismal Instruction* 10.5–16. On the latter, see *Catéchèse* 3.12–19 (SC 50.158–62).

training in the Creed and the Lord's Prayer would have been given to the candidates in their formal instruction from the bishop, Chrysostom did give them some instruction in the Statement of Faith that they would have to make during the baptism ceremony. He told them how they must 'first believe in God and then speak the word [I believe] out loud and clear' because 'I believe' was a word that was 'a foundation of stone which holds up an unshaken edifice' (*Catéchèse* 3.3 (SC 366.225) = Harkins, *Baptismal Instruction* 11.15–16).[25] In another baptismal sermon Chrysostom outlined this Statement of Faith in more detail for the candidates for baptism by recounting the formula they would have to learn and repeat. He described how the candidates would have to state their belief in 'the God of the universe, the father of our Lord Jesus Christ, the cause of all things . . . who has . . . created all things, and in Jesus Christ, His only-begotten Son'. They also had to repeat the Nicaean formulation of the relationship between father and son and to accept both the role of God as timeless creator and belief in the crucifixion and resurrection of Christ (*Catéchèse* 1.20–1 (SC 50.118–19)).[26] Accepting this faith in Christ would also, Chrysostom taught, give his audiences a new way of seeing 'with the eyes of the soul' that would 'make the unseen visible from the seen' (*Catéchèse* 2.9 (SC 50.138)). This way of seeing was one of the defining features of being a believer that enabled those who had been baptized to understand even the most complex and mystical of Christian teachings (*Catéchèse* 3.3 (SC 366.221) = Harkins, *Baptismal Instruction* 11.11).[27]

Chrysostom also wanted his audiences to see baptism as a process that marked off Christian from non-Christian through an irreversible change.[28] The language of transformation is found throughout the *Catechetical Sermons* as Chrysostom called on the candidates to 'be transformed' as they took on their new Christian identity.[29] Chrysostom wanted this change to be a complete turn around for the candidates that would last for their whole lives and not just a few days (*In Ep. ad Rom. Hom.* 10 (PG 60.480)). In talking about this kind of transformation, however, it was not possible for Chrysostom to describe only what Christians were changing to: he also had to describe what they were changing from. Marking out firm boundaries between the Christianity of the newly baptized and any previous religious allegiances was not possible unless one first defined those previous religious

---

[25] See also *Catéchèse* 1.19–22 (SC 50.118) and 2.9–10 (SC 50.138–9).
[26] See also *In Ep. ad 1 Cor. Hom.* 40.2 (PG 61.347–8)).
[27] See also *In Ep. ad 2 Cor. Hom.* 2 (PG 61.391–404).
[28] On the catechumenate more generally, see Dujarier 1979; Finn 1992; Riley 1974; and Yarnold 1994.
[29] See Sandwell 2001: 185–91 on Chrysostom's language of conversion.

allegiances. For this reason Chrysostom contrasts the new state of the catechumens after 'marriage' to Christ with the practice of idolatry and blood sacrifice that had supposedly characterized their pre-baptismal state:

> let us ascertain clearly the deformity of the bride [the catechumen] before this time ... What could be more unshapely than that soul which has abandoned the privilege appropriate to it, forgotten the nobility of birth it gained from above, made a show of worshipping stone, wood, senseless animals and less honourable things and which has increased its deformity by the smell of the sacrificial victim, the filth of blood, and the smoke? (*Catéchèse* 1.5 (SC 50.111))[30]

After baptism, in contrast, he who had once 'worshipped stones thinking they were gods would suddenly rise up to such a height of virtue that ... he sees that the stones are stones' (*Catéchèse* 4.15 (SC 50.190)). He would thus leave behind 'idolatry, error and the worship of demons' (*Catéchèse* 1.9 (SC 50.112–13)).[31]

By painting a vivid image of the supposed idolatrous past of the catechumen, Chrysostom could exaggerate and clarify the boundary between idol-worshipper and Christian. The ritual of exorcism that the candidate underwent regularly in the weeks prior to baptism included a 'renunciation of the pomps of Satan (*Catéchèse* 2.20–1 (SC 50.145)).[32] Because *pompa* originally referred to the processions in which statues of the gods were carried through the cities of the ancient world, a rejection of one's idolatrous past was implicit in the very process of becoming Christian.[33] By the fourth century the Christian understanding of *pompa* had shifted slightly so that as well as traditional festivals it now included less clearly 'religious' aspects of the convert's previous life such as: 'every form of sin, spectacles of indecency, horse racing ... portents, oracles, omens ... amulets and incantations' (*Catéchèse* 3.6 (SC 366.233–4) = Harkins, *Baptismal Instruction* 11.25).[34] Reference to the *pompa* of traditional Graeco-Roman religion could become shorthand for everything in their normal lives that Chrysostom wanted catechumens to leave behind on their conversion. In fact, Chrysostom defined a range of practices that the catechumens were using as 'Greek' to emphasize

---

[30] See also *Catéchèse* 1.9 and 25 (SC 50.112–13 and 121).
[31] See also *Catéchèse* 1.25 and 32 (SC 50.121 and 125).
[32] See also *Catéchèse* 2.12 and 17–21 (SC 50.139 and 143–5); *Catéchèse* 4.32 (SC 50.199); *Catéchèse* 3.4–6 (SC 366.227–35) = Harkins, *Baptismal Instruction* 11.19–26); *Catéchèse* 3.6 (SC 366.233–4 = Harkins, *Baptismal Instruction* 11.25); and *Ad Illum. Catech.* 2.5 (*PG* 49.239 = Harkins, *Baptismal Instruction* 12.48 and 51). And with H. A. Kelly 1985: 94–105.
[33] Harkins 1963: 223–4 and Daniélou 1956: 26, 28–9. See also H. A. Kelly 1985: 97–9.
[34] A very similar list is found at *Ad Illum. Catech.* 2.5 (*PG* 49.239) = Harkins, *Baptismal Instruction* 12.52 (*PG* 49.239).

that they should be given up after baptism. Chrysostom berated his audience for using omens and amulets and for still attending the racecourses – all of which he defined as Greek (*Catéchèse* 1.39–43 (SC 50.128–30), 6.1–8 and 15 (SC 50.215–19 and 222) and *Ad Illum. Catech.* 2.5 (*PG* 49.239–40) = Harkins, *Baptismal Instruction* 12.53–9).

Chrysostom's ordinary preaching was also concerned with constructing Christian identity. On many occasions Chrysostom emphasizes that belief in Christ, his crucifixion and his resurrection were central to being Christian and to distinguishing Christians from Jews and Greeks: 'For Jews ask for signs and Greeks seek after wisdom: but we preach Christ crucified, which for the Jews is a stumbling block and for Greeks a foolishness, but for those that are called, both Jews and Greeks, is Christ the power of God . . .' (*In Ep. ad 1 Cor. Hom.* 4.5 (*PG* 61.33) quoting 1 Corinthians 22–4). Christians accept the resurrection of Christ while Greeks do not – Greeks 'do not know God and disbelieve the resurrection' (*In Ep. ad 1 Thess. Hom.* 7 (*PG* 62.436–7)).[35] Conversely, anyone who did not accept the resurrection of Christ was, by implication, a Greek.[36] Christian acceptance of Christ and Greek rejection of him were also embedded in acceptance or rejection of certain ways of understanding the world. As we saw in the *Catechetical Sermons*, a defining feature of being Christian was to see with the 'eyes of faith'; Chrysostom asserted this idea throughout his preaching as an essential feature of being Christian that enabled Christians to believe in Christ's crucifixion and resurrection (*In Ep. ad Ephes. Hom.* 12 (*PG* 62.92)).[37] Greeks, in contrast, emphasized 'wisdom', reason and rationality as modes of understanding and therefore denied the resurrection of Christ (*In Ep. ad 1 Cor. Hom.* 7.1 (*PG* 61.53–5).[38] They lived 'according to the flesh . . . according to what is in sight now' and so could not accept the defining elements of the Christian faith (*In Ep. ad 1 Cor. Hom.* 5.1–2 (*PG* 61.39) and 7.2 (*PG* 61.55)).[39] As Chrysostom puts it, 'I for instance, feel differently upon these subjects from an unbeliever. I hear "Christ was crucified" and . . . I admire his loving kindness . . . the other hears and esteems it weakness . . .' (*In Ep. ad 1 Cor. Hom.* 7.2 (*PG* 61.55)). Greeks were also unable to believe in these

---

[35] See also *In Ep. ad 1 Cor. Hom.* 4.1 and 11 (*PG* 61.29 and 38); *In Ep. ad 2 Cor. Hom.* 8.2 (*PG* 61.30) and 24.4–8 (*PG* 61.580–4); *In Ep. ad Ephes. Hom.* 12 (*PG* 62.91–2); *Hom. de Stat.* 7.4 (*PG* 49.93) and 16.9 (*PG* 49.167); *In Ep. ad Coloss. Hom.* 2 (*PG* 62.316–17).
[36] As at *In Ep. ad 1 Cor. Hom.* 4.1–4, 7.2 and 17.2 (*PG* 61.29–32, 55 and 141); *In Ep. ad 2 Cor. Hom.* 8.2 (*PG* 61.30) and *Hom. de Stat.* 16.9 (*PG* 49.167).
[37] For an example of the use of the eyes of faith see *Hom. in Gen.* 12.11–12 (*PG* 53.102–3).
[38] See also *In Ep. ad 1 Cor. Hom.* 20.7 (*PG* 61.164); 33.7 and 41.2 (*PG* 61.283–4 and 355); *In Ep. ad 2 Cor. Hom.* 12.2 (*PG* 61.483); *Hom. de Stat.* 16.9 and 9.4 (*PG* 49.166–7 and 105) and *In Ep. ad Ephes. Hom.* 12 (*PG* 62.91–2).
[39] See also *In Ep. ad 1 Cor. Hom.* 7.6 (*PG* 61.58).

crucial aspects of Christian doctrine because they did not accept the one other form of proof that there could be for them: scripture (*In Ep. ad 2 Cor. Hom.* 8.2 (*PG* 61.30)).[40]

Belief in Christ and his crucifixion and resurrection were also necessary for acceptance of Christian attitude to life and death (*In Ep. ad. 1 Cor. Hom.* 4.5 (*PG* 61.33) and 17.2 (*PG* 61.141–2)). The resurrection of Christ became a model for the resurrection of all Christians and the participation of Christians in Christ at baptism and the Eucharist was a sign that they would be resurrected as he had been. Resurrection of ordinary Christians in turn supported the doctrine of judgement in the afterlife. It allowed for the bodies of Christians to remain intact so that they could be judged for their sin and virtue along with their souls (*In Ep. ad I Cor. Hom.* 39.4 and 12 (*PG* 61.336 and 342)).[41] Belief in judgement after death and the fires of hell were essential for ensuring good Christian behaviour in the present life.[42] If one did not believe in the system of rewards and punishments in the afterlife then there was no reason to behave properly in the present life. Having the faith to believe in the resurrection and judgement was what made Christians act like Christians (*In Ep. ad 1 Cor. Hom.* 4.4 (*PG* 61.31–2)).[43] These ideas, too, were reinforced by comparison with Greeks or Gentiles, who did not believe in the resurrection or the torments of hell because they were 'darkened in their understanding' (*In Ep. ad Ephes. Hom.* 12 (*PG* 62.91–2)). This meant that Chrysostom could describe members of his audience who did not believe in the judgement, the resurrection or afterlife as Greeks, who could be excluded from church for as long 'a time as we do the idolater' (*In Ep. ad Heb. Hom.* 4 (*PG* 63.44)).[44] By continuing to sin and by continuing to mourn the dead such 'Christians' belied the truth of the resurrection and this, in turn, amounted to denying Christ, so undermining the basis of their Christian identity: 'How is it that you say you are a Christian? . . . If you do not believe in Christ I would not say that such a person is a Christian, God forbid, but worse than a Greek (*Hellēnōn cheirōnes*)' (*In Ep. ad Coloss. Hom.* 2 (*PG* 62.315)).[45]

---

[40] *In Ep. ad 1 Cor. Hom.* 17.2–3 (*PG* 61.141–2) and 41.1 (*PG* 61.355); *Hom. de Stat.* 9.4 (*PG* 49.105) and 12.12 (*PG* 49.133); and *Hom. in Gen.* 2.10 (*PG* 53–4.30). See also Jackson 1990.
[41] See also *In Ep. ad 2 Cor. Hom.* 9.3 (*PG* 61.463).
[42] *In Ep. ad 1 Cor. Hom.* 9.1–3 (*PG* 61.75–7) and 14.5–6 (61.117–18); *In Ep. ad 2 Cor. Hom.* 9.4 (*PG* 61.464–5) and 22.4 (*PG* 61.551); and *Hom. de Stat..* 7.4 (*PG* 49.93–4).
[43] *In Ep. ad 2 Cor. Hom.* 10 (*PG* 61.465–74) and *Hom. de Stat..* 1.20 (*PG* 49.27–8).
[44] See also *Hom. in Gen.* 54.28 (*PG* 54.478); *In Ep. ad 1 Thess. Hom.* 6 (*PG* 62.430–1); and *In Ep. ad 1 Cor. Hom.* 28.4 (*PG* 61.235).
[45] See also *In Ep. ad 1 Tim. Hom.* 10 (*PG* 62.551–2) and *In Ep. ad 1 Cor. Hom.* 3.9 (*PG* 61.28–9).

Belief in the one Christian God was the other central defining feature of being Christian that had to be asserted constantly. One of Chrysostom's most common arguments for God's existence and for his all-powerful nature was his creation of the world. Chrysostom constantly asserted that the wonder of creation should lead the onlooker directly to God the Creator (*Hom. in Gen.* 2.11 (*PG* 53.30); 4.12 (*PG* 53.44); *Hom de Stat.* 9.4 and 8 (*PG* 49.105) and *In Ep. ad 2 Cor. Hom.* 9.3 (*PG* 61.463)). At the same time, God's creation of the world could be used as proof that the resurrection of Christ and all Christians was possible (*In Ep. ad 1 Cor. Hom.* 17.3 (*PG* 61.141–2)) and that once resurrected all Christians would face judgement (*In Ep. ad 2 Cor. Hom.* 9.3 (*PG* 61.463)). These ideas about the nature of God were again reinforced by contrast with Greeks who believed in many gods (*In Ep. ad 1 Cor. Hom.* 20.7 (*PG.* 61.164)).[46] Chrysostom criticized Greeks for using their own reasoning to explain the creation of the world instead of accepting it on faith or believing what was written in scripture about the matter (*Hom. in Gen.* 2.5 and 10–11 (*PG* 53.28 and 29–30));[47] Particularly objectionable were Greek philosophical conceptions that the world was created out of pre-existing matter or by chance (*Hom. in Gen.* 2.6, 10–11 (*PG* 53.28 and 29–30)).[48] Chrysostom also criticized misguided Greek ideas about the creation of the world because they led the Greeks to worship the universe, the earth and the sun as if they were gods. In doing this, Greeks were worshipping the creatures of God instead of God who had created them (*Hom. in Gen.* 2.10 (*PG* 53.29–30)).[49] Such assertions of God's power and existence often went hand in hand with Chrysostom's denigration of Greek ideas about the divine. Chrysostom could use the idea of the Christian God as creator of the world to mock the Greek idea that gods could live in temples made by men (*Hom. in Gen.* 2.7 (*PG* 53.28)). Or, he could use description of Greek ideas about the gods to highlight the true, all-powerful, benevolent nature of the Christian God. The sun could not be a god because it required the aid of the other elements to exist: 'God must be independent and not stand in need of assistance, be the source of all good things to all and be hindered by nothing' (*Hom. de*

---

[46] See also *In Ep. ad Coloss. Hom.* 2 (*PG.* 62.316).
[47] See also *Hom. in Gen.* 3.10 (*PG* 53.35); 4.6 (*PG* 53.40); 5.12 (*PG* 53.51); and *Hom. de Stat.* 10.10 (*PG* 48.118).
[48] See also *Hom. in Gen.* 3.12–13, 7.10 and 18 (*PG* 53.35–6, 65 and 68) and *Contra Jud. et Gent.* 11.7 (*PG* 48.828).
[49] See also *Hom. in Gen.* 2.10–11, 3.13–13, 4.12, 6.20 and 7.18 (*PG* 53.30, 35–6, 44, 60 and 68); *Hom. de Stat.* 10.6 (*PG* 49.115); and *In Ep. ad 1 Cor. Hom.* 5.3 (*PG* 61.40–1). See also J. Kelly 1995: 58 and Schatkin and Harkins 1983: 234, note 7.

Stat. 10.8 (*PG* 49.117)).⁵⁰ Similarly, the sun's needing moisture in order to avoid 'a universal conflagration' meant that the sun could not be a God: 'to do harm is foreign to God's nature; to do good is his property' (*In Ep. ad Ephes. Hom.* 12 (*PG* 62.90)). It was only by describing the Greek views that Chrysostom could truly make clear that the Christian conception of the all-powerful, benevolent God was the correct and normative view.

It was important for Chrysostom to get across to his audiences a true understanding of the Christian conception of divinity and its relationship to man. Chrysostom had to assert God's difference from the human race due to his all-powerful nature in order to counteract his audience's misinterpretations of Genesis on this matter (*Hom. in Gen.* 8.4–8 (*PG* 53.70–2) on Genesis 1.26). When Genesis recorded that God created humans in his 'image and likeness' this meant in terms of their 'control over everything on earth' not in terms of their bodily form (*Hom. in Gen.* 8.9–11 (*PG* 53.72–3)). In fact, according to Chrysostom, those who 'ascribe an arrangement of limbs to God' (i.e. make him like humans) are a short step from idolatry and worshipping humans as gods; they are thus 'in danger of falling into the Greek impiety (*hellēnikēn asebeian*)' (*Hom. in Gen.* 13.9 (*PG* 53.107)). For the same reason Chrysostom mocks the divinization of men by the Greeks and Romans.⁵¹ The arrogance of Greeks makes them 'refer all to themselves' and so makes men into gods (*In Ep. ad 1 Cor. Hom.* 5.4 (*PG* 61.42–3). It leads philosophers to make themselves gods and encourages others to try to make gods of the Apostles or even, according to Chrysostom, to divinizing dead children (*In Ep. ad 1 Cor. Hom.* 35.8 (*PG* 61.301); *Hom. de Stat.* 1.17 (*PG* 49.25–6), 10.7 (*PG* 49.115–16) and 11.4 (*PG* 49.121); and *In Ep. ad Ephes. Hom.* 18 (*PG* 62.125)).⁵² This is again used to highlight a feature of God's all-powerful nature: men are made weak and able to suffer, even Paul and the other Apostles and saints, because in this way it is possible to distinguish them from the true God, who cannot suffer (*Hom. de Stat.* 1.17 (*PG* 49.25–6)).⁵³ At the other end of the spectrum, Chrysostom could also highlight the special place given to man in God's creation by mocking Greek worship of animals, sticks and

---

⁵⁰ *In Ep. ad Ephes. Hom.* 12 (*PG* 62.91) and *Hom. in Gen.* 6.16 (*PG* 53.59).
⁵¹ This is the Euhemerist theory. See Schatkin 1988: 115, note 182. See also Clement of Alexandria, *Prot.* 30, Athenagoras, *Leg.* 29 and Theodoret, *Affect.* 3. 24–33 and 8.12–28.
⁵² On this, see Schatkin 1988: 115. On Chrysostom's criticism of the 'Greek' practice of divinizing its heroes and rulers, see Straub 1962: 310–26. For a reference to the worship of Antinous, see *In Ep. ad 2 Cor. Hom.* 26.4 (*PG* 61.581).
⁵³ See also *Hom. de Stat..* 10.7 (*PG* 49.115–16) and *In Ep. ad 2 Cor. Hom.* 26.4–5 (*PG* 61.576–7).

stones (*Hom. in Gen.* 7.18 (*PG* 53.68)).[54] Greeks who did this betrayed the privileged place they were given, as reasoning humans, over other living things that had been created as lesser beings, at least according to Christian thinking.

Christian adherence to correct ideas about the divine was important for Chrysostom because it was intimately linked to the good behaviour of Christians. In his construction of Christian identity, Chrysostom placed great emphasis on visible behaviour and external appearances among his Christian audiences. For Chrysostom, Christian identity, and thus also the differences between Greek and Christian, should be marked not only in internal terms of what one believed but also in terms of one's outward behaviour and of how this appeared to others. Chrysostom was concerned that his audiences held the right theological beliefs about certain key features of Christian doctrine. However, very often he related these beliefs to practice and behaviour among his audiences: belief in the afterlife and resurrection was crucial because it ensured that his audiences thought about the consequences of their actions. It was only through the expression of beliefs in behaviour that Christian difference could be shown and that Greeks could be convinced of Christian superiority (*In Ep. ad 1 Cor. Hom.* 18.4 (*PG* 61.149)). When heathens, Jews and heretics saw Christians mourning the dead it made them laugh because it belied Christian teachings about the afterlife (*In Ep. ad Heb. Hom.* 4 (*PG* 63.43)). Seeing such behaviour could even lead Greeks to think that Christians were not really Christian at all, but that they were adhering to 'the very errors to which they themselves are subject' (*Hom. in Gen.* 7.3 (*PG* 53.63) or were only being Christian for political reasons.[55] This would make Christianity appear a falsehood and hypocritical: 'I mean, when they see some of those drawn up on our side, who name themselves Christians in what they say and in address, stealing like themselves, claiming more than their share, being envious and plotting . . . they consider our way of life to be deception and all of us to be guilty of these things' (*Hom. in Gen.* 7.10 (*PG* 53.68–9)).[56] Chrysostom's audience 'should cease from adhering to the world to put the Greeks to shame', but instead they 'bring upon ourselves much derision by the comparison of our way of life, seeing that [the Greeks] indeed who tend to error and have no such conviction abide by philosophy but we do just the

---

[54] See also *Hom. de Stat.* 10.6 (*PG* 49.115) and *In Ep. ad Rom. Hom.* 3 (*PG* 60.414).
[55] See also *In Ep. ad Coloss. Hom.* 2 (*PG* 62.315).
[56] *In Ep. ad 1 Cor. Hom.* 25.2 (*PG* 61.207) and *Hom in Gen.* 7.2 (*PG* 53.62). On Greeks thinking Christianity to be a fable see also *In Ep. ad 2 Cor. Hom.* 8.2 (*PG* 61.456); *De S. Bab. Contra Jul. et Gent.* 16 (*PG* 50.538); and *Contra Jud. et Gent.* 17.8 (*PG* 48.836).

contrary' (*In Ep. ad 1 Cor. Hom.* 7.12 (*PG* 61.61)).[57] Only visual and outward displays of Christian belief and of Christian difference could ward off such criticisms.

Throughout his preaching, Chrysostom wished to impress on his audience the defining features of what it meant to be Christian, namely accepting that God was the all-powerful creator of the world and that Christ was his son who had been crucified but was now resurrected. It also meant accepting that ordinary Christians would be resurrected in order to face judgement and either rewards in heaven or punishment in hell. Accepting these things resulted from having a particular way of 'seeing' that enabled an 'understanding' of the more difficult to explain aspects of Christianity. However, being Christian should also, according to Chrysostom, entail showing these differences in one's behaviour. Chrysostom reinforced these essential features of being Christian by reference to, and in comparison with, Greekness. Constructing the defining features of Christian identity also inevitably meant that Chrysostom was involved in constructing a Greek identity. Chrysostom's *Catechetical Sermons* associate Greek religion with sacrifice, the worship of idols, demons and the use of amulets and omens. In his sermons more generally, he defines Greek religion as worship of the sun, water, animals and divinized humans and associates it with Greek philosophy (*Hom. de Stat.* 19.5 (*PG* 49.190)).[58] While there is some basis for these ideas in the forms that Graeco-Roman religion took in the ancient world, we should recognize that Chrysostom focused on these characteristics more because they suited his needs in defining Christianity than because they referred to reality. While blood sacrifice had once been a defining feature of Graeco-Roman religion, it is not at all clear that this was any longer the case in the fourth, or even the third, century.[59] Similarly, while worship of animals could be related to Egyptian religion and worship of the sun to the Graeco-Roman god Helios, it is not clear how central these still were.[60] It is true that philosophical and religious ideas could be

---

[57] See also *Hom. in Gen.* 5.17 (*PG* 53.54) and *In Ep. ad 1 Cor. Hom.* 15.1 and 23.1–2 (*PG* 61.121 and 189–90).
[58] *In Ep. ad 1 Cor. Hom.* 7.14–16 (*PG* 61.62–4). Conversely, Plato and Socrates are described as idolaters and as taking part in Greek religion (*In Ep. ad Rom. Hom.* 3 (*PG* 60.414) and *In Ep. ad 1 Cor. Hom.* 7.15 (*PG* 61.63–4)).
[59] On the centrality of sacrifice, see S. R. F. Price 1999: 33–6; Beard, North and Price 1998: vol. 1, 36–7; and North 2000: 44–5. For the decline of importance of sacrifice in the third and fourth centuries, see Veyne 1986.
[60] Libanius, *Or.* 13.35 (F.II.75); *Or.* 18.240 (F.II.340); and *Or.* 19.42 (F.II.404). There is also a possible indication that Libanius saw Earth as a divinity, *Or.* 18.292–3 (F.II.364–5). On the emperor Julian's worship of the sun, see Athanassiadi 1992: 113–14. On the role of Helios in Libanius, see Misson 1914: 67–83.

connected in the ancient world but Chrysostom ignored any reference to more recent ideas of Neoplatonic philosophy and instead relied on references to natural philosophy.[61] Behind this lay a larger contrast between Greek religion as polytheistic and Christianity as monotheistic, which was not borne out in reality. Many adherents of forms of Graeco-Roman religion held to monotheistic conceptions of divinity that could not so easily be placed in direct contrast to Christianity, and despite all the struggles over the relationship between God and Christ Christians never found an answer on which they could all agree in reply to accusations that they worshipped more than one divinity.[62] Chrysostom's representation of Greek religion or Greekness consisted of disparate elements of Graeco-Roman religious practice brought together in so far as they suited Chrysostom's goals of constructing Christianity by comparison with an antithetical 'Greek' religion.

GREEK RELIGION AND THE CONSTRUCTION OF RELIGIOUS DIFFERENCE

In the previous section I considered how Chrysostom began to define or construct Greek religion almost as a by-product of his construction of what it was to be Christian. Direct and prolonged discussion of the religion of the Greeks in Chrysostom is relatively rare; he simply was not interested in Greek religion for its own sake. For the little explicit discussion of Greek religion that there is, we have to turn to what might be considered Chrysostom's most outwardly directed works, his treatises addressed to pagans the *Discourse on Blessed Babylas and Against the Greeks* and the *Demonstration against the Gentiles and Jews that Christ Is God*.[63] These treatises were probably written in AD 378 and AD 382–6 respectively, both before Chrysostom became a priest.[64] The *Discourse on Babylas* is a panegyric of the martyr Babylas but also becomes an apologetic work that seeks to prove the superiority of Christianity. As such, it answers some of the claims of Greek philosophers and writers about Greek prophecy, in particular the works of Porphyry and Hierocles, as well as Libanius' *Monody on the Shrine at Daphne*. The *Demonstration against the Gentiles and Jews*, in contrast, was intended to be an apologetic work from its inception. Its stated goal was to demonstrate to

---

[61] On Chrysostom and Greek philosophy, see Coleman-Norton 1930: 305–17. When describing Julian's mystical education, Libanius referred to the writings of philosophers as educating people about the gods (*Or.* 18.18 (F.11.244)).
[62] Athanassiadi and Frede 1999 and North 2005.   [63] See Schatkin and Harkins 1983.
[64] For the dating of these treatises, see Schatkin and Harkins 1983: 15–16 and 181–4.

both Jews and Gentiles that Christ was God, especially through arguments based on the deeds of Christ and fulfilled biblical prophecy, but it appears that Chrysostom only got as far as addressing the Gentiles (*Contra Jud. et Gent* 1.4 (*PG* 48.813)).[65] It is often assumed that the audience of these treatises were educated Greeks.[66] However, recent work on earlier examples of Christian apologetic has shown that Christians were often the intended readers of apologetic works.[67] Chrysostom's treatises against the Greeks and Gentiles might well have been intended to act as a form of edification for Christian audiences, or as education in how to argue against Greeks, as much as to act as an apologetic text.[68]

These treatises still give us the most prolonged focus on Greek religion in Chrysostom's writings. Chrysostom uses them to present Graeco-Roman religion in his present day as defunct and in decline: 'Even if impiety (*tēs asebeias*) still makes progress among a few people, the altars, the temples, the idols, are gone and so are all the things they are attached to. Gone too are the festivals, the rituals of initiation, the smoke, the smell and the accursed assemblies' (*Contra Jud. et Gent.* 15.4 (*PG* 48.833)).[69] He describes how the temples and cult statues in his time were covered in cobwebs, dust and grass (*De S. Bab. Contra Jul. et Gent.* 41 (*PG* 50.544)) and celebrates the fact that divination at the oracle of Apollo at Daphne had been silenced by the power of Babylas (*De S. Bab. Contra Jul. et Gent.* 127 (*PG* 50.570–1)).[70] Worship of the idols was kept alive in his day only because of the entertainment and enjoyment it afforded, namely the expenditure on revelry, feasts and drunkenness (*De S. Bab. Contra Jul. et Gent.* 43 (*PG* 50.544)). Chrysostom occasionally accepts that there might be a few small cities that 'display the same superstition and madness of idolatry' as in earlier times (*De S. Bab. Contra Jul. et Gent.* 43 (*PG* 50.544)) and that it was possible that there could be a non-Christian emperor again (*Adv. Oppug.* 2.9 (*PG* 47.344)). However, on the whole, he suggests that sacrifice was no longer being practised at all 'for no Greek is required to sacrifice to demons anymore' (*De S. Bab. Contra Jul. et Gent.* 6 (*PG* 50.535)). This picture of Greek religion as defunct did not stop Chrysostom from describing certain aspects of the religion in

---

[65] On this see Schatkin and Harkins 1983: 163–9. Although it has been argued that Chrysostom's sermons against the Jews can be seen as the part of the speech addressed to the Jews (see the discussion in Harkins 1979, introduction to his translation of the *Against the Jews*).
[66] J. Kelly 1995: 41–2 and Wilken 1983: 161. Although it is also likely that they were meant for Christian consumption so that Christians could learn arguments with which to combat Greeks.
[67] See Edwards, Goodman and Price 1999.   [68] Schatkin 1988: 27.
[69] See also *De S. Bab. Contra Jul. et Gent.* 13–14 and 41 (*PG* 50.537 and 544) and *In Ep. ad 1 Cor. Hom.* 20.8 (*PG* 61.165).
[70] See also *In Ep. ad 2 Tim. Hom.* 8 (*PG* 62.508).

very vivid terms. The deception of demons (the Greek gods) had in the past led Greeks to 'redden their altars with human blood' (*De S. Bab. Contra Jul. et Gent.* 3–5 (*PG* 50.534–5)) and the demons had lapped up the 'savour, smoke and blood' sacrificed to them (*De S. Bab. Contra Jul. et Gent.* 74 (*PG* 50.553)).[71] He gives a vivid description of the sacrifices made by the emperor Julian, recounting how he caused 'torrents of blood to flow from the slaughter of cattle' when he went to the shrine of Apollo at Daphne (*De S. Bab. Contra Jul. et Gent.* 80, 100, 103 (*PG* 50.555, 561 and 562)). The fact that Chrysostom could describe the ritual of sacrifice so vividly suggests that it played an important role for him. There appears to have been some tension in Chrysostom between wanting to present Greek religion as dead and gone and between wanting to keep alive vivid images of Greek worship. On the one hand, in works directed against Greeks he would hardly want to emphasize the survival of Greek religion. On the other hand, blood sacrifice was essential to Chrysostom as it was the feature that distinguished Greek religion most clearly from Christianity: by continually referring back to the blood sacrifice that characterized Greek religion at its height Chrysostom could give Greek religion defining features that were incontestably different from Christianity.

Vivid images of sacrifices appeared at regular, even if not frequent, intervals throughout Chrysostom's ordinary preaching too. These descriptions of sacrifice most often referred to Jewish contexts from the past – whether in exegesis of passages of the Old Testament or when making comparisons between the Old Covenant and the New (*In Ep. ad 1 Cor. Hom.* 27.5 (*PG* 61.229)).[72] However, Chrysostom did discuss Greek sacrifice when it was alluded to in New Testament texts, for example Paul 1 Corinthians 8–10 on meat sacrificed to the idols (*In Ep. ad 1 Cor. Hom.* 20–5 (*PG* 61.159–212)).[73] Scholars have long noted the importance of Paul and his writings to Chrysostom and to his engagement with the social and rhetorical context of the fourth century.[74] As Mitchell points out, the primary point of Chrysostom's interpretation and representation of Paul's works was not to achieve some 'true' exegesis of the saint's writings, but to answer contemporary

---

[71] See also *Conciones de Lazaro* 2.2 (*PG* 48.983). See Schatkin's footnote to her translation (1983), footnote 10, 77.
[72] See also *In Ep. ad 2 Cor. Hom.* 7.3 and 20.3 (*PG* 61.444–5 and 538–9) and *Hom. in Gen.* 27.5–6 (*PG* 53.242).
[73] On Chrysostom's exegetical goals and methods, see Malingrey 1975; Garret 1992; Gorday 1983: 104–35; and Amirav 2003. On how Chrysostom made apostolic times relevant to his own audience, see Wylie 1992.
[74] See *In Ep. ad 2 Cor. Hom.* 11.1 (*PG* 61.473). See also Ritter 1990; Hartney 2004: 14–16; Jackson 1990: 349; and, most recently, M. Mitchell 1998 and 2002: 22–8 and 401–4.

problems.⁷⁵ Paul wrote 1 Corinthians 8–10 for a particular socio-historical context, in which traditional Graeco-Roman religion was still the dominant religion and in which Christians were living among Greeks and Jews who still practised blood sacrifice.⁷⁶ In his exegesis of this passage Chrysostom discusses Paul's words to the Corinthians on the dangers of eating meat sacrificed to idols (*In Ep. ad 1 Cor. Hom.* 24.3–5 (*PG* 61.200–1)), explaining Paul's argument that the strong should hold back from eating this meat, despite the fact that the wooden idols were powerless.⁷⁷ The weak, both newer converts and the Greeks, still believed in the power of the idols and if they saw the strong eating the meat sacrificed to these idols, they might 'stumble' or be 'scandalized' (*In Ep. ad 1 Cor. Hom.* 20.1–6 (*PG* 61.159–64) and 25.3 (*PG* 61.208)).⁷⁸ Seeing a Christian eat meat that they knew had been sacrificed to the idol might cause the weak to think Christianity was a fable and hypocritical. As Chrysostom says, they 'conclude that not for truth's sake, but through ambition and love of power [Christians] have betaken themselves to this doctrine' (*In Ep. ad 1 Cor. Hom.* 25.2 (*PG* 61.207)). Despite the use of the rhetorical trope of addressing his audience in the vocative as if they were Paul's Corinthians, Chrysostom does not see the situation faced by Paul as directly comparable to the religious situation in his own time. He has to ask his audiences to use their imagination to understand the religious context that Paul faced precisely because it was so different from their own context: 'Do not tell me about the present establishment, and that you have received piety from your ancestors. But carry back your thoughts to those times ... impiety was still powerful, and altars were burning and sacrifices and libations were offered up and the greater part of men were Greeks (*Hellēnōn*) ...' (*In Ep. ad 1 Cor. Hom.* 20.8 (*PG* 61.165)). This understanding of the gap between Paul's time and Chrysostom's own is what allowed Chrysostom to turn Paul's words to the fourth century social context.

This can be seen when Chrysostom elucidates Paul's comparison between eating meat sacrificed to the idols and drinking the blood of Christ in the Eucharist (*In Ep. ad 1 Cor. Hom.* 24.3–6 on Paul 1 Corinthians 10.1–21 (*PG* 61.199–202)). Chrysostom recounts how Paul used this comparison to show that knowingly eating meat sacrificed to idols brought one into communion with devils just as the Eucharist brought one into communion with Christ. For Chrysostom this discussion of the significance of

---

[75] M. Mitchell 2002: 18–22 for the former point and 22 for the latter point. [76] Thiessen 1982.
[77] See also *Catéchèse* 4.15 (SC 50.190); *In Ep. ad 1 Cor. Hom.* 29.1–2 (*PG* 61.239–42); *In Ep. ad Ephes. Hom.* (*PG* 62.90); and *Hom. in Gen.* 7.18, 8.4–11 and 47.14 (*PG* 53.69, 70–3 and 54.433).
[78] See also *In Ep. ad 1 Cor. Hom.* 20.8–11 (*PG*.61.165–8).

the Eucharist provides an entrance into discussion of his present situation ('These things therefore knowing, let us also brethren . . .'). He encourages his audience to recognize the significance of Christ's body and of Christian contact with it in the Eucharist ceremony (*In Ep. ad 1 Cor. Hom.* 24.7 (*PG* 61.203–4)). However, this is not accompanied by a plea to flee from contact with idols and sacrifices, as Paul had ask the Corinthians. Instead Chrysostom asks his audiences 'to leave behind worldly things' so replacing the prohibition against eating meat sacrificed to idols with a more generic exhortation to good Christian behaviour (*In Ep. ad 1 Cor. Hom.* 24.7–8 (*PG* 61.203–6)). On this occasion, Chrysostom uses the contrast with animal sacrifice to assert more inward defining features of Christian identity (the meaning of the Eucharist) and a general withdrawal from the world. Elsewhere he uses Paul's discussion of the dangers of eating meat sacrificed to the idols as a lesson about the external boundaries between Greek and Christian in his own day. In one of his baptismal sermons, Chrysostom uses reference to this passage of Paul to show what was wrong with attending the races.

> Is it not appropriate to say to them what blessed Paul said to the Corinthians who kept going to the temples of idolatry after they had received the word of piety? *For if a man sees you who 'have knowledge' reclining at table in an idol place*, he says. But we shall change the words slightly and say: 'If a man sees you who have knowledge of piety passing the day in those foolish and harmful associations, will not the conscience of this weak man be given the excuse to pursue such actions with more enthusiasm?' (*Catéchèse* 6.15–16 (SC 50.222–3))[79]

The problem with attending the races in Chrysostom's own time was directly akin to the problem posed by people eating meat sacrificed to idols in Paul's time. In both cases people might imagine that Christians were not what they said they were, so attending the races or eating meat sacrificed to idols could become a 'stumbling block' to Christians and 'cause of scandal' to Greeks.[80] Members of Chrysostom's audiences who attended the races 'deserve this condemnation because they have turned a deaf ear to the blessed Paul when he says, 'do not be a stumbling block . . . to the Church of God' (*Catéchèse* 6.14 (SC 50.222). They could also be mocked by Greeks (*In Ep. ad 1 Cor. Hom.* 18.4 (*PG* 61.149)). In a world where sacrifice was no longer common Chrysostom could use reference to Paul's words on meat sacrificed to the idols to show that there were many practices in his own time that might at first look harmless, but that in fact involved

---

[79] See also *Hom. in Gen.* 7.2 and 40.18 (*PG* 53.62 and 54.374).
[80] On Chrysostom's use of the concept of scandal, see Schatkin 1988: 111–13.

the practitioner in idolatry. In doing so, he could draw a clear distinction between Christian and Greek and could make his contemporary situation appear as black and white as Paul's situation in first-century Corinth.

Chrysostom associated a wide range of practices with blood sacrifice. As he states, 'The devil never proposes sins to us in their proper colour, he does not speak of idolatry but he sets it in another dress' (*In Ep. ad Ephes. Hom.* 22 (*PG* 62.158)). Chrysostom's audiences denied that sin and idolatry could be brought together in this way, arguing that they 'never made an idol . . . nor set up an altar, nor sacrificed sheep nor poured libations of wine . . .' Chrysostom disagrees:

> When you pass by the altar of the idols you shall see it reeking with the blood of bullocks and goats; but when you pass by the altar of covetousness, you shall see it cruelly breathing human blood. If you stand before it here, you shall see, not the wings of birds burning, no vapour, no smoke exhaled, but the bodies of men dying. (*In Ep. ad Ephes. Hom.* 18 (*PG* 62.124))[81]

Chrysostom uses a similar technique to make clear that popular religious practices, such as the use of amulets, were not Christian and were, in fact, equivalent to the act of sacrifice. Talking of a woman who had used amulets to cure a sick child, he says: 'So is that other one an idolatress. For it is clear that she would have done sacrifice, had it been allowed to her to do sacrifice. In fact, even now, she has carried out the act of sacrifice' (*In Ep. ad Coloss. Hom.* 8 (*PG* 62.358)).[82]

The other side of the coin of comparing unacceptable practices to sacrifice was to compare the avoidance of these practices to martyrdom. Although martyrdoms rarely happened in the fourth century, aligning good Christian behaviour with martyrdom could tap into a traditional source of Christian identity: 'And does anyone say, what am I to do, for now is not the time of martyrdom? What do you say? Is now no time for martyrdom? . . . For it is not the hanging on a cross only that makes a martyr . . .' (*In Ep. ad 2 Cor. Hom.* 1.6 (*PG* 61.388)).[83] Refusing to use an amulet when one's child was sick could make someone a martyr (*In Ep. ad Coloss. Hom.* 8 (*PG* 62.357)).[84] If the comparison between using amulets and sacrifice was meant to draw clear-cut boundaries between Greek and Christian then the comparison

---

[81] See also *In Ep. ad Titus Hom.* 5 (*PG* 62.689); *Adv. Oppug.* 3.2 (*PG* 47.351), for envying a friend making someone worse than a Greek; and *In Ep. ad 1 Cor. Hom.* 23.1–2 and 4 (*PG* 61.190 and 192), for gluttony as idolatry.
[82] *Adv. Jud.* 8.5.6 (*PG* 48.934) and *In Ep. ad Coloss. Hom.* 8 (*PG* 62.357–8).
[83] On martyrdom and persecution as a marker of Christian identity before the fourth century, see Markus 1990: 19–63.
[84] See also *Adv. Jud.* 8.7.3 and 13 (*PG* 48.938 and 939) and *In Ep. ad 1 Thess. Hom.* 3 (*PG* 62.412–13).

between refusing amulets and martyrdom was meant to shore up Christian identity. While blood sacrifice and Christian martyrdom were no longer common in his time, Chrysostom could still use these as vivid images in order to draw boundaries between Greek and Christian. Either you were a sacrificing Greek or you were a Christian martyr and there was no state in between. Everything that Chrysostom considered to be non-Christian was associated with sacrifice, idolatry and Greekness while good Christian behaviour was associated with martyrdom.[85]

What might at first seem more surprising is that elsewhere in his preaching Chrysostom used sacrifice and other characteristic Greek practices to describe aspects of *Christian* worship. We find some of the longest descriptions of sacrifice on one occasion when Chrysostom refers to sacrifice as a ritual that was replaced by Christ's ultimate sacrifice, an image taken from the New Testament.[86] This comparison is made to show the superiority of the Christian sacrifice. However, it can also suggest an interest in making Christianity more familiar to those from a Greek background. In explanations of the Eucharist, Chrysostom emphasizes that Jesus' offering of his own blood on his altar gave those from a Greek background a form of blood sacrifice if they needed it (*In Ep. ad 1 Cor. Hom.* 24.3–5 (*PG* 61.200–1)).[87] This desire to appeal to those from a Greek background can also be seen in Chrysostom's use of metaphors of sacrifice and other Greek rituals to describe aspects of Christianity.[88] Avoiding sin could become 'an acceptable sacrifice to God' and, just like a blood sacrifice, this spiritual sacrifice would be rejected if it had a flaw – in this case the flaw would be the presence of sin instead of the absence of an ear or a tail (*Hom. in Gen.* 60.15 (*PG* 54.524)).[89] Similarly, he could describe prayer in the very vivid imagery of sacrifice:

So too in prayers we can stay sober . . . if we reflect that we are offering a sacrifice and that we have in our hands a knife and fire and wood . . . if we . . . taking the knife of the Spirit, infix it in the throat of the victim: make our sober attitude the sacrifice and our tears the libation to him. For such is the blood of this victim, such is the slaughter that reddens the altar. (*In Ep. ad 2 Cor. Hom.* 5.4 (*PG* 61.432))[90]

---

[85] On blood sacrifice continuing to be emblematic of Graeco-Roman religion, see Bradbury 1995: 332.
[86] For the idea of Christ's sacrifice in early Christian thought, see Young 1979.
[87] See also, *In Ep. ad 1 Cor. Hom.* 27.5 and 42.4 (*PG* 61.230 and 365). On the 'sweet savour of Christ' in his sacrifice of himself, see *In Ep. ad 2 Cor. Hom.* 5.2–3 (*PG* 61.429–31) and *Contra Jud. et Gent.* 8.4 (*PG* 48.823–4).
[88] On Chrysostom's use of metaphor, see Garret 1992: 207–10.
[89] See also *Hom. in Gen.* 9.12 (*PG* 53.80) and *In Ep. ad 2 Cor. Hom.* 20.3 (*PG* 61.540).
[90] See also *Hom. in Gen.* 13.3 (*PG* 53.106).

What is strange about these examples is that they appear to contradict Chrysostom's desire to present sacrifice and Greek religion as the complete opposite of Christianity.[91] Just as Chrysostom could not avoid describing what it meant to be a Greek when he was outlining characteristic features of Christianity, so he could not avoid describing internal features of Christianity when characterizing Greekness. Chrysostom's metaphorical use of the image of sacrifice maintained sacrifice as a meaningful symbol for his audiences long after it had ceased to be a common practice.[92] It was something that had to be kept alive to maintain a clear distinction between the two religions, but was also a symbol that was used as a means of communication across this divide.

CHRISTIANS VERSUS JEWS, GREEKS AND HERETICS

Chrysostom's sermons against the Jews can be seen as a model example of identity formation. We can read them as a textbook of Chrysostom's identity-constructing techniques, which we can then compare with how he refers to Greeks. The sermons *Against the Jews* were probably delivered in Antioch in two series, Sermons 1–3 in 386 and 4–8 in 387.[93] It is now usually accepted that the prime target of these sermons was Judaizing Christians not the Jews themselves.[94] The reason for their delivery was the divisions caused within the Church at Antioch by the actions of Judaizing Christians who were attending Jewish festivals and synagogues, practising Jewish fasts, and even treating Easter as Passover and Lent as preparation for the Jewish Pasch.[95] In acting in this way, these Judaizing Christians seriously challenged the self-definition of Christianity as distinct from Judaism – an issue that had first arisen at Antioch in the first century AD (in the debates over the admittance of Gentiles to Christianity).[96] As Wilken notes, in the minds of these 'Judaizers' 'there was no contradiction between going to the synagogue on Saturday to hear the reading of the law and coming to Church on Sunday to participate in the Eucharist'.[97] They wanted 'fellowship with the Jews' and 'fellowship at the holy table sharing the precious blood' (*Adv. Jud.* 2.3 (*PG* 48.861)). There have been various attempts to define

---

[91] On use of the image of sacrifice by other Christians, see Young 1979: 145–229; R. J. Daly 1978; E. Ferguson 1980; and Bradbury 1995: 333–4.
[92] Young 1979: 296.
[93] For the dating of these sermons, see Harkins 1979: l–lix and van de Paverd 1991: 255–93.
[94] Harkins 1979: xlix and Wilken 1983: 158–9.
[95] Wilken 1983: 73, 75 and 93; Harkins 1979: xxxv–xlii; and Soler 1999: 272–328.
[96] See, for example, Zetterholm 2003 (on Antioch) and Boyarin 2004 and Lieu 2004 (more generally).
[97] Wilken 1983: 75. See also Harkins 1979: xlii and *Adv. Jud.* 4.3.6 (*PG* 48.875).

who these Judaizers were: either they were uneducated half-Christians who indiscriminately mixed Jewish and Christian elements or they were a different group of Christians in their own right.[98] This will not be our concern here. Instead, we shall consider the ways in which Chrysostom sought to reaffirm Christian identity in this situation through stark contrast between what it was to be a Jew and what it was to be Christian. We shall see that in order to shore up the boundary between Jew and Christian Chrysostom sought to characterize Judaism as the opposite of Christianity and to make very clear distinctions as to what characterized Christian or Jewish practices.

Chrysostom argued that the Judaizers inappropriately confused the boundaries between Judaism and Christianity. He berates 'those who seem to belong to our ranks, although they observe the Jewish rite' saying that 'they deserve stronger condemnation than any Jew' (*Adv. Jud.* 4.3.4 (*PG* 48.875)). In his first homily *Against the Jews*, Chrysostom describes a situation that he had encountered just three days earlier in which a supposedly Christian man had dragged a Christian woman into a synagogue in order to make her swear an oath on a matter that they were disputing (*Adv. Jud.* 1.3.4 (*PG* 48.847)). The woman was a 'free woman of good bearing, modest and a believer (*pistos*)' (*Adv. Jud.* 1.3.4 (*PG* 48.847)). The man, in contrast, was brutal and unfeeling and only 'reputed to be a Christian (*dokountos einai Christianou*)' – because, says Chrysostom 'I would not call a person who could dare to do such things a sincere Christian (*Christianos eilikrinēs*)' (*Adv. Jud.* 1.3.4 (*PG* 48.847)). Chrysostom used this contrast between the good believer and the Judaizing half-Christian to highlight for his audience what counted as being Christian and what did not.[99] As a result, he refused the name of Christian or believer to anyone he labelled a Judaizer.[100] To support his notion that Judaizers were not acceptable and that they were failing in their Christianity in some way, Chrysostom referred to them as 'sick' throughout these sermons.[101] As a result, he argued that his audience should watch over each other and correct each other if they noticed anyone with this sickness (*Adv. Jud.* 1.4.9 (*PG* 48.850)).[102] Chrysostom wanted to use communal shame as a way to put a stop to the practices of the Judaizers. Just as he had done with those who continued to attend the races and the

---

[98] For the former view, see Simon 1964: 374 and Harkin 1979: xliv–v. For the latter view, see Wilken 1983: 94.
[99] He goes on to describe this man as a 'mule'. [100] *Adv. Jud.* 1.4.3 (*PG* 48.849).
[101] *Adv. Jud.* 1.1.4–5, 1.4.4, 2.3.6, 3.1.4, 4.3.5 and 5.12.12 (*PG* 48.844–5, 849, 861, 862, 875, 904).
[102] See also *Adv. Jud.* 1.3.6, 4.6.7 and 4.6.9, 1.4.8, 6.7.7 and 6.10 (*PG* 48.848, 880, 881, 849, 915 and 916).

spectacles, he used Paul's words to the Corinthians (1 Corinthians 8–10) to rebuke the Judaizers.

> And let me say: if someone sees you who have knowledge entering the synagogue and participating in the festival of the trumpets, shall not his conscience, being weak, be emboldened to esteem what the Jews do? (*Adv. Jud.* 1.5.7 (*PG* 48.851))

Again, we see Paul 1 Corinthians being turned to Chrysostom's contemporary context.

To ensure that his audiences understood his message Chrysostom had to make completely clear what kind of behaviour was unacceptable for Christians because it was were Jewish rather than Christian.[103] He mocked Christians who attended Jewish feasts and festivals and told them that it was not fitting that they should also attend church (*Adv. Jud.* 1.5.7 (*PG* 48.851)).[104] He attacked the participation of his audience in Jewish fasts, arguing that they might as well show their allegiance for Judaism publicly as they were only 'half-Christians' anyway (*Adv. Jud.* 1.4.6 (*PG* 48.849). Elsewhere Chrysostom contrasted Jewish fasts with Christian ones to show the superiority of the latter (*Adv. Jud.* 3.4.1–3 (*PG* 48.867)). Because fasting was a shared feature of both religions, he sought to differentiate the Christian fast by showing that it was to be carried out for repentance from sins and to achieve a state of purity rather than because of the time of year (*Adv. Jud.* 3.4.7 (*PG* 48.867)).[105] This included the Christian Lenten fast in which the moral reasons for fasting were supposed to dominate. Throughout the third sermon *Against the Jews* Chrysostom berated those who celebrated the Pasch according to the Jewish dating as it put them out of time with the festivals of the Church. He also berated those who celebrated the Passover, because this undermined the new dispensation of Christ, which made the Passover irrelevant (*Adv. Jud.* 3.5.7 and 4.4.3–5 (*PG* 48.876–7)).[106] Finally, Chrysostom accused those who attended the synagogues of 'sharing with those who crucified Christ' (*Adv. Jud.* 1.5.1 (*PG* 48.850)). Chrysostom was trying to show the Judaizers that they were 'mixing what cannot be mixed', because they seemed to think that 'the two religions [were] one and the same thing' (*Adv. Jud.* 4.6 (*PG* 48.579–81)). His goal was to show that Christianity and Judaism were two completely distinct religions that were mutually exclusive. Judaism had to be distinguished from, and opposed to, Christianity in every way in order for Chrysostom to construct Christianity as a discrete identity. As he says at one point, 'both the ceremonies of the

---

[103] See Wilken 1983: 75.   [104] See also *Adv. Jud.* 1.6.2 (*PG* 48.852).
[105] See also *Adv. Jud.* 3.5.1 and 4.4.2–5 and 5.1.3–5 (*PG* 48.868, 876–7 and 883).
[106] See Wilken 1983: 76–7.

Jews and of us cannot be holy': his audience would have to come down on one side or the other (*Adv. Jud.* 1.6.5 and 4.4.1 (*PG* 48.852 and 876)). To reinforce this idea Chrysostom made a comparison with the way that a Roman soldier would not mix with barbarians and Persians. He argued that this was how Christians should feel about Jews (*Adv. Jud.* 1.4.8 (*PG* 48.849)).

Chrysostom also denigrated Judaism in comparison to Christianity. He could not ridicule the Jewish God, as he did the Greek gods, because the Jewish God was the God of the Christians too.[107] But he could present the Jews as perverting the will of God because they continued to follow the law and refused to accept Jesus Christ and the new dispensation that he had brought. In the sixth and seventh sermons *Against the Jews* Chrysostom mocks the Jews for adhering to the Law when the temple and priesthood of Jerusalem, on which the Law's legitimacy were based, had been destroyed.[108] He then compares this with being Christian, which meant imitating Christ and obeying his laws and the New Covenant (*Adv. Jud.* 8.9.3 (*PG* 48.941)). As a result, Chrysostom often contrasts Jewish rituals, such as fasting, offerings and sacrifice, with their new Christian equivalents to show how superior the latter were (*Adv. Jud.* 3.4.1–3; 1.7.2 and 5.12.6–7 and 7.2.6 (*PG* 48.866–7, 853 and 918–19)).[109] Throughout these references we can clearly see the beginnings of the strand of anti-Semitic thinking that Jewish religion was all about the externals of ritual practice while Christianity was the true spiritual choice. Thus, as with the comparison between Greekness and Christianity, we can see that the superiority and essence of what it was to be Christian was partly constructed out of comparison with what it was to be Jewish.

Throughout this comparison between Jewish and Christian identity Chrysostom places great emphasis on animal sacrifice. He presents Jewish blood sacrifice as part of the Old Covenant, which was made irrelevant with the coming of Christ's New Covenant, and as inextricably tied up with the temple and priesthood in Jerusalem ((*Adv. Jud.* 5.12.6–7 and 7.2.6 (*PG* 48.853 and 918–19)). He presents Jewish sacrifice as at fault because it could only take place in the city of Jerusalem (*Adv. Jud.* 5.12.4–5 (*PG* 48.853)) and because it was an 'impure' offering of 'smoke, fat and blood' (*Adv. Jud.* 5.12. (*PG* 48.853)). He also compares it with gentile sacrifice because both could be sacrifice of 'material things' (*Adv. Jud.* 7.2.6 (*PG* 918–19)). What is most interesting, however, is the way in which Chrysostom uses

---

[107] For Chrysostom's polemic against the Jews, see Wilken 1983: 95–127.
[108] See also *Adv. Jud.* 6 and 7 (*PG* 48.903–15 and 915–27) and 1.2.3 (*PG* 48.845–6).
[109] See also *Hom. in Gen.* 39.16–19 and 40.16 (*PG*. 53.367–8 and 373–4).

animal sacrifice as a defining feature of Judaism despite his being clear that Jewish sacrifice ended with the destruction of the temple in AD 70. We can see why this might have been so if we now turn to Chrysostom's representation of Judaism in his ordinary preaching. Here too Chrysostom often uses reference to the change from animal sacrifice to the sacrifice of Christ's body as a crucial feature of his comparison between Jew and Christian. He talks in very vivid terms of the 'cup of the Old Covenant' as 'the libations and blood of brute creatures' and compares this to Christ's offering of his own blood (*In Ep. ad 1 Cor. Hom.* 27.5 (*PG* 61.230)). He also explores the difference between the Jewish and the Christian dispensation as part of his explanation of the difference between spiritual and temporal considerations in Paul (*In Ep. ad 2 Cor. Hom.* 20.1–3 (*PG* 61.535–40) on 2 Corinthians 9.10). Christians have an invisible altar available to them at all times, 'both in lanes and in market places', because it is made of flesh of the Lord, while the Jews have only the stone altar found in the holy of holies. Similarly, Christian sacrifice is an offering of souls and of good deeds that can be compared to and equated with the savour of sacrifice (*In Ep. ad 2 Cor. Hom.* 20.3 (*PG* 61.539–40)). Christian sacrifice is far superior to Jewish sacrifice due to its spiritual rather than ritualistic nature. Where Chrysostom does talk in more positive terms of Jewish sacrifice, as he does in descriptions of sacrifice carried out by biblical characters in his exegesis of Genesis, he describes it as prefiguring Christian sacrifice. Thus he spends much time enunciating how it was Noah's good intentions in making his animal sacrifice to God that made it acceptable, not the sacrifice of an animal in itself (*Hom. in Gen.* 27.5–6 (*PG* 53.241–2)). We can thus see that while Chrysostom must have been very aware that Jews no longer practised animal sacrifice, it suited him to talk as if they did. As we saw to be the case with Greek sacrifice, this allowed Chrysostom to make a direct contrast between Jews and Christians. It also allowed him to suggest an essential kinship between Greek and Jew by holding up animal sacrifice as a defining feature of both their religions. In one sermon on 1 Corinthians 10.13 Chrysostom alternates between comparing Christian sacrifice with the idolatry of the Greeks and with the Old Covenant of the Jews (*In Ep. ad 1 Cor. Hom.* 24.5 (*PG* 61.201–2)). It can thus be hard to tell whether he is referring to Jewish or Greek sacrifice; the two become interwoven as idolatrous sacrifice to demons.

This tendency to posit a lack of distinction between people who were not Christian is a typical feature of Chrysostom's writings. Chrysostom did have specific labels for Greeks and Jews and for the various heretical groups. However, he also had two more general labels, 'those on the outside' and 'unbelievers', that could be applied to any of these groups[110] because he saw those outside Christianity as sharing many characteristics. Jews were contrasted with Christians because they did not accept Christ as God but continued to follow the Old Law when it was no longer valid.[111] For this reason the 'godlessness (*asebeia*) of the Jews and the Greeks [was] on a par' (*Adv. Jud.* 1.6.4 (*PG* 48.852)). Similarly, Chrysostom suggested that Jews and Greeks and Anomoeans (a group of Arian Christians in Antioch who were in opposition to the Nicene Christianity favoured by Chrysostom) all shared the same weakness of thinking that Christ was only a man who had been set up as a god (*Adv. Jud.* 5.3.2–4 (*PG* 48.886–7) and 1.1.6 (*PG* 48.886–7)). Jews could also be accused of idolatry in a similar way to Greeks. Chrysostom describes how in the Jewish synagogue 'stands an invisible altar of deceit on which they [the Jews] sacrifice not sheep and calves but the souls of men' (*Adv. Jud.* 1.4.4 (*PG* 48.849)).[112] Or, at other times, he expresses the fear that those using Jewish amulets and other 'magical' cures might more easily be persuaded to become involved in the use of Greek religious cures and so in the worship of the Greek gods (*Adv. Jud.* 1.7 (*PG* 48.854)).[113] Finally, Jews, like the Greeks, did not see things clearly with the 'eyes of faith' but as 'in a mirror darkly' (*In Ep. ad 1 Cor. Hom.* 34.3 (*PG* 61.288)) and disputed the validity of the Gospels (*In Paralyticum demissum per tectum* 3 (*PG*.51.53)). Greeks, Manichees, Marcionites and Valentinians also shared the mistaken idea that the world was created out of pre-existing matter rather than out of nothing by God (*Hom. in Gen.* 2.10 (*PG* 53.29–30)) and Greeks and heretics both denied that the human body was made by God (*Hom. de Stat.* 11.2 (*PG* 49.120)). Greeks, Jews and heretics could thus collectively be characterized as 'enemies' because they all disagreed with Christians on these points (*Hom. in Gen.* 2.5 and 11 (*PG* 53.28 and 30)). Chrysostom could align all non-Christians and tar them with the same brush: they were all other and therefore the opposite of everything that was Christian, good and acceptable.[114] As soon as someone stepped outside the boundaries that Chrysostom drew around the Christian community it did not really matter which other category of religion he or she belonged to: they were all equally wrong.[115]

Christians in the ancient world often conceived of heresies as resulting from either Judaizing or Hellenizing tendencies among Christians.[116] In the

---

[110] Schatkin 1988: 54 and *De Incomp. Dei Nat.* 3.356–7 (SC 28.216). For a definition of Gentiles as 'those without' in contrast to Christians as 'those within', see *In Ep. ad 1 Cor. Hom.* 16.2 (*PG* 61.130).
[111] See also *Adv. Jud.* 1.2.3–4 (*PG* 48.846) and *In Ep. ad 2 Cor. Hom.* 7.3 (*PG* 61.445–6).
[112] See also *Adv. Jud.* 1.6.3 (*PG* 48.23) and 6.7.1 (*PG* 48.914); and *Hom. in Gen.* 2.7 (*PG* 53.28).
[113] See also *Adv. Jud.* 4.4.3–5 (*PG* 48.876–7).   [114] Schatkin 1988: 27–30.   [115] Schatkin 1988: 28.
[116] Boyarin 2004: 1–33. He argues that heretical groups were often seen as Jews or Judaizers.

third sermon against the Judaizers Chrysostom berated those who followed the Jewish way of dating the Pasch because they had rejected the decision made at Nicaea on this issue: that is, he saw it in terms of a Christian decision about orthodoxy that aligned Judaizers with the Anomoeans.[117] Chrysostom had interrupted his sermons *Against the Anomoeans, On the Incomprehensibility of God* to turn to address the Judaizers, saying that he did not see it as an interruption precisely because the Jews, like the Anomoeans, refused to accept Christ as the son of God (*Adv. Jud.* 1.1.6 (*PG* 48.886–7)). Jews and Greeks could also easily become aligned in Christian minds because they both used (or had used) animal sacrifice and because of Julian's attempt to restore the Jewish temple in Jerusalem. For this reason Wilken has argued that we can see Chrysostom's sermons against the Judaizers as addressed not only to Judaizing Christians but also to Greeks.[118] Wilken claims that references to Julian's failure to rebuild the Jewish temple in his *Demonstration to the Gentiles and Jews that Christ Is God* were used in order to symbolize the failure of Jewish religion a whole (as at *Contra Judaeos et Gentiles, quod Christus sit deus* 16 (*PG* 48.835)). Such references show that the 'status of the temple was not simply a matter that concerned Christianity and Judaism but that it also entered into disputes with pagans'. It was in fact less relevant to Jews, for whom the 'religious crisis provoked by the loss of Jerusalem was resolved before the end of the first century'.[119] As Julian had sought to align Jews and Jewish sacrifice with Greeks and Greek sacrifice in order to combat Christianity, so Chrysostom too was led to see Jews and Greeks as a common enemy.

The final step in this pushing together of Greeks, Jews and heretics was that Chrysostom could label all these groups as demonic. He spoke of apostolic times as the time when 'all men were worshipping demons' (*In Ep. ad 1 Cor. Hom.* 4.10 and 25.2 (*PG* 61.37 and 206–7)).[120] In his day too he described the worship of Graeco-Roman idols as the worship of 'stones and demons' (*In Ep. ad 1 Cor. Hom.* 20.4 (*PG* 61.163)).[121] Demons tricked people into thinking that statues of deities could deliver oracles in order to convince people that they were not just dumb idols.[122] Chrysostom thus equated worship of Graeco-Roman gods with service to Satan.[123] We have

---

[117] Harkins 1979: xlii.
[118] Wilken 1983: 131–59. On the relationship between these two works, see also Harkins 1979: l–lix.
[119] Wilken 1983: 132 and 151. On Julian's attempted restoration of Jewish sacrifice and the Jewish temple, see Wilken 1983: 138–45.
[120] See also *De S. Bab. Contra Jul. et Gent.* 13 (*PG* 50.537).
[121] *In Ep. ad 1 Cor. Hom.* 20.4 (*PG* 61.162–3). See also, *In Ep. ad 1 Cor. Hom.* 4.9–10 (*PG* 61.36–7); *In Ep. ad Coloss. Hom.* 2 (*PG* 62.316) and *Catéchèse* 1.9 (SC 50.113).
[122] *In Ep. ad 1 Cor. Hom.* 29.2 (*PG* 61.241–2).
[123] See *Interpretatio in Isaiam Prophetam* 8.1 (*PG* 56.88–9).

already seen in his *Catechetical Sermons* that he labelled the various activities as pomps of the devil.[124] In fact, Chrysostom characterized the worship of the Greek idols as worship of demons throughout his writing and preaching and even sometimes characterized Greeks themselves as demons (*De S. Bab. Contra Jul. et Gent.* 73–5, 79, 93, 96, 103 and 109 (*PG* 50.553–4, 555, 559, 560, 562 and 564)).[125] He described Graeco-Roman prophecy and divination as equivalent to possession by a demon. The Pythia sat astride the tripod while an 'evil spirit' entered her and filled her with 'madness' causing her to 'play the bacchanal' (*In Ep. ad 1 Cor. Hom.* 29.2 (*PG* 61.241)). Chrysostom also referred to Greek religion as superstition (*deisidaimonia*) (*De S. Bab. Contra Jul. et Gent.* 13 and 76 (*PG* 50.537 and 554)), and he even referred to 'the sophist who taught [him] as the most superstitious (*deisidaimonesteros*) – of all men', which surely must refer to Libanius (*A une jeune veuve* 2 (SC 138.120)).[126] Chrysostom described Greeks as being 'proficient in the theory and practice of magic' and represented the priests of the emperor Julian as magicians and sorcerers.[127] When he described Greek religion itself, he represented it as working by 'certain mystical rites and bewitchments' (*In Ep. ad 1 Cor. Hom.* 29.2 (*PG* 61.241–2)). He described necromancy as one of the central rituals in Graeco-Roman religion and spoke of how 'wonderworkers evoked apparitions of the departed and phantoms of certain dead men' (*In Ep. ad 1 Cor. Hom.* 29.2 (*PG* 61.241–2)).[128] In this way Chrysostom associated Greek religion with magic and witchcraft and so with the worship of demons.

Because Chrysostom saw Greek religion as encompassing every cultural and social aspect of living as a Greek, he also applied this ascription of the label demonic to every aspect of Greek life. Any aspect of the world outside the Church could find itself labelled as demonic if Chrysostom had reason to rail against it.[129] By characterizing Greek religion as magical and demonic in these ways, Chrysostom was trying to distance it as far as possible from being a legitimate religious choice.[130] However, it also allowed him to show very

---

[124] See also *Catéchèse* 2.20 (SC 50.145), 4.32 (SC 50.199) and *Catéchèse* 1.11–15 (SC 366.135–43) = Harkins, *Baptismal Instruction* 9.19–26, 12.52 ((*PG.* 49.239). See H. A. Kelly 1985 on renunciation.
[125] *In Ep. ad 1 Cor. Hom.* 4.9–10, 25.2 and 29.1–2 (*PG* 61.36–7, 207 and 239–42); *In Ep. ad 2 Cor. Hom.* 8.4 (*PG* 61.458); and *In Ep. ad Coloss. Hom.* 2 (*PG* 62.316–17). See also *Interpretatio in Isaiam Prophetam* 8.1 (*PG* 56.88–9) and the discussion of Garret 1992: 241–2. For Greeks as demons, see *In Ep. ad Coloss. Hom.* 7 (*PG* 62.250) and also Mayer and Allen 2000: 82.
[126] On this, see Hunter 1988: 4.
[127] For witchcraft, see *In Ep. ad 2 Tim. Hom.* 8 (*PG* 62.648) and *In Ep. ad 2 Cor. Hom.* 8.4 (*PG* 61.458). For Julian and witchcraft, see *De S. Bab. Contra Jul. et Gent.* 77 and 83 (*PG* 50.554–5 and 556).
[128] For necromancy, see *De S. Bab. Contra Jul. et Gent.* 1 and 79 (*PG* 50.533 and 555).
[129] *In Kal.* (*PG* 48.954); *Contra Ludos et Theatra* (*PG* 53.23–270); *Conciones de Lazaro* 7.1 (*PG* 48.1045); *In Ep. ad 1 Cor. Hom.* 18.3 and *In Ep. ad Coloss. Hom.* 3 (*PG* 62.306–7).
[130] See, for example, Phillips 1991; Rives 2003; Janowitz 2001; and Beard, North and Price 1998: vol. 1, 214–36.

clearly how being Greek was completely beyond the pale and completely incompatible with being Christian. Similar processes can be seen in the way he described Jews and heretics: Jewish synagogues were the homes of demons, the Jews themselves were demons and the Anomoeans were possessed by demons.[131] The association of Jewish synagogues with demons meant that Chrysostom could again present them as just as idolatrous as the Greeks because anywhere that demons inhabited was a place of idolatry even if no idols stood there (*Adv. Jud.* 1.6.2 (*PG* 48.851–2)).[132] Thus, he was able to present the choice between being a Christian, a Jew and a Greek as a choice between whole different ways of life but also as a cosmic choice between siding with God and siding with demonic powers.

Chrysostom was attempting to construct a clear-cut Christian identity for his audiences and to draw firm boundaries between Greeks and Christians. He wanted there to be an absolute choice between the Christian way of life and the Greek way of life – including social, moral and cultural characteristics as well as more strictly 'religious' ones. As a result, he wanted the differences between the two groups to be made constantly public and visible through the behaviour of Christians. As we saw in his *Catechetical Sermons*, the step from one religion to another was supposed to involve a great turn around and a great change. Chrysostom was not just asking his audiences to think about Greek and Christian identities in particular ways; he was also asking them to use distinct religious categories in thinking about the world in the first place. This was a way of thinking in which individuals had to define their whole existence in terms of their religion and make choices between distinct religious options that were seen to be in conflict with one another. We need to remember, however, that Chrysostom was not preaching the use of categories of 'Greek', 'Christian' and 'Jew' in a positive way to offer people new ways of being. Rather, he was speaking from a position as a Christian leader, at the centre of a Church-focused world and in order to impose an ideologically laden way of thinking. For this reason we, as modern scholars, should be wary of taking Chrysostom's strict categories of religious identity as representative of fourth-century society as a whole.

---

[131] On the Jews, see *Adv. Jud.* 1.3.1, 1.4.6, 2.3.2, 5.12.12, 6.6.7–11 and 8.8.6–7 (*PG* 48.847, 849, 860, 904, 913–14 and 940). On the Anomoeans, see *De Incomp. Dei Nat.* 3.347–52 (SC 28.216–17). See also Schatkin 1988: 55–6.
[132] See also *Adv. Jud.* 6.7.1 (*PG* 48.914).

CHAPTER 4

Libanius and the strategic use of religious allegiance

LIBANIUS' LABELLING AND DEFINITION OF RELIGIOUS ALLEGIANCE

References to religious allegiance are the exception rather than the rule in Libanius' writings. He wrote orations and letters on a whole range of topics including education, social reform (on behalf of prisoners and peasants, for example), civic life and imperial administration, almost without mentioning religious issues in any significant way. Libanius' sense of himself as someone who adhered to traditional religion simply did not impose on these matters in a consistent way and was rarely something he thought relevant to mention. Against this background, the examples where Libanius does mention religious allegiance and does explore religious difference are striking. The largest body of Libanius' writings that give a central place to religious issues are the Julianic orations (particularly *Oration* 13 *An Address to Julian* and *Oration* 12 *An Address to the Emperor Julian as Consul* written during Julian's stay in Antioch (the latter at the emperor's request); and also *Orations* 17 *The Lament over Julian*; 18 *The Funeral Oration*; and 24 *On Avenging Julian*) and the letters written during and around the reign of Julian. Julian sought to restore Graeco-Roman religion as the state-sponsored religion, to convert people back from Christianity and to emphasize the most visual features of Graeco-Roman cult practice, such as blood sacrifice, which meant that Libanius was forced to discuss religious issues.[1] The other occasion on which Libanius places great emphasis on questions of religious allegiance and on the difference between Graeco-Roman religion and Christianity is in his *Oration* 30 *To Theodosius in Defence of the Temples*. In this case, the actions of Christian monks against traditional Graeco-Roman religion in the countryside around Antioch have forced Libanius to talk about the relationship between the two religions. On three other occasions issues of

---

[1] On Julian's religious policy, see Athanassiadi 1992: 109–11 and 181–91; R. Smith 1995: 198–218 and Bradbury 1995.

religious allegiance and religious difference appear in Libanius' writings. In his *Oration 2 To Those Who Call Me Tiresome* Libanius presents the change from the religious revival of Julian's reign to the dominance of certain Christians in the early 380s as characteristic of the decline of the period. In his *Oration 1 The Autobiography* (written in the late 370s (up to *Or.* 1.155) and throughout the period of 380–93 (from *Or.* 1.155 onwards)) he looks back on his life and at various points mentions religion and the religious allegiance of individuals when relevant. This could be in his description of Julian's reign, in references to his enemies – where their Christianity was just another negative factor – or as a way to commend those close to him who also shared his religious allegiance. Finally, Libanius mentions issues of religious allegiance in his orations on the Riot of the Statues (*Oration 23 Against the Refugees*; *Oration 19 To the Emperor Theodosius, about the Riots*; *Oration 20 To the Emperor Theodosius, after the Reconciliation*; *Oration 21 To Caesarius, Master of Offices*; and *Oration 22 To Ellebichus*), where the Christians are just one of the groups he blames for causing the riot.

In these orations we see Libanius' most consistent use of references to religious allegiance but even here, he uses less distinct labels than John Chrysostom did. Libanius speaks of those who share his religious allegiance as 'those on our side (*tēn merida tēn hēmeteran*)' (*Or.* 14.42 (F.II.102)), those who have 'recognition of the ones truly ruling heaven (*tēn gnōsin tōn hōs alēthōs ton ouranon echontōn*)' (*Or.* 18.125 (F.II.289)) and 'those honouring the affairs of the gods (*tous ta tōn theōn timōntas*)' (*Or.* 30.26 (F.III.100–1).[2] Their religion is 'the affairs of the gods (*ta tōn theōn*)' (*Or.* 24.21 (F.II.523)), the 'worship of the gods (*hē tōn theōn latreia*)' (*Or.* 18.22 (F.II.246) or *hē therapeia* (*Or.* 12.69 (F.II.34)), or the 'the divine rites (*hiera theia*)' (*Or.* 1.219 (F.I.180)).[3] Libanius does not once use the words 'Christian' or 'Christianity' and does not make use of the other current terms for Christians, such as 'Galileans'.[4] Instead he speaks of the 'irreligious' or 'impious ones (*hoi dussebeis*)' (*Or.* 1.207 (F.I.175)), 'atheists (*hoi atheoi*)' (*Ep.* F.607 and *Ep.* B.147 (*Ep.* F.695)), 'the polluted ones (*hoi miaroi*)' (*Or.* 18.287 (F.II.362)) and 'the uninitiated (*hoi amuētoi*)' (*Or.* 1.39 (F.I.103)).[5] Or he talks of those 'not knowing the gods (*eidōs oud' theous*)' (*Or.* 1.255 (F.I.193)) and those having 'a false opinion about the gods (*doxan de peri theōn ouk alēthē*)' (*Or.* 18.122 (F.II.287–8)).[6] Finally, he speaks of the 'enemies' of the gods

---

[2] See also *Or.* 1.219 (F.I.180) and *Or.* 16.48 (F.II.179).
[3] See also *Or.* 62.8 (F.IV.350); *Or.* 12.69 (F.II.34) and *Or.* 13.26 (F.II.72).   [4] P. Petit 1955: 204.
[5] See also his sarcastic references to Christians as the 'holy ones (*hoi semnoi*)' (*Or.* 18.286 (F.II.362)) and (*Or.* 23.18 (F.II.502).
[6] See also *Or.* 18.124 (F.II.289).

(*Ep.* N.120.3 (F.1220)) and of the temples (*Ep.* B.154.3 (F.1425)), 'men who intimidate us (*androi phoberoi*)' (*Ep.* N.143.4 (F.1534)) and 'our opponents (*hoi hēmin enantioi*), (*Ep.* N.103.5 (F.819)).[7] At other times, Libanius could refer to Christians in much more neutral terms simply as those who were 'different' or 'other' on religious matters in some way (*Ep.* N.144.1 (F.1543), *Or.* 18.19 (F.II.245)) and *Or.* 14.42 (F.II.102)). The only group for which Libanius had a clear-cut terminology was the Jews, who were as much an ethnic as a religious group. He used the traditional and well-accepted label in the Greek term *Ioudaios* (*Or.* 47.13 (F.IV.410)) and (*Ep.* N.131 (F.1251)) or referred to them, without any derogatory implications, as 'the race of that kind' – *toiouton* or *ekeinon genos* (*Ep.* N.160 (F.914) and *Ep.* F.1084).[8] When Libanius was forced to mark out the difference between Christians, Jews and adherents of Graeco-Roman religion, he had the language to do so.

Particularly noteworthy in Libanius' terminology for religious allegiance is his constant reference to 'the gods' in the plural, which could suggest that he saw a polytheistic conception of divinity as a defining feature of the difference between Christianity and Graeco-Roman religion.[9] Throughout his writings Libanius does refer to 'the gods' generally and to numerous specifically named gods, in particular the gods Tyche, Apollo, Calliope, Zeus and Helios.[10] He also occasionally characterizes Christians by the fact that they worship only one God: in the orations on the Riot of the Statues he talks of the people who call on 'the God' or 'their God' as causing the riot (*Or.* 19.25 (F.II.397), *Or.* 20.3 (F.II.422) and *Or.* 22.5 (F.II.473–4)). In one of these examples he makes a direct contrast between these people and those who share his own religious allegiance and call on 'the gods' (*Or.* 22.5 (F.II.473–4)). Usually, however, Christians were described negatively according to their failure to worship the gods. They were simply those *not* worshipping, *not* knowing the gods, the *un*initiated or those who were enemies of traditional religion. What Libanius has given us is not a contrast between two positively constructed religions, one polytheistic and the other monotheistic, but rather a contrast between a presence, worship of the gods, and an absence, no worship of the gods. He also showed no sign of excluding from adherence to Graeco-Roman religion anyone

---

[7] See also *Or.* 2.59 (F.I.258); *Or.* 18.12 and 34; *Or.* 1.165 (F.I.160); *Ep.* N. 47.5 (F.81); and *Ep.* F.695.
[8] See also the translations of these letters in Meeks and Wilken 1978: 59–66.
[9] As Misson suggests (Misson 1914: 23).
[10] For Libanius' polytheism, see Schouler 1984: vol. II, 939–40; Liebeschuetz 1972: 15; P. Petit 1955: 192–3; and Misson 1914: 23–39. For local deities of Antioch, see *Or.* 15.79 (F.II.152) and *Or.* 18.162 (F.II.306). For times when Libanius does use a singular of the divine, see Misson 1914: 25 and 29.

who thought of the traditional gods in a more syncretic, henotheistic or monotheistic way. Libanius' use of terminology such as 'those who worship the gods' is far more inclusive than use of a single definitive term for practitioners of Graeco-Roman religion, such as 'Greeks' or 'pagans'. All that this terminology suggests is that an individual needed to offer worship to the gods generally, or to one of the gods in particular, in some way. It does not imply that this worship had to take a particular form. In fact, Libanius at times himself made use of the singular terminology for the divine.[11] He could use the singular for the divine completely interchangeably with the plural, or when it was not possible to specify which god was acting – something that Greeks and Romans had been doing since the time of Homer and Herodotus.[12] For example, he described Julian's pious actions towards the gods and the gods' protection and care of Julian using both singular and plural forms of *ho theos* and *ho daimōn* interchangeably.[13] He could also use a monotheistic conception of the divinity ('the god (*ho theos*)' or 'the higher power (*ho kreittōn*)') when it suited him, when praising Christian emperors in his *Oration 59 In Praise of Constans and Constantius*, for example.[14] As a *basilikos logos* (an imperial oration), delivered before Constantius' highest officials in the 340s, this oration sought to smooth over the religious differences between Libanius and Constantius. The aim was not for Libanius to define himself as a Christian in any sense.[15]

We can now move beyond Libanius' labels for religious allegiance to understand his broader representations of worship of the gods and Christianity. In the Julianic orations and letters *Oration* 30 and *Oration* 2 Libanius was driven to define and contrast the two religions far more than he normally did, by focusing on certain recognizable and traditional features. In his Julianic orations Libanius often characterizes the Graeco-Roman religion promoted by Julian as a 'restoration' or a 'revival' (*Or.* 13.45 (F.11.79) and *Or.* 17.9 (F.11.210)). This was a revival of a religion of festivals, temples and idols.[16] In particular, it was a revival of a religion of blood sacrifice.

---

[11] Quiroga Puertas has recently argued, in an unpublished PhD dissertation, that Libanius held a stronger concept of monotheism than this: a 'cultural monotheism' that was part of a 'third way' that existed in the fourth century (Quiroga Puertas 2006: 148–57). Quiroga Puertas kindly sent me his dissertation but I received it at too late a stage to incorporate it more fully into this current work.
[12] See Misson 1914: 232–8 and 25 and also P. Petit 1955: 193. See also West 1999.
[13] The references for this are too many to List. See Misson 1914: 67–83 and P. Petit 1955: 193.
[14] *Or.* 59.16, 48, 74, 122 125, 142 and 169 (F.IV.216, 232, 244–5, 269, 273, 281 and 294).
[15] On the genre, see Lieu and Montserrat 1996: 159–61. On the dating and context of the delivery of *Oration* 59, see Wiemer 1994: 512–13 and Lieu and Montserrat 1996: 158 and 161–4.
[16] *Or.* 13.45–7 (F.11.79–80); *Or.*12.69 (F.11.34); *Or.* 17.1–9 (F.11.206–11); *Or.* 18.126, 287–8 and 298 (F.11.290, 362–3); and *Or.* 24.36 (F.11.530).

Libanius eulogizes Julian's restoration of sacrifice describing how 'everywhere there were altars, fire, blood-offerings, fat and smoke' and how 'the same ox served as worship for the gods and a feast for men' (*Or.* 18.126–7 (F.II.290)).[17] He also gives very vivid descriptions of Julian's own sacrifice, describing how Julian 'runs about and gets the wood and holds the knife; he opens the birds and inspects their entrails' (*Or.* 12.82 (F.II.38)).[18] He places particular emphasis on the public sacrifices that Julian carried out in Antioch itself (*Or.* 1.121 (F.I.141)).[19] Similar constructions of Graeco-Roman religion can be seen in *Oration* 30 and *Oration* 2. In many places in *Oration* 30 Libanius presents Graeco-Roman religion in traditional terms as worship of idols in temples and by blood sacrifice (*Or.* 30.4–5, 8, 9 and 31 (F.III.89–90, 91, 92 and 103–4)). He argues that because sacrifices were still allowed in Rome and Egypt and they were clearly considered beneficial, they should also be allowed in the countryside near Antioch (*Or.* 30.33–6 (F.III.104–6)). In *Oration* 2 Libanius again characterizes Graeco-Roman religion, which he now presents as in decline, in traditional terms of 'sacrifices in plenty', temples 'full of worshippers' and the 'good cheer, music, songs and garlands' of public festivals (*Or.* 2.30 (F.I.248)).

These same orations also give some characterization of Christians and Christianity. In the Julianic orations Libanius refers to the 'wicked and disobedient' people who caused much destruction to Graeco-Roman altars and temples in Constantius' reign (*Or.* 15.53 (F.II.140) and *Or.*18.23 (F.II.246)), objected to Julian's rule and perhaps even murdered the emperor who so visibly worshipped the old gods (*Or.* 15.77 (F.II.151) and *Or.*18.275 (F.II.356)).[20] In *Oration* 17 *The Lament over Julian*, written after Julian's death, Libanius describes those who 'put out the sacred fire, put an end to the sweet sacrifices . . . and closed the altars and temples or demolished them' (*Or.* 17.7 (F.II.209–10)).[21] On a number of occasions he also stereotypes Christianity as a religion for women. In his *Oration* 16 *To the Antiochenes, on the Emperor's Anger*, in which he seeks to blame Christians in the city for Julian's anger, he ridicules elite Christians for placing trust in the doctrines of their 'wives', 'housekeepers' and 'cooks' and for thus 'following the lead of those [they] should command' (*Or.* 16.47 (F.II.178–9)).[22] He also appears to have seen the cult of the martyrs as characteristic of Christianity. In one

---

[17] See also *Or.*13.47 (F.II.80); *Or.* 12.69 and 79 (F.II.34); *Or.* 14.69 (F.II.112); *Or.* 15.79–81 (F.II.152); *Or.* 18.126–7 (F.II.290); *Ep.* N.80.7 (F.694); *Ep.* N.100.4 (F.*Ep.* 1351); and *Ep.* B.181.1 (F.712).

[18] See also *Or.*17.9 (F.II.210).   [19] See also *Ep.* N.97.3 (F.797) and *Ep.* B.43 (F.739).

[20] See also *Ep.* 120.2 (F.1220) and Julian, *Mis.* 361b.

[21] See also *Or.* 17.34 (F.II.220); *Or.* 18.286–7 (F.II.362–3); *Or.* 24.1–2 and 21 (F.II.514–15 and 523); *Ep.* B.46 (F.1449); *Ep.* B.104.4 (F.1223); and *Ep.* B.159 (F.1458).

[22] See also *Ep.* F.1411.

of his Julianic orations he makes derogatory reference to Christian worship of 'dead men's tombs' (*Or.* 18.282 (F.II.360)) and, in a letter defending a Christian, he points out that persecution might lead to his becoming a martyr (*Ep.* N.103.5–8 (F.819)). Later, in his *Oration 2 To Those Who Call Me Tiresome* Libanius refers to the influential courtiers and bureaucrats whom he saw as a corrupting influence on government (*Or.* 2.59–61 (F.I.258)). He describes how they spend their time at 'disgraceful' parties 'where there is plenty of iced water laid on' and 'where instead of the gods, those responsible for our present woes receive hymns of praise' (*Or.* 2.59 (F.I.258)).[23] This notion of Christians as involved in drunken parties could have arisen from a Graeco-Roman misunderstanding of the Eucharist ritual. Libanius also presents these Christian officials and courtiers as involved in sexually dubious activity (*Or.* 2.61 (F.II.258)). In his series of orations on the Riot of the Statues Libanius describes those who worshipped their own God and gathered outside the church as one of the groups who were to blame for fermenting the riot (*Or.* 19.25 (F.II.396–7)).[24] Finally, in his *Oration 30 In Defence of the Temples* Libanius argues that it was the monks and the Christian governor Cynegius who were responsible for the destruction of temples in the countryside around Antioch in the 380s (*Or.* 30.11–12 (F.III.93–4)).[25] Libanius present the monks as extremists who have left their proper work on farms and makes innuendoes about 'how they spend their days and how they spend their nights' (*Or.* 30.21 (F.III.98–9)). This is similar to the picture he gives of Christian monks in his *Oration 62 Against Critics of his Educational System*, probably written in 382. He describes the monks as 'sallow-faced people, enemies of the gods, who hang around tombs and tear to pieces the solemnity of Helios and of Zeus and of those who rule with him' (*Or.* 62.10 (F.IV.351)).

On certain occasions Libanius was capable of constructing a relatively well-defined version of Graeco-Roman religion. He could emphasize the most traditional and most distinctive aspects of Graeco-Roman religious practice in order to make a contrast with the competing religion of Christianity. Blood sacrifice played a key role in this process because it was the most visually striking and visible feature of Graeco-Roman religion and had once been the central ritual of that religion. In the past, Libanius' focus on this ritual of blood sacrifice has led scholars to assume that it

---

[23] On the Christian decurions of Antioch playing dice, see *Or.* 35.17 (F.III.218–19) with Pack 1935: 41.
[24] See also *Or.* 20.3 (F.II.422–3) and *Or.* 22.5 (F.II.473–4).
[25] For other negative references to the monks, see *Ep.* B.75.4 (F.1367); *Or.* 7.10 (F.II.375–6); and *Or.* 23.18 (F.II.501–2).

was a ritual that he particularly favoured;[26] we can now see that other explanations are possible. The Julianic orations were highly rhetorical and formulaic speeches composed with the explicit goals of praising and pleasing Julian. By mentioning blood sacrifices so often in these orations, Libanius might simply have been saying what was expected of him in view of the importance that Julian placed on blood sacrifice.[27] At the same time, Julian's reign, with its uncompromising position on religious affairs, led to emphasis on the differences between different religious allegiances.[28] We can argue that Libanius was simply responding to this situation when he marked out differences between adherents of Graeco-Roman religion and Christians. The same is true of *Oration* 30, which he wrote at a time of heightened conflict between Christians and worshippers of the gods, in this case caused by the aggressive measures of Christians. Large parts of the oration take the form of a traditional defence of Graeco-Roman religion because it was the most traditional features of this religion that were being attacked by the Christians. Again, Libanius was responding to an image of Graeco-Roman religion that was created by someone other than himself. It is only in *Oration* 2 that Libanius himself seems to fashion a direct contrast between the traditional religion of the past and the Christianity of the present. He emphasizes the negative impact of certain Christian groups and policies as characteristic of the decline of his current times. In this oration Libanius presents himself as the 'grumpy old man', dissatisfied with every aspect of contemporary life, and is not trying to convey his true views in a straightforward way.[29]

In fact, there is evidence to suggest that Libanius did not favour blood sacrifice himself and that he might not have approved of the prominent role it played in Julian's so-called religious revival.[30] Except when he referred to Julian's reign, Libanius never mentioned himself or anyone else taking part in blood sacrifice. As he did refer to his own use of divination, which imperial legislation also outlawed, this lack of reference to blood sacrifice cannot be put down simply to a desire to hide his taking part in an illegal practice. It is possible that, like various other adherents to traditional religion, Libanius simply no longer saw large-scale sacrifice as the most appropriate form of religious expression. Ammianus Marcellinus famously disapproved of the scale of sacrifices carried out by the emperor Julian,

---

[26] P. Petit 1978: 75.
[27] R. Smith 1995: 19, 169, 184, 198, 200–8, 211, 216–17 and 222 and Bradbury 1995.
[28] R. Smith 1995: 179–218 and Athanassiadi 1992: 24–7, 133–4 and 161.
[29] On the comparable self-representations of second-sophistic orators, see Whitmarsh 2001: 30–4.
[30] Burr 1996: 32 and Swain 2004: 395.

saying that it made Julian 'superstitious rather than truly religious' (Amm. Marc. 25.4.17).[31] Bradbury has also suggested that Julian followed the teachings of Iamblichus, which advocated blood sacrifice as an appropriate offering to the gods of the material world, whereas other Neoplatonists (those who followed the teachings of Porphyry) spurned it completely.[32] Other Neoplatonists, therefore, let alone other worshippers of the gods, may not have agreed with Julian that such a strong emphasis on blood sacrifice was necessary in the fourth century. Libanius might be making a more explicit reference to disapproval of Julian's sacrifices when at one point he describes Julian as not 'complying with the dictates of convention' because he carried out sacrifices every day instead of only on certain demarcated days (*Or.* 12.80 (F.II.37)).[33] This is ostensibly intended as praise but as Libanius is usually critical of such changes of convention it is possible that it veils 'a disguised intention' (the phrase is Malosse's) to criticize Julian.[34]

While Libanius did include references to Christian groups and their actions in speeches where he was concerned with creating an image of Graeco-Roman religion, what is most striking is how underplayed these were. In his references to Christians and Christianity, Libanius spent very little time elaborating on what it meant to be Christian. It is interesting that he saw martyrdom as a characteristic feature of Christianity, since Chrysostom too singled this out as a defining feature of the religion. However, much of what Libanius said about Christians came directly from the traditions of anti-Christian polemic that had developed in earlier centuries. It was, for example, stereotypical to focus on sexual impropriety at Christian meetings and on Christianity as a religion for women. There was little attempt to create a coherent picture of Christianity that could be opposed to Graeco-Roman religion and very often, as we saw, he simply defined the Christian religion as an absence of worship of the gods. These ideas are supported by the fact that Libanius rarely spoke of the Christians *en masse* or as a cohesive group; here his lack of a single term for them is significant. Rather, on each occasion that he spoke of those who do not worship the gods he was referring to a particular group of Christians: those who destroyed temples in the reign of Constantius or after Julian's death (in the Julianic orations); Christian courtiers and officials under Constantius (in

---

[31] See also Amm. Marc. 22.12.6 and 7 and 22.14.3–4 and the views of Themistius as summarized by L. J. Daly 1980. See also Bradbury 1995: 331 and 342.
[32] Bradbury 1995: 340–1; E. G. Clark 2000: 3; and also Porphyry, *Abst.* 2.5.332, especially 2.7.1–3 (animal sacrifice is a perversion of true Greek religion), 2.42–58 (blood sacrifice is to bad *daimones* not to the gods).
[33] Bradbury 1995: 342.   [34] On disguised intention, see Malosse 1997: 519.

Oration 2); and the Christian monks (in *Oration* 30). While there might be some overlap between these groups of people, it is not at all clear that Libanius consistently referred to one united, clearly identifiable collectivity. He did not represent the religious situation around him in terms of a great conflict between two distinct religions. Rather, he represented it in terms of a series of smaller battles against particular groups of people who caused religious problems in certain contexts.

At times Libanius was placed in the position of having to define what it meant to be a worshipper or an enemy of the gods, but this does not mean that he was interested in constructing permanent categories of 'pagan' or 'Greek 'and 'Christian' throughout his writings. In fact, very often it is hard to distinguish the religious allegiance of those in Libanius' letters. Paul Petit's *Les fonctionnaires dans l'œuvre de Libanius: analyse prosopographique* tried to ascertain as many of these religious allegiances as possible but very often Libanius' writings themselves confuse rather than clarify matters. In one letter of thanks to an important official in 358 Libanius writes:

When people get something good from the gods, they must give thanks not only to them but also to their priests. Since you are counted by us as being among the priests, you fairly share in their rewards ... (*Ep*. N.31 (F.370))

In most circumstances Petit would take such a reference as evidence that someone was a 'pagan'. However, in this particular case we know that the letter was addressed to the infamous official of Constantius, Paul the Chain, whom we know from other sources to have been a Christian. Clearly the reference to Paul being like a priest was not meant to be a reference to his religious identity but rather a literary compliment – Libanius is thanking Paul for encouraging the emperor Julian to write to him in Gaul.[35] In another example Libanius identifies Anatolius 9/6, a senator in Constantinople 390–3, as Christian because his father, Anatolius 4/2, was a Christian and because he had a connection with John Chrysostom (Chrysostom, *Ep*. 205). However, in Libanius' letters to Anatolius we see references both to prayer (*Ep*. N.175 (F.1001)) and to the fact that Anatolius would be 'praised by the gods' for the help he had given to Libanius' son Cimon (*Ep*. N.179.2 (F.1023)). As Petit himself states, in examples such as this 'allusions aux Dieux ... curieuses' disrupt any easy ascription of Christian identity to men such as Anatolius when there is no external evidence to confirm it.[36]

---

[35] Norman 1992: vol. 1, 453, note b. Burr gives a similar interpretation of this passage to that given here (Burr 1996: 13).
[36] P. Petit 1994: 39 and 233.

There are in fact many problems with Petit's ascriptions of religious identity to individuals in Libanius' writings and rather than continue along this course it is better to accept that Libanius' writings simply did not, most of the time, need to divide the world into people with distinct religious identities. This will allow us to explore why Libanius refers to religious allegiance on the occasions that he does do so and what purposes these references might serve other than stating whether someone was 'pagan' or 'Christian'. At times, however, it will still be useful to allow ourselves to compare Libanius' way of referring to people's religion with the religious allegiances usually associated with them in modern scholarship or ancient literature.

THE STRATEGIC USE OF REFERENCES TO RELIGIOUS ALLEGIANCE

The reign of Constantius was a time when it was not useful or appropriate for adherents of Graeco-Roman religion to emphasize their religious allegiance publicly. References to religion between Libanius and those who shared his religious allegiance are rare in letters from this period, and most of the references that we do have are oblique and difficult to interpret.[37] In a letter written to Anatolius 3/1, Constantius' praetorian prefect, at the end of 359 (*Ep.* N.47 (F.81)) Libanius makes reference to the consul of the time 'who elevated himself to the heavens, spoke boastfully and, despising the gods, imposed upon others, crouching in fear of men who were not even comparable to the slaves he had procured' (*Ep.* N.47.5 (F.81)). The consul in question was Datianus 1. On first sight this passage might be taken as evidence for a shared religious allegiance between Libanius and Anatolius that contrasted with the way that Datianus 'despised the gods'. As Norman puts it 'in criticising so openly the highest official of the day' Libanius 'must have been sure of Anatolius' sympathy and discretion'.[38] In fact, the situation was not as simple as this. *Epistle* N.47 (F.81)) was written just before Anatolius' death in 360 and was the last letter in an exchange between Libanius and Anatolius. Anatolius was an old acquaintance of Libanius' uncle Phasganius and eventually became praetorian prefect of Illyricum for 357–60.[39] In the early days of their relationship Libanius and Anatolius appear to have been on very good terms: they were connected

---

[37] See *Ep.* F.504 of 355–6 with P. Petit 1994: 118–19. An exception is *Ep.* N.67.2 (F.195) of AD 360, which recommended the philosopher Hierius in religious terms.
[38] Norman 1992: vol. 1, 521, note j.
[39] See Bradbury 2000: 177. For Libanius' letters concerning Anatolius, see Bradbury 2004: 227–8.

to one another through Anatolius' friendship with Libanius' beloved uncle Phasganius and shared an interest in sophistic culture, which they had discovered when they met in Constantinople in the early 350s.[40] Because of this friendship, Anatolius was a useful contact for Libanius, and Libanius wrote many letters to him asking for favours for friends and ex-pupils. At some point, however, the playful sophistic banter that had always been a characteristic of the relationship between the two men began to turn sour and took on a more serious tone.

The problem started in spring 357 when Libanius received a letter from Anatolius.[41] This was a reply to an earlier letter from Libanius, written in February 357 (*Ep.* N.22. (F.552)), complaining that Anatolius had not contacted him since he had become praetorian prefect. In this earlier letter (*Ep.* N.22. (F.552)) Libanius had jokingly suggested that Anatolius was avoiding writing to him because he thought Libanius would try to extract favours from him after he had gained his new post. From Libanius' response (*Ep.* B.60 (F.578) of spring 357) to Anatolius' reply to this earlier letter, we can tell that Anatolius had answered Libanius' humorous suggestion in an offensive way by accusing Libanius of being a flatterer (*Ep.* B.60.3–6 (F.578) of spring 357). For a while after this the friendship between the two men was restored and Libanius continued to write to Anatolius in order to promote his friends and acquaintances.[42] However, after a letter sent by Libanius to Anatolius in the summer of 358 (*Ep.* B.6 (F.333)) the two men fell out again. This letter was carried to Anatolius in Sirmium (a town in Illyricum) by Libanius' cousin Spectatus 1 (who is usually thought to have been a Christian), along with a speech praising Spectatus' actions as an ambassador to the Persian court.[43] Anatolius replied to this letter and presumably again caused offence as it took Libanius six months to respond. In the eventual reply we see Libanius' pique and learn that what had upset him was that Anatolius had accused him of not praising Spectatus enough (in the speech that had accompanied his last letter) and of praising other people too much (*Ep.* N.40.4 and 7 (F.19)).[44] This was then followed by two more strained letters from Libanius to Anatolius in 359 (*Ep.* N.46 (F.80)) and finally the letter that we started with (*Ep.* N.47 (F.81)), in which Libanius shows us that Anatolius had accused Libanius of not writing long enough letters to him.

---

[40] Bradbury 2000: 173 and also Libanius *Or.* 1.80 (F.1.122).
[41] For a description of these events, see Bradbury 2000: 175–6.
[42] Bradbury 2000: 177. See also *Ep.* F.314; *Ep.* B.59 (F.563); *Ep.* B.62 (F.339); *Ep.* B.175 (F.582); *Ep.* B.61 (F.583); and *Ep.* B.64 (F.362).
[43] Bradbury 2000: 177–8. We shall hear more of Spectatus.   [44] Bradbury 2000: 178–9.

What is interesting throughout this semi-hostile exchange of letters is the pattern of accusations and counter-accusations of flattery and abuse of power. After Anatolius' first accusation of flattery against him in spring 357 (*Ep.* B.60.3–6 (F.578)), Libanius had replied by saying that it must surely be Anatolius himself who had been guilty of flattery in order to achieve such high office, not Libanius, who lived in poverty (*Ep.* B.60.3–6 (F.578)). In the later exchange of letters Libanius continued this tactic of counter-accusation as he charged Anatolius with helping only his own family members to gain promotion (*Ep.* N.40.16–17 (F.19)), with 'throwing his weight about so that people 'kow-towed' to him, and with needing a flatterer not a friend (*Ep.* N.46.5–6 and 4 (F.80)). Bearing in mind this context, we can now turn back to the letter containing the reference to Datianus as someone despising the gods in *Epistle* N.47 (F.81). Here Libanius suggests to Anatolius that his offensive comments to Libanius were the result of Anatolius' fear that he was about to lose his own position and therefore the result of insecurity (*Ep.* N.47.3 (F.81)). Libanius then goes on to illustrate this with a complex example of Anatolius' influence over one of Libanius' own ex-pupils. It is in this context that we find the reference to Datianus as 'despising the gods'. Libanius first describes how Julianus 9/9, his pupil, had left his school to 'associate with' Anatolius. He implies that this association would have a bad influence on Julian's oratory and then argues that Julian had been 'encouraged to become a military man from the fact that he saw as consul one who elevated himself to the heavens, spoke boastfully and, despising the gods, imposed upon other men' (that is, as we have seen, the consul Datianus). However, Libanius then goes on to suggest that Anatolius too was 'hankering after' the kind of 'power' that Datianus had and that Anatolius only remained in his 'position of influence through' men like Datianus (*Ep.* N.47.6 (F.81)). Here the implication is that Anatolius' sycophancy and flattery had been directed towards Datianus in particular. Libanius' comments thus fit into the pattern of the previous hostile letters in accusing Anatolius of being a flatterer. Once we understand the point of the reference to Datianus in this letter, we can assess the true significance of the reference to Datianus as 'despising the gods'. This shows that Libanius cannot have included this reference in order to make a connection between Anatolius and himself or to contrast Anatolius with Datianus' faulty attitude to religion. Rather, Libanius was trying to suggest an association between Anatolius and Datianus' rejection of the gods and in so doing to cast a slur on Anatolius' character. While it might have been bold of him to refer to Datianus as 'despising the gods', the reference was used not to make a bond of religious allegiance between himself and Anatolius but rather to associate Anatolius with someone of a different religious allegiance.

This is a particularly striking example of the care that we must take when assessing the significance of references to religion and religious allegiance in Libanius. A general lesson can, however, be drawn from this example. It teaches us that we must seek to understand what Libanius' purposes were in mentioning religious issues rather than simply assume that these references tell us about an individual's religious allegiance in a straightforward way. We can see this in another very different example. In a letter of 357 Libanius wrote to his friend Aristaenetus 1/1, assessor to the prefect Anatolius 3, to recommend the young philosopher Iamblichus 2 to him. Iamblichus was from a prominent Apamean family with whom Libanius had connections. Iamblichus' grandfather Sopater 1 had been a pupil of the philosopher Iamblichus of Apamea and this started a family tradition of love of philosophy that the young Iamblichus 2 was continuing. In the letter of 357 Libanius praises Iamblichus 2 in the highest terms, starting with:

> The greatest of the qualities in him is that, thinking the greatest necessitating factor in the practice of virtue to be the gods, honouring them he will choose to become an Irus [the beggar in the *Odyssey*] rather than not honour them and become a Cinyras [a proverbial millionaire]. (*Ep.* N.24.2 (F.571))

In this example, we see almost the opposite of what we saw in the case of Anatolius. Whereas with Anatolius Libanius used reference to religion to slur his character, in the case of Iamblichus he uses it to compliment him. Whereas Anatolius was accused of flattering people, including Christians such as Datianus, for his own personal gain, Iamblichus is praised for his refusal to change his religious practice to benefit himself. Although Iamblichus' religious allegiance and Aristaenetus' approval of it are important factors here, the central point about Libanius' comment is that he is able to praise Iamblichus' strength of character, sincerity and lack of greed through praising his unwillingness to bend his religious principles. Just as a reference to someone's seeking for personal gain to please a person who despises the gods could be a way to discredit him as a flatterer, so a reference to someone's refusing to bend their own religious allegiance could be a sign of the greatest virtue and strength of character. We can make a more direct comparison between the language Libanius uses to describe Iamblichus and the language he uses to describe Anatolius by placing passages from two letters, both written in 357, alongside one another (*Ep.* B.60 (F.578) and *Ep.* N.24 (F.571)). While Iamblichus was described as compelled to virtue by the gods, Anatolius was described as compelled to virtue by praise,

> thinking the greatest necessitating factor in the practice of virtue to be the gods. (*Ep.* N.24.2 (F.571))

And

> You lust after praise and rightly do so, for it is a great necessitating factor in the practice of virtue. (*Ep.* B.60.5 (F.578))

Libanius regarded Iamblichus and Anatolius as at opposite poles of the spectrum of the appropriate approach to virtue: one through fidelity to the gods even to his own detriment, the other by acting in a way that would please others and make them praise him even when this meant associating with someone who 'despised the gods'. The fact that he sent *Epistle* N.24 about Iamblichus to Aristaenetus while he was Anatolius' assessor suggests that Libanius might have intended Anatolius to make this comparison too.

During Constantius' reign, Libanius did not make statements about allegiance to the Graeco-Roman gods in a straightforward way to show on which side of the religious divide people stood. Rather, he used such statements to play the game of recommendation so common to elite social circles. In a period when people often changed their religious allegiance with the change of emperor, to imply that someone held firm on this issue became the greatest compliment on strength of character. References to religious allegiance during Constantius' reign were as much about commenting on the characters of individuals as about stating religious solidarity and religious allegiance for its own sake.

Compared to the infrequent references to allegiance to the gods in letters written during Constantius' reign, it is striking that a number of letters written once Julian came to power refer back to people as true worshippers of the gods during Constantius' reign. This retrospective attribution of religious allegiance must make us suspicious.[45] In his *Oration 14 In Defence of Aristophanes* Libanius describes the religious practice of his friend Aristophanes of Corinth under Constantius' reign. In 357–9 the young Aristophanes had received some favour from Constantius. He had been made an imperial courier and had been sent on business to Egypt with the new prefect of the region, Parnassius. While in Egypt, Aristophanes and Parnassius had made use of some kind of divination and were accused under the treason trials during Constantius' reign and exiled on charges of magic. When Julian

---

[45] As Drinkwater has also already suggested (Drinkwater 1983: 349).

came to power, Libanius had the chance to persuade the new emperor that Aristophanes should be called back from exile and given a position again (in his *Oration* 14). Not surprisingly, Libanius defended Aristophanes against the charge of magic. However, he also appears at certain points to be very concerned to show Julian that Aristophanes had not betrayed the worship of the gods during Constantius' reign. Libanius first describes how Aristophanes had 'never won honour by dishonouring the gods' (*Or.* 14.64 (F.II.110)). He then goes on to talk of the desire of Bishop George of Cappadocia, (bishop of Alexandria while Aristophanes was in Egypt) to see Aristophanes become a Christian preacher (*Or.* 14.65 (F.II.110)). Libanius argues that if Aristophanes had succumbed to George's wishes, he would have 'embraced the cause of Constantius too' (*Or.* 14.65 (F.II.110–11)). However, in the face of this threat, Aristophanes had remained steadfast in doing honour to the gods and so should be praised. As Libanius says:

> Yet neither for power nor money, nor security, nor ambition did he let out for hire the best things of the Greeks, but even in the very trials themselves, whenever it was necessary, he took the oath by our gods ... not persuaded by concerns for his safety but rather thinking piety (*eusebia*) to be a good epitaph. To him the danger was easier to bear than a complete turnaround.[46] (*Or.* 14.66–7 (F.II.111))

Libanius' phrasing of this point suggests that there had been some doubt about Aristophanes' religious allegiance at this time. It is perhaps even possible that he had become too close to Bishop George, or had been tempted to show some allegiance to the Christian God in order to gain a position from Constantius or to get off the charges of magic. Libanius then had to excuse this activity. There are elements in the passage above that are very reminiscent of the trials of Christian martyrs who refused to sacrifice to the gods to ensure their own safety, as well as of the pagan martyrs who stood up to tyrannical Roman powers. Scholars of the second sophistic have shown how influential such models of behaviour were on elite male self-representation during the imperial period.[47] In the first to second centuries AD elite men used this topos to present themselves as heroic and courageous individuals who would not give up their own beliefs to ensure their safety.[48] Libanius' use of this topos to describe the experience of certain people under Constantius, allowed him to suggest that such people had heroically supported Julian and the traditional gods at a time of great

---

[46] Julian particularly disliked George (Julian, *Ep.* 60).
[47] I must thank an audience in the department of Classics at Exeter for this suggestion. See also Whitmarsh 2001: 134–5 and Geffcken's arguments discussed by Seiler (Seiler 1998: 180).
[48] Whitmarsh 2001: 134–5.

danger. Like Iamblichus 2 in an earlier year, Libanius praised Aristophanes for not giving up his true religious allegiance for personal gain and for the strength of character that this revealed. In the reign of Julian, however, this form of recommendation for an individual gained extra significance. It became a way to assert the loyalty of individuals to Julian when in fact their acquiescence in the rule of Constantius might have put this in doubt.[49] This seems to be how Julian saw the situation. In a letter he wrote to Libanius about Aristophanes after the delivery of *Oration* 14, he states that Libanius had 'requited Aristophanes for his piety towards the gods ... transforming what was formerly a reproach against him ...' (*Ep.* 97).

We can bear these ideas in mind when we turn to references to religious allegiance and religious actions during Julian's reign. In numerous letters of this period Libanius refers to people carrying out blood sacrifice under Julian. In a letter to Maximus of Ephesus, Libanius describes the religious activity instigated in Antioch when Pythiodorus brought news of Julian's accession from Constantinople (*Ep.* N.80 (F.694)).[50] Again, in a letter to Maximus of Ephesus, Libanius claims that he had prayed for Maximus not to be harmed under Constantius (*Ep.* N.80.3 (F.694)). Or again, in a letter to Julian's governor of Syria, Alexander 5/3, Libanius states that the city of Apamea had sacrificed when it was dangerous to do so (*Ep.* N.104.3 (F.1351)). None of these references should be seen as straightforward descriptions of religious practice, because there was usually a particular reason for making them. The addressees in these letters were men very close to Julian and his religious policy: Maximus of Ephesus was the Neoplatonic philosopher said to be responsible for Julian's apostasy from Christianity, and Alexander, as governor of Syria, was responsible for implementing Julian's religious policy there. In the case of Maximus of Ephesus, there is also some evidence that Libanius and Maximus did not get on and did not have similar ideas about what was an appropriate way to worship the gods: Maximus' extreme Neoplatonism is often thought to have been anathema to Libanius. Libanius thus might well have emphasized this shared religious practice in letters to Maximus in order to smooth over any differences with him. This is particularly the case with the description of sacrifices that supposedly took place in Antioch when the city heard of Julian's accession. The city as a whole was far from supportive of Julian or his religious policy and Julian explicitly complained about the lack of public sacrifice at the shrine of Apollo in Daphne when he visited the city (Julian, *Mis.* 362b). Thus, to emphasize that the city had sacrificed once they heard that Julian had come

---

[49] See also *Or.* 1.27 (F.1.96) and *Ep.* B.183.1 (F.1338).   [50] For Pythiodorus see Jones, *PLRE*: 756.

to power could be a way to show the city's loyalty to the emperor; the sacrifices mentioned might never actually have taken place.[51]

After Julian's death in the summer of 363 Libanius wrote many letters expressing sorrow at Julian's death and describing the hardship faced by those who had supported Julian and his religious policy (*Ep.* N.129 (F.1187) and *Ep.* B.161 (F.1196)).[52] In a letter written to his friend Fortunatianus 1/1 at the end of 363 Libanius encourages him to introduce the poet Philippus 3 to Secundius Salutius 3, praetorian prefect of the east under Julian and retained by Jovian and Valens in this position (*Ep.* B.154 (F.1425)). Libanius recommends Philippus by saying that he was 'among those who sacrificed often when it was possible and has now been caught round the middle by those who were aggrieved when he did sacrifice' (*Ep.* B.154.3 (F.1425)). He then goes on to argue that it would be especially noble to help Philippus for these very reasons because in doing so Fortunatianus would not 'by being inadequate, bring delight to the enemies of the temples' (*Ep.* B.154.3 (F.1425)). We see here a threefold process in which Libanius uses references to religious allegiance to achieve certain goals. Libanius recommends Philippus by saying he was being persecuted for his support of Julian's religious policy, he puts moral pressure on Fortunatianus to help Philippus or be thought of as a traitor to Julian's cause and, finally, he suggests that the defence of people who had supported Julian could be a way to quietly challenge the new regime. All this gives the impression that Philippus had been a loyal and steadfast supporter of Julian and his religious policy and that he now continued to be so after Julian's death. It also gives the impression that Salutius and Fortunatianus shared in these ideals. However, if we take a closer look we can see that again the situation is more complicated than it first appears. Salutius and Fortunatianus had held positions under Julian (Salutius had been close to Julian, acting as his prefect of the east, and Fortunatianus had probably been Salutius' assessor) but they had also held positions under Constantius and continued to hold high office once Julian had died and Christian emperors were in control again. Salutius had been proconsul of Africa under Constantius and was retained as praetorian prefect of the east by Jovian and Valens; Fortunatianus had been influential at Constantius' court and was probably Valens' *comes rerum privatarum* in 370. The situation is far from simple with Philippus too. We have another letter, this time written to Philippus, in which Libanius shows a very different view of him. Here Libanius refers to the fact that on Julian's death

---

[51] Libanius' use of references to religious allegiance during the reign of Julian will be discussed in chapter 8.
[52] See also *Ep.* B.46.2 (F.1449); *Ep.* B.104.4 (F.1223); *Ep.* B.154.1 (F.1425); and *Or.* 1.136–8 (F.1.148–9).

Philippus had removed his sons from Libanius' school out of fear that association with Libanius would not be looked on favourably by the new regime (*Ep.* B.104 (F.1223)). This is precisely the kind of 'being inadequate' that might 'bring delight to the enemies of the temples' and suggests that Libanius did not always see Philippus as such a loyal supporter of Julian and his religious policy. Thus what we see in *Epistle* B.154.3 (F.1425) is not a straightforward description of the religious allegiance of the individuals involved. Rather the references to Philippus' loyalty to Julian's religious policy can be seen as a way to recommend his strength of character and also to build up religious links between a number of men when all this might, in fact, have been in doubt.

Passages such as these have sometimes been taken as straightforward representations of the difficulties faced by men such as Libanius after Julian's death or as Libanius' nostalgia for Julian's reign (Petit's 'remembrance of past deeds').[53] However, if we shift our perspective we can see that expressing grief about Julian's death allowed Libanius and his friends to show their loyalty to Julian and his religious ideas just at a time when they were having to adjust to living under Christian emperors again and to hiding their true religious colours. It could act as a counterweight to the fact that in public they were again under pressure to act in a way more acceptable to Christian emperors and so could bolster their self-image at time when this was being eroded.

After a gap in his letter-writing during the difficult years of the reign of Valens and Valentinian in the mid 360s to the late 370s, Libanius started to keep a record of his correspondence again in the 380s. In this period we do see him occasionally using references to religious allegiance as a way to recommend people but this was far less common than before.[54] Much more typical of the 380s are vague references to the gods and the general influence of divine powers and the gods of eloquence (*theoi logoi*), the muses or other classicizing and literary references to the gods.[55] These are the kind of neutral religious references that could be applied to Christians as much as to those who worshipped the gods. There is a large number of Libanius' correspondents who might be worshippers of the gods, but we cannot be sure because the kind of references made to religion could be just as applicable in addressing Christians. This is, for example, the case with Panhellenius, an admirer of Libanius' *epideixeis* (*Ep.* F.863), who had studied

[53] See Malosse 1995a: 260.
[54] *Ep.* F.936.1; *Ep.* F.841.2; *Ep.* F.948.3; *Ep.* F.993.2; *Ep.* F.1037.2; *Ep.* F.932.2; and *Ep.* F.1032.1.
[55] Such references are too many to list (see, for example, *Ep.* N.173 (F.972); N.1522–3 (F.868); *Ep.* N.157 (F.907); and *Ep.* N.177.5 (F.1004)).

at Athens and Antioch before becoming a citizen of Antioch (*Ep.* F.861) and who was consular of Lydia in 382. Libanius described Panhellenius as having the favour of Poseidon on his journey from Antioch (*Ep.* F.863.1 of 388), which might suggest he was a worshipper of the gods.[56] However, as Petit points out, such references could be of a more literary nature and in reference to Christians.[57] In the 380s, long after Julian's death, it was no longer useful to Libanius to build up links with others who shared in the worship of the gods. It became more useful, instead, to develop a neutral language that could be shared by those who worshipped the gods and by those who did not.

This does not mean that Libanius did not use references to religion in a very sophisticated way at this time. In his *Oration* 42 Libanius requests that the emperor Theodosius enrol Thalassius 4, Libanius' secretary, in the senate at Constantinople in order to prevent him from being forcibly recruited to the civic council in Antioch.[58] As part of his argument for Thalassius Libanius describes how Thalassius avoided dicing and drinking and how he was always helping his friends. He also emphasizes Thalassius' religiosity saying that 'he believes that gods exist and that they observe happenings on earth, and he behaves as one of such convictions should do' (*Or.* 42.7 (F.IV.152)). As a result of these religious convictions, wrote Libanius, Thalassius had given up marriage, sexual activity, love of money and attending the racecourse and the theatre. It is unlikely that this oration was delivered before its named addressee, the emperor Theodosius. However, Norman, following Sievers, has suggested that it might have been 'designed to attract attention from interested parties at court' who might then subtly pass the important arguments on to the emperor – as was the case for *Oration* 30.[59] Thus it appears that Libanius was presenting Thalassius' worship of the gods in Christianized terms that would be acceptable to the Christian courtiers and a Christian emperor. Libanius could recommend someone who was a worshipper of the gods to Christians in religious terms, as long as he presented his or her religion in Christianized terms of morality and celibacy. This adds a new twist to the old technique of using references to religion to recommend someone. Here, having a good attitude to the divine and to religion (however that might be defined) was what was important, not where one's religious allegiance lay.

Also referred to in *Oration* 42 is Optatus 1/2, a senator in Constantinople in the 390s who also appears to have been a worshipper of the

---

[56] See also *Ep.* F.842.3 and *Ep.* F.977.3.   [57] P. Petit 1994: 253.
[58] For a full description of events, see Norman 2000: 145–8, introduction to *Oration* 42.
[59] Norman 2000: 148

gods.⁶⁰ Optatus had become Libanius' enemy because of his opposition to the nomination of Thalassius 4, Libanius' secretary, to the senate.⁶¹ Libanius had first written a polite letter to Optatus himself to try to persuade him to give up his opposition (*Ep.* N.162 (F.923)) but this failed and Libanius resorted to writing *Oration 42 On Behalf of Thalassius* to Theodosius. As we have just seen above, he intended this oration to have some impact at the court of a Christian emperor, even if it was not delivered directly before Theodosius. Having characterized Thalassius in glowing terms (see above), Libanius goes on to describe all that was wrong with Optatus (*Or.* 42.11–20 (F.IV.154–7)). From his early childhood Optatus is presented as an unlikable boy whom even his parents could not love (*Or.* 42.11 (F.IV.154)). A large part of this character assassination concerns religious matters. Libanius describes Optatus as a youth who engaged in sorcery against his elder brother out of jealousy of the favour he was given. This improper religious action is contrasted with how 'prayers were offered on behalf of the brother' (*Or.* 42.12 (F.IV.154)). Then, later, Libanius describes Optatus' continued religious misdemeanors while based in Alexandria as *praefectus Augustalis* in 384. Optatus had flogged many of the decurions of Alexandria, including the Neoplatonic philosopher Ptolemaeus, so violating the 'holiness' of this educated man (*Or.* 42.16 (F.IV.156)).⁶² He 'tore [Ptolemaeus] away from the very images, under whose eyes he lived a life that proceeded by prayer, libation, sacrifice and books' (*Or.* 42.15 (F.IV.155)). In addressing a Christian courtly audience, Libanius found it useful to present Optatus as acting in a sacrilegious way that challenged the rules of proper living just as he had found it useful to present Thalassius as reaching the peaks of pious virtue.⁶³ Even though Libanius referred to non-Christian examples in making this argument he could feel confident that the Christian court would understand the contrast between pious and impious behaviour, so they would be able to translate it into Christian terms and be sympathetic towards it. What we see in such references is the ultimate blurring of religious boundaries in the fourth century. Worshippers of the gods whom Libanius sought to recommend could be described in Christian terms while those he sought to condemn could be presented as sacrilegious in terms that matched any of his hostile descriptions of Christians. In certain circumstances at least, calling on notions of piety and sacrilege shared by Christians

---

[60] On Optatus' religious allegiance, see Norman 2000: 152, note 15 and Socrates, *HE* 6.18.
[61] See *Epp.* N.161–4 (F.922–3); *Ep.* F.924; *Epp.* F.927–30; *Ep.* F.932; and *Ep.* 936–7.
[62] Norman 2000: 153, note 16.
[63] For other descriptions of governors who appear to have been adherents of Graeco-Roman religion as sacrilegious, see *Or.* 221–2 (F.I.180–1) and *Or.* 10.6–7 (F.I.403)).

and worshippers of the gods was more important than emphasizing religious differences. References to religious differences were becoming less useful as a networking tool in the 380s and 390s, but the other side of the coin was that more could be gained from appeal to shared ideals. Just as there was much less use in emphasizing allegiance to the worship of the gods so there was greater appeal to ideals shared by Christians and worshippers of the gods.

REFERENCES TO THE RELIGIOUS ALLEGIANCE OF CHRISTIANS AND JEWS

Throughout his career Libanius corresponded with large numbers of elite men; many of these would have differed from him in religious allegiance and must have worshipped the Christian God. Despite this likelihood, Libanius rarely referred to the fact that certain individuals did not share his religious allegiance. On the few occasions when he did think it worth mentioning we need to understand why this was so. The situation with regard to Libanius' cousin Spectatus is one such example. In almost all of his letters to and about his cousin Spectatus, Libanius makes no mention at all of Spectatus' religious allegiance. Spectatus was primarily useful and an object of pride to Libanius because he was a notary in the court of Constantius and had played an influential role in an embassy to Persia that had succeeded in securing peace in 358.[64] For Libanius these were the most important features of Spectatus' personality, and his religious allegiance was not worth mentioning. One letter, however, reveals that Spectatus did not share Libanius' religious allegiance and that this difference in the gods they chose to worship could be a significant factor. Early in 360 Phasganius, uncle of Spectatus and Libanius, died and left his two nephews as co-heirs to his estate （*Ep.* N.56 (F.115) and *Ep.* N.57 (F.126)）. Libanius inherited the land and Spectatus the family home, and as both were free from curial duties (Libanius because he was a sophist, Spectatus because he worked for the imperial bureaucracy) they hoped to keep these for themselves.[65] However, the city council of Antioch contested the will of Phasganius in order to regain control of the land left to Libanius, arguing that, as a possession of a curial family, it had originally been subject to curial obligations. As part of this battle, it appears that someone from the civic council had asked Spectatus to assist the council in taking the land from Libanius. In

---

[64] For the latter see *Ep.* F.513 and *Ep.* B.27 (F.514) and also Amm. Marc. 17.5.15.
[65] Norman 1992: vol. 1, 23–4, notes a and b.

response Libanius wrote to Spectatus in order to keep him on side (*Ep.* N.56 (F.115)). What is interesting about this example is that religious allegiance was brought into the dispute. Libanius describes how his opponent from the city council will approach Spectatus and seek to turn him against Libanius by 'also mentioning the gods, against whom he is consumed by hatred each day' (*Ep.* N.56.5 (F.115)). Here Libanius suggests that the councillor would try to use a shared religious allegiance to Christianity in order to form a bond with Spectatus against him; in turn, Libanius tries to lay emphasis on the links of family loyalty between himself and Spectatus (*Ep.* N.56.1–2 (F.115)). He was seeking to argue that these bonds of family loyalty should precede the bonds of shared religion between Spectatus and the councillor. It thus seems that Christians as well as Libanius and his coreligionists could emphasize ties of religion when it suited them in order to make links with one another. For Libanius the only way to counter such contact was by asserting the prior connection of family bonds.

The religious allegiance of Christians also became an issue when Libanius defended them against charges of appropriating or harming temple property. Libanius defended his relatives Thalassius 2/2 and Bassianus 2 from the actions of Julian's zealous governor, Gaianus 6 governor of Phoenicia (*Ep.* N.105 (F.1364)), and his friend Orion of Bostra from Belaeus, governor of Arabia (*Ep.* N.103 (F.819) and *Ep.* B. 130 (F.763)). He also wrote on behalf of Eusebius 17/21, the son of Asterius a man of curial rank in Antioch with whom Libanius was friendly (*Ep.* B.98 (F.1411)); in defence of Basilicus and Aemilianus from Bacchius of Tarsus, who was restoring the cult of Artemis in the city of Tarsus (*Ep.* N.91 (F.757)); and in defence of Theodulus, an Antiochene Christian, against Hesychius, who was priest under Julian (*Ep.* B.182 (F.724)). On each of these occasions Libanius openly referred to the fact that these men held a different religious allegiance from his own.[66] He did not mind his links with Christians being known, even to the most zealous of Julian's governors and supporters, but he did try to play down the purely religious nature of these links. In each case, he argues that the Christian figure in question was not guilty of the crimes of which they were being accused and that in fact they were moderate Christians who had never harmed anyone else because of their religion. Thus, for example, in one letter to Bacchius of Tarsus about his restoration of the cult of Artemis he writes of the Christian Aemilianus, 'no one had complained of [his] conduct . . . for he was not one of the aggressors, though he could have been if he had wished' (*Ep.* N.91.2 (F.757)). Similarly, in the letter to Belaeus,

---

[66] See also *Ep.* N.107 (F.1376), in which he defended Vitalius.

Libanius and religious allegiance 113

governor of Arabia 362–3, Libanius argues that Orion had often previously helped those who were now accusing him (*Ep.* N.103.2–3 (F.819)).[67] He also often emphasized that he was writing on behalf of these Christians primarily due to a connection of family or friendship and thus toned down the question of religion. This is the case with his two letters to Belaeus on behalf of Orion (*Ep.* N.103.1 (F.819) and *Ep.* B.130.1 (F.763)) and the one letter to Gaianus on behalf of Thalassius and Bassianus (*Ep.* N.105.2 (F.1364)).[68] He started the two letters on behalf of Orion by emphasizing that Orion was an old friend of his and devoted the second paragraph of his letter on behalf of Thalassius and Bassianus to his family connections with them. By presenting his links with these men as ones of family and friendship, he could downplay his connections with Christians to Julian's governors. Just as religious allegiance could be emphasized when it was necessary, it could also be pushed into the background if it caused dissension.

On a small number of occasions Libanius also referred to the religious allegiance of Jews whom he knew. In these cases it is unclear how far Libanius was referring to the Jews as a religious group as opposed to an ethnic or social group because he described them as a race – *genos*. In two of eight letters that he wrote to the Jewish patriarch in Jerusalem he made the 'race' of the Jews an issue. In one letter to the patriarch of 388 Libanius sympathizes with the persecution faced by the Jews at the time, saying 'who would not be distressed that such a race suffers so long' (*Ep.* N.160.1 (F.914)). He goes on to say that he would never side with those who persecuted this race, even if they asked for his assistance, so he reaffirms his link with the Jews in question (*Ep.* N.160.2 (F.914)). Again, in another letter to the patriarch, this time of 393, Libanius dwells on the humanity of the Jewish race and the value they put on someone who had lived virtuously (*Ep.* F.1084.1). However, he does this with the specific purpose of recommending his friend Theophilus to the patriarch. In doing so, he was suggesting that Theophilus lived up to the high Jewish standards of virtue – so creating a bond in much the same way as in his presentation of Thalassius' worship of the gods in Christian terms when addressing Christians. He was also suggesting that the patriarch himself would not be living up to the humane ideals of his own race if he did not help Theophilus as requested (*Ep.* F.1084.2–3). It is interesting to compare these very positive descriptions of the Jewish race in the letters to the patriarch with how Libanius wrote about the Jews among his tenant farmers in *Oration* 47, delivered sometime in 386–92. These

---

[67] See also *Ep.* B.130.1 (F.763); *Ep.* N.107.2 (1376); *Ep.* B.98.2–3 (F.1411); and *Ep.* B.182.2 (F.724).
[68] For a similar interpretation of *Ep.* N.105 (F.1364) see Burr 1996: 20–1.

Jewish peasants angered Libanius when they sought to challenge the terms of employment under which he held them (*Or.* 47.13 (F.IV.410)). To find support for their claim, after Libanius had brought them to trial before the governor in Antioch, they turned to a military patron for protection (the Jews are just one group that Libanius describes as turning to military patrons in *Oration* 47).[69] Libanius refers to this group of Jews in much less positive terms. He describes how they 'presumed to define how' Libanius 'should employ them' and used bribery so as to escape the charge made against them (*Or.* 47.13–14 (F.IV.410–11)). There is, however, little suggestion that Libanius used their religion as a way to vilify these Jewish farmers. The only mention of religion comes in Libanius' criticism of the governor for showing favour to the views of the general who was acting as patron for the Jews. He describes this favour as in enmity to the gods (*Or.* 47.14 (F.IV.411)) and says that the governor preferred 'impiety to the gods' to disobeying the general in question. As we do not know the identity, and religious allegiance, of the governor and general involved we cannot say anything decisive about the significance of the references to religion in this context. However, it is almost certain that the governor and general were not Jews, so that what we see here is not a simple contrast between Libanius who had the gods on his side and Jews who were unholy. It is much more likely that this is another example in which Libanius used charges of impiety against a governor who shared his own religious allegiance when he did not like the course of action the governor had chosen.

A FEEL FOR THE FOURTH-CENTURY RELIGIOUS GAME

Fourth-century imperial society was a complex world in which to function. Loyalty to the Roman state had always entailed loyalty to the gods of the Roman state in some form. What changed in the fourth-century context was that the Christian God could now be the God of state religion, and people had the additional option of showing allegiance to this God. The fact that different emperors held different religious allegiances as they chose to support different factions of Christianity or, in Julian's case, to turn back to Graeco-Roman religion, further complicated the situation. Those who worshipped the traditional gods in some form and those who worshipped the Christian God both held positions in civic and imperial life and had to find a way to interact. As well as all the normal problems of getting on politically and socially in the world, religious issues were becoming

---

[69] See Wilken 1983: 53–4 and Liebeschuetz 1972: 122 and 203.

more pressing. To be successful in this situation, individuals had to be very adept at managing issues of religious difference and religious allegiance. They had to have a good 'feel for the game'; a good sense of what was appropriate in certain circumstances. They had to be tactful and timely enough to know when one should make no mention of religious allegiance and when it could be acceptable to do so. They also had to be able to judge well the impact, what would 'get done', if they mentioned religious allegiance. This meant taking great care in how one represented one's own religious allegiance in relation to how one represented the allegiance one gave to the gods of the state and the emperor. It also meant finding ways to get on with people who might not share one's religious allegiance in normal interaction. Getting the balance right between these various factors was a delicate matter and those who did so could have the longest and most successful careers. The emperor Constantine, the man who did so much to change the religious situation of the fourth century, and the self-styled philosopher Themistius exemplify those who achieved success in the fourth century through getting this balance right. Constantine was one of the longest-ruling emperors of the period and this was due partly at least to his ability to handle religious issues in a subtle way. He managed to balance his own stated allegiance to Christianity, and the state support he gave to it, with acts of compromise and of continuity with Graeco-Roman religion in order to 'win agreement, mobilize support and gain consensus'.[70] Similarly, Themistius succeeded in being an influential courtier and senator throughout the reigns of the Christian emperors Constantius, Jovian, Valens and Valentinian and Theodosius, partly because of his skill at praising the actions of these emperors, often using a monotheistic religious terminology that mediated between his allegiance to Graeco-Roman religion and their allegiance to Christianity.[71] None of this has to mean that Constantine and Themistius did not have sincere religious beliefs or allegiances of their own. To oppose true religious belief to the strategic use of religious allegiance is to miss the point.[72] Most members of fourth-century imperial society were working within a framework of expectations in which religion was always political: religion was always about 'getting things done' not about fulfilling ideals.[73] While these people might well have had strong personal feelings about which religion they favoured, they knew that in fourth-century imperial society it was often appropriate to play these down. It was precisely Constantine's lack of willingness to give total support to

---

[70] Drake 2000: xvi. See also Salzman 1987.   [71] Heather and Moncur 2001: 3–4, 24, 40 and 61–6.
[72] Drake 2000: 20 and Heather and Moncur 2001: xii–xiii.
[73] Drake 2000: 12–20, particularly 14–16 on Eusebius, *VC* 1.26–7, and Drake 2000: xvi.

Christianity, the insincerity of his allegiance to Christianity as some would once have put it, that allowed him to work so well as an emperor ruling over an empire of mixed religious allegiances.[74]

It is in the company of men such as Constantine and Themistius that we must see Libanius. Like them, he too survived the vicissitudes of the fourth century because he had a good 'feel' for playing the religious game. He had a good sense of when it was best to let his allegiance to the Graeco-Roman gods fall into the background and when he should emphasize it. He could adjust how he represented divinity when addressing Christian emperors but could also refer to an individual's piety towards the Graeco-Roman gods when this could work to recommend them to someone. Perhaps most importantly, however, Libanius had the confidence to push the bounds of what was appropriate by referring to religious allegiance when this was dangerous or contentious. The letter to Anatolius 3/1, which was studied earlier in this chapter, referred to the consul Datianus as 'despising the gods' (*Ep.* N.47.5 (F.81)). Doing so might have been dangerous under Constantius but it also bordered on the tactless. In fact, it was the tactlessness of the comment that made it so cutting: it took a very skilled player of the fourth-century religious game to feel comfortable doing this. By not insisting on the constant need to assert religious difference or to maintain a clear-cut, well-defined religious allegiance at all times Libanius was very well equipped to deal with the subtle and complex expectations of the fourth century, hence he sustained a successful career during a large part of it. None of this meant that Libanius did not have his own true religious allegiance. To think of everything Libanius says about religion in terms of a stark choice between politically motivated insincerity and true expression of religious allegiance is mistaken. Having his own religion did not have to be incompatible with Libanius' strategic and practical use of references to religious allegiance.

Constantine, Themistius and Libanius played the fourth-century religious game well. It was however, easy to play this game badly: to make errors of judgement and to get the balance wrong between personal religious allegiance and its public expression. On the one hand, the 'untimely' demands of Julian and Christian leaders to state which gods they worshipped (Amm. Marc. 22.10.2) or to adopt clear-cut religious identities forced people to declare themselves in a way that created difficulties for social interaction. On the other hand, the over-zealous performances of allegiance to the God or gods favoured by imperial power at the time were tasteless and disrupted easy social relations. They made too obvious the

---

[74] Drake 2000: 27.

way that people suddenly switched from performing sacrifices to claiming allegiance to the Christian God: people alter their 'rituals with more ease than Euripus... the same people are seen at the votive altars and sacrifices, at shrines of the gods and altars of God' (Themistius, *Oration* 5.67d–68a). This caused difficulties for the subtle shifts of external religious allegiance that most people found so useful in the fourth century just as the desire to maintain a true and firm religious identity did. In the first section of his *Oration* 1 *The Autobiography*, written between 374 and 380, Libanius criticizes such a tendency among those who took part in the sacrifices that the emperor Julian performed in Antioch. He describes how there 'were always many attending' Julian 'and flattering him as usual through worship of the gods' (*Or.* 1.121 (F.1.141)).[75] These people had intended to display their true religious allegiance to Julian by their overt support for his public sacrifice, but instead they managed to achieve the opposite goal: to appear as flatterers. The two poles of getting wrong 'the feel for the game' of the fourth-century religious situation were tasteless displays of overt religious identity, on the one hand, or base and unsubtle political flattery, on the other. The difficulty of getting the balance right between the two extremes is revealed by how easily the one could collapse into the other.

The strategic use of references to religious allegiance did not have to mean that someone had no true personal religion of their own. However, accusations of the disparity between inner religious allegiance and outward displays of worship could be used as a way to single out people who erred too much on the side of religious flattery. Libanius could only accuse those who gathered around Julian's sacrifices of flattery because he was accusing them of not being sincere supporters of Julian's religious policy. In a similar way, when Libanius chastises a rival sophist Bemarchius for writing a speech in praise of Constantius, he does so by highlighting the contrast between what Bemarchius said and what he did 'personally (*autos*)': 'he delivered a speech in praise of the one who had set himself up against the gods, while personally sacrificing to the gods, teaching and describing in full about things such as the shrine Constantius had built for him' (*Or.* 1.39 (F.1.103)). It was precisely the difference between a person's internal religious position and his or her outward appearance that Libanius wanted to highlight when accusing them of religious flattery. In the fourth century, the opposition between inner beliefs and outer appearance became a rhetorical tool for blackening the character of enemies or for praising friends. If you did not like someone, you could point to his flattery in the field of religion in order to besmirch his

---

[75] See also *Ep.* N.97.3 (F.797) and *Ep.* B.43 (F.739).

character. At the same time, however, showing that some individuals were maintaining their true inner beliefs in situations where they were forced to adopt a different outward religious loyalty could be a way to praise them. Libanius conceives of Julian's apostasy from Christianity by describing how the emperor Julian had to keep secret that he had 'grasped . . . our old gods instead of the new one' (*Or.* 13.12 (F.II.67)) because he was living in the Christian household of the emperor Constantius (*Or.* 18.19 (F.II.245)). In so doing, Libanius emphasizes the contrast between Julian's outward appearance and his inner state: 'although he was different concerning these things he took the same outward form as before' (*Or.* 18.19 (F.II.245)). The same distinction between outward appearance and inner belief could also be used to highlight how people could maintain their inner personal religious allegiance after forced conversion. Force only resulted in 'seeming' conversions rather than 'ones that actually happened' because people would consciously deceive their Christian proselytizers and say they had changed to being Christian when actually they had not (*Or.* 30.28 (F.II.101–2)). Libanius says:

> They take part in their religious displays and their noisy assemblies and go through the other things that those people do but, placing themselves in the outward appearance of prayer, they either call on no one or they call on the gods and although they do not call on them properly from this place, they do call on them. (*Or.* 30.28 (F.III.102))

As in the example of Julian, the Christian appearance of these peasants was like a mask that an actor would wear while remaining the same underneath (*Or.* 30.28 (F.III.102)). The notion of an inner or private religious state itself becomes a rhetorical tool for Libanius to use to attribute praise or blame or to make a specific point. Just as one's outward religious presentation of one's religious allegiance could be adjusted to suit the circumstances, so at times the sphere of internal personal religious belief could be valued over outward appearance when benefit could be gained from it. Thus while Libanius was not working with a straightforward distinction between politically decided religious allegiance and personal belief, we do see an increased valorization of the personal sphere as the place where true religious opinion lies. This in itself was one of the responses open to individuals in the fourth century. We have seen that those from a Graeco-Roman background would have thought it quite normal to offer their loyalty to the divinity supported by the state without there being any question about personal belief. Unfortunately the fast turnover of emperors in the 360s (Constantius to Julian to Jovian to Valens and Valentinian) highlighted the strategic nature of these changes in a way that might have made some people uncomfortable. In such a situation, in which overt outward displays of religious allegiance were suspect, it is not surprising that we see an emphasis on the inner sphere as the place of true religious opinion.

Libanius' writings take us into a very different world from those of Chrysostom. He reveals people functioning in imperial society rather than in the world of the Church. As a result, Libanius does not show us religious ideals but the complex ways in which people could represent their religious allegiance in order to get on in that imperial society. We can wonder how far Chrysostom's audiences would have shared the world depicted by Libanius rather than the one we see in the writings of Chrysostom.

PART III

Religious identities and other forms of social identification

INTRODUCTION

In the previous part, I considered Chrysostom's and Libanius' ways of writing about religious identity and religious allegiance. We saw that Chrysostom was trying to construct for his audiences clear-cut identities of Christian, Greek and Jew and of believer and unbeliever. He demanded that they adopt being Christian as an identity that dominated their whole lives and that would be externally visible at all times. He required not only that they be Christian but also that they display their Christianity. In doing this, Chrysostom not only presented a stark contrast between what it was to be Christian and what it was to be Greek or Jewish but also suggested that all non-Christian identities could be aligned and characterized as demonic. This allowed Chrysostom to present his audiences with the starkest of choices: either they accepted being Christian on his terms or they were the total antithesis of what was Christian and godly. There was absolutely no room for compromise and no room for having a different understanding of what it meant to be Christian. In the case of Libanius, in contrast, we saw that most of the time he was not interested in marking out permanent religious identities. His habitual sense of the appropriate ways to represent religious allegiance in each situation gave him 'a feel for the game' for when it was right to refer to this factor and for when it was better to let it fade into the background. This allowed him to use references to religious allegiance strategically in order to benefit himself and those he knew. We also saw that the notion of inner religious belief or disposition as opposed to outward religious appearance was developing as a rhetorical or strategic tool for Libanius. He could praise individuals for holding to an unpopular religious allegiance in secret while presenting themselves externally in a different way. But he could also condemn individuals for flattery if they hid their true religious allegiance to benefit themselves. In either case there was a sense that Libanius valorized the internal religious state above appearances.

Chrysostom's and Libanius' representations of religious identity and religious allegiance can be contrasted in a number of ways. While Chrysostom valued opposed and mutually exclusive religious identities, Libanius was happy to work with much more fluid notions of religious allegiance. While Chrysostom saw Christian identity as something that was supposed to determine every aspect of one's life, Libanius saw religious allegiance as something that could be used strategically as and when it was of benefit. Finally, while Chrysostom wanted his audiences to display their Christianity outwardly at all times, Libanius, almost paradoxically, was beginning to develop the notion of the inner sphere as the place where true religious opinion was expressed.

To take our understanding of these opposed conceptions of religious identity and religious allegiance further we now also need to see how our two authors wrote about other kinds of social identity and social allegiance. Religious identities and allegiances do not exist on their own in society but only in relation to other ways in which individuals in society might identify themselves. There are a number of different possible social identities and social allegiances to which they can devote themselves, for example those of family, state, city, work or gender group. At the same time, the sphere of religious identity itself cannot be seen as an objective category that exists in the same way and covers the same territory in every society. Rather, it is created and defined differently in each social context. The importance that individuals place on religion will largely depend on how far they see it to dominate, be coextensive with or be separate from other kinds of social identity. The closer the relationship that is conceived of between religious and other kinds of social identity, the greater the influence people will see religion to have. Concomitantly, an ability to partition religious identity or religious allegiance from other ways of defining oneself can lead to religion having a less fundamental place in society. We in modern western societies tend to assume that 'religion' and 'religious' identity are easily definable as distinct from the fields of political, social, national and other forms of identity. As Asad's work shows, this distinct category of 'religion' is not, however, a universal feature of all societies but rather a result of western liberal thinking about religion as a personal choice that should have little impact on public life. We must beware of assuming that Libanius and Chrysostom will share the same view that 'religion' is a category distinct from other social spheres and other forms of social identification. This is particularly the case for the ancient world, which traditionally assigned religion a very different place in society from that to which we are accustomed. It has become almost a commonplace of scholarship on Graeco-Roman religions to state that Greeks and Romans hardly conceived of religion as a category that could be separated from political allegiance and from civic and ethnic identity. Rather than make any assumptions about how Chrysostom and Libanius conceived of religious identity/allegiance in relation to these other forms of identity we must take this as the area to be explored. This also has a direct bearing on our exploration of how much importance Chrysostom and Libanius placed on questions of religious identity in the first place, because there can be a correlation between the extent to which religious identity is seen as independent of other social identities and the emphasis laid on the strength of the boundaries of that identity. Where a social identity is seen to be supported by political power and associated with the dominant national or social identity, this will often correlate with the notion that the boundaries of that social identity are firm, fixed and not easily changed. On the other hand, where a social identity is seen to be independent of the dominant power in society and distinct from other forms of identification, it will often correlate to a more fluid understanding of that identity as something that can be adjusted, changed or given up at will. Or, to put this the other way round, we might say that those who have a very firm notion of identity will tend to associate that identity with power and other dominant forms of identification and those who have a much looser sense of religious allegiance will tend to see that allegiance as somehow distinct from power and other dominant forms of identification.

Much has been written about whether the fourth century was a time of conflict between distinct religions or a time of toleration and coexistence. What is less often noted is that having an understanding of how far religion is seen as a separate sphere from others and as a private rather than a public and political matter is crucial to answering this question. It is only when choice of religion is seen as a private matter and one of personal preference that toleration is possible. On the other hand, seeing a close relationship between power and religion and between political and religious identities will tend to lead to a model of conflict between different religions. Exploring how far Chrysostom and Libanius saw religion to be related to other forms of identification, or independent from them, will also help us to understand their preferred vision for interaction between religions at this time. In particular it will allow us to see from a more analytical perspective the often-stated notion that Libanius was 'tolerant' on religious matters. In part III we shall thus explore the way that Chrysostom and Libanius understood religious identity to relate to political, civic and ethnic identity and allegiance, which were the most important forms of identification in the ancient world.

CHAPTER 5

Religious identity and other social identities in Chrysostom

RELIGIOUS IDENTITY AND POLITICAL IDENTITY

From the time of Constantine's adoption of worship of the Christian God the question of the relationship between Church and state was one that Christians had to confront. Should the Church and the Christian community be subject to the authority and rule of the emperor and be part of the *politeia* of the Roman empire? The archetypal formulation of a solution to this question is Eusebius of Caesarea's notion of Christian *imperium* and of the emperor as God's image or representative on earth.[1] In this formulation the emperor could ultimately be leader of both the empire and the Church and so there is seen to be no real contradiction between being a Christian and being a citizen and subject of the empire. For a long time it was assumed that Eusebius' model was shared by all Christians but in recent years this view has been questioned.[2] Chrysostom could reject secular rule as valid or relevant to Christians because heaven was their true *politeia*; he, as other Christians had done before him, used the metaphor of citizenship to describe what it meant to be Christian.[3] In so doing, he presented Christianity in a way that was familiar to Greeks but that also sought to transform their notion of citizenship from an earthly one in an earthly *politeia* to citizenship in a heavenly *politeia*. Chrysostom thus constantly reminded his audience not to think about the present life but to refer themselves only to 'future things' and 'love of the kingdom' (*Hom. de Stat.* 5.9 (*PG* 49.72)).[4] The Christian had to accept that he was 'a stranger and a

---

[1] Although the notion that even Eusebius himself accepted this model is now being questioned by some scholars.
[2] I have argued this view in greater detail in Sandwell 2001: 87–108 and 2004. See also Stephens 2001 for similar arguments.
[3] See O'Daly 1999: 53–62. See also, to give just two examples, Tertullian, *De Corona*, 13.1–4 and Ambrose, *Ep.* 63.
[4] The references to such statements are too numerous to be listed. See, for example, *In Ep. ad 1 Cor. Hom.* 15.11 and 42.1 (*PG* 61.127 and 363) and *Hom. de Stat.* 5.4–5 and 6.8 (*PG* 49.70–1 and 86).

sojourner (in this world)' and so should not expect too much of the present world (*In Ep. ad. Rom. Hom.* 23 (*PG.* 60.618) and *In Ep. ad 2 Cor. Hom.* 16.5 (*PG.* 61.518)).[5] These ideas were partly the result of Antiochene theological thinking on the achievability of human perfection on earth. Despite the fact that Antiochene Christianity placed great emphasis on human free will and the ability to choose to do good rather than to sin, perfection was seen as achievable only in the life to come.[6] This led to a constant emphasis on the heavenly life and a certain lack of interest in worldly affairs.[7]

This total rejection of the earthly *politeia* was very different from Eusebius' more positive formulation of the relationship between Church and state. Chrysostom had a very strong sense of the failings of the Christian state and of the fact that imperial support and 'peace' for Christianity actually caused Christians to be lax (*In Ep. ad 2 Cor. Hom.* 26.4 (*PG* 61.580)).[8] In fact, for Chrysostom, persecution was a much better state for Christians as it allowed them an ideal means for achieving perfection (*In Ep. ad 2 Cor. Hom.* 26.4 (*PG* 61.580)). Unlike Graeco-Roman religion, Christianity did not need to be 'shored up by human honours' (*De S. Bab. Contra Jul. et Gent.* 41–2 (*PG* 50.544)). In these views too Chrysostom was typical of the Antiochene school of Christianity.[9] Despite the very negative views that he expressed towards imperial rule, we do not have to see him as apolitical or as uninterested in politics.[10] In fact, on a number of occasions Chrysostom did tackle the question of the role and function of worldly authorities in relation to the Church. It is simply that he formulated the relationship between religion and politics in these passages very differently from Eusebius' understanding of it.

At times Chrysostom could express the view that human secular government was not evil in itself but was a necessary institution for human life ((*In Ep. ad Rom. Hom.* 23 (*PG* 60.615) and *In Ep. ad 1 Cor. Hom.* 34.7 (*PG.* 61.291)).[11] In his sermons on *Romans* 13.1 he states that 'it was not for the subversion of the commonwealth that Christ introduced his laws' (*In Ep. ad Rom. Hom.* 23 (*PG* 60.615)). Secular power is not something evil and completely antithetical to the rule of God but is simply human rule on earth. This is especially the case when secular rulings have something in common with the divine rulings of Christianity. In a passage from the sermons *On the Statues* Chrysostom discusses the problem of how it was

---

[5] See Meeks 1993: 50.   [6] See Wallace-Hadrill 1982: 62 and 118–25.
[7] Wallace-Hadrill 1982: 57–61.   [8] See also *In Ep. ad 1 Cor. Hom.* 36.7 (*PG* 61.219).
[9] See Wallace-Hadrill 1982: 155–7.   [10] As Stephens convincingly argues (Stephens 2001).
[11] *Hom. de Stat.* 6.2 (*PG* 49.82) and *In Ep. ad Rom. Hom.* 22 (*PG* 60.615). For more detailed discussion, see Sandwell 2004: 4–5.

possible for 'Gentiles' to know about good and evil without having the law (and here he means the Judaeo-Christian laws), or any prophecy or the Bible. He argues that there must be a natural law implanted in all human consciousness or Gentiles would not have made 'laws . . . concerning marriages, concerning murders, concerning wills . . . concerning abstinence from encroachments on one another, and a thousand other things' (*Hom. de Stat.* 12.12 (*PG* 49.133)).[12] Some laws, such as those concerning the burial of the dead, are 'laws of nature common to all men' (*Hom de S. Bab.* 2 (*PG* 50.534)). Despite this ability to view human government and secular rulings in a positive way, Chrysostom did on the whole make distinctions between the two forms of *politeia*. Thus in his exegesis of 2 Corinthians he describes three categories of rule: political rule, the individual's rule over the self and the spiritual rule of the Church (*In Ep. ad 2 Cor. Hom.* 15.5 (*PG* 61.507)). Chrysostom sees political rule as inferior because it was merely concerned with earthly matters such as meting out punishments to the body and organizing financial transactions ((*In Ep. ad 1 Cor. Hom.* 40.2 (*PG* 61.349), *In Ep. ad 2 Cor. Hom.* 15.6 (*PG* 61.509 and *Hom. in Oziam, Vidi Dominum* 4 (*PG* 56.126)). Divine rule, on the other hand, has the much more important area of concern of care of the soul and punishment of sin (*Hom. in Oziam, Vidi Dominum* 4 (*PG* 56.126) and *In Ep. ad 2 Cor. Hom.* 15.5 (*PG* 61.509).[13]

This division of labour between political rule and divine law might suggest that the two spheres could exist side-by-side without coming into conflict, particularly in this most extreme form. However, this is not how Chrysostom envisages the situation: the fact that divine laws came from God made them superior to secular law and we often see Chrysostom setting up a hierarchy of the two ((*In Ep. ad 2 Cor. Hom.* 15.5 (*PG* 61.507)). As Stephens has argued, for Chrysostom Christian leaders were superior to earthly ones precisely because they based their rule on divine laws that came directly from God.[14] In a sense, they were thus God's mouthpiece on earth. The contrast can easily be seen here with Eusebius' model, in which it was the emperor himself who was God's representative on earth, whereas for Chrysostom Christian holy men, bishops and priests had this function. It should thus not be surprising that for Chrysostom divine law should always take precedence over political rule and it was according to divine law that people should live their lives, including the Christian emperors themselves.

---

[12] See also *Hom. de Stat.* 13.7 (*PG* 49.139).
[13] For more detailed discussion of the differences between political rule and divine rule, see Sandwell 2001: 98–9 and 2004: 5–6 and Stephens 2001: 81–105.
[14] Stephens 2001: 81–105.

In this way, he again shows how emperors are lower in the hierarchy than Christian bishops. Chrysostom's ideal was not only that Christian rule be seen as superior to secular but that secular rule should also be submissive to Christian rule. In the final instance, the emperor should thus submit to the bishop or priest (*Hom. in Oziam, Vidi Dominum* 4 (*PG* 56.126)). This ideal hierarchy is given fuller elaboration in Chrysostom's account of the martyrdom of Saint Babylas and the events preceding it. Chrysostom's *Discourse on Blessed Babylas* was written in approximately AD 378, before he became a priest.[15] In it he describes the life, death and works of the local martyr Babylas, who was believed to have been an earlier bishop of Antioch. Babylas' first great deed was that he stood up to a (Christian) emperor who had murdered the son of an allied king (*De S. Bab. Contra Jul. et Gent.* 23–7 (*PG* 50.539–40)).[16] After the murder the emperor had gone to Babylas' church without showing any remorse, and in response Babylas had ejected him. Chrysostom praises Babylas for his great courage in standing up to the 'ruler of the greater part of the whole world' and turns this praise into a statement about the relationship between bishop and emperor: 'thus the subordinate gave orders to the chief and the subject judged the ruler of all' (*De S. Bab. Contra Jul. et Gent.* 31 (*PG.* 50.541)).[17] In so doing, Babylas showed that 'one appointed to the priesthood is a more responsible guardian of the earth and what transpires upon it than one who wears the purple' (*De S. Bab. Contra Jul. et Gent.* 51 (*PG* 50.547)). Thus Chrysostom depicts Babylas as standing next to God, the judge, in heaven and expelling the 'defiled excommunicate' from the holy flock for transgressing the laws of God (*De S. Bab. Contra Jul. et Gent.* 34, 51 and 107 (*PG* 50.541, 547 and 563–4).[18] Because Babylas 'was instructed by divine teaching that all worldly activities are a shadow and a dream' no earthly authority could 'made him cower' (*De S. Bab. Contra Jul. et Gent.* 34 (*PG* 50.541)).

This depiction of a priest confronting an emperor is certainly how Chrysostom would have liked things to be.[19] Thus when a bishop in his own lifetime comes into direct contact with a Christian emperor during

---

[15] For the dating of the treatise, see Schatkin and Harkins 1983: 15–16.

[16] In the version of the story given by Chrysostom, Eusebius and the *Chronicon Paschale* the emperor is identified as Christian and as either Philip the Arab or Numerian. Other sources present him as a Greek.

[17] For fuller discussion of Chrysostom's treatment in Babylas, see Sandwell 2001: 100–10 and Stephens 2001: 17–49.

[18] Stephens' dissertation made clear to me the importance of the reference to divine laws in these passages (Stephens 2001: 39–40 and 47).

[19] For a similar view, see Stephens 2001: 39.

the events following the Riot of the Statues, we can see Chrysostom mapping some of his ideas about Babylas' authority onto the situation.[20] In 387, as we saw above, Theodosius had imposed some particularly harsh taxes and the people of Antioch rioted to show their anger: they smashed the statues of the emperor and his family and, in doing so, brought the wrath of the emperor down on them. The city lost its status as a metropolis, and the baths, theatre and circus were all closed. In response to this situation Chrysostom preached his sermons *On the Statues*, in which he tells us that the Antiochene bishop, Bishop Flavian, went as envoy to the emperor Theodosius to ask forgiveness for the city of Antioch.[21] It is now generally recognized that his representation of Flavian's role in these events is far from objective and that we should not accept it at face value.[22] What is important however, is how Chrysostom presents Flavian's relationship with Theodosius. We see here that, as was the case with Babylas, he depicts Flavian as having the force of divine law behind him (*Hom. de Stat.* 3.1 and 2 (*PG* 49.48 and 50). This could then be used by Chrysostom in the days just after the riot to reassure his audience that Flavian would be successful because the emperor would have to submit to divine law as embodied in Flavian (*Hom. de Stat.* 3.1 and 2 (*PG* 49.48 and 50).[23] In the last sermon in this series Chrysostom describes Flavian's success at persuading Theodosius to forgive the city of Antioch, saying how impressive it was that 'a single old man invested with the priesthood of God, taking the situation in hand, reproved the emperor by his aspect alone and by his unadorned conversation. And, that favour which he granted to no one else, he gave to this one old man, so reverencing God's law' (*Hom de Stat.* 21.16 (*PG*. 49.219)).[24] The rule of Christian emperors was not heavenly rule on earth and could not be the means for achieving true Christian piety on earth but was just a practical way to keep order in the world.[25]

These ideas are also reflected in some very negative depictions by Chrysostom of earthly or 'secular' laws in opposition to Christian ones. Political or 'secular' laws should only be followed if they do not come into conflict with divine laws. In his Homily 12 on 1 Corinthians Chrysostom criticizes his audience for caring more about the' ridiculous' and 'corrupt' judgements of the 'mob' of common people than about the judgement of God (*In Ep. ad 1 Cor. Hom.* 12.9 (*PG* 61.20)). He then goes on to sharpen

---

[20] My discussion here has been taken from Sandwell 2001: 101–3, but my arguments on divine law have been given greater nuance from reading Stephens 2001: 49–80.
[21] This can be compared with Libanius' descriptions of the riots in his *Orations* 19–23.
[22] Van de Paverd 1991: 135–56 and French 1998.   [23] Stephens 2001: 59–60.
[24] See also *Hom. de Stat.* 21.13 and 16 (*PG* 49.217 and 219).   [25] Markus 1970: 75–8.

the point by showing that the judgements of even the wisest men, 'those considered worthy of legislating for cities and peoples' (*In Ep. ad 1 Cor. Hom.* 12.9 (*PG* 61.20)), were completely contrary to what was right. He says that the laws of these men do not censure fornication, dice-playing, drunkenness or blasphemy but see a petty crime such as theft as more serious offences (*In Ep. ad 1 Cor. Hom.* 12.9 (*PG* 61.101)). At the same time Chrysostom says that these legislators 'enforce by law' the use of 'harlots and child prostitutes in the theatre' and all the other scandals of public spectacles (*In Ep. ad 1 Cor. Hom.* 12.10 (*PG* 61.102)). Here, then, no common ground of natural law can be found between secular and Christian laws, and something which was 'clearly and confessedly abominable, seemed not so to the legislators from the outside' (*In Ep. ad 1 Cor. Hom.* 12.11 (*PG* 61.103). Where there were laws in common between Christians and non-Christians, non-Christians perverted them: marriage, which is 'accounted an honourable thing both by us and by those without', is ruined by the customs and rules of the heathen legislators (*In Ep. ad 1 Cor. Hom.* 12.11 (*PG* 61.103)).

This is so much the case that Chrysostom even tried to deter his audience from using secular courts at all. Christians did have their own courts and Constantine had given these courts official sanction.[26] He even appeared to allow any defendant or plaintiff involved in a lawsuit in an ordinary court to appeal to the court of the bishop at any moment and have his case transferred there.[27] Libanius describes the action of these courts in the region of Antioch.[28] Chrysostom's most important reference to the use of Christian courts comes after his exegesis of Paul 1 Corinthians 5 on Christians going to law before the unrighteous and the Greeks (*In Ep. ad 1 Cor. Hom.* 16.3–10 (*PG* 61.131–9)). Most of this passage consists of a historical exegesis of Paul's words to suit the Corinthians in the context of their times. However, as is usual with Chrysostom's sermons, he also applies Paul's words to his own context and his audience in fourth-century Antioch. He says: 'Knowing these things, beloved ... let us flee the tribunals of the outsiders in the agora; and the noble birth which God has blessed us with, let us guard closely. For think how shameful it is that a Greek should sit down and deal out justice to you?' (*In Ep. ad 1 Cor. Hom.* 16.9 (*PG*. 61.135–6)). Christians are too good to be judged by non-Christians because, as Paul says, in the final days Christians will judge unbelievers ('Do you not know that the saints will judge the world?') (*In Ep. ad 1 Cor.*

---

[26] *CTh* 1.27.1. See also Drake 2000: 322–5 and Liebeschuetz 1972: 240.
[27] Drake 2000: 323 and 325.   [28] Libanius *Or.* 30.19 (F.III.97).

Hom. 16.5 (*PG* 61.132–3)). If there were disputes between Christians, then Chrysostom, following Paul, argues that these should be quietly resolved by the priest and should not bring ill repute on the Church by being publicized in the courts outside the Church.[29]

Despite the support given to Christian religion by imperial law, Chrysostom allowed little leeway for coexistence between obedience to imperial authority and obedience to Christian authority. Christian, divine law was supposed to offer guidance for living in every area and there was supposed to be little room to appeal to any other source of authority. Chrysostom did not simply want Christians to choose between a Christian *politeia* and a Roman imperial *politeia*. He also wanted the Christian *politeia* to replace or take over the Roman *politeia*. In this sense, being Christian could also be seen as being political since it meant having a *politeia* and one that sought to be dominant in the Roman world. This Christian *politeia* was seen as superior to the Roman state but also as all-defining for those who claimed to be Christian, which left little room for compromise for Christians as their Christian identity was supposed to govern every aspect of their life.[30] It was thus not so much that Chrysostom saw the state in religious terms but rather that he saw the Church in political terms.

Up to this point I have focused on Chrysostom's understanding of the relationship between the Christian *politeia* and the Roman imperial *politeia*. However, there was one other *politeia* that Christians, and others, in Antioch might have seen as available to them: that of the Jews.[31] Chrysostom was clearly worried that the Jewish law and way of life appealed to members of his audiences. He describes how 'many ... respect the Jews and think that their present way of life (*politeia*) is a venerable one' (*Adv. Jud.* 1.3.1 (*PG* 48.847)). Judaism was not simply a religious belief: it also offered a whole way of life and had some institutions of government (for example law courts and council, or *gerousia*, and its own hierarchies that were connected to those in Jerusalem).[32] Judaism could offer his audiences much that he was hoping his Christian *politeia* would offer them and in many ways provided more ancient and established guidance for living. In particular, Chrysostom complains of his audiences turning to the Jewish *politeia* in two ways. He describes how the Judaizers in his audience respected Jewish synagogues because of the presence there of the scrolls containing Law (*Adv. Jud.* 1.5.2

---

[29] For more on this idea see Chrysostom's sermons *Against Publishing the Errors of the Brethren*.
[30] Stephens 2001: 104–5 makes a similar point.   [31] Soler 1999: 245–9 has also noted this.
[32] Zetterholm on the first century AD (Zetterholm 2003: 38–40) and Wilken on the fourth century AD (Wilken 1983: 50–1, 56–7, 60–2 and 64). See also *CTh* 16.8.2 and 16.8.8. On the limits on the powers of these Jewish institutions generally after the second century AD, see Schwartz 2001: 119–28.

(*PG* 48.850)) and saw the Jewish courts to be more binding than Christian ones (*Adv. Jud.* 1.3.4 (*PG* 48.847)). For some people who called themselves Christians, Jewish Law and Jewish courts offered another set of guidelines for living that were alternative to those offered by the Church and, to some degree at least, by the Roman government. Chrysostom does accept that God gave Jewish Law to the Jews, so it had divine status equivalent to that of Christian divine Law (*Adv. Jud.* 6.4.2 (*PG* 48.909)). However, to combat the appeal of Jewish Law he argues that since the coming of Christ and the destruction of the Jewish temple this Law was no longer valid (*Adv. Jud.* 4.4 and 7.1.3 (*PG* 48.876–7 and 915). He thus invalidates their whole *politeia* so that it can no longer be a true competitor with Christianity (*Adv. Jud.* 5.1.5 (*PG* 883–4)). He also mocks the supposed solemnity of oaths taken in the courts of the Jews and forbids his audiences to make use of these courts (*Adv. Jud.* 1.3.4 (*PG* 48.847)). Despite the elements of continuity between Jewish and Christian ways of life, Chrysostom rejects Jewish *politeia* and Jewish Law and will not allow his audiences any acceptance of, or allegiance to, them.

CIVIC IDENTITY AND RELIGIOUS IDENTITY, I: THE TRANSFORMATION OF THE CITY

The civic context was the place in which ancient Christian communities were located and grew up.[33] It was in the challenging environment of the Graeco-Roman city that Christians first had to define themselves and construct their own identity. Before the fourth century they had largely envisaged themselves as a minority group (or groups) under constant threat from those who sought to suppress their religion.[34] In the fourth century, however, the relationship between Christians and the city began to change. The dominance of Christianity and the support given to it by the state from the time of Constantine onwards, in the form of church building (such as the Great or Golden Church in Antioch) and funding, for example, cannot but have brought changes to these traditional aspects of civic religion. At the same time, and because of these changes, Graeco-Roman religion was losing its hold over the city and over public and communal forms of worship. Christians could now compete with Greeks as to which religion represented the city and over the symbolic capital that went with this. One response was for Christians to disengage themselves from civic life. The metaphor of heavenly citizenship could be used to transcend and

---

[33] Meeks 1993: 37.   [34] Meeks 1993: 30, 37 and 50.

replace civic identity as the main point of reference for the Christian. In one example Chrysostom states, 'If you are a Christian, you do not have an earthly city. Of our city "the Builder and Maker is God". Though we may gain possession of the whole world, we are strangers and sojourners in it all. We are enrolled in heaven and we are citizens there' (*Hom. de Stat.* 17.12 quoting *Hebrews* 11.10 (*PG* 49.177–8)). Chrysostom thus compares the Church to a city, but one that was built by God, not by human hands, and one that has its true existence in heaven. It was a little piece of heaven on earth amid all the temptations of daily life (*In Ep. ad 1 Cor. Hom.* 36.8 (*PG* 61.313)). Early Christianity is often thought to have transcended localized civic and national identities in its focus on heavenly citizenship and in the universalizing message this implied.[35] The Church is supposed to have offered a new point of identification and reference that could be shared by all Christians throughout the empire and even beyond, wherever they had originated from. In this sense, we might think that civic identity and being a citizen of Antioch would mean little to Chrysostom and that he would present this as unimportant in his preaching. However, on a number of occasions he showed an interest in the city of Antioch and spoke of it as a context for Christian living in a positive way. He saw that it was necessary to discuss the relationship between Church and city and saw the benefits of gaining some hold over the city for Christianity. Chrysostom could, on occasion, envisage the city as a God-given institution that provided a necessary site of human interaction (*In Ep. ad 1 Cor. Hom.* 34 (*PG.* 61.291)).[36] He also showed great pride in the fact that Antioch was the first place in which disciples took the name 'Christians'.[37] He used this to present a Christianized history of the city and went on, on one occasion, to list other good Christian actions related to the city. He also focused attention on local Christian saints and holy figures.[38] These include the sainted bishops Meletius and Philogonius, who were pro-Nicene bishops in the fourth century, Babylas, bishop in the third century and Ignatius, the renowned second-century bishop.[39] It also included the local martyrs Juventius and Maximinus, Julianus (who had been a bishop of a town in Cilicia but who had been buried near Antioch),[40] Pelagia,[41] Drosis and Thecla, of Paul and Thecla fame. Saint Babylas was clearly especially important as Chrysostom

---

[35] Mann 1986. [36] See also *Hom. de Stat.* 16.17 (*PG* 49.172).
[37] See also *Hom. de Stat.* 3.3; 14.16 (*PG* 49.48 and 153) and *In. Ep. ad 1 Cor. Hom.* 21.9 (*PG* 61.178).
[38] On Chrysostom's theology of martyrdom, see Christo 1997.
[39] On Philogonius, see the translation by Mayer and Allen 2000: 184–95. On Babylas, see Schatkin and Harkins 1983. For the view that these bishops also counted as martyrs for Chrysostom, see Christo 1997: 156–78. On Ignatius, see *In S. Ignat. Mart.* 4 (*PG* 50.587–96).
[40] Leemans *et al.* 2003: 126–40. [41] See Leemans *et al.* 2003: 148–57.

devoted to him a long treatise, *Discourse on Blessed Babylas and against the Greek* as well as a shorter sermon.[42] Through these local Christian figures and the stories told about them, Chrysostom could construct a Christian 'mythology' for Antioch that could rival the Greek foundation myths told by men such as Libanius and could be found on the mosaics throughout the city. He could use these myths to instil in his audience a quite different, Christian way of thinking about their city and asks his audience to 'immerse themselves perpetually' in the stories of the martyrs' struggles (*Hom. in Mart.* (*PG* 50.664)). This reinterpretation of civic life in Christian terms through the lives of local figures could also be linked to changes in the physical layout and use of the city in terms of martyr shrines and festivals. As Baldovin has argued, the ability of Christians to lay claim to the city was tied to their ability to lay claim to the city as a Christian space.[43] Thus we can see that Chrysostom understood that Christianization of the city accompanied the transformation of civic space.

Chrysostom's interpretation of the conflict between the Saint Babylas and Apollo in his *Discourse on Blessed Babylas* reveals this well. After his death at the hands of the murderous emperor, Saint Babylas had been buried in Antioch but was later moved to Daphne by Constantius' Caesar Gallus with the specific intention of purifying the site that had been polluted by immoral festivals such as the Maiumas. Chrysostom describes how Babylas' remains, once they had arrived in Daphne, brought sobriety to the region, which before had been the meeting place of 'dissolute youths' and the 'abodes of demons' (*De S. Bab. Contra Jul. et Gent.* 70–2 (SC 362.185–7)). The very presence of the saint could help to Christianize Daphne. However, this was not the end of Babylas' activities. According to stories circulating at the time, the remains of the saint also caused the Oracle of Apollo at Daphne to be silenced (*De S. Bab. Contra Jul. et Gent.* 73 (SC 362.189)). Chrysostom presents this as a particularly sweet victory for the Christian saint because it happened during Julian's reign when the cult of Apollo had been revived and the god was receiving sacrifices again (*De S. Bab. Contra Jul. et Gent.* 70–2 and 74 (SC 362.185–9 and 191–2)). Julian had the body of Babylas moved away from Daphne, but this simply gained an even greater victory for the Christian saint as, according to Chrysostom, Babylas caused the shrine of Apollo to catch fire and be badly damaged (*De S. Bab.*

---

[42] For a recent translation, see Schatkin 1988. For other versions of the martyrdom of St Babylas, see Eusebius, *HE* 6.29.1 and 4 and 6.34–39, The *Chronicon Paschale* 1.503.9–504 as well as Chrysostom, *In Juventinum et Maximinum Martyrem* 1 (*PG* 50.571). On all these, see Schatkin and Harkins 1983: 46–70.

[43] Baldovin 1987. See also Mayer and Allen 2000: 17.

Contra Jul. et Gent. 93–7 (SC 362.219–25). Chrysostom presented this story of Babylas' actions during the late fourth century as a battle between the saint and the god Apollo to lay claim to space in the city. For Chrysostom the victors were clearly the Christians.

Chrysostom's sermons in honour of martyrs can also inform us about the transformation of the civic space in Antioch – as well as themselves playing an active role in that transformation. They were usually delivered on the occasion of the saint's festival so, by their nature, they were occasional sermons to mark a specific day and must be seen in that context. In these sermons Chrysostom gives us less information than we would like about the festivals but he does give some indication of the context in which each sermon was delivered. In the sermon on Philogonius, delivered on 20 December, the saint's day, Chrysostom describes how he was speaking on the occasion of the festival of the martyr and gives some description of the accompanying market day (*Hom. de S. Phil.* (*PG* 48.747 and 749)). In the same sermon Chrysostom also refers to the approaching Christmas festival, introduced in 376 on the day of Sol Invictus. He describes this as the 'metropolis of all feasts' *(Hom. de S. Phil.* (*PG* 48.752)) and refers to the fact that people would come into the church in especially large numbers to see 'our Master lying in the manger, dressed in swaddling clothes'.[44] Again, in the sermon in honour of Ignatius, Chrysostom compares the festivals and achievements of local martyrs to the entertainments of the city and describes this festival as a time for particular piety (*In S. Ignat. Mart.* 1 (*PG* 50.587)). He also gives some indication that this sermon was delivered at the tomb of Ignatius, which was in the cemetery outside the city and beside the road that led to the suburb of Daphne. This delivery of martyr sermons at the site of the tombs and shrines of the martyrs in question was normal practice (*In S. Ignat. Mart.* 5 (*PG* 50.594)) and the crowning feature of a procession to the saint's tomb.[45] The homily on Saint Julian describes how the site of the saint's tomb provided a pleasant place for picnics after the sermon had been delivered (*In S. Jul. Mart.* (*PG* 50.673)).[46] Similar examples are Chrysostom's delivery of his sermon on Babylas (to be distinguished from the treatise discussed in the previous paragraphs) at the Church of Babylas to the east of the city on the occasion of his feast day (24 January); and the festival of the sainted bishop Meletius, which

---

[44] See also *In diem Natalem* 1 (*PG* 49.351), composed in 386, and also Theodorou 1997 and Brottier 2004: 442–3. Large numbers also came at Pentecost, see *De Pentecoste* 1.1 (*PG* 50.453).
[45] On procession to the martyr shrines see also *In S. Jul. Mart.* (*PG* 50.672) and *In S. Ignat. Mart.* (*PG* 50.595).
[46] See Mayer and Allen 2000: 19, note 6.

was also held there.[47] Later in his sermon on Babylas Chrysostom presents the festival of the saint as a popular and a communal event. He says 'all our city poured forth into the road, and the market-places were empty of men' (*Hom. de S. Bab.* (*PG* 50.527–34)). A short sermon entitled *Homily on Martyrs* and delivered in the Old or Great Church of Antioch also asserts the popularity of these occasions (*Hom. in Mart.* (*PG* 50.661–6);[48] In this sermon Chrysostom states that the 'entire city,' whether rich or poor, old or young, man or woman, had 'transferred itself' to the suburb and shrine where the festival was taking place (*Hom. in Mart.* (*PG* 50.663)). He also describes night vigils (*Hom. in Mart.* (*PG* 50.663)) and prayers, tears and anointment with holy oil as the kind of rituals that should take place at the shrines of martyrs alongside the Eucharist ceremony (*Hom. in Mart.* (*PG* 50.664).[49] What is most interesting, though, is that the sermon mentions that the governor attended – Chrysostom states that 'madness for power' did not keep him away (*Hom. in Mart.* (*PG* 50.663)).[50]

The large numbers of martyrs' and saints' festivals that took place in Antioch throughout the year reveal the way that Christianity was imposing itself on the city.[51] Chrysostom could talk of the numerous martyr shrines around the outside of city that acted like its 'protecting wall' (*Hom. in Egyp. Mart.* (*PG* 50.694)). Similarly, processions to the tombs and shrines of the saints, along with feasts, celebrations and market days in honour of the saints' days, were becoming a central feature of civic life.[52] A festival would often start before the saint's feast day with a night-time, candlelit vigil at the tomb or shrine of the martyr. Psalms and hymns would be sung during the night and a sermon might even be delivered. The next day the Eucharist would be taken at the martyr's shrine, and another sermon in praise of the martyr would be delivered.[53] Chrysostom could present these festivals as replacements for traditional civic festivals (*In S. Jul. Mart.* 4 (*PG* 50.672–3)) or could speak of them using metaphors of public entertainment (*Hom. in Mart.* 1 (*PG* 50.645) and *In S. Jul. Mart.* 1 (*PG* 50.665–6)). He could also use them to reinforce the power of the Christian God because of the miracles and cures performed by the martyrs (*Hom. in Mart.* (*PG* 50.664)).[54] The martyr festivals would have been additions to the normal liturgical calendar of Church celebrations and were sometimes even interwoven with this. We

---

[47] On this sermon, see Leemans *et al.* 2003: 14–18.   [48] See Mayer and Allen 2000: 93–7.
[49] See also Leemans *et al.* 2003: 10 and Chrysostom, *De Ascensione Domini* (*PG* 50.443) on the popularity of martyr shrines as places of personal prayer.
[50] See, Leemans *et al.* 2003: 18.
[51] On the Christian calendar in Antioch, see Soler 1999: 445–75.   [52] Leemans *et al.* 2003: 15.
[53] For this description of a martyr festival, see Leemans *et al.* 2003: 15 and 114.
[54] Leemans *et al.* 2003: 9, 12 and 14.

have seen how Chrysostom referred to the celebration of Christmas Day in his sermon for Saint Philogonius. There is also some evidence that the celebrations of Good Friday and Ascension involved processions to the shrines of the martyrs.[55]

Despite expressing his interest in the city in homilies on the martyrs Chrysostom devoted large parts of these to presenting the martyr as a moral example, someone whose behaviour his audience should imitate. He also often suggested that the best way to honour the martyr was not to go to the festivals at all but rather to transform one's whole life so that it was carried out in honour of the martyr through proper Christian behaviour.[56] Thus in the *Sermon on Blessed Philogonius* Chrysostom used an extended metaphor of a festival and market day to describe heaven as the true site of celebration that the Christian should look towards (*Hom. de S. Phil.* (*PG* 48.749–50)). In another set of sermons, however, delivered during the Riot of the Statues of 387, Chrysostom was forced to deal with the city in a much more whole-heartedly positive way. He realized that the aftermath of the riot provided a special occasion on which the Church could lay claim to representing the city and so present it in a Christian light. Throughout the sermons *On the Statues* Chrysostom sought to represent the Church as the saviour of the city in troubled times. The Church itself is described as 'the mother' of the inhabitants of the city and the Christians as the city's 'guardians, its patrons and teachers' (*Hom. de Stat.* 6.1 (*PG* 49.81));[57] Chrysostom often calls on his audience to remember and associate with the 'greatness of the city' of Antioch and its past; as he says, 'the manners of this city have noble characters from old times' (*Hom. de Stat.* 2.10 (*PG* 49.37)).[58] He recognizes Antioch's political status as the leading city of Syria and thus expresses his concern 'not for one city only but for the whole of the east' (*Hom. de Stat.* 3.1 (*PG* 49.47)). He also uses very affectionate images to describe the city, for example he compares the forum with how it used to be, before the desolation caused by the expected punishment. He says, 'As bees buzz around their hive, so previously the inhabitants of the city flew about the agora every day, and everyone esteemed us happy in being such a crowd' (*Hom. de Stat.* 2.3 (*PG.* 49.35)). That the city was deserted and fearful after the riots is something that Chrysostom regrets as now the

---

[55] Mayer and Allen 2000: 19 and Leemans *et al.* 2003: 16 and also Chrysostom, *De Ascensione Domini* (*CPG* 4342).
[56] *Hom. in Mart.* (*PG* 50.666).
[57] Bishop Ignatius is also described as the guardian of the whole city in Chrysostom's encomium to him (*In S. Ignat. Mart.* 4 (*PG* 50.596)).
[58] See also *Hom. de Stat.* 3.3 (*PG* 49.48–9).

city 'stands desolate, stripped of almost all her inhabitants' (*Hom. de Stat.* 2.3 (*PG* 49.35)).[59]

At other times in these sermons, however, Chrysostom presents the aftermath of the riot as having had a positive impact on the city. On the one hand, he describes how all the inhabitants of the city came into the church as if driven by waves and a storm (*Hom. de Stat.* 4.1 (*PG* 49.59)).[60] On the other hand, he presents the church and its values as extending outwards to the whole city so that the city can be described as purified and 'like a church' (*Hom. de Stat.* 15.3 (*PG* 49.154–5)) or a monastery (*Hom. de Stat.* 17.8 (*PG* 49.175)).[61] As a result of these transformations the city could, like the church itself, gain the status of being heavenly rather than earthly as its Christian credentials made 'it a metropolis not on earth, but in heaven' (*Hom. de Stat.* 17.10 (*PG* 49.177)).[62] In answer to classical ideas about the city being equal to its inhabitants, Chrysostom gives a specifically Christian conception of why it is the virtue of the citizens, not any external aspect of the city, that really matters. He says that a normal encomium of Antioch that praised the beauty of the suburb of Daphne was praise only in 'an outward sense' and for 'the present life' alone. Real praise could instead be found by describing 'modest and temperate' inhabitants and their 'virtue, meekness and almsgiving; all things that pertain to the 'true wisdom of the soul'; that is, in inward qualities (*Hom. de Stat.* 17.13 and 14 (*PG* 49.178–9)). As a man must be considered blessed owing to the 'beauty of the soul' and not outward 'comeliness', so a city must be judged by its inner virtue and not its outward appearance (*Hom. de Stat.* 17.10 and 13–14 (*PG* 49.176 and 178–9)).[63] In such passages Chrysostom was attempting to change the significance of the city for his audience. To be a citizen of Antioch was to be Christian and vice versa.

Chrysostom's attempt to take over the city for the Christian cause at the time of the riot can also be seen in the way that he described the monks coming into the city from the mountains around Antioch. The monks usually represented the height of Christian goodness and the antithesis of the civic, with their solitary living and complete lack of worldly goods and desires – at least as Chrysostom presented the monks around Antioch.[64] They supposedly lived a heavenly life on earth and had almost won the battle against temptation, because they lived completely outside the bounds of

---

[59] See also *Hom. de Stat.* 13.2 (*PG* 49.136), 17.5 (*PG* 49.174) and 21.14 (*PG* 49.217–18) and also Libanius, *Oration* 23 *On the Refugees*.
[60] See also *Hom. de Stat.* 21.2 (*PG* 49.211).   [61] See also *Hom. de Stat.* 6.3 (*PG* 49.82).
[62] See also *Hom. de Stat.* 14.16 (*PG* 49.154).
[63] See also *Hom. de Stat.* 21.20 (*PG* 49.220) and 17.8 (*PG* 49.175).   [64] Mayer 1999.

the city:⁶⁵ They lived, often as hermits, in the mountains around Antioch and they did not uphold any of the values that were most central to city life; they did not hold public office or fit into the fixed structures of status and they reversed expectations of what was considered honourable or dignified behaviour. Their entrance into Antioch thus allowed the city to become its own antithesis 'as then might one see the city likened to heaven, while these saints appeared everywhere' (*Hom. de Stat.* 17.3 (*PG* 49.172–3)). This was especially so because Chrysostom described all those who were normally powerful and 'held the first offices' in Antioch as leaving for the desert in the exodus of citizens who feared the revenge of the emperor (*Hom. de Stat.* 17.5 and 18.12 (*PG* 49.102–3 and 186)). The monks replaced them and became the first citizens of the city. In fact, it is not clear that the monks, including their leader Macedonius, played any pivotal role in securing forgiveness for the city after the riot. However, as M. Maas states, during these events after the riot, 'Christian models of authority had taken a grip of the imagination. Antioch's political profile had become Christian.'⁶⁶

Peter Brown, as so often, was the first person to explore in detail the relationship between attitudes to the body, asceticism and the city in early Christianity. He noted that the tendency towards extreme bodily practices, and in particular sexual abstinence, could have a great impact on traditional civic values.⁶⁷ In his study of Chrysostom's attitude to sexuality and the city, Brown argued that Chrysostom used his privileging of monastic life to undermine traditional Graeco-Roman values and civic life.⁶⁸ Because Chrysostom favoured ascetic modes of existence, Brown argued that his ideal was that all people should live in cells and monasteries in the deserts and mountains rather than in the comfort of the city. However, the notion that Chrysostom wanted to bring about the end of civic life has recently been challenged from a number of perspectives.⁶⁹ In a recent study Hartney has argued that rather than try to do away with civic life altogether, Chrysostom was trying to transform it through the application of true ascetic values to an urban context. As Hartney states:

> He [Chrysostom] asks for a reinterpretation of existing models in a Christian framework . . . His ascetic leanings . . . became part of a blueprint for living for an entire congregation. Not content to simply exhort the advisability of self-denial and celibacy, Chrysostom had definite ideas about how these aims might be realized within the urban environment.⁷⁰

---

[65] Hunter 1988: 13–14 and 51.
[66] Maas 2000: 19. On the authority of monks, see Brown 1982b: 103–52.
[67] Brown 1988: 305–22.   [68] Brown 1986: 306.   [69] For example, see Mayer 1999: 275–8.
[70] Hartney 2004: 11 and 28.

Chrysostom would have liked all his audience to live like monks in relation to the rest of the city. He often cited monks and saints as the model for every member of his community and he encouraged them to strive to change and perfect their behaviour. This often meant that he wanted his audience to hold attitudes very different from those normally held by inhabitants of the city. Chrysostom's ideal was that the disdain of riches and the charitable works that characterized the behaviour of monks would replace *philotimia*, patronage and competition for status. He wanted honour to become associated with avoiding all worldly things and for people to look to heavenly rewards instead of present ones;[71] he stated that Christians should give their money to the poor rather than spend it on display and the entertainments in the city.[72] He told his audiences that poverty and manual labour should no longer be reasons for shame and he encouraged the rich to give charity to the poor of Antioch rather than to put up buildings for the city purely for the sake of honour.[73] In a sermon on 1 Corinthians Chrysostom asked his audience to imagine two cities, one inhabited by rich people alone, one by poor people alone. He argued that the city of the rich would not be able to survive on its own without poor people to carry out manual work. The city of the poor, on the other hand, would be an almost ideal city that would not gain anything if rich people lived there too.[74] Attitudes to wealth and spending money could transform the type of city that humans lived in and could therefore produce a Christianized version of civic life and a Christian version of citizenship.

It would be wrong to dismiss Chrysostom's use of metaphors of the city and civic life as mere rhetorical play, as has sometimes been suggested. Instead it can be seen to be partly the result of the difficulties that beset Christians who lived in the cosmopolitan urban environments of the ancient world. Bringing together Christianity and civic life in these metaphors allowed Chrysostom, in preaching to his audience, to manipulate the idea of what the essence of a city was. He used terms and language that his audience would have understood but transformed their meaning by placing them in a different frame of reference. By talking of the city in positive terms he claimed for the Church some of the symbolic power of the classical idea of the city but at the same time gave it a Christianized

---

[71] Leyerle 2001: 44–60. See Chrysostom's *On Vainglory and the Right Way to Bring up Christian Children*; *Homiliae in Iohannem* 42.4 (*PG* 59.243) and *Hom. in Matt.* 19.2 (*PG* 57.275). See also Meeks 1993: 62.
[72] Leyerle 2001: 58–9 and Hartney 2004: 151–70.
[73] Natali 1975: 45, with reference to Chrysostom, *Homiliae in Iohannem* 3 (*PG* 59.38–45) and *Adv. Oppug. 3 (PG* 47.359).
[74] *In Ep. ad 1 Cor. Hom.* 34.8 (*PG* 61.292).

interpretation. Chrysostom followed classical theorists in seeing virtue and the city as interlinked but he substituted Christian virtue for the virtues normally associated with membership of a city. As Daley says of the use of such language about the city in the Cappadocian fathers, 'it was not simply inflated fourth-century rhetoric' but was part of a 'drive on the part of these highly cultivated bishops and some of their Christian contemporaries to reconstruct Greek culture and society along Christian lines, in a way that both absorbed its traditional shape and radically reoriented it'.[75] This kind of enterprise was particularly important in a competitive context in which the persuasion and conversion of non-Christians was of paramount concern. It has thus been proposed that what often drove Christian authors to use metaphors from civic life to describe Christianity was the context of interaction with adherents of Graeco-Roman religion. As O'Daly says of Augustine, '[he] was attracted to discourse about humans in society in terms of the city because it allowed him to engage with pagan critics of Christianity and those who, while attracted to or influenced by Christianity, were steeped in Graeco-Roman culture . . . [he] engages in debate with a pagan on the basis of common assumptions about cities, real and ideal'.[76] The use of civic metaphors could be a way for Chrysostom to represent Christianity to recent converts and to appeal to those Christians who still played an active role in civic life. He could represent the novelty of the Christian way of life in terms that were reassuringly familiar and might even encourage people to become Christian (*Hom. de Stat.* 21.4 and 13 (*PG* 49.213 and 217)).[77] Chrysostom could not completely avoid references to civic life; they were a useful communicative tool. However, he sought to use them to Christianize and transform civic life so that it could be conceived of in Christian terms.

Similar ideas can be seen played out in Chrysostom's attitude to the Jews. The focus on heavenly citizenship could be used not only to direct Christians' attention away from their lives in the earthly city of Antioch but also to denigrate the privileged place given to the earthly city of Jerusalem by the Jews. Throughout his sermons on the Jews Chrysostom constantly links the invalidity of Jewish ritual in the present day with the destruction of the Jewish temple (*Adv. Jud.* 3.3.6–7 and 4.4.3–9 (*PG* 48.865–6 and 876–7)). In particular, he argues that God destroyed Jerusalem precisely because he did not want the Jews to continue to observe their traditional

---

[75] Daley 1999: 432. See also Hunter: Chrysostom had to 'redefine virtue in terms of the heavenly *politeia*' (Hunter 1988: 65).
[76] O'Daly 1999: 23 and also Markus 1970: 59–61.
[77] *Hom. de Stat.* 21.13 and 19 (*PG*. 49.217 and 220) and also *In Ep. ad Rom. Hom.* 23 (*PG*. 60.615).

rites (*Adv. Jud.* 4.6.1 (*PG* 48.879)). The corollary of this is that Jews who continue to practise their traditional rites show a perverse attachment to the earthly city of Jerusalem and expect that one day it will be rebuilt (*Adv. Jud.* 5.1.6, 5.2.14–15 and 5.4.3 (*PG* 48.884, 884–5 and 889)). One of the faults of Judaism is that it cares more about a physical and earthly space than about more spiritual matters. Thus, Chrysostom states that 'among the Jews little account was made of the season of the Pasch, but they cared greatly about the place, namely Jerusalem' (*Adv. Jud.* 3.5.5 (*PG* 48.868)). Christian perceptions that Julian's attempt at rebuilding the temple was meant as an attack on Christianity would have fuelled all these debates about the significance of Jerusalem.[78] This could be the case for the Judaizing Christians as much as for the Jews themselves. Chrysostom had to work harder to show why the physical city of Jerusalem was not an appropriate focus for Christian piety and, conversely, why membership of the heavenly city meant that respect for the earthly Jerusalem was no longer necessary. In addressing Judaizing Christians he sought to make these distinctions clear, 'What do you have in common with the free Jerusalem and with the Jerusalem above? You choose the one below; be a slave with that one. For according to the word of the Apostle that one is a slave with her children' (*Adv. Jud.* 1.4.6 (*PG* 48.849)). He could also contrast the earthly city of Jerusalem with God's city above just as he contrasted the Jews' old form of worship with the Christians' new one. As he says:

What are old things? He says they are sins and impieties, or all the Jewish observances. Rather, he says they are both these things . . . But behold both a new soul and a new body, and a new form of worship and promises new and covenant and life and table and dress and all things completely new. And in place of Jerusalem below we have received that mother city above . . . instead of tables of stone, flesh; instead of circumcision, baptism. (*In Ep. ad 2 Cor. Hom.* 11.4 (*PG* 61.475–6))

Focus on the heavenly city above could thus very clearly act as part of the broader refocusing of Christianity away from the earthly religion of the Jews.

Chrysostom did not simply seek to reject the Jewish focus on the earthly city of Jerusalem. He also sought to ensure that his own city of Antioch could not be seen as a Jewish city in any sense. The cult of the martyrs gave Christians the opportunity not only to Christianize Antioch as a Greek city but also to take over Jewish space within the city. The Maccabean martyrs (seven brothers and their mother) were martyred by Antiochus IV

---

[78] Wilken 1983: 128–60.

(Epiphanes) in the second century BC, probably over a refusal to eat pork.[79] It is disputed whether this took place in Antioch. However, it is likely that the martyrs were buried at Antioch by the first century AD, probably in the site known as the Cave of Matrona near the Jewish synagogue at Daphne.[80] From that time, the cult of the Maccabean martyrs was an important focus for Jewish piety in Antioch. We know that there had always been some degree of competition between Jews and Christians in the city since the time of early Christian debates about the level and nature of distinction between the two religions. However, in the fourth century, this competition became much keener and Chrysostom clearly saw the Jewish synagogues as rival sites that might attract his audiences away. He thus sought to denigrate the Jewish temple and to describe the impieties that took place at the Cave of Matrona (*Hom in Act.* 35.1 (*PG* 60.252)). At the same time there was a growing Christian interest in the cult of the Maccabean martyrs as a precursor to, and exemplum for, the flourishing Christian cult of the martyrs.[81] As a result of this growing interest, at some point during the fourth century the Christians in Antioch sought to take over the cult of the Maccabees in the city and to transform it into a Christian form of worship. They seem to have built a church to the Maccabean martyrs in the Jewish quarter of the city as a rival to the cult at the Cave of Matrona in Daphne.[82] This was accompanied by the setting up of a Christian festival of the cult of the Maccabean martyrs, which was celebrated on 1 August, and Chrysostom describes the popularity of this one urban martyr festival as people poured in from the countryside for the celebration (*Hom. in Mart.* (*PG* 50.663)). In this way a prominent Jewish site could become Christianized and the Christian Church could take over for themselves the power of the Maccabean martyrs, the archetype of those who suffered for their religious belief. As Chrysostom said, rather tendentiously, the Maccabean martyrs had 'poured out their blood for the sake of Christ' (*Hom. de Eleazaro* 1 (*PG* 63.525)). As we have no Jewish writings from Antioch we cannot know how Jews in the city would have reacted to this aggressive move but we can imagine it would not have been well received. Ideas about citizenship and the city could thus also be used to clarify the distinction between Christians and Jews and to allow no room for compromise between the two.

---

[79] 2 Maccabees 7. See Wilken 1983: 36 and 88.
[80] Vinson 1994: 179–86. See also Wilken 1983: 36 and 88 and Downey 1961: 110.
[81] First exemplified in Gregory of Nazianzen, *Oration* 15. See Vinson 1994.
[82] Vinson 1994: 182–5. See also Wilken 1983: 88 and Augustine, *Sermo* 300.

CIVIC IDENTITY AND RELIGIOUS IDENTITY, II: THE
DEMONIZATION OF CIVIC LIFE

It has been suggested above that Chrysostom wanted to transform and Christianize government and civic life as a whole. In his ideal world Christians would live according to God's law and in a Christianized city. It was inevitable, however, in a city such as Antioch and in the Roman empire, that Chrysostom would be far from successful in this goal. One option open to Christians striving to live the heavenly life on earth was to see the world around them in demonic terms. They could thus construct their battle to live as good Christians as a battle of good against the evil powers that could exist in almost any aspect of daily life. Apocalyptic ideas based on Revelation, in which the emperor was the anti-Christ and the world outside the Church was demonized, were prevalent in some circles even in the fourth century even if this was among groups labelled as heretical.[83] At certain points Chrysostom explicitly rejects the notion that the 'secular' (that is, non-Christian) parts of Roman rule were demonic. In discussion of Romans 13.1 in one of his homilies on 1 Corinthians, he states:

When he speaks of 'rulers of this life' Paul speaks not of certain demons, as some clearly suspect, but of those in authority, those in power, those who think the matter to be worth debating about, philosophers, rhetoricians and writers of speeches. For those were the ones who were ruling and who often became leaders of the people. (*In Ep. ad 1 Cor. Hom.* 7.1 (*PG* 61.55))

Similarly, he rejects the proposition of 'many at this day' who say 'that God takes no care for the visible order of things, but has delegated your affairs to demons' (*In Ep. ad 2 Cor. Hom.* 2.9 (*PG* 61.402)).[84] One of his prime goals here was to combat the notion that humans had no power of free-will to do good as a result of the power of demons. The passage also suggests that Chrysostom did not see the earthly world as the sphere of demonic powers, whether these are conceptualized as malign forces, lesser divinities or Fate.

At other times, however, Chrysostom was less forgiving of the world around him. For Chrysostom civic life posed a real threat to his attempt to instil Christian values in his community and provided a great source of temptation for Christians to fall back into traditional Graeco-Roman

---

[83] For example, the Donatists with their strong emphasis on martyrdom and opposition to the state had some of these tendencies.
[84] See also his three sermons on contemporary attitudes to demons and free will, *That Demons Do Not Govern the World* (*PG* 49.243–76).

and 'pagan' ways. The theatre, racecourses and other entertainments were sites of immorality and were a great danger to the Christian soul.[85] The sexual element in many theatrical shows led Chrysostom to describe the theatre as a veritable school of immorality where one could learn about adultery and fornication (*Hom. in Act.*. 42.4 (*PG* 60.301)).[86] At the same time he poured deep scorn on some of the basic values that undergirded civic life,[87] for example he did not regard *philotimia* as a beneficial use of private wealth for the public good, as did traditional Greeks and Romans.[88] Instead, he saw it as an ugly form of vainglory and conspicuous display that showed a typical Graeco-Roman love of wealth (*Adv. Oppug.* 3.7 (*PG* 47.359).[89] Even the buildings and central spaces of the city were caught up in this negative portrayal of the basic institutions and values of the city. Chrysostom describes the courts, the council chamber and the forum as places that will distract the Christian from spiritual contemplation and keep him tied to concern with 'earthly and corruptible' matters such as merchandise, feasts, taxes, contracts and wills (*Hom. de Stat.* 10.2 (*PG* 49.112)).[90] People who came to church from these places would have the wrong attitude for worship of God and might even bring their earthly concerns into the church with them. In a passage from his sermons on 1 Corinthians Chrysostom describes how the Church in his time in Antioch has deteriorated from the Corinthian Church in the time of Paul, which 'was a heaven'. He first makes a rhetorical comparison between Paul's day when the houses were churches and his own day when the Church has become like a house in its worldly concerns. He then extends this comparison to the rest of the city and describes the deterioration in terms of an invasion of the Church by values and activities from the city. It has taken on the tumult and confusion of a vintner's shop, the baths, the stage or a market place when it should be 'a place of angels' (*In Ep. 1 ad Cor. Hom.* 36.8 (*PG* 61.313)).[91] The very physical imagery of the buildings and spaces of the city is used to show the opposition between Church and city and how the two have been wrongly brought together. In this way Chrysostom gives very negative and uncompromising depictions of all the places in which his

---

[85] Vandenburgh 1955: 36–41 and Leyerle 2001: 1–74.
[86] See also *Hom. in Matt.* 7.7 and 37.6 (*PG* 57.81 and 426–7); *Contra ludos et thēâtre* 2 (*PG* 56.267) and *De Davide et Saule* 3 (*PG* 54.696–7) and also Leyerle 2001: 69–71.
[87] Leyerle 2001: 49–53. See also Hartney 2004: 29–30 and 48.
[88] Aristotle, *EN* 4.2 and Libanius, *Or.* 11.134–8 (F.1.480–2).
[89] See also *In Ep. ad Ephes. Hom.* 12.1 (*PG* 62.89); *Hom in Matt.* 20.2 (*PG* 57.289); and *In Ep. ad 1 Cor. Hom.* 40.5 (*PG* 61.354).
[90] See also *Hom. de Stat.* 10.1, 12.2, 15.7 and 20.3 (*PG* 49.111, 127, 156 and 199).
[91] See also *Hom. de Stat.* 2.11 and 20.3 (*PG* 49.38 and 199) and *In Ep. ad 1 Cor. Hom.* 36.9 (*PG* 61.314).

congregation spent their ordinary lives and makes it clear that it was very difficult to live a good Christian life in them.[92]

It was partly the corrupt nature of civic life and the continued existence of many 'pagan' civic institutions that led Antiochene Christians generally to be negative about the possibility of achieving Christian perfection in the present life.[93] Despite the increased presence of Christian institutions, buildings and festivals, many of the old institutions of the city still existed. Because of the dangers posed to the purity of the Church and the Christian community by civic institutions and civic spaces Chrysostom was forced into giving a negative religious interpretation to civic life. Only in this way could he mark out clear boundaries for his Christian audiences between proper Christian behaviour and all other ways of being that were now to be considered improper. A good example of this is Chrysostom's interpretation of civic festivals in his sermon *On the Kalends*.[94] The Kalends festival was still being celebrated in Chrysostom's day to mark the turn of every new year. It was a joyous festival in which all members of society took part and one that particularly allowed for a temporary reversal of the normal social orders.[95] The Kalends festival was also characterized by gift giving and feasting and it appears to have been one of the most popular festivals in the Graeco-Roman calendar. Many of Chrysostom's audience were involved, which prompted Chrysostom to write his sermon against the festival. He could not allow the Kalends, as the remnant of a Graeco-Roman festival, to be seen as an acceptable event for Christians to attend. Not only were images of the gods still paraded through the city (the *pompa*), but the festival was also a time of unholy singing and dancing and of other moral sins that involved too much expenditure on extravagances and the gaudy decoration of the city.[96] To make it clear that attendance at such a festival was incompatible with being Christian, Chrysostom presents the Kalends as demonic: 'demons parade in the agora' and 'diabolical night festivals' take place (*In Kal.* 1 (*PG* 48.954)).[97] Christians should remember their 'citizenship of heaven' and 'should do all for the glory of God' rather than attend the festival (*In Kal.*

---

[92] See also *In Ep. ad 1 Cor. Hom.* 16.1 (*PG* 61.129–30).

[93] Theodoret of Cyrrhus, *Therapies for Hellenic Maladies*; Wallace-Hadrill 1982: 59 and 61 and Hartney 2004: 115.

[94] On Greek festivals in Chrysostom, see *De S. Bab. Contra Jul. et Gent.* 73 and 77–9 (*PG* 50.553 and 554–5); *Hom. in Gen.* 1.2 (*PG* 53.21), 48.30 (*PG* 54.443), 55.1 (*PG* 55.448); *In Ep. ad I Cor. Hom.* 33.5–7 (*PG* 61.282–4); *In illud vidi dominum* 1.2 (*PG* 56.99), 22.5 (*PG* 62.37); *Conciones de Lazaro* 1.1 (*PG* 48.963) and *Hom. de Stat.* 21.20 (*PG* 49.220).

[95] On the Kalends festival in fourth-century Antioch, see Gleason 1986.

[96] *In Kal.* 2 (*PG* 48.954–5).

[97] These probably refer to the pomps, the processions of pagan statues that were carried through the city, see Gleason 1986: 109–10.

3 (*PG* 48.956–7)). As well as staying away from the festival this 'doing all for the glory of God' includes a whole host of other daily activities (*In Kal.* 3 (*PG* 48.957)). Whereas we saw above that appeals to heavenly citizenship were used to construct a separate transcendent sphere in which Christian perfection was possible, here Chrysostom uses them in a slightly different way to argue that heavenly values should be brought into civic life or else it must be characterized as demonic.

Chrysostom could see civic festivals as religious only in negative terms, as demonic and antithetical to being Christian. The only antidote was for the whole of civic life to be given a Christian and heavenly interpretation by Christians and for no one to attend the festival. As Harl argues, Christian critiques of Graeco-Roman festivals had the goal of highlighting the proper Christian way of life and true Christian festivals.[98] The presentation of traditional festivals as demonic and the heavenly values of Christianity as the only antidote did not allow any space for the festivities to be left free of religious significance. As Harl states: 'En connotant la fête des kalendes d'une signification démoniaque, et en faisant une manifestation du Mal, l'Eglise révélait clairement sa volonté de n'accepter aucune mitigation, aucune conciliation entre de telles pratiques et la profession de chrétien'.[99] Chrysostom also labelled a whole host of other normal civic activities as idolatrous and demonic in his attempt to draw boundaries around the proper Christian life and to isolate it from the dangers of living in the city. Theatrical shows and festivals were labelled as idolatrous because they aroused demonic passions in his audience. The only cure was for the theatre to be disbanded and for the city to be completely Christianized.[100] Although Chrysostom's theology sought to avoid conceptualizing the earthly world in religious terms, he could not help envisaging the earthly city as either heaven or the realm of the devil. As Markus has argued, this was the inevitable result of a fourth-century context, in which the Church was dealing with a large influx of new converts from Graeco-Roman religion. As he says, it developed a tendency to absorb what had previously been 'secular' into the realm of the 'sacred', turning secular into Christian or dismissing it as 'pagan' and idolatrous or demonic.[101] At such moments it was particularly important for Chrysostom to assert that there was no neutral, secular space that both pagans and less zealous Christians could inhabit. Either civic identity was supposed to be totally at one with Christian identity or it had to be extinguished. In

---

[98] Harl 1981: 123–47.   [99] Meslin 1970: 97. See also Harl 1981: 132.
[100] *Homiliae in Iohannem* 1.4 and 32.3 (*PG* 59.29 and 188); *Hom. in Act.* 42.1 (*PG* 60.297) and *Hom. in Matt.* 7.8 (*PG* 57.82). See also Leyerle 2001: 45.
[101] Markus 1990: 16.

this way Chrysostom sought to reinforce the notion that religious identities were all decisive and not something that could at times be utilized and at times ignored. He also disallowed any possibility of a neutral secular sphere or of arguments for religious toleration.

ETHNIC IDENTITY AND RELIGIOUS IDENTITY

We have seen that Chrysostom labelled those who worshipped the gods as *ta ethnē* and *Hellēnes*. He called them 'children of the Greeks (*paides Hellēnōn*)' (*Hom. in Gen.* 2.10 and 6.12 (*PG* 53.29 and 58)), a permutation of the biblical 'children of Israel', in contrast to 'the race of Christians (*to tōn Christianōn ethnos*)' (*Hom. in Gen.* 7.2 (*PG* 53.62)). In using this kind of language to describe religious allegiance Chrysostom raises the question of the relationship between religion and ethnic and cultural forms of identification. Christians had inherited the use of the term *ta ethnē*, the tribes or peoples, from the Jews who had used it alongside the term *genos*, or 'race', to describe the non-Jewish people of the world. This included Greeks but also other peoples such as the Egyptians and the Canaanites.[102] Jews also referred to themselves as an *ethnos* or a *genos*, usually during, or in reference to, interaction with Greeks and Romans.[103] Christians took over the use of these labels from the time of Paul, who used them to refer to non-Christians, and they went on to become the most common terminology by which Christians referred to those outside the Judaeo-Christian tradition.[104] The use of the term 'Greeks' also goes back to Jewish usage.[105] As Jews encountered Greeks during periods of Hellenistic rule and in the Greek cities of the Roman empire, it was natural for them to talk in terms of a contrast between the two peoples.[106] This contrast between the Jewish and the Greek races was again picked up by Paul in his famous statement about Jews and Greeks all being 'one in Jesus Christ' (Galatians 3.28). It can also be found at various points in Acts where the Jews and the Greeks were

---

[102] 1 Maccabees 1.11, 13, 14; 2.68 and 3.10, 45, 48; 2 Maccabees 8.5, 12.13 and 14.14–15; *Letter of Aristeas* 139 and 3 *Sibylline Oracle* 381–400. See Gruen 2001: 365 and Bowersock 1990a: 10–11.

[103] 1 Maccabees 8.23, 10.25, 11.30, 12.3, 13.36, 14.28 and 15.1–2; 2 Maccabees 11.27; Josephus, *AJ* 12.141–2 and *BJ* 7.43. See Gruen 2001: 365.

[104] For Paul's use of these terms see Romans 3.29, 9.24, 11.11–12 and 25; 1 Corinthians 1.22–4; 2 Corinthians 11.26 and Galatians 2.14–15 and also Gruen 2001: 365. For later usage, see Tertullian, *Ad Nationes* 1; Clement, *Str.* 6.39 and 42; Pseudo Cyprian, *De Pascha Comptus*; and Athenagoras, *Leg.* 1.1–3. See also Bowersock 1990a: 10–11 and Buell 2001: 461–2.

[105] As Bowersock has shown, there was some Jewish tradition of using *hellēnikos* as well as *ethnikos* to describe Gentiles (Bowersock 1990a: 11).

[106] See, for example, 4 Maccabees 4–18; Josephus, *Ap.* 2.161, 168 and 72 and *BJ* 7.43; and also *The Letter of Aristeas* 138.

described as the two groups who were the object of Paul's proselytizing mission (Acts 6.1; 9.29; 11.19; 11.20; and 18.4).[107] It is also in the writings of Paul that we find a rare early example of Greeks being defined as direct opposites of Christians – 'but we preach Christ crucified, to the Jews a stumbling block and to the Greeks a foolishness' (1 Corinthians 1.22–3).[108] Occasionally Christian writers in the centuries after Paul would use the term 'Greeks' to refer to non-Christians but the word did not enter into common parlance as *ta ethnē* did.[109] It was only from the beginning of the fourth century that the terms *Hellēnes, hellēnikos* and *hellēnismos* came into common usage among Greek-speaking Christian writers such as Athanasius and Eusebius.[110] From then onwards these terms appear to have been used interchangeably with *ta ethnē* to designate those who were neither Jews nor Christians and who worshipped the Graeco-Roman gods in some form.

The question that we thus have to ask is how Christians, and Jews before them, understood the ethnic connotations of these terms. Only in this way can we understand what they tell us about how Christians conceived of the relationships between ethnicity and religion. To have any chance of doing this successfully we first need to understand what we mean by the term ethnicity and how it relates to the concepts of race and culture more generally. Frederick Barth long ago defined ethnicity simply as the construction of similarities and differences between different groups of people. He argued that the essence of ethnicity lay in the boundaries constructed between groups rather than in any essential features or the 'content' of the characteristics of different groups.[111] The problem with this view is that to focus on form (the boundaries) at the expense of content makes it impossible to distinguish ethnic identity from any other kind of social identity.[112] While accepting that a sense of ethnic identity will always be constructed and fictional, we need to be able to identify the particular aspect of human existence it takes as its focus. Often ethnic identity is assumed to be synonymous with either cultural identity (language, education, artistic expression, etc.) or with race. However, John Hall in a recent work on Hellenic identity in the ancient world has argued against this view. As he says, 'biological features, language, religion or cultural traits may appear to be highly visible markers of identification but they do not ultimately define the ethnic

---

[107] Gruen 2001: 353–4.
[108] It is interesting that Paul then goes on to characterize those who accept Christ as 'them which are called both Jews and Greeks'.
[109] Exceptional examples of use of 'the Greeks' can be seen in Justin's *Discourse to the Greeks* and his *Hortatory Address to the Greeks*.
[110] Eusebius, *VC* 2.44 and Athanasius, *Ar.* 3.16 and 4.10. See also Bowersock 1990a: 10.
[111] Barth 1969: 13.   [112] S. Jones 1997: 61 and Jenkins 2003: 100–1.

group'.¹¹³ Instead, Hall insists on a strong distinction between ethnicity and culture and argues that the most important of the 'definitional *criteria*' of ethnicity is a 'putative subscription to a myth of common descent and kinship'.¹¹⁴ He then distinguishes ethnicity from race by emphasizing the fictive, mythical and constructed nature of ideas about descent in ethnic categorizations.¹¹⁵ We need to keep these distinctions between race, ethnicity and culture in mind.

Jews clearly perceived themselves in terms of shared descent and kinship as well as in terms of a shared religion and culture.¹¹⁶ They called themselves an *ethnos* and compared their *ethnos* to that of other *ethnē*. Jewish sources rarely give extensive descriptions of how they characterize other *ethnē* but there seems to be the assumption that Canaanites, Egyptians and Greeks were all, like themselves, groups that could be defined according to their blood ties to one another as much as by their religion and their culture. There is some evidence that, for a short while in the fifth century BC, Greeks also held this view of themselves as defined by their blood ties to one another. Hall has recently argued that before the fifth century BC the only truly ethnic categories to have emerged were those of the tribal affiliations of the Achaeans, the Ionians, the Aeolians and the Dorians.¹¹⁷ However, in the fifth century the terms 'Hellas' and 'Hellenes' began to be used to denote the whole of Greece and the whole of the Greek people as related by a common descent.¹¹⁸ At this time Herodotus could define the Greeks as a unified people 'speaking the same language', having 'the same way of life', 'having common (*koina*) shrines and sacrifices' but also, most importantly, 'sharing the same blood' (Herodotus, *Hist*. 8.144.2). This truly ethnic usage of the term Greek was, however, Hall states, very brief. In the fifth to fourth centuries BC, under the influence of Athens, 'Hellenic identity shifted from ethnic to broader cultural criteria.'¹¹⁹ As Isocrates announced, in his famous statement in the *Panegyricus*, 'the name "Greek" does not seem to indicate common descent (*genos*) any longer' nor a 'common nature (*phusis*)' but rather a 'frame of mind' and a shared 'culture (*paideia*)' (Isocrates, *Paneg.* 50). From Isocrates' time onwards it is this cultural conception of Greekness that seems to have dominated and that still seems to be favoured by Greeks living under Roman rule.¹²⁰ Throughout these changes,

---

¹¹³ Hall 2002: 9.   ¹¹⁴ Hall 2002: 8–9.   ¹¹⁵ Hall 2002: 13–15.
¹¹⁶ Boyarin 2004: 2–8.   ¹¹⁷ Hall 2002: 6 and chapter 3.
¹¹⁸ As opposed to its previous use to describe one region of central Greece and its inhabitants, see Hall 2002: 7 and chapter 5.
¹¹⁹ Hall 2002: 7–8, chapter 6 and 226–8. See also Said 2001: 280–5.
¹²⁰ Hall 2002: 220–6; Said 2001; and Whitmarsh 2001.

religious elements of Hellenic identity continued to be stressed by Greek writers: Greek religion was clearly seen to be part of the package of Greek culture.[121] Perceptions of shared descent were, however, far less important to definitions of 'Greekness' in the Roman period; people once defined as 'barbarian' as well as Romans were now able to take on all the accoutrements of Greek culture to become 'Greek' if they so desired.[122] This means that Greeks in this period no longer defined themselves as an ethnicity, in Hall's strict sense of the term, but more as a culture.

Where does the thinking of Christians fit into this picture? Buell has recently argued that Christians conceived of themselves and of their relations to others in ethnic and racial terms.[123] It soon becomes clear, however, that Buell is not using ethnicity and race in the strictest sense of the terms to mean common descent and kinship, as outlined by Hall. Rather, she is using the terms ethnic and racial in a looser sense that follows later Greek conceptions of Greekness as accessible to everyone because it is defined in cultural terms. She argues that Christians chose to represent themselves in ethnic terms because this fitted into Graeco-Roman, and Jewish, perception that having a distinct religion was a normal part of the package of having a distinct culture.[124] They could then argue for tolerance for their *'ethnos'*, including the religious aspects of this, just as any other *ethnos*, notably that of the Jews, was tolerated in the ancient world. Buell argues that Christians also, like Greeks, conceived of their 'ethnicities' as something that were open to all, rather than being confined only to a group of people related by blood, because this could act as model for conversion to Christianity. What Buell does not recognize is that we can only accept this argument if we first jettison the strictly ethnic (sharing ideas about common descent) characteristics of Greekness. Doing so allows us to see that just as anyone could take on Greek cultural identity so any one could take on Christian cultural identity. Christians did often use the language of race and kinship to describe themselves but they did so in only the loosest and most metaphorical sense. Much more useful to them were ideas about the interconnectedness of culture and religion that were commonplace in the Graeco-Roman world. It is these ideas that fourth-century Christians were building on in their use of ethnic/cultural terminology to describe religious allegiance *but* the fourth-century situation meant that the significance and impact of using such terms began to change. In the fourth century Christian leaders began to make increasing use of Greek culture to

---

[121] Isocrates, *Paneg.* 180; Dion. Hal. *Ant. Rom.* 1.89.4 and Dio Chrys. *Or.* 38.46 and 40.28.
[122] Whitmarsh 2001.   [123] Buell 2001: 449–76.   [124] Buell 2001: 458–60 and 562.

promote Christian aims. *Paideia*, and the power it held in Graeco-Roman society, was something that these fourth-century Christians were increasingly laying hold of as they sought to convert elite Greeks and Romans and to represent themselves as a serious force in Graeco-Roman society.[125] This entailed a re-evaluation of the relationship between Christianity and Greek culture. Christians who wanted to be able to make use of Greek rhetoric and literature for their own purposes had a vested interest in separating off Greek culture from Greek religion. The emperor Julian's ruling on Christian teachers intensified these debates by suggesting that Christians should not teach Greek literature because they did not worship Graeco-Roman gods (Julian, *Ep.* 61), which raised the ire of many educated Christians. As Gregory of Nazianzus says: '[Julian] wrongfully transferred the meaning of Greek, as though the Greek speech belonged to religious worship exclusively and not to the tongue' and despite the fact that 'words' were the 'common property of all rational beings, he begrudged' them 'to the Christians' (Gregory of Nazianzus, *First Invective against the Emperor Julian* 4–5). The question of the relationship between Greek cultural identity and allegiance to Greek religion was thus a highly charged one in the fourth century.

On this matter, Chrysostom's thinking is clear: he had very little time for the literature and learning of classical culture. While Basil of Caesarea was able to allow Greek learning to be a 'shadow outline' of Christian virtue if used carefully, Chrysostom totally rejected its use and favoured education from scripture only.[126] It is this position that gives special significance to Chrysostom's use of the terms *Hellēnes* and *ta ethnē* to describe non-Greeks. He could use such terminology to reassert the difference of Christianity from Greek culture and religion as a whole package. By labelling worshippers of the gods as Greeks he was arguing for the rejection not just of Greek religion but also of Greek language, culture, history and moral and social values. As a result, there would be little room for compromise between religious identity and ethno-racial identity: a person could not be Christian and at the same time Greek so had to choose not only one religion but also the whole way of life that went with it. By maintaining the association between ethnicity and religion, Chrysostom was showing how central he wanted religion to be as a defining feature of people's identity. Just as Graeco-Roman religion had once been a key and defining feature of what it meant to live in the Greek world, now Chrysostom wanted Christian

---

[125] Av Cameron 1991.
[126] See Chrysostom, *De Inani Gloria et de educandis liberis* 28–47 (SC 188) and *Adv. Oppug.* (*PG* 47.367). On Basil's view, see Moffat 1972 and Rousseau 1994: 27–60.

religion to be a defining feature of what it meant to be human and to live in the new Christian world as part of the race of Christians. There had to be a stark choice between being Christian and being Greek, with no possibility of overlap or indeterminacy. Just as Chrysostom allowed no room for a non-Christian civic identity and little room for a non-Christian form of government, he also allowed little room for a non-Christian form of ethnic identification. While he did use the metaphor of race, the main purpose of his use of the terms *Hellēnes* and *ta ethnē* was to show the incompatibility of Greek culture and Christianity. Chrysostom's demands for such separation were, of course, quite unrealistic and we know that he himself often made use of techniques taken from classical Greek education. However, the statement of his ideal is worth noting because it contrasts so strongly with the policy of many other Christian leaders.

Chrysostom sought to associate religious forms of identification very closely with political and ethnic-cultural forms. Christianity was supposed to become the political, civic and ethnic identity of Christians as well as their religious identity. Where this was not successful, these spheres of life were defined as Greek and demonic and were rejected, so Chrysostom left little room for manoeuvre between different types of social identity or for a neutral or secular sphere where religion did not matter. This also meant he did not leave much space for religious toleration or for the idea that one's choice of religious allegiance could be a purely private matter.

CHAPTER 6

Religious allegiance and other social identities in Libanius

RELIGIOUS ALLEGIANCE AND THE POLITICAL SPHERE

The religious and the political spheres were traditionally inseparable in the Graeco-Roman world. Good functioning of religion was seen as indispensable for good functioning of the state, and dysfunction in the state was seen as a religious problem too. Political allegiance to the state was often simultaneously religious allegiance to the gods of the state and the divine person of the emperor. It is not surprising that we see this attitude in some of Libanius' writing about the fourth century. He eulogized the emperor Julian's rule as divinely ordained and as exemplifying the 'correct relationship between gods and empire' and praised his restoration of blood sacrifice as beneficial to the whole world.[1] When Julian died, possibly murdered, Libanius could then blame all the woes of the Roman empire on this event (*Oration* 24 *On Avenging Julian* (of 378)).[2] In the 380s Libanius could continue to exploit these traditional ideas such as when he attributes Roman success in conquest to worship of the gods (*Or.* 30.5 and 33 (F.III.90 and 104–5)). On other occasions he could express very similar views about Christian emperors: in his oration *In Praise of Constans and Constantius* he praises the rule of Constantius as having divine favour and being divinely inspired: 'the reigns of the present empire lie in the hand of the power above...' (*Or.* 59.48 (F.IV.232)).[3] He could also praise Theodosius and his rule as divine in nature.[4] Whatever the religious allegiance of the emperor, in *basilikoi logoi* praise of his rule in divine terms was always appropriate and expected. The very fact that *Orations* 24 and 30 were, nominally at least, addressed to

---

[1] *Or.* 13.20, 33 and 47 (F.II.70, 74 and 80); *Or.* 14.3 (F.II.88); *Or.* 12.38 and 59 (F.II.21–2 and 30–1).
[2] On this oration, see Criscuolo 1994.
[3] See also *Or.* 59.18, 72, 125, 140, 142 and 169 (F.IV.18, 244, 273, 280–1 and 294). Lieu and Montserrat cite this praise of Christian emperors in traditional terms as the reason for Libanius' divergences from Menander's model for a *basilikos logos* (Lieu and Montserrat 1996: 161). See also Schouler 1984: 939–40; Liebeschuetz 1972: 15; and Misson 1914: 29.
[4] *Or.* 20.11, 22, 28 and 48 (F.II.426, 431, 434 and 443) and *Or.* 21.17 (F.II.458).

Theodosius, a Christian emperor, must make us doubt that Libanius saw a return to state-sponsored worship of the Graeco-Roman gods as the only option for the fourth-century empire. At the level of high fourth-century rhetoric he was able to accept the Christian takeover of Graeco-Roman models of state–divine relations.

On other occasions Libanius shows disapproval of Christian attempts to compete with, or take over, aspects of public life. In *Oration* 30 *In Defence of the Temples* he objects to the way that Christian monks, bishops and officials sought to take the law into their own hands[5] by destroying temples and stealing their property when Theodosius had not sanctioned this by law (*Or.* 30.11–13; 24–7 (F.III.169–70 and 100–1)). Libanius explicitly recognizes and accepts the Christian bias of Theodosius' laws, saying that if the monks had stayed within the bounds of these laws no one would have criticized them: '[They] should have achieved this with you [Theodosius] on their side and have shared their ambition with the ruling power. It would have been better, I think, to gain the things which they wanted doing nothing wrong according to the law, rather than by abusing it' (*Or.* 30.27 (F.III.101)). However, the monks not only went beyond what was allowed by law but also sidestepped secular law altogether by making charges against the peasants in the ecclesiastical court of the bishop Flavian in Antioch. Libanius opposes his own correct appeal to secular law (even secular law that was against aspects of Graeco-Roman religion) to the monks' incorrect appeal to the ecclesiastical court: the monks made charges about the peasants in 'Flavianus' court of law' not 'in real courts of law (*en tois hōs alēthōs dikastēriois*)' (*Or.* 30.19 (F.III.97)). It was wrong that the Christians should have a separate court dealing only with its own matters but it was even worse that the Christian ecclesiastical court sought to compete with the secular rule of the emperor and take over some of its functions. If the monks had evidence that the peasants had broken the law by sacrificing, they should have taken this evidence to the magistrate who was in charge of the secular court because it was his 'job to impose the penalty' (*Or.* 30.20 and 25 (F.III.98 and 100)). Instead of this due process of law the monks used illegal force that was sanctioned by the Christian court and the bishop (*Or.* 30.26 and 11 (F.III.101 and 93)). As Libanius says, the Christians were 'the only ones ever to judge the cases of those whom they accuse and, having passed judgement, themselves play the hangman's part' (*Or.* 30.26 (F.III.101)). In an oration that purports to have the emperor Theodosius as its intended

---

[5] Libanius seems to have shared this disapproval of separate Christian courts with some of Constantine's advisers and officials, see Drake 2000: 324–5.

audience, and whose basic message probably reached the emperor in some form, Libanius appeals to the authority of secular laws and seeks to keep these distinct from forms of authority based in the Church.[6]

Libanius also shows favour to Christian emperors who did not confuse their personal religious allegiance with their public policy. At the beginning of *Oration* 30 he states of Constantine, the first Christian emperor, that he 'thought it advantageous to himself to recognize some other god' (*Or.* 30.6 (F.III.90)). In so doing, he refers to Constantine's greed for personal gain from the wealth stripped from the temples and to the traditional comparison between Constantine's personal adoption of Christianity and Constantius' far more offensive attempts to impose it as state religion.[7] He then praises Theodosius for following the better examples of Constantine and Julian in not seeking to impose his personal religious beliefs on the public through any programme of enforced conversion: 'Nor, then, have you imposed this yoke upon the souls of men. But, while you think this way of worship to be better than that other one, you do not think the other to be impious or that someone could justly be punished for it' (*Or.* 30.53 (F.III.116–17)).[8] Like Julian, Theodosius did not persecute those of his subjects 'who held a belief contrary to his own' (*Or.* 30.54 (F.III.117)).[9] This approach should ideally apply to the officials of Christian emperors as well as to Christian emperors themselves. Libanius complains that Cynegius, the praetorian prefect of the east, had tricked Theodosius into supporting the destruction of temples by the Christian monks.[10] He states that in doing this Cynegius and the monks had been 'zealous for personal things of their own (*ta de idia sphisin espoudastai*)' (*Or.* 30.48, (F.III.114)) and that Cynegius had put his private pleasures (*tas oikeias hēdonas*) before [the emperor's] interests' by 'becoming servile' to the religious extremism of his wife (*Or.* 30.48 (F.III.114)).[11] To act for the common good Cynegius should have eased or avoided religious tensions, not incited them. Libanius makes a similar point in his *Oration* 45 to Theodosius *On the Prisoners*, probably delivered in 386 either before the emperor Theodosius or those close to him. He argues

---

[6] On the delivery and audience of *Oration* 30, see P. Petit 1956a: 495–8 and 507.

[7] Libanius was part of a shared 'persistent pagan tradition which insisted that Constantine, although he adopted Christianity for himself, nevertheless did not persecute pagans' (Wiemer 1994: 522).

[8] Or we could argue that by presenting Constantine in a positive light Libanius could suggest to Theodosius, the addressee of the oration, that there was some precedent for the preservation of traditional cult by a Christian emperor (Wiemer 1994: 522–3). Compare with Barnes 1981: 377, note 11).

[9] Compare with Themistius' view that God made religious choice 'depend on individual inclination' (*Or.* 5.68a).

[10] For the identification of Cynegius, see P. Petit 1951: 295 and 1994: 73–4.

[11] For the influence of his wife and the monks on Cynegius, see *Or.* 30.46–7 (F.III.113).

against the detention of prisoners for great lengths of time before their punishment and he gives the scruples, possibly religious scruples, of those involved as one reason for these delays.[12] He says:

> they say that it is not in their nature to put a man to test by flogging him or by giving him over to the sword in public. I would say to these people that they should know themselves and *stay in private life* (*idiōteuein*) and should not hope for office, when they are incapable of dispensing office. (*Or.* 45.27 (F.III.372), my emphasis)

It is likely that we see reference here to Christian officials whose personal religious beliefs were stopping them from performing their duty properly.[13] Libanius emphasizes that such personal beliefs should be kept in private and not brought into public life. The Christian establishment of the Church and some Christian individuals were drawing the boundaries between the sacred and the secular in a way that could potentially cause conflict between religious and political allegiances.[14] In response, Libanius identifies personal adherence to Christianity with the private and personal in order to leave the civic and the political as an autonomous, neutral public space that would not constantly be the site of religious conflict.

The flip side of Libanius' argument that the public and political sphere should be kept free of personal religious allegiances was that the private sphere should be a safe haven for personal religious views. In *Oration* 30 Libanius accepts that Theodosius' legislation on religious matters was not going to change and instead argues that the peasants who were being attacked by the Christian monks were not doing anything illegal:[15] they had not sacrificed an animal on the altars or given offerings of meal or libations, because they knew that this was forbidden (*Or.* 30.16–17 (F.III.96)). They *had* killed an ox away from the altar, used incense and invoked the gods but none of this was illegal because 'by banning the performance of one specific action you [Theodosius] automatically permit everything else' (*Or.* 30.18–19 (F.III.96–7)). In the midst of this Libanius makes one very particular type of defence of the practices of the Greek peasants:

---

[12] On this speech, see Norman 1969–77: vol. II, 155–9; Pack 1935: 39; and P. Petit 1956: 479.

[13] For the view that this passage refers to Christian officials see P. Petit 1955: 214. On Christian objections to corporal punishment, see *LRE*: 983 and, for example, Augustine, *Ep.* 100 in Atkins and Dodaro 2001: 134–6 (although Augustine did think corporal punishment was acceptable on some occasions for reform and deterrence). See also *Or.* 30.20 (F.III.98) and *Or.* 4.36 (F.I.314–15).

[14] On the kinds of crimes tried in the courts of bishops, areas of overlap with secular courts and limits to their authority, see Mathisen 2001: 3–4; Harries 2001: 68–82; Lenski 2001: 83–97; and Dossey 2001: 98–114.

[15] For fuller discussion of this passage and others like it, see Sandwell 2005: 98–118.

So even if they drank together amid the scent of all sorts of incense, they did not overstep the law, nor if in their toasts they all sang and invoked gods, unless indeed you accuse *the way of life that takes place in private (tēn oikoi diaitan gignomenēn)*.[16] (*Or.* 30.18 (F.III.96))

He makes a similar defence in his *Oration 14 In Defense of Aristophanes*, when he describes how Aristophanes had been accused of introducing a soothsayer to a man called Parnasius during the reign of Constantius. Parnasius had been accused of inquiring 'about one of those matters where information is forbidden' but Parnasius and Aristophanes defended themselves by saying that 'the matter had only to do with Parnasius' *private affairs (epi tōn idiōn)*' (*Or.* 14.16 (F.II.93–4)). Similarly, in his *Oration 1 The Autobiography*, Libanius bemoans Valens' failure to recognize the proper distinction between someone's using a soothsayer 'to learn from the gods something *of his own fortunes (peri tōn idiōn tōn autou)*' and someone's using a soothsayer 'for some matter of greater moment' (that is for political reasons) (*Or.* 1.171 (F.I.163)). It was possible to distinguish between treasonous divination/soothsaying to find out about politics and acceptable use of these practices for personal reasons. Ammianus Marcellinus makes a similar contrast on a number of occasions, for example during the magic trials under Valens when Valentinian and Libanius' relative Bassianus 'was accused of trying to gain foreknowledge of higher power' and defended himself thus saying 'that he had merely inquired about the sex of a child which his wife was expecting' (Amm. Marc. 19.2.5).[17]

Libanius formulated the private sphere as a place where people should be able to practise their religion freely and where those persecuted could express their true religious allegiance. He presented a turn to more private and less visible religious practices as one way for adherents of Graeco-Roman religion to avoid persecution under Christian emperors. In his *Oration 14 In Defence of Aristophanes*, he recounts that his friend Aristophanes was not allowed to bring offerings of incense, blood sacrifice or wine to the ruins of temples under Constantius. Instead he simply came 'with a sorrowing heart and grief-filled prayers', so as not to give anyone reason to attack him (*Or.* 14.41 (F.II.102)). In *Oration 18, The Funeral Oration over Julian*, Libanius again uses reference to people praying 'to the gods in silence and without the altars' for Julian to come to power in the reign of Constantius (*Or.* 18.112–16 (F.II.283–4)). Later, in the part of his *Oration 1 The Autobiography* that was written in the 380s Libanius describes how his brother was losing his sight and the measures he took to help him (*Or.* 1.199–201

---

[16] See *Or.* 30.18–19 (F.III.96–7).   [17] See also Amm. Marc. 19.12.12.

Other social identities in Libanius 159

(F.I.173–4) describing events of 381–2): seeing doctors and using charms but as a last resort going to the altars of the gods to mourn silently 'for it was not possible either to look upon the images or to utter a single word to them' (*Or.* 1.201 (F.I.173–4)). These compromises of religious practice were forced on Libanius but his acceptance of the turn to more private practices shows that he preferred to respond to persecution by making his allegiance to Graeco-Roman religion less visible in order to avoid religious conflict.

The notion of the private sphere of religion could also be used when Libanius sought to defend Christian friends. He wrote to Belaeus, Julian's governor of Arabia, to defend his friend Orion from accusations of possessing property taken from destroyed temples. He first defends Orion in pragmatic terms, by saying that he was now very poor and owned nothing that could be taken back. However, he then goes on to defend the very fact of Orion's allegiance to Christianity because this was Orion's private affair: 'if he differs from us in his opinion concerning the divine he harms himself only' (*Ep.* N.103.2 (F.819.2)).[18] In fact, he tells us in another letter, those persecuting Orion were only doing it for their personal gain under the guise of loyalty to the gods: 'these people are not secretive about the fact that they desire other people's property while they pretend that they are helping the gods' (*Ep.* B.130.6 (F.763)). On another occasion Libanius defends a Christian family friend, Eusebius, from the accusations of Julian's zealous governor Alexander 5/3 that he had undermined attempts to restore sacrifice. Libanius argues that Eusebius should be shown toleration because he was the kind of Christian who did not impose his religious allegiance onto others: 'in honouring *in his own way* he did not dishonour those who took their oath by Zeus' (my italics) (*Ep.* B. 98.3 (F.1411)).[19] The private nature of religious allegiance could also become an argument against forced religious conversion. In *Oration* 18 Libanius argues that Julian was right not to use force to convert people to the worship of the gods because such conversions result in 'a rough sketch of change not a real conversion of opinion' (*Or.* 18.122 (F.II.287–8)).[20] In a passage praising Julian's dislike of enforced conversions, he says: 'But a false opinion about the gods can never be driven out by chopping and burning: for even if the hand sacrifices, the conscience reproaches the hand and condemns its bodily weakness and values the things which it valued before' (*Or.* 18.122 (F.II.287–8)). Christians

---

[18] See also *Ep.* B.130 (F.763).
[19] See also *Ep.* F.1414, where Libanius defended the Christian Eusebius from a tax that Julian's governor of Syria, Alexander, was trying to impose on him. See also P. Petit 1955: 214.
[20] See also *Ep.* N.104 (F.1351) and *Or.* 5.67b–c and 68b and Eusebius, *VC* 2.48–60.

forced to sacrifice by Julian's governor Alexander would soon regret what they had done: even if 'in public (*exō*) he is persuaded by you who counsels good things and approaches the altars ... in private (*oikoi*) the wife, her tears and the night change their minds by persuasion and drag them away from the altars' (*Ep.* B. 98.1 (*Ep.* F.1411)). Religion imposed by the state will never work because the state cannot reach the personal sphere in which people make decisions about religious allegiance. This is true also for the forced conversion of non-Christian peasants under Theodosius. External displays of religious allegiance achieved by the violence of the monks are little more than a mask that barely conceals the old religious allegiance underneath: like an actor who 'is just the same as he was before putting on a mask, so here each of these people keeps himself unchanged but seems to those others to be changed' (*Or.* 30.28 (F.III.102)).

When it suited him, Libanius was able to articulate the religious sphere as a private matter that should be separate from political allegiance and public policy. In this Libanius was drawing on a traditional Graeco-Roman opposition of private and public religion.[21] By suggesting that the private sphere could be the appropriate space for religion, Libanius was turning this opposition to a new purpose that was suitable for the fourth century.

CIVIC IDENTITY AND RELIGIOUS ALLEGIANCE, I: THE SEPARATION OF CIVIC AND RELIGIOUS LIFE

Graeco-Roman religion has often been characterized as 'civic religion'.[22] Greeks and Romans did not define 'religion' as a category distinct from civic life but saw them as interwoven. Every city had its own array of divinities and its own temples, sacrifices, rituals, processions and festivals that laid claim to civic space and imbued the whole city with religious connotations.[23] The participation in festivals to their city's gods was a way for inhabitants of a city jointly to express their civic loyalty and their loyalty to the civic gods. It maintained communal solidarity among all levels of the population and enabled the community to represent itself as a whole.[24] This inextricable bond between civic and religious identity existed in Antioch as elsewhere.[25] Civic identity was still one of the central means by which

---

[21] As at Festus, *De Significatione Verborum* 245. See also Bakker 1994: 3–4; Rives 1995: 173–94; and Beard, North and Price 1998: vol. 1, 48–54.
[22] On 'religion of place,' see Zaidman and Schmitt-Pantel 1992; Rives 1995: 5, 9, 12–13 and Beard, North and Price 1998: vol. 1, 167–81. For some discussion of the civic model, see Davies 2004: 3–4.
[23] S. R. F. Price 1984: 101–32.   [24] S. R. F. Price 1984: 112–13.
[25] See Norris's fuller description of the gods, festivals and temples of early Roman Antioch, Norris 1990. See also Takács 2000: 199; Zetterholm 2003: 24–8; and Downey 1963: 120.

Libanius in the fourth century defined himself and those around him.[26] He was very proud of Antioch's place as a leading city in the ancient Graeco-Roman world. In his *Oration* 11 *In Praise of Antioch* he presents it as an equal to Rome and Athens and praises what he saw as its characteristic features.[27] He extols Antioch for being a centre of education, welcoming to strangers, temperate and attractive – especially the suburb of Daphne with its springs and groves – and for giving humans a safe place to live.[28] He spent much of his life defending the city of Antioch and its institutions, especially the civic council (*Oration* 48 *To the City Council* and *Oration* 49 *To the Emperor for the City Council*).[29] The communal feeling that civic life provided enabled sociability and friendship, which in turn provided the context for a moral and virtuous existence (*Or.* 19.157 (F.I.489) and *Or.* 23.26 (F.II.506)).[30] In the middle of a passage from *Oration* 11 Libanius describes the many beautiful stoas of the city that provide an ideal place for 'meetings and mixings with other [people]' and says that it is this characteristic that makes a really good city (*Or.* 11.213, 217 and 266 (F.I.510, 512 and 532)). In fact, many of the institutions of Antioch, such as the hippodrome, theatre and baths were beneficial precisely because they contributed to this communal sociability: they were in the middle of Antioch and therefore easily reachable by all (*Or.* 11.215 and 218–19 (F.II.511 and 512–13)). Libanius also often uses civic festivals as an image of societal happiness and as one of the ideal places for people to meet (*Or.* 11.172, 230 and 266 (F.I.494, 517 and 532)). Libanius' *Oration* 11 *In Praise of Antioch* shows us that as late as in 356 Antioch's sacred myths could still be seen as a binding factor for the civic community and civic identity.[31] Libanius gathers together all the main myths of the foundation of the city to show that divine will was behind this foundation and that the city was loved by the gods. He also describes how the foundation of the city was accompanied by the construction of a shrine or temple and how, as a result, the city continued to be guarded by divine protection throughout its

---

[26] For Libanius' use of models of civic life drawn from the classical past, see P. Petit 1955: 191, 193, 195; Liebeschuetz 1972; and also Schouler 1984: 836, 574–607; 608–11 and 836–49.
[27] Nock 1954: 76–82. On this oration and the idea of the city in Libanius, see also the recent work of Francesio 2004.
[28] *Or.* 5.13 (F.I.308); *Or.* 11.68, 103, 163 and 167 (F.I.458, 469, 491 and 492); *Or.* 18.187–8 (F.II.318–19); and *Or.* 23.27 (F.II.506–7). See also Downey 1961: 363.
[29] See also *Or.* 33.23–5 (F.III.177–8); *Or.* 20.40 and 49 (F.II.440 and 443); *Or.* 2.69 (F.I.260); *Or.* 11.2 (F.I.438); *Or.* 48.34–5 (F.III.444–5); and *Or.* 49.11 (F.III.458). See also Downey 1966b: 359 and 361 and Schouler 1984: 983.
[30] See also Schouler 1984: 601, 836–8, 916 and 964.
[31] See Norman 2000: 3 for the dating of this oration.

history (*Or.* 11.124 (F.I.476–7)).³² This link between the building of temples and the foundation of civilization and cities is also found in *Oration* 30 *For the Temples* where he argues that the first acts of primitive men were to build cities and simultaneously conceive of worship of the gods (*Or.* 30.4 (F.III.89)).³³

Libanius' love of civic life and the close association that he sometimes posits between civic life and religion have led some to characterize his religion as essentially traditional, civic and classical.³⁴ As Petit says, 'sa religion est avant tout civique et antiochéenne. Il croit et raisonne comme les Athéniens du Ve siècle, qui concevaient la sagesse du monde sous les traits de leur Athéna poliade.'³⁵ Libanius is presented as constantly harking back to a classical idea of civic religion and as being unable to conceive of any alternative. At moments when this civic religion appears to be lost Petit can only imagine Libanius to be distressed by 'le désordre d'un esprit confiné dans l'exaltation du passé'.³⁶ Petit was able to create this picture of Libanius because he chose to focus only on certain orations and certain points of view found in them. Clearly, Libanius did at times talk of civic religion as an ideal to which he would like to return. However, this does not mean that he was unable to envisage any alternative to the civic model of religion. Saying that Libanius was only able to conceive of his religious allegiance in the most civic and traditional sense means accepting that Libanius was unable to adjust to a situation in which Christianity was making inroads into civic religion. In fact, in the demands of daily life, Libanius was forced to have a more flexible attitude to the relationship between city and religion. Events of the fourth century had caused a rupture in the once coextensive fields of Graeco-Roman religion and civic life. Christianity was staking a claim to the city, and civic populations were no longer bound together by both communal feeling and religious allegiance. In such a context, Libanius' 'feel for the game' of what was appropriate for easy and successful social relations could only mean that at times he adjusted how he represented the relationship between civic and religious allegiance to suit the context. At certain times it was most appropriate and useful for Libanius to represent religion as civic and traditional; at other times, it was more appropriate for him to

---

³² For shrines and temples, see *Or.* 11.84 and 94 (F.I.464 and 467) and *Or.* 11.76 (F.I.461). For divine protection, see *Or.* 11.125 (F.I.477) and *Or.* 11.63 (F.I.456).
³³ See *Or.* 1.48 (F.II.107), where he describes Nicaea as the city of Dionysus and Nicomedia as the city of Demeter; see also *Or.* 1.102 (F.I.132–3); *Or.* 31.40 (F.III.143), where he describes Calliope as Antioch's guide; and *Or.* 2.69 (F.I.260), where all the gods are credited with protecting Antioch.
³⁴ P. Petit 1955, 191–3 and 196. See also Liebeschuetz 1972: 12; Schouler 1984: 918 and 1006; and, more recently, Swain 2004: 370.
³⁵ P. Petit 1955: 192.   ³⁶ P. Petit 1955: 211 and also Liebeschuetz 1972: 13.

take a different view. No one single representation characterizes Libanius' religion as a whole because his approach to the relationship between civic and religious identities was not idealized and monolithic but strategic and practical.

Oration 11 was a formal speech in praise of a city (a panegyric) in which it was appropriate for Libanius to describe Antioch in classicizing terms and to ignore the presence of Christians in the city: representing civic religion as if it had never changed was 'a normal part of compositions glorifying a city'.[37] During the reign of Julian too there were times when it was best to represent religion as civic and traditional. In a letter to the emperor Julian after he had left Antioch for his campaign in Persia Libanius reports the success of the religious restoration carried out by Julian's governor Alexander 5/3 (*Ep.* N.100 (F.811)); he confesses that he disapproved of Alexander's harsh methods at first but now approved of them as he could see that they were achieving results: the festival of Calliope had been restored, sacrifices were now taking place in the theatre and the gods were invoked in the applause of the audience (*Ep.* N.100 (F.811)). This should not be taken at face value as a 'true' description of the situation in Antioch or of Libanius' own religious ideals. Not long before, Julian had left Antioch in disgust at the city's resistance to his religious policy, and Libanius himself had played an active part in seeking to restore the relationship between his city and the emperor. Emphasizing the return of civic festivals to Antioch in the very last letter he sent to Julian was part of Libanius' attempt to convince him that he should no longer be angry at the city. On other occasions we see Libanius doing the same for other cities: he refers to the religious loyalty of cities when addressing those who shared his religious allegiance or who were close to Julian (*Ep.* B.159 (F.1458) to Acacius 8/1 in 365 about Athens and *Ep.* N.104.3 (F.1351) to Julian's governor Alexander 5/3 about Apamea).[38] Under Julian it was important for cities to present themselves as full supporters of Julian and of the revival of civic religion.

In an oration asking Julian to forgive Antioch for its bad attitude towards him Libanius argues that many temples were still standing in Antioch when Julian came to power and that people in Antioch had resisted those who had sought to destroy them under Constantius (*Or.* 15.53 (F.11.140)). This was the best way to convince Julian that Antioch was worthy of his attentions and should not be punished for its apparent resistance to him (and to counteract Julian, *Mis.* 361a). In the *Funeral Oration* written after Julian's

---

[37] Nock 1954: 77–9 and Downey 1966b: 363. See also Libanius, *Or.* 11.163, 167, 182–192 and 270 (F.1.491, 492, 498–502).
[38] See also *Or.* 15.34 (F.11.132).

death, in contrast, Libanius emphasizes that many temples in Antioch had been destroyed under Constantius and needed to be restored when Julian came to power in November 361 (*Or.* 18.126 (F.II.290)). Libanius' depiction of Constantius as a villain in *Oration* 18 required that he had destroyed the temples. Neither statement about the destruction or survival of the temples under Constantius was completely incorrect, but Libanius could put a slightly different spin on each in order to suit the point he was making. In the 380s Libanius could also represent the state of the temples in different ways in different contexts. In a letter to the general Richomer written in 392 he describes 'the many temples [of the gods] that we have in and around the city' (*Ep.* N.180.4 (F.1024)). In a letter to the priest Hierophantes, also written in the early 390s, however, Libanius refers to a 'great blow that the statues [of the gods] have been trampled underfoot' (*Ep.* N.171.2 (F.964)).[39] In the former context Libanius sought to present his friend Richomer with an Antioch that was still full of the temples of the gods, because Richomer was a pious worshipper of the gods (*Or.* 1.219 (F.I.180)). In the latter, Libanius wanted to highlight the reverse in his fortunes brought about at the time when he received Hierophantes' letter (*Ep.* N.171.4 (F.964)). As part of this he exaggerated all that was wrong with religion in Antioch, alongside a list of other problems (*Ep.* N.171.2–3 (F.964)). Libanius' representations of civic religion were not ideal statements that should be taken at face value but were used as a practical and rhetorical means to make a particular point or to have a particular effect.

At some moments we do see Libanius talking in mournful and vengeful terms of the harm done to the traditional cults. After Julian's death Libanius describes how 'the temples were either demolished or half-finished' and became the laughing stock of 'those accursed people' (*Or.* 18.287 (F.II.362)). His *Oration* 30 *On the Temples* includes another very vivid and emotionally charged reaction to the destruction of temples, this time in the reign of Constantius. The family and friends of Constantius were punished for his destruction and pillaging of the temples by the violence and death that befell them after the death of Constantine (*Or.* 30.38–9 (F.III.107–8)).[40] In his *Oration* 60 *Monody on the Shrine at Daphne* Libanius again shows great sadness and anger at the loss of the temple and he attributes similar emotions to the gods. In full rhetorical language he describes the distress of the Nymphs of Daphne, of Zeus, who also had a temple near by, and of Calliope, as they saw the shrine destroyed (*Or.* 60.12–13 (F.IV.319–20)).

---

[39] That this refers to the destruction of the statues of the gods, see Norman 1992: vol. II, 367, note b.
[40] See also the argument that the Riot of the Statues was a punishment for the destruction of the Temple of Nemesis (*Or.* 19.7 (F.II.387)).

Such passages are striking but they should not be seen as characteristic of a desperate and vengeful attitude in Libanius, as Petit might suggest, but simply as the appropriate representation of religion for the particular moment. The reference in *Oration* 18 was part of Libanius' denigration of Constantius and his exaggeration of the horror of the loss of Julian. That in *Oration* 30 was made in order to pin the whole blame for the destruction of the temples on the bad policies of Constantius and to appeal to Theodosius to allow them to stand (*Or.* 30.6–8 (F.III.90–1)).[41] *Oration* 60 *Monody on the Shrine at Daphne* was bound to be negative and to have a despairing tone: that was the whole point of a monody. Libanius himself shows us that this was not a straightforward representation of his own views when he describes to us the circulation of the oration. In one letter to his friend Demetrius 2/1 of Tarsus, Libanius mentions that he had sent Demetrius a copy of 'the lament I delivered on the fire and its ravages' (*Ep.* N.96.2 (F.785)). We also know from other letters that Libanius received similar orations from Demetrius and his circle in Tarsus in return. Libanius had requested that Demetrius send him his two speeches on the destruction of the shrine of Asclepius at Aegea (*Ep.* B.146.3 (F.727) of summer 362). He had also received a speech on this shrine of Asclepius from Acacius 7 of Tarsus, a friend of Demetrius', via Acacius' son, Titianus, who was a pupil of Libanius (*Ep.* B.147 (F.695) and *Ep.* B.148 (F.1342)). The tone of the letters about these orations is generally humorous and their primary concern is with the literary quality of the texts rather than the destruction of the temples.[42] The contrast between the grief expressed in *Oration* 60 and Libanius' attitude to the destruction of the temples described by Demetrius and Acacius must again make us wary of seeing any 'true' religious representation in his writings.[43] This simply was not the purpose of Libanius' writing and we should not look for it.

When it was more useful for him to do so and when it enabled him to promote toleration and coexistence over religious conflict, Libanius could separate out religion from aspects of civic life. In 363 he was appointed by Julian to the tribunal of three who were given the task of finding the culprit for burning the shrine of Apollo. While in this position Libanius showed great concern that the tribunal not be used as an excuse to persecute Christians.[44] In doing so he defended a Christian accused of the burning

---

[41] See also *Or.* 7.10 (F.1.376).
[42] See the discussion of divination in chapter 9 for more on these passages.
[43] Although this does not mean that Libanius and his friends from Tarsus did not believe in the powers of these divinities and their shrines.
[44] *Ep.* F.1376.

of the shrine by arguing that the gods were more concerned for 'souls than for shrines', so would not support their attacks (*Ep.* N.107.3 (F.1376)). Putting the good of people before the temples was what it meant to be truly religious and it was quite possible to worship the gods and to be religious without putting the temples first. Similar examples can be seen on the occasions when Libanius defended Christian friends and relatives who had built houses from materials taken from destroyed and pillaged temples (*Ep.* B.182.2 (F.724) on his friend Theodulus). Although Libanius says that the ideal situation would be to conserve and rebuild temples, he goes on to say that sometimes other considerations must be taken into account: the house 'by its beauty and its size contributes to making our city more beautiful than the others' (*Ep.* B.182.2 (F.724)). Rather than destroy the house, Julian's officials should find a way to show themselves 'to be concerned about the god' as well as 'not unconcerned about the city' (*Ep.* B.182.2 (F.724)).[45] A slightly different distinction between the sacred and the secular spheres can be seen in events in the 380s when Libanius had to defend the existence of Graeco-Roman temples to the Christian emperor Theodosius. In *Oration* 30 *To Theodosius In Defence of the Temples* he argues that it would be wrong to destroy the temples, because they were an essential physical part of the city: 'if our cities owe their fame to the temples' then people must be 'zealous for their maintenance as part of the body of the cities' (*Or.* 30.42 (F.III.110)). But Libanius does allow that it would be acceptable for these temples to lose their religious functions if by this they could continue to stand: temples could, for example, be used as buildings for tax collection and not for any religious function (*Or.* 30.42 (F.III.110)). In the examples involving Christians and the possession of temple property, the temples were separated out from, and presented as less important than, the good of the whole city. In the example from Theodosius' reign, the close relationship between the temples and the city and civic good is emphasized but only by playing down the overtly religious characteristics of the temples ('even though not used as temples' (*Or.* 30.42 (F.III.110)).

In cities that were now often of mixed religious allegiance and in which public aspects of Graeco-Roman cult were in decline, religion could no longer act as a binding feature of civic life and civic community in any straightforward way. The point of many civic festivals had originally been to assert the shared civic and religious values of the community. The New Year, or Kalends, festival, which was held every year on the first and third day of

---

[45] See also *Ep.* B.130 (F.763); *Ep.* N.103 (F.819); and *Ep.* N.105 (F.1364). Contrast these with his more negative comments about money now being spent on private homes in *Or.* 7.

January, is a good example of this: it was intended to reassert communal life in opposition to the social divisions and classifications of society.[46] There was gift giving across social classes and people could ridicule and make jokes about their social superiors.[47] Libanius' *Oration 9 On the Kalends* is a traditional *encomium* of the festival that describes it in almost idyllic terms, listing all the good things it had brought to civic life. It was a time of joy and enhanced communal feeling, when enmities were forgotten, people forgave each other and even prisoners could be happy.[48] As Libanius states, 'it reconciles citizen with citizen, stranger with stranger, child with child and woman with woman' (*Or.* 9.14 (F.1.396)). However, in the last two sentences of the oration, the idyll is broken and Libanius shows us that the overtly religious elements of the festival are no longer practised: the gods no longer enjoyed sacrifice at the festival because this was forbidden by law (*Or.* 9.18 (F.1.398)). While the Kalends did still help to reinforce communal feelings in fourth-century Antioch, the traditional, quintessential aspect of public religion, blood sacrifice, was no longer part of this. By deviating from the encomium form, which need not make any mention of unpleasant realities, Libanius must have been making an intentional point. It is possible that he was using this oration to answer Chrysostom's criticisms that the festival was an occasion for idolatry and for 'devils to parade around the agora'.[49] If this were the case, Libanius might see benefit in emphasizing the fact that the more overt aspects of Graeco-Roman religion were no longer part of the festival.

Even if public festivals such as the Kalends no longer combined religion with the communal good, they could still be given some religious interpretation by Libanius albeit in a personal form. Libanius' *Oration 5 In Praise of Artemis*, like his oration on the Kalends, at first appears to be a traditional oration, this time in praise of a goddess. The main body of the oration lists the goddess's main attributes and achievements with full references to classical literature (*Or.* 5.1–41 (F.1.305–17)). It then goes on to describe the festival of Artemis as it was celebrated in his own day: with boxing matches in the suburb of Meroë and the tribes of the city were willing to spend large amounts of money on providing the boxers (*Or.* 5.42–4 (F.1.317–8)). It is here that we begin to see an element of fourth-century reality imposing itself. At one time the whole city had attended the festival because it had been considered impious not to go, but now the 'festival had become dull' and people did not attend in such large numbers (*Or.* 5.43 (F.1.317–8)). The

---

[46] *Or.* 9.11 (F.1.395–6). See Gleason 1986: 109–11   [47] *Or.* 9.9 and 15 (F.1.395 and 397).
[48] See Schouler 1984: 916 and Pack 1935: 78.   [49] See Chrysostom *On the Kalends*.

public, communal element of this festival to Artemis had deteriorated but this did not mean it had become totally irreligious or meaningless to Libanius. The end of the oration moves even further away from the traditional encomium form by recounting a personal experience that he had at the time of the festival. A doorway in his school had collapsed and Libanius and his students were only just saved, something that he attributed to the goddess. His students had stayed away from class because the festival of Artemis was taking place that day and they 'felt the fear of the goddess', and Libanius himself was saved because the goddess made him move away from the doorway just before it fell down (*Or.* 5.45–52 (F.I.318–20)).[50] By reinterpreting a public festival, in personal terms Libanius was giving it a significance that was more suitable for the fourth-century context. Except during the reign of Julian, it was quite common for traditional civic festivals no longer to have their religious as well as their communal functions. This is true of the Olympic festival of Antioch. It was only under Julian that it was possible to offer full worship to Zeus at this festival, and after Julian's death Libanius describes how worshippers of the gods could no longer live up to their expectations for the festival but must 'fulfil our duty to the god in the best way we can' (*Ep.* N.125 (F.1180)).[51] This 'best way we can' could mean giving an offering of an oration on Zeus' altar, in 384 (*Or.* 1.222 (F.1.181)), or placing a picture of Asclepius in the Temple of Zeus Olympias, in 365 (*Ep.* N.143.4 (F.1534)).[52] In this way the festival could still be seen as religious to those who worshipped the gods in more personal ways, even after sacrifice was forbidden.

It was no longer possible for Libanius to identify community, civic life and religion with each other at all times, as had once been the case. Men no longer 'served their city' and in doing so 'served the gods'; the two were no longer synonymous.[53] In response to this, Libanius at times adjusted traditional associations between religiosity and temples and festivals – the basic features of civic religion. At other times, he could articulate the relationship between temples, festivals and the good of the civic community differently so that they no longer had to be seen as aligned. Such adjustments and re-articulations present very different views of the relationship between religion and civic community from those found in *Oration* 11 as well as from the moments of despair that we have considered above. At certain times, when it was appropriate and useful, Libanius represented religion in civic and traditional terms. At other times, however, he was able

---

[50] Compare with Swain 2004: 369–70.   [51] See also *Ep.* N.47 (F.81).
[52] On hymns as a gift to the gods and the importance of cult hymns, see S. R. F. Price 1999: 37.
[53] Ward-Perkins 1998: 393.

Other social identities in Libanius 169

to rethink the relationship between religion and civic life as this too became useful.

CIVIC IDENTITY AND RELIGIOUS ALLEGIANCE, II: RELIGIOUS DIFFERENCE AND THE CIVIC COMMUNITY

The ability to distinguish civic community and religious community was absolutely essential in the fourth-century situation, in which cities contained people of different religious allegiances. This was particularly important when Libanius had to represent the city of Antioch to Christian and non-Christian emperors. The emperor Julian came to Antioch soon after coming to power, hoping to use the city as the base for his military campaigns in Persia and for the heartland of his religious restoration. The city was, however, not very responsive to Julian's personality or his religious policies and in February AD 363 an angry Julian left the city to embark on his Persian campaign threatening never to return. Libanius' *Oration 15 The Embassy to Julian* and *Oration 16 To the Antiochenes on the Emperor's Anger* were both written in response to this situation. *Oration 16* was ostensibly addressed to the people of Antioch, although it is not clear that it was actually delivered.[54] Its purpose was to chastise the Antiochenes for their treatment of Julian and to persuade them to beg forgiveness from him. *Oration 15* was addressed to Julian and was written after a delegation of the city council and Libanius himself had met with Julian and failed to gain his forgiveness. It was sent on to Julian on campaign but would probably not have reached him before his death in June of that year. If it did, then Julian never responded. In these orations Libanius, as a worshipper of the gods, sought to argue for an emperor who also worshipped the gods before a city of mixed religious allegiance (*Oration 16*) and to represent a city of mixed religious allegiance to an emperor who worshipped the gods (*Oration 15*). This caused him certain difficulties as he could not address or refer to the citizen body as a unified whole with a shared religious identity as would once have been possible. At one point in *Oration 16* Libanius is forced to address those of different religious allegiance in the city separately. He turns first to address the Christians and says that to gain forgiveness from Julian they should 'surrender (their) city to Zeus and the other gods' (*Or.* 16.46 (F.II.178)). Their choice was, 'either to continue to be hated or to profit twofold by procuring the good will of the emperor and by recognising those ones who really occupy heaven' (*Or.* 16.48 (F.II.179)). He then goes on to

---

[54] See P. Petit 1956: 486–7.

address the worshippers of the gods saying, 'To those of you who feel that they are treated unjustly, because even though they do not share in the other charges and even though they sacrifice to the gods, they are to be punished with the impious and with those called to account for other offences' (*Or.* 16.50 (F.II.179)). Libanius separates those who worship the Graeco-Roman gods from the Christian majority who refuse to do so and, according to him, are really guilty of making Julian angry. This is one of the few points where Libanius directly contrasts those who worship the gods with those who do not recognize them. At first, this appears to be a way of excusing from blame those who shared Julian's religious allegiance. However, Libanius goes on to point out that Julian was not going to accept this distinction between Christians and those who worshipped the gods because he was going to hold the whole city responsible for not implementing his religious policies. Libanius describes how at his personal meeting with Julian to ask him to forgive the city, Julian retorted by quoting a line of Hesiod: 'often a whole city has been punished for one wicked man'.[55] To show what Julian meant, Libanius then outlines to the city various examples from classical literature of whole communities being punished for the sins of a few.[56] In this way, Julian and Libanius use examples from the classical past to explain the present situation, in which there was no longer a united religious-civic community and in which pagans might be punished for the crimes of Christians.

Oration 15 shows similar concerns. At one point in the oration Libanius seeks to defend the city for the support it gave to Constantius and his religious policies and argues that in fact many who worshipped the gods had taken a stance against Constantius' actions. Libanius argues that while many in Antioch had been involved in demolishing temples, there were also people who saved temples from demolition (*Or.* 15.53 (F.II.140)). He goes on to describe how a friend of his, Celsus 3/1 (Julian's *praeses Ciliciae* in 362), could give evidence of this. He says,

Here too there were some who were telling and teaching what they knew of your nature ... Do you want me to call as witness of this someone [Celsus] who was long ago given a place to stay by you ... Or does it harm myself and my witness that we are both citizens here? We are, majesty, *part of the larger number of people and related to them*, yet certainly we would never be so devoted to family or country as to put them before truth and you. (*Or.* 15.50–51 (F.II.139), my italics)

---

[55] Hesiod, *Op.* 240. See also Libanius, *Or.* 16.50 (F.II.179).
[56] On Libanius' use of the archaic concept of collective responsibility, see Schouler 1984: 837–40.

Libanius again singles out the worshippers of the gods from the 'larger number of people' in Antioch and suggests that their loyalty to Julian was greater than their loyalty to this now largely Christianized civic population, hoping to gain Julian's favour for them. However, as we saw in the discussion of *Oration* 16, it is also clear in this passage that Julian was not easily going to accept this distinction between Christians and worshippers of the gods in the city. Libanius clearly fears that his and Celsus' appeals would be harmed by the fact that they lived among Christians. In this oration too Libanius tells us that Julian was intending not to punish individuals but the 'whole city', because rather than seeing just a few (Christian) individuals as responsible, he claimed that 'the corruption has permeated the whole' (*Or.* 15.66 (F.11.145)). Libanius thus clearly knew that he also needed to try a different tactic from simply singling out those in the city who shared Julian's religious allegiance. To understand this we have to turn back to *Oration* 15, where Libanius tries to excuse the people of Antioch for not praying 'as a community (*dēmosiai*)' to the gods for Julian to become emperor, arguing that the restrictions and hostility of the reign of Constantius had prevented this. These restrictions meant that they had been forced to pray for Julian secretly and privately instead: 'each either on his own or in groups with this desire' prayed 'ceaselessly to Zeus to put an end to all that was ruining the empire' (that is, Constantius' reign) (*Or.* 15.45 (F.11.137–8)).[57] Here Libanius tries to suggest that everyone in the city had *wanted* to offer Julian public prayers but was not able to, so turned to private forms of prayer. He does not separate out worshippers of the gods as a private group within the community of Antioch as a whole but rather opposes the private worship of each Antiochene individually for Julian to the public worship they would have carried out if it had been possible. Libanius continues by arguing that once Julian had become emperor the whole city did pray for him publicly, filling the theatres and hillside to do so (*Or.* 15.48 (F.11.138)). In such statements, Libanius was trying to present the community of Antioch as if it were unified in support of Julian and the gods, despite all evidence to the contrary. It was a rhetorical ploy to suggest to Julian that the whole city was not as bad as it seemed, because it was the whole city that Julian was threatening at that moment. Thus Libanius describes how, if Julian forgave the city and came back to winter in Antioch, he would be escorted into the city 'with cries of gladness and the usual acclamations from the people' (*Or.* 15.19 (F.11.126)). He argues that the civic gods of Antioch still

---

[57] See also *Or.* 13.14 (F.11.68), in which Libanius describes how elite men throughout the empire 'united' in their wish for Julian to come to the throne with 'hidden prayer and secret sacrifice'. This can be contrasted with *Ep.* B.75.4 (F.1367).

cared for the city, so ignoring the loyalty that many Antiochenes now had to the Christian god, in order to persuade Julian that he should forgive a city protected by such gods (*Or.* 15.79 (F.II.152)).

In *Oration* 15 and *Oration* 16 Libanius was trying to appease Julian and to make the city of Antioch come round to the emperor's views; he did not have to guess what Julian was most angry and concerned about because he had first-hand knowledge from the emperor's own words. We know that Julian's *Misopogon* was publicly displayed in Antioch, so Libanius could have read it even if he had not received a copy personally from Julian. We also know, though, that Julian personally addressed his complaints about the city to Libanius in conversation.[58] Libanius himself would thus have been very aware of the nature of the emperor's views and objections to Antioch. Because Julian would probably have written in the *Misopogon* something similar to what he told Libanius in person, we can see there the complaints to which Libanius was responding in his own works.[59] We learn from the *Misopogon* that, among other things, Julian objected specifically to the fact that Antiochenes had adopted 'Christ . . . as the guardian of [their] city instead of Zeus, the god of Daphne and Calliope' (*Mis.* 357c) and that they were unified in their Christianity. It is this difference in religious allegiance between the city and himself that Julian posits as the reason for their bad relationship. As Julian himself states, the 'common people' of Antioch hated him because of their 'atheism' while the wealthy citizens did so because he adhered to 'the ordinances of the sacred rites which (their) forefathers observed' (*Mis.* 357d). The civic, but Christian, unity of the city becomes something negative for Julian. At one point Julian sarcastically praises the population of Antioch for their 'unanimity' and for being a 'city at one' in their preference for licentious festivals and bad behaviour rather than the solemn religious festivals that Julian preferred (*Mis.* 356b). This Christian, anti-Julian unanimity of the city also resulted in the citizens of Antioch not worshipping the gods and not celebrating the festivals properly. Julian was particularly upset about the state of the festival of Apollo when he visited the shrine of Apollo at Daphne. He was shocked that the only offering was a single goose brought by the priest from his home and that the city as a whole had offered nothing to the god (*Mis.* 362b). For Julian this was a clear example of the disruption of the normal civic-public form of the festival. Every tribe of the city and the city as a whole should have brought offerings 'on (their) behalf and on behalf of the

---

[58] *Or.* 15.52 (F.II.139).
[59] Gleason states that in *Oration* 16 Libanius tried to refute the *Misopogon* point by point (Gleason 1986: 107).

city's welfare' (*Mis.* 362d). The one 'private' sacrifice by the priest was not sufficient because 'it befits the city to offer both private (*idia*) and public (*dēmosia*) sacrifices' (*Mis.* 363a). It was not lack of wealth that prevented the Antiochenes from making these offerings, because there were lands owned both by the city and privately (*idia*) from which offerings could have been provided (*Mis.* 362c). Instead of spending their money on these offerings as they should have done, says Julian, the people of Antioch have spent it on 'private dinners (*idia deipna*)' or let their wives carry it off to the Christians (*Mis.* 362d). In these passages, Julian berates the city of Antioch for not fulfilling its religious duties and for letting its Christian majority dominate. By manipulating ideas of the private and the public Libanius could answer some of these concerns put forward by Julian.

During the reign of Valens and Valentinian, Libanius rarely sought to address the emperors and spoke out less on matters of public concern. It was in the reign of Theodosius that he again attempted to represent the city of Antioch to an emperor and his officials in his orations on the Riot of the Statues of 387. Libanius wrote five orations on the subject of the riot. One of these was delivered after the riot when Antiochenes were fleeing the city in fear of the emperor's punishment (*Oration* 23) and two were simply speeches praising officials involved in gaining the emperor's forgiveness for the city (*Oration* 21 and *Oration* 22).[60] The other two orations, however, purport to have been delivered to Theodosius as part of the process of gaining his forgiveness even though they were actually written after the event (*Oration* 19 and *Oration* 20). While it is no longer thought that Libanius was directly mimicking Chrysostom's sermons on the riot it is likely that he presented himself as playing an active role in the situation precisely because he was competing with Christian claims to represent the city. We do not, however, have to see Libanius' orations as purely literary or fictional constructs that had nothing whatsoever to do with resolving the problems caused by the riots. In his autobiography Libanius describes how he presented petitions to the imperial commission that came to Antioch to apprehend the guilty (*Or.* 1.253 (F.1.192)). It is quite possible that he did this and that he wrote up these petitions as formal orations readdressed to the emperor himself for publication after the situation had been resolved. Some of Libanius' arguments made at the time to the commission might thus have found their way into the orations that we have now. Certainly all the orations on the riot show Libanius dealing with the problem of how he, as a worshipper of the gods, could represent the mixed religious population of Antioch in

---

[60] For a recent study of these orations, see Quiroga Puertas 2006.

the reign of an emperor of one particular religious allegiance – this time, the Christian Theodosius.

One of the most pressing problems in these orations was the question of who was responsible for the riot.[61] Libanius tried to argue to Theodosius that the whole city was not to blame, but that a small minority had started the trouble, variously named as foreign inhabitants of the city, the circus claque, Christians and evil spirits. Modern historians have attempted to identify one of these groups as particularly responsible for the riot.[62] However, as French has shown, Libanius' attempt to blame the riot on a minority was a rhetorical ploy to excuse the city and should not be taken as a direct description of reality.[63] Foreigners, the circus claque and evil spirits were all stereotypically blamed for any form of social disruption and we clearly cannot identify one rather than the other as being responsible. What is interesting for present purposes is that the Christians were one of the groups on whom Libanius tried to pin the blame. At two points in the orations addressed to Theodosius Libanius presents the riot as starting when Christians turned to pray to their God for relief from the heavy tax impositions made by Theodosius. In *Oration* 19 Libanius describes how the majority of citizens realized that they would be incapable of paying the tax and started supplicating to their God outside the courtroom: 'They had recourse to the help coming from the God, calling on him in case it was possible to persuade you to diminish the burden of the tax' (*Or.* 19.25 (F.II.397)). The supplications to the Christian God were not themselves a problem but from the supplications a group of people went on to 'cause a disturbance' and went in search of Flavianus, bishop of Antioch, which suggests that the group involved was Christian in the majority.[64] When they did not find Flavian they turned to violence. A similar chain of events is *Oration* 20, where Libanius described reports that an 'unscrupulous gang' pushed the worried Christians into violence. Libanius says,

Our city was careless towards a good emperor when, after the reading of the rescript, they shook off the bonds of his rule to have recourse in appearance to the God (*en tōi dokein epi ton theon*) for it is clear that these words could not remove any of the complaints. An evil gathering made a start to this in the courtroom and increased more and more in number from outside its doors.[65] (*Or.* 20.3 (F.II.422))

---

[61] As at *Or.* 19.8–9 (F.II.388); *Or.* 21.5 (F.II.451–2); and *Or.* 22.9 (F.II.475).
[62] See, for example, Browning 1952.   [63] French 1998: 469–71.
[64] Although Libanius also blames an evil spirit and those who love the pantomime.
[65] This is one of the examples of Libanius' use of a pluralist conception of divinity in an oration addressed to Theodosius.

In another oration Libanius again blames the Christians, this time in a more forthright way,

> First, near the throne and view of the governor they let out a rebellious shout. This had the appearance of supplication, but, in reality, was disobedience. As when we are in great trouble we are accustomed to call upon the gods and ask them to help us, thus, on that occasion, those shouting called upon their God to pity them for reaching this state worthy of pity because of these decrees. (*Or.* 22.5 (F.II.473–4))

These people calling out to the Christian God then turned to violence and encouraged others to join them, so acting as the primary instigators of the riot (*Or.* 22.6 (F.II.474)). The obvious explanation for this is that Libanius was trying to shift blame for the riot from the minority in the city who worshipped the gods onto the Christians but something more complicated seems to be going on – he seems to be excusing the fact that people in such a situation appealed to divine powers of any kind, whether the gods or God, instead of turning to the secular power of the emperor (*Or.* 22.5 (F.II.473–4)). This is what lies behind his comments in *Oration* 20 and *Oration* 19 that calling to the God could not 'remove the grievances' or 'diminish the burden'. Thus Libanius also has to excuse those who called on a Graeco-Roman god for the same reasons: 'What if they said these things not to you [the emperor] but to Helios? Shall we punish those mourning for their lamentations too?'[66] (*Or.* 19.42 (F.II.404)). Libanius is less worried that Theodosius would punish these people for appealing to a Graeco-Roman god than that he would be angry because they appealed to any god rather than to him.[67] Making specific reference to the fact that many in Antioch called on the Christian God did still, however, serve a specific purpose for Libanius. He emphasizes that the Christians were calling on the same God as Theodosius himself 'personally prayed' to, so making a strong link between the city and the emperor through their shared Christian religion. As Libanius says, 'majesty, you have not been wronged by anyone, for what wrong is done when someone wants to have as a helper the one from whom you personally pray for good things?' (*Or.* 19.27 (F.II.397)). Theodosius could not punish the whole city, because it would mean also punishing those who shared his religious allegiance. As Libanius says later in the oration, 'How can you punish these people with a fine when it is not possible to prove they have been wrongdoers? Especially because, if

---

[66] This is an example of Libanius' use of reference to Helios when making a contrast with Christians.
[67] If this reading is correct and if Libanius had accurately assessed the concerns of Theodosius, this is a striking example of Theodosius' expression of a secular view of the role of government as late as 387.

this is applied to all, you will be seen punishing those whom you value as friends because they honour God' (*Or.* 19.43 (F.II.404)). Those calling on the Graeco-Roman god were mentioned so that Libanius could be sure that they would be excused, but it was only those calling on the Christian god who could be really useful to Libanius at this time. In blaming the Christians for starting the riot, he was thus doing something subtler than simply using them as scapegoats in order to exonerate non-Christians in the city. He was also trying to make it harder for Theodosius to inflict any serious punishment on the city by calling on his religious sentiments, even though these sentiments were different from Libanius' own. Libanius was able to do this only because he could manipulate the relationships between religious groups within the city, the city as a whole and an emperor of one particular religious allegiance. By being able to disengage Graeco-Roman religion from the city and by presenting Christians as the majority religion in Antioch he could better represent and ensure the safety of the city as a whole. Religious difference in the city became a rhetorical ploy for Libanius, something he could use at a particular rhetorical and diplomatic juncture in order to save the city that was so precious to him.

In this section we have seen Libanius thinking about and seeking to make sense of what constituted the civic community in the fourth century AD. He had to rethink how religious allegiance related to civic identity and to consider what happened when religious identity and civic identity could no longer be considered as synonymous. Rather than formulating answers consistently or writing an explicit treatise on the matter, we see Libanius reacting in a more subtle way to these changes. Concerns about public and private worship instead impact on how he formulates the problems that confront him in fourth-century Antioch and on the different answers that he gives to these problems in different situations. As we have seen, he could give what appear to be contradictory answers at different times because he would often present the most appropriate argument for the moment rather than try to work out any consistent position on these matters. What is common to the way he formulates these answers though is the opposition between communal and personal or private religious expression.

RELIGIOUS ALLEGIANCE AND ETHNIC IDENTITY

'Ethnic' or cultural identity is the final form of social identity that we must examine in relation to Libanius' understanding of religious allegiance. He clearly saw being a Hellene as an important part of his identity. He placed a very high value on Greek *paideia*, Greek culture and education, and praised those who were well versed in it. The question that we have to ask is how this love of *paideia* related to Libanius' religion. Modern scholars have made much of the relationship between 'Greekness' and adherence to the worship of the traditional gods in the fourth century. Some have aligned being Hellenic with a shared culture that could ease conflict between those of different religious allegiances, while others have seen it as a unifying feature of a revived Graeco-Roman religion and so as the antithesis of Christianity. Both views can be supported by material from ancient writings. Bowersock argues that the term *Hellene* first came into common usage among adherents of Graeco-Roman religion to describe their religion in conjunction with their culture. He suggests that we first see this in the writings of Iamblichus of Apamea but that for most other non-Christians too Greek language and literature became the binding feature of the traditional cults in the eastern part of the Roman empire.[68] This notion of the importance of the term *Hellene* to religious matters can be supported by Julian's use of it to describe allegiance to the Graeco-Roman gods as well as to refer to knowledge of classical literature.[69] Julian was making a strong statement that there could be no compromise between being Christian and being truly Greek. One had to choose whether one was Christian or Greek, and Christians should not be allowed to 'nibble at the learning of the Greeks': they should be content with the use of their own scripture.[70] Not all adherents of Graeco-Roman religion agreed with Julian in this. Athanassiadi has shown that many elite men of the late Roman world disagreed with Julian over what it meant to be Greek and saw it as a purely cultural matter that could be detached from religion.[71] Ammianus, like many others, saw it as 'harsh' and 'inhumane' that Julian forbade 'Christian rhetoricians and grammarians to teach unless they consented to worship the divinities' (Amm. Marc. 25.4.20 and 22.10.7).

It is clear from this that just by saying that Libanius was a Hellene we do not learn very much. We still have to ask what kind of Hellene he was. Many have assumed that Libanius followed Julian wholeheartedly in his definition of Greekness as synonymous with worship of the Graeco-Roman gods. Festugière, for example, has argued that Libanius, like Julian, saw a close link between classical culture and Graeco-Roman religion because both came

---

[68] Bowersock 1990a: 10 and 13 and also Trombley 1994: vol. 1, 127–8 and 277.
[69] Athanassiadi 1992: 8 and 121–8.
[70] Julian, *Against the Galileans* 229c and *Ep.* 61. See also R. Smith 1995: 198–9, 208 and 212–15. I must also thank Gillian Clark for an illuminating discussion on the intentions of Julian's edict on the Christian teachers.
[71] Athanassiadi 1992: 1–12 and 121–60.

under attack in the reign of Constantius.[72] Those who support this view have made much of Libanius' statement that 'religion and oratory are ... interconnected and interrelated' (*Or.* 62.8 (F.IV.350)). However, occasional assertions of the religious nature of oratory do not prove that Libanius saw being Greek as directly associated with allegiance to the Graeco-Roman gods. Rather than extrapolate general conclusions from such occasional statements and categorize him ourselves we need to explore Libanius' own conception and use of the term.[73] Haubold and Miles have shown that he was interested in comparing what Hellenism meant in his own time with what it meant to Aelius Aristides in the second century AD.[74] Schouler has shown that the term *Hellene* appears frequently in Libanius' work even if a reasonable proportion of these uses refer to historical contexts.[75] He has argued that for Libanius Greekness is mainly a geographic entity, 'une *réalité ethnique*' and a linguistic community.[76] As such, it could be confined to those born in Greece but through the notion of educational ideals could also be made accessible to a much wider group of people.[77] With regard to the role of religion in Hellenic identity, Schouler suggests that there were many literary aspects to Libanius' understanding and representation of religion: he often used references to classical culture and traditional literary topoi to describe the religious situation.[78] However, Schouler stops short of saying that for Libanius religion was a defining feature of being Greek. This subtle distinction between allowing that Libanius could see Greek culture in religious terms and assuming that he saw Greekness as defined by religion is important. Libanius did not use the term *Hellenes* to describe religious allegiance but used it to refer to a person's racial origins,[79] their cultural and literary background,[80] or, finally, to those key Hellenic qualities of humaneness and forgiveness.[81] The cultural, ethical and ethnic

---

[72] For this argument, see Festugière 1959: 25–39.

[73] This subject requires much greater exploration than space allows here. An in-depth study of how Libanius uses the term *Hellene* in relation to how Julian uses it would also be very worth while.

[74] Haubold and Miles 2004: 24–34.   [75] Schouler 1991: 267.

[76] Schouler 1991: 267–8 and 270–2.   [77] Schouler 1991: 268–9.   [78] Schouler 1991: 275.

[79] *Ep.* B.6 (F.333); *Ep.* B.20 (F.801); *Ep.* B.69.1 (F.108); *Ep.* N.66.1 (F.192); *Ep.* N.94.4 (F.760) – sons of the Greeks; *Ep.* N.109.1 (F.1402); *Ep.* F.188.1; *Ep.* F. 203.1; *Ep.* F.652.1; *Ep.* F.823.3; *Ep.* F.950.2; *Ep.* F.1504.3; *Or.* 5.33 (F.I.314); *Or.* 10.14 (F.II.405); *Or.* 11.58, 63, 103, 119, 184 (F.I.455, 456, 470, 475 and 499); *Or.* 14.12 (F.II.92); *Or.* 15.25 (F.II.129); *Or.* 17.1 (F.II.206); *Or.* 19.13 (F.II.389–90); *Or.* 32.23 (F.III.159); *Or.* 59.65 (F.IV.240); and *Or.* 64.6 and 12 (F.II.424 and 428). On the use of the term 'children of the Greeks' in classical Greek texts as a racial/ethnic designation, see Schatkin's footnote in her translation of *De S. Bab. Contra Jul. et Gent.* 1 (PG 50.533, Schatkin and Harkins 1983). See also Swain 2004: 397.

[80] *Ep.* N.15 (F.469); *Ep.* N.99.2 (F.810); *Ep.* B.118 (F.75); *Ep.* F.347.2; *Ep.* F.606.1; *Ep.* F.859.3; *Ep.* F.1085.1; *Or.* 2.74 (F.261–2)); *Or.* 14.12 (F.II.92); and *Or.* 58.3 (F.IV.33).

[81] *Ep.* N.71 (F.217); *Ep.* N.113 (F.1120); *Ep.* F.411.4; *Or.* 15.22, 25 and 27–37 (F.II.128, 129–34); *Or.* 43.18 (F.III.347); and *Or.* 59.94 (F.IV.255). At times Greek values can be described as being 'god-like' but

aspects thus appear to have dominated Libanius' understanding of Greekness and there is little evidence that Libanius shared the desire to make Greek religion synonymous with Greek culture and literature.[82] As Petit has shown, Libanius, like many others, did not approve of Julian's ban on Christian teachers and did not once mention it in his praise of Julian.[83] Libanius did not want his beloved Greek culture to be dragged into religious conflicts and did not want religious difference to be made a point of conflict between groups who were asserting their control over Greek language and literature. Classical culture was for him a way to ease the differences between religious groups rather than a point of difference that could lead to conflict. Through his *Oration* 11 *In Praise of Antioch*, he could suggest a sense of continuity with Antioch's classical past precisely because it concealed the religious conflict and competition that characterized the last years of Constantius' reign and the first months of Julian's rule. Using classical references in orations addressed to the Christian emperors was also a way to draw on a shared classical heritage and so to gloss over religious differences. Libanius' use of the term *Hellene* to describe shared cultural and moral values can thus be contrasted with the terminology he employs to describe religious allegiance, in which distinctively religious factors were prominent.[84] The Jews provide the only case where we probably do see an alignment of religious and ethnic identity in Libanius' writings. The distinctive status of the Jews as people who were simultaneously both a religious and an ethnic group is recognized by ancient and modern alike, and Libanius seems to go along with this view. The only time that we might see Libanius take a different approach is when he refers to the Jewish tenant farmers who worked his land as 'real' or 'proper' Jews – *Ioudaioi tōn panu* (*Or.* 47.13 (F.IV.410)). This has led some scholars to debate whether he was using these words to designate a particularly religious group of Jews or he was simply mocking them and their difference from others in general because they were causing him problems.[85] The later view is now accepted as the most likely. Aside from the exceptional example of the Jews Libanius usually sought to make a clear distinction between religious and ethnic or

---

this is very different from saying that there was a direct association between Greekness and religious allegiance (*Ep.* N.113 (F.1120) and *Or.* 15.27–37 (F.II.129–34)). Norman's suggestion that a 'good (*chrēstos*)' *Hellene* in *Ep.* N.114.5 (F.1431) refers to this man's religious allegiance as well as his ethnic origin and education is not provable, especially as we do not know to whom it refers.

[82] As Festugière tried to argue on the basis of passages *Or.* 13.1 (F.II.63) and *Or.* 14.27 (F.II.97). These, however, are clearly used in contexts when Libanius would want to show his loyalty to Julian.
[83] P. Petit 1955: 208. See his interpretation of *Or.* 18.158 (F.II.304).
[84] As Bowersock has noted (1990a: 10).   [85] See Norman 1969–77: vol. II: 497.

cultural identities. One could thus easily be a Greek as well as a Christian and did not have to adopt the worship of the gods to be seen as a Greek.

Because of the traditional Graeco-Roman association between religious allegiance and other forms of social identification, Libanius had even more vested in understanding this relationship than Chrysostom did. What we have learnt is that it was Libanius who was most willing to disengage loyalty to particular gods from political, civic and cultural loyalties and identifications by manipulating traditional rhetorical dichotomies such as communal versus individual and public versus private. This was partly out of necessity because of the encroachments that Christianity was making on many areas of life. It was also, however, out of a desire for a less confrontational approach to the religious situation. Rather than seek to assert the identity of traditional religion or to argue that allegiance to the old gods should dominate people's lives, Libanius reacted by emphasizing the private sphere of religious life. In this way, he was able to present a world in which there was room for coexistence and manoeuvring between different kinds of social identity. Worshipping the gods, or allegiance to the Christian God could, at times, be placed in a private sphere that need not have an impact on these other kinds of social identities. This allowed for a distinction between religion and power that enabled a great scope for toleration of those who did not share Libanius' religious allegiance.[86]

---

[86] Modern literature recognizes that religious toleration and the privatization of religion go hand in hand (Griffiths 2001: 82–4; Asad 2002: 116 and 121–2; and Yalçin-Heckmann 2001: 335).

PART IV

Religious identity and social organization

INTRODUCTION

In the previous part we explored how Chrysostom and Libanius conceived of the relationship between religious identity and religious allegiance and other forms of social identity and social allegiance. We saw that Chrysostom sought to present Christian identity as all encompassing and as equivalent to political, civic and ethnic identity, whereby he could suggest that there was no alternative to being Christian and no sphere of life in which one's Christian identity should not be dominant. We saw that he presented the authority of the Church as superior to that of the state, ideally at least, and that he presented Christianity as a *politeia* that could replace both the *politeia* of the Roman state and that of the Jewish people. We also saw that he sought to align Christian identity with civic identity and citizenship of Antioch by suggesting that the city be totally Christianized or else rejected as demonic. Finally, we saw that Chrysostom also presented religious identity and ethnic identity as aligned. He presented Christianity as a form of ethnicity that should replace Greekness and presented Greekness in religious terms so that it was clear to his audiences that they could not be both Greek and Christian: they had to choose between the two. By closely associating religious identity with political, civic and ethnic identities he was allowing no room for neutral secular spheres of life in which people's Christian identity could matter less. Rather, for Chrysostom, being Christian was supposed to permeate every aspect of the lives of his audiences. If we turn to Libanius the situation is very different. What characterizes all of Libanius' writings is his ability to distinguish religious allegiance from political, civic and ethnic allegiance when it was useful or appropriate to do so. At times he rejected the notion that the personal religious beliefs of individuals should have an impact on public policy or that Christianity should develop institutions to rival that of the state. He was also able to disarticulate religious allegiance from civic identity and accept that there was no longer a straightforward relationship between people's worship of particular gods and their membership of a city. Finally, he did not see Hellenic cultural identity in religious terms but rather as something that could be shared by all whatever their religious allegiance. Underlying these ways of thinking was an opposition between the public and the private sphere that was a characteristic ancient approach but adapted by Libanius to the fourth-century context. This was articulated by Libanius on a number of occasions and in a number of different contexts to suggest that the appropriate sphere for religion was the private one. This allowed him to work with a model of social interaction in which there were many spheres of life that could be considered as religiously neutral and as untouched by religious conflict.

As in part II, we thus saw in part III that Chrysostom and Libanius were pulling in two different directions. Chrysostom, who saw religious identities as mutually exclusive, also saw Christian identity as determinative of every sphere of life. Libanius, who had a more strategic approach to religious allegiance, could allow for a world in which one's religious allegiance might matter in certain contexts but not in others. To take our understanding of these different approaches further we now need to turn to the question of social organization. It is by exploring the relationship between religious identity and social organization that we will begin to understand how far Chrysostom's attempt at imposing a clear-cut Christian identity on his audience was successful. It is also by exploring this relationship that we will be able to develop our understanding of Libanius' use of religious allegiance. It is easy to assume that because Chrysostom used the label Christian and we use the term 'pagan' there were also well-defined 'pagan' and Christian groups or communities in Antioch that could be attached to these labels. This relates to a broader problem within the study of social identity. Barth's model can lead to the assumption that every time there is a categorization or a labelling of a social identity we will also find a distinct and well-organized social group (S. Jones 1997: 75 and Eriksen 1993: 156). It also relates to an issue within the study of the religions of the Roman empire. In recent years there has been great interest in identifying religious groups, in outlining their social structure and in the realignment of social organization after religious conversion. It is thus all too easy to see religious groups everywhere and to slip into the assumption that we can talk in terms of these whenever it suits us.

Identity theorists have shown that identity relates to social organization in a manner that can be much more variable and indeterminate than the social group model assumes. Handelman has shown the variety of ways that social organization can, in fact, relate to ethnic or other social forms of identification. He outlines four different levels: ethnic category; ethnic network; ethnic association and the ethnic community (Handelman 1977: 187–200. For similar formulations see also Parkin 1974: 126–7). Ethnic association and ethnic community are clearly the most developed form of social organization. They involve those sharing a social identity in meeting together regularly and having shared goals and a public and visible presence. They also entail a strong degree of social cohesiveness between those people that is directly based on the social identity in question and that can be easily and publicly articulated by them (so, for example, religious groups will be based on shared religious ideas that all members adhere to and see as the factor binding the group together). The presence of ethnic networks and ethnic categories in Handelman's list, however, enables us to see beyond the normal group- or community-based models of social organization. Wellman and Berkowitz, in their *Social Structures: a Network Approach*, argue that sociologists have for too long focused on the study of groups or 'aggregated sets of individuals'. They argue that instead we should see 'relations as the basic units of social structure'. These relations or connections between individuals are seen *primarily* to build up *networks*. Groups or communities can come about when very dense sets of relations (or 'clusters') build up in one area, but are not seen as inevitable. Because network theorists look beyond the group to find the basic unit of social life in personal interaction, they are able to look beyond the communal and the public spheres that normally dominate models of society. While networks do not function as visible groups and have little public impact, they do create lasting personal links between people and allow for the transfer of resources through those ties. Network members can also belong to, and even move between, a 'wide variety of groups' rather than having to be focused on membership in just one group. Precisely because networks are more loosely organized and less public they can intersect more easily with other networks and with more organized groups. (On these characteristics of networks, see Eriksen 1993: 42 and Handelman 1977: 269; Wellman and Berkowitz 2003: 17; and Wellman 2003: 21.) Finally, we can even conclude that a social identity does not have to have any correlation with social organization and can simply remain at the level of a category. We thus need to be open to the idea that there are alternatives to thinking in terms of a Christian community or a 'pagan' group in Antioch.

Another problem with assuming that we can talk in terms of Christian and 'pagan' groups and communities arises from the ancient writings on which these assumptions are based. Discussions of Christian communities and Christian social organization in the ancient world are often based on the study of the very Christian texts that were responsible for trying to instil rules and guidelines for those communities. There is thus a risk of circularity as we take the texts responsible for constructing Christian communities as evidence for those communities. Similarly problematic can be the notion of the textual community, which links the formation of communities to specific texts, and the idea that literary representations of groups will be descriptive. The writings left to us from antiquity in fact put up many barriers to the study of social organization and it can be very difficult to get beyond their representations and constructions. This is as true of the writings of Libanius and Chrysostom as of any others. For this reason, we need to be aware that the written texts of these authors might give the impression of developed forms of social organization based on religious identity and religious allegiance when this was not the case. Again, we need to be aware of the looser forms of social organization that were possible.

It is these ideas that will be explored in part IV. Chapter 7 will explore how relevant the notion of the textual community is to Chrysostom's preaching and to Christians in Antioch. It will consider Chrysostom's attempts to create a sense of community among his audiences and how successful he was in this. It will explore the variety of ways in which those in his audiences related to being 'Christian' as well as the alternative social commitments that drew them away from a unified Christian community. Chapter 8 will then turn to Libanius' writings and the assumptions that have been made about a 'pagan' group in Antioch. It will explore Libanius' relationship with Julian as a supposed focus of this 'pagan' group and will investigate the uses that Libanius made of representations of social links between worshippers of the gods. In so doing, it will suggest that the model of the network works much better as a way of understanding the form of social organization we see in Libanius' writings.

CHAPTER 7

Chrysostom and social structure among Christians in Antioch

CHRYSOSTOM'S PREACHING AND TEXTUAL COMMUNITIES

It is easy to assume that we can talk of a Christian community at Antioch in the fourth century. We see that there were people who called themselves Christian in the city and take for granted that this means we can talk about them as a cohesive group. Often this is simply a convenient way of speaking and does not entail our making a strong statement about the degree of social organization among those Christians. It is precisely through such references made in passing and without much thought that the notion of the Christian community becomes reified as fact. Because we are so accustomed to using the term we no longer question its propriety but use it as if it describes an objective reality. Technically, according to the definitions of social theorists, the term 'community' refers to a high degree of social organization. It means that community members meet together regularly, have some kind of shared social space and a visible presence and that they are united by shared goals that they can articulate publicly.[1] In fact, for many social theorists the term community actually entails the 'collectivity' in question having a shared political organization' and 'a territory with more or less physical boundaries', such as modern nation states.[2] We need not accept this strongest understanding of 'community' but can still recognize that we need to be more careful about how we use the term. For the present example of Christians in fourth-century Antioch, we simply do not know enough about how they lived to be sure that we can define them as a community in even the weaker sense outlined above. We do not know, for example, if there were Christian areas in which they lived in close proximity to one another or if they had many meeting places exclusive to them. All we have are texts written by Christian leaders, so we have to ask whether

[1] Eriksen 1993: 42–3.   [2] Eriksen 1993: 43.

we can use these texts to tell us anything about the social organization of ordinary Christians. In recent years, the thinking of Brian Stock has been very influential on scholars of early Christianity because he posited a way in which texts could be opened again to social analysis after this had been brought into question by post-structuralist approaches.[3] Stock has argued that, at least for the medieval period, we can see 'microsocieties organized around the common understanding of a Script' – what he called 'textual communities' that were 'interpretive communities' but also 'social entities'.[4] According to Stock, a literate preacher with knowledge of certain texts would instruct a group in this knowledge and in his message and this, in turn, would alter the behaviour of the group. As Stock states, 'if the force of the word is strong enough, it can supersede the differing economic and social backgrounds of the participants, welding them together . . . into a unit' and so bring about a greater sense of solidarity among members and of separation from non-members.[5] Textuality thus becomes 'the script for the enactment of behavioural norms' and causes a permanent change in the way that people relate to each other: 'the social lives of the group's members will from that moment be determined by the rules of membership in the community'.[6] At first sight, these ideas might appear easily applicable to Chrysostom's preaching.

Chrysostom can be described as the educated leader who had detailed knowledge of a set of biblical texts and used preaching from these texts to lay down the rules by which he wanted his congregation to live. By teaching them about the Bible and how to interpret it Chrysostom was creating a new literary corpus and a new literary canon for his audiences.[7] His continual preaching of certain biblical texts and of certain modes of interpretation of these texts had the potential to lead to 'something happening' to his audiences, as Stock puts it, and to their forming a greater sense of unity because of their shared knowledge. We might say that Chrysostom's congregation were united around a shared knowledge of the writings of Paul and the Book of Genesis, which recurred in Chrysostom's exegetical preaching.[8] It was only by knowing these texts that they were able to know

---

[3] Stock 1990: 21–2 and 157.   [4] Stock 1990: 150. In particular, see also Stock 1990: 21–2 and 157.
[5] Stock 1990: 150 and also Stock 1983: 90 and 101.
[6] Stock 1990: 23 and 150.   [7] Hartney 2004: 50.
[8] Chrysostom's preaching on Pauline letters, such as 1 and 2 Corinthians and Romans, probably took place in his later years as preacher in Antioch, in the 390s (Brändle and Jegher-Bucher 1995: 291 and 292). However, quotations and lessons from Paul's works are also scattered throughout Chrysostom's earlier preaching. For his preaching on Genesis we have the long series of sixty-seven sermons that were probably delivered in 385–8 (*PG* 754.580) as well as a shorter series of nine sermons that were probably delivered in 386 (*PG* 54.580–630). There are also some signs that the series of sermons *On*

what behaviour counted as sinful (*Hom. in Matt.* 14.4 (*PG* 57.221)). At the same time Chrysostom's preaching about particular ways of thinking and of living their lives could be seen as the 'rules' by which he sought to change the behaviour of those listening to him and so to institutionalize the sense of shared identity between them (*Adv. Oppug.* 3.5 (*PG* 47.357)). As Stock says 'the Scriptures are not the rules . . . It is the rules [of the community as laid down by Church leaders], not the Scriptures, that transcend pre-existing economic and social bonds.'[9] Chrysostom's guidelines for moral living, giving to the poor and regular attendance at church could be seen as examples of these rules, as could his teachings about the importance of having a distinct Christian identity. The imposition of these rules on his audiences could then be said to lead to the formation of a textual community around him. The problem with this model as proposed by Stock is that, as Bourdieu might object, it suggests a very simplistic relationship between the 'rules' of a society and the behaviour of individuals. To assume that Chrysostom's audiences formed a community around him would mean accepting that they put into practice all the rules he laid down for them, but this is precisely what we are questioning.

It is not even clear in the first place that Chrysostom's sermons can be related to one particular group of people on whom he might impose his 'rules'. Mayer and Allen have shown that we too often assume that his sermons were delivered in the form of the series that we now have, which may not have been the case.[10] It was once thought that most of Chrysostom's preaching took place while he was a priest in Antioch, as he would have had more time to preach there than he would have had as bishop in Constantinople.[11] Conversely, certain series of sermons were once thought to have been delivered in Constantinople, often as a result of mistaken notions about an episcopal tone. These assumptions are being undermined by the recent work of Mayer and Allen and it is now impossible to say with any confidence that Chrysostom's audience in Antioch would have heard a particular set of sermons and those in Constantinople another.[12] This present work has tried to use series of sermons whose provenance in Antioch is more certain, but even among these we cannot be sure that

---

the *Riot of the Statues* was intended to have been the exegesis of Genesis that was suitable for the Lenten season but that the events of the riot changed its emphasis. Sermons 7–13 all involve exegesis of Genesis or discussion of issues raised by Genesis.

[9] Stock 1990: 150.
[10] Mayer and Allen 1994: 21–39; Mayor 1995b: 309–48 and 1995a: 27–89. See also Allen 1997: 3–21.
[11] Mayer 1998: 113.
[12] Mayer 2005: 1–465 in particular. See also Mayer and Allen 1994; Mayer 1995a: and 1995b; and Allen 1997.

every sermon was delivered there. Even if we can specify sermons that were preached in Antioch, there are still problems with linking them to a particular group of Christians. It was once assumed that the 'Great' or 'Golden' Church was the focus of most of the liturgy and preaching of the Antiochene Church and that Chrysostom simply aided Bishop Flavian in delivering the service there through the contribution of his preaching.[13] It is now known, however, that the Old Church in the city was also a site of active and regular church services and that for a while John Chrysostom was the regular preacher there.[14] Assigning particular sermons and series of sermons to Chrysostom's time of preaching in the Old Church is even harder than assigning particular sermons to Antioch. Some sermons do explicitly tell us that they were delivered in the Old Church, or in particular *martyria*. Others speak of Chrysostom as preaching prior to Bishop Flavian in the service, which would suggest delivery in the Great Church, although even this is not certain, because Flavian was quite capable of visiting other churches.[15] However, many sermons give no indication at all of where they were preached and although it is likely that some series of sermons were preached in the Old Church we cannot speak confidently about specific sermons.

We also cannot say that a particular audience was attached to Chrysostom rather than to a place of worship.[16] On two occasions, at least, Chrysostom had to apologize to his audiences in the Old Church for his absence (*In illud: In Faciem ei restiti* (*PG* 51.371) and (*In Princ. Act.* 2 (*PG* 51.77–8)).[17] As Mayer has pointed out, this suggests that the congregation that he addressed in the Old Church was attached to the church rather than to him and that it remained in the church to hear a locum preach when he was absent. The congregation in the Old Church would thus have been exposed to the ideas of more than one preacher, so they cannot be said to have formed a textual community around Chrysostom and his preaching, at least not in any simplistic way. Similarly, Chrysostom himself could at times have more than one audience, something that further complicates the idea that there was a well-defined textual community around him.[18] Because some of the sermons that are being considered in this present study might have

---

[13] Baur, 1959–60: vol. I, 190. For a different view, see Eltester 1937: 217–18.
[14] Mayer 1997: 72 and 1998: 110.
[15] On the Old Church, see *In illud: In Faciem ei restiti* (*PG* 51.371) and *In Princ. Act.* 2 (*PG* 51.77–8). On *martyria*, see *In S. Ignat. Mart.* 5 (*PG* 50.594) and *In S. Jul. Mart.* (*PG* 50.673). See also Mayer and Allen 2000: 19, note 6 and Leemans *et al.* 2003: 6. On Chrysostom's preaching in conjunction with Flavian, see *In illud: In Faciem ei restiti* (*PG* 51.371) and also Mayer and Allen 2000: 7 and 41.
[16] Mayer 1997: 71–2. [17] See also *In Cap. ad. Galat. Comment.* 2.11 (*PG* 51.371).
[18] Mayer 1997: 75.

been delivered to one group of people and some to another, we cannot be sure that all of the ideas in them would have been transmitted to the same group of people.

Yet another problem that militates against the idea of a textual community around Chrysostom is that it is very hard to know how regularly people attended Chrysostom's preaching, even within one congregation.[19] We know that at times of major liturgical festivals, such as Lent, Easter and saints' days, much greater numbers than normal filled the church.[20] On these occasions it seems likely that, as Mayer puts it, 'a composite mass audience was involved'.[21] In addition, sermons preached during Lent, in the lead up to Easter, were delivered daily, in the late afternoon or early evening, rather than on Sundays only.[22] This meant that more people came more regularly to hear Chrysostom preach at just one time of the year. We can thus imagine that the sense of community and the social links between Christians varied during the year: at Lent Christians met together more regularly and in greater numbers to share the experience of Chrysostom's preaching, so that was a time when they would have been more closely bonded together. Perhaps this was why Chrysostom reserved preaching on the most fundamental ideas about Genesis and God's creation for Lent, as is evidenced by his homilies on Genesis and the series of sermons on the statues (*The Homilies on Genesis* (*PG* 53.21–54.580), *The Sermons on Genesis* (*PG* 54.580–630) and the *Homilies on the Statues* 1–21 (*PG* 49.15–222).[23] We can imagine that after Lent, when attendance at Chrysostom's preaching fell off, the sense of community and the common bonds between Christians would also have declined. Chrysostom spoke of the large numbers who attended Christian festive occasions such as the martyr festivals, Christmas and Lent;[24] he also complained that attendance dropped off aside from these special occasions, at the time of ordinary preaching and services. On two occasions he implied that some people attended only once or twice a month, or even less (*In Ep. ad 2 Thess. Hom.* 5 (*PG* 62.498 and *De Bapt.*

---

[19] See, for example, Hartney 2004: 47–50.
[20] Mayer 1998: 131 and Allen 1997: 4. See also *Hom. in Act.* 29 (*PG* 60.218); *In Princ. Act.* 1 (*PG* 51.65); *De Bapt. Christ;* (*PG* 49.363); and *Hom. de Stat.* 4.1 (*PG* 49.59) (where numbers were greater not only because these sermons were delivered at Lent but because of the events after the riot).
[21] Mayer 1997: 72. See also *In Sanctum Meletium* (*PG* 50.415) and *Hom. in Mart.* (*PG* 50.663).
[22] On ordinary preaching on Sundays, see Maxwell forthcoming: 5 and Harkins 1979: xxiv. On the increased regularity of Lenten preaching, see Mayer and Allen 1993: 263; van der Paverd 1991: 161–2 and 164; and also Bradshaw 2002: 183–5 and 223–4.
[23] Van der Paverd has shown that readings from Genesis were a normal part of the Lenten services (1991: 189–90). This appears to have been a universal custom of the eastern Church (van der Paverd 1991: 190).
[24] See chapter 5 above.

Christi 1 (*PG* 49.363 and 364).²⁵ One factor hindering the regular attendance of certain people at Chrysostom's preaching would have been the demands of work.²⁶ It is possible that artisans might have had to work every day of the week, including Saturday and Sunday when his ordinary (non-festive) preaching was delivered.²⁷ As van der Paverd has pointed out, Chrysostom himself at one point described how people used their poverty (*penia*) 'as an excuse for staying away from the weekly Sunday mass' (*De Bapt. Christi* 1 (*PG* 49.363–4)). Chrysostom also spoke of the difficulty for tradespeople of attending church regularly because of the demands of their professions (*In Kal.* (*PG* 48.957) and *In Princ. Act.* 1 (*PG* 51.69)).²⁸ We might thus imagine that there was a small group who attended Chrysostom's preaching regularly throughout the year and gained in-depth knowledge of the full range of his preaching. The majority, however, would have attended only intermittently throughout the whole year and so gained a breadth of knowledge of what Chrysostom said but in a very erratic and patchy way. There would also have been others who attended only at Lent and so learnt, and then re-learnt each year, only the basic teaching on Genesis that Chrysostom gave at this time. The different knowledge of biblical texts and of Chrysostom's preaching shared by separate groups would have led to different levels of social bonding between them and this would have been a factor that divided Chrysostom's audience as a whole.

It is unlikely that one textual community would have formed around Chrysostom's preaching. We thus need to explore other ways in which it might be possible to relate Chrysostom's writings to a community in Antioch. In the next section I shall study Chrysostom's active attempts to construct a sense of community for his audiences.

CONSTRUCTION OF A SENSE OF COMMUNITY

The notion of community had been important to Christian leaders from the time of Jesus as they sought to bring about a strong feeling of social support among Christians.²⁹ Christians as the body of Christ and the Church as the bride of Christ were concepts used to create a strong sense of the unity and communality of Christians. As early as Paul's letters to the eastern churches, especially to the Corinthians, we see a concern with building up the community: Paul exhorted those who 'had knowledge' to put their

---

²⁵ Van der Paverd 1991: 180.   ²⁶ Mayer 1998: 121 and 129.
²⁷ Libanius' hyperbolic statement that artisans were compelled to work night and day might give some support to this notion (van der Paverd 1991: 177–8). See also Baldovin 1987: 261 and Allen 1997: 7.
²⁸ Mayer 1998: 124.   ²⁹ See, for example, Meeks 1993.

superior wisdom aside for the good of the community. In these earlier centuries, having a strong sense of community was important to Christians because they were an isolated group in a largely hostile world. In the fourth century the significance of this sense of community shifted as it was now used to combat the dilution of the Church's principles at a time of increased conversion and Christianization. We should not be surprised to find this focus on community-building among Christians who were also concerned with marking out Christian identity. As Cohen has shown, one important aspect of identity construction is the creation of a sense of shared communality within group boundaries.[30] Creating a sense of community was part of constructing the feeling of similarity that could then be contrasted with differences from others.

Chrysostom often spoke of 'the community' or 'shared things' (*to koinon*) of the Christians (*Hom. de Stat.* 3.5 and 12, and 16.17) and referred to members of his audience as 'brothers' or 'neighbours' (*Hom. de Stat.* 2.12 5.20, 9.11, 12.16, 13.12, 16.17, 20.23).[31] Through his preaching on Paul 1 and 2 Corinthians he used Paul's ideals of communal life among Christians in Corinth to teach his audiences how they should be living with one another.[32] Early in the sermons on 1 Corinthians Chrysostom mentions that Paul used the metaphor of the body and of marriage to describe the close unity between Christ and Christians. Christ was the head while Christians were the body; Christ was the bridegroom while Christians (or the Church) were the bride (*In Ep. ad 1 Cor. Hom.* 30.1 (*PG* 61.250)).[33] In fact, the body provided the perfect metaphor for the ideals of unity, equality and community that Chrysostom wanted to promote: 'all the members of the one body, being many are one' (*In Ep ad 1 Cor. Hom.* 30.1 (*PG* 61.250)). Just as there should be 'no schism in the body' there should be 'no schism in the Church'. Instead all Christians should love and look after one another (*In Ep ad 1 Cor. Hom.* 31.3 and 6 and 32.1 and 44.5 (*PG* 61.259, 262, 263–4 and 578)). In the *Homilies on the Riot of the Statues* Chrysostom used the image of members of his audience losing or hurting a limb of their body to show them how they should feel when a Christian brother had become their enemy or was acting in unchristian ways (*Hom. de Stat.* 13.12 and 20.12 (*PG* 49.142 and 204)). Chrysostom could also describe the problem of Judaizing Christians as 'an illness, which has become implanted in the

---

[30] Cohen 1985.
[31] See also *Hom. in Gen.* 41.1 and 43.10 (*PG* 53.374 and 54.398) and *In Ep. ad 1 Cor. Hom.* 24.4 (*PG* 61.200–1).
[32] See, for example, *In Ep. ad 1 Cor. Hom.* 31 on 1 Corinthians 12.21.
[33] See also *In Ep. ad 1 Cor. Hom.* 8.5 (*PG* 61.70).

body of the Church' (*Adv. Jud.* 1.1.4 (*PG* 48.844)). The very physical image of the body encouraged the idea that good relations between Christians were something tangible and permanent that should stretch beyond their shared moments in church. It could be used to override the particular problem of differences of class and wealth among Chrysostom's audiences. Recent work on Chrysostom's audiences has shown that they were probably of mixed social status from reasonably well-to-do shopkeepers to the upper classes and perhaps also including some slaves who accompanied their masters.[34] In one passage Chrysostom argues that just as the body needs all its parts, even those that seem less important, such as the hair, eyebrows and eyelids, so the Christian community needs its more lowly members such as the beggars and the poor (*In Ep. ad 1 Cor. Hom.* 30.6–7 (*PG* 61.253–5)). He also particularly berates members of his audience who ignore the welfare of ordinary workers and treat them as slaves. For Chrysostom such men, whether 'a shoemaker, a dyer or a brazier', were each 'a believer and a brother' and should be treated as equal members of the Christian community (*In Ep. ad 1 Cor. Hom.* 20.11 (*PG* 61.168)).[35] He then goes on to use the resemblance of such lowly craftsmen to the Apostles, who were fishermen, tentmakers and tax-collectors, to enhance his point (*In Ep. ad 1 Cor. Hom.* 20.11–12 (*PG* 61.168–9)). Just as Christianity's founding fathers had come from ordinary backgrounds, so the Christian community in the fourth century should embrace such people.

Chrysostom also sought to create a sense of brotherhood and concern for each other among those in his audiences and used Paul's teachings to impart this message. After reference to Paul's lesson to the Corinthians that eating meat sacrificed to the idols could act as a stumbling block to the weak, Chrysostom states: 'But it would be timely for these things to be said not only to them [the Corinthians], but also to us, we who are disdainful of the salvation of our neighbour and who utter such satanical words, saying, "what do I care if such a person stumbles, or if another perishes?"' (*In Ep. ad 1 Cor. Hom.* 20.11 (*PG* 61.168)).[36] In this way he attempts to develop among his audiences a sense of responsibility for monitoring the Christian behaviour of their neighbours. He argues that Christians should care for each other because the unbeliever would not do so (*In Ep. ad 1 Cor. Hom.* 44.5 (*PG* 61.578)). Putting one's Christian 'brothers' first in all one's actions is the primary goal of the good Christian (*Hom. de Stat.* 9.6, 15.14, 18.13

---

[34] See, for example, Hartney 2004: 43–7.
[35] See also *In Ep. ad 1 Cor. Hom.* 5 (*PG* 61, 47) and *In Ep. ad Ephes. Hom.* 2 (*PG* 62.22). See also Hartney 2004: 171–81 and Leyerle 1994: 29–47.
[36] See also *In Ep. ad 1 Cor. Hom.* 25.3–4 (*PG* 61.208–10).

(*PG* 49.106–7, 160 and 188)). Christians should always set a good example for another and always do good to one another rather than harbour evil or envious feelings.³⁷ They should 'edify one another' (Paul 1 Thessalonians 5.2), instruct one another, and chide one another when they see each other using oaths, attending the racecourses, or taking part in Jewish festivals.³⁸ As Chrysostom says:

> For the remaining time, you should be teachers and guides of one another; friends should instruct and encourage their neighbours; servants their fellow servants and youths those of their own age ... For this is the reason we live with others, that we inhabit cities and that we meet together in churches, in order that we may bear one another's burdens and that we may correct one another's sins. (*Hom. de Stat.* 16.17 (*PG* 49.170–1))

In saying that 'they had nothing in common with [their] own members' his audiences were denying their shared nature and therefore lost their membership in Christ: 'But if you have nothing in common with your member (*pros to melos*) then you have nothing in common with your brother, nor do you have Christ as your head' (*Adv. Jud.* 1.3.6 (*PG* 48.848)).³⁹ Chrysostom knew he could not be with his audiences at all times. He thus tried to encourage Christians to watch over each other and to ensure each other's good Christian behaviour through community feeling and vigilance.

Another means by which Chrysostom sought to create a more permanent sense of community in his audience was through his exhortation that they should continually talk about what they had heard in church with family, friends and neighbours. In the fifth homily *On the Statues* Chrysostom states that the whole point of gathering together in church is to bring about some kind of permanent change in his audiences (*Hom. de Stat.* 5.21 (*PG* 49.79)). To think of what he says only while they are in church is a 'temporary admonition' and instead 'the husband' should 'hear these things from the wife and the wife from the husband' 'at home also' (*Hom. de Stat.* 5.22 (*PG* 49.80)).⁴⁰ Those who are absent from his preaching for any reason should also be taught what he had said by those who had been present. Instead of going to the racecourse Christians should meet together

---

³⁷ *Hom. de Stat.* 3.12–16, 6.15, 8.5, 13.12 and 20.2 (*PG* 49.53–6, 89–90, 101, 141–2 and 198) and *In Ep. ad 1 Cor. Hom.* 24.4, 31.6–7 (*PG* 61.200–1 and 262–3)).
³⁸ On oaths, see *Hom. de Stat.* 5.20, 9.11 and 12.16–17 (*PG* 49.79, 110 and 135–6). On the racecourses, see *Hom. in Gen.* 41.4 and 43.10 (*PG* 53.376 and 54.398). On Jewish festivals, see *Adv. Jud.* 1.2.6 and 1.4.8 (*PG* 48.846 and 849)).
³⁹ See also *Adv. Jud.* 4.6.7 and 8.5.2–3 (*PG* 48.880 and 934)).
⁴⁰ See also *Hom. de Stat.* 6.18, 8.7, 13.10, 14.14, 20.23 (*PG* 49.88–9, 102, 141, 151 and 210) and *Hom. in Gen.* 2.11 and 14.22 (*PG* 53.30 and 117).

and read scripture (*Hom. in Gen.* 6.22 (*PG* 53.61)).[41] While in the forum or involved in business or when making a journey or taking part in any other public activity they should keep the divine word present in their minds and allow it to guide their actions (*Hom. de Stat.* 6.18 (*PG* 49.88–9)) and *Hom. in Gen.* 35.10 (*PG* 53.325)). Chrysostom also suggests that forming small groups with other Christians for the correction of oaths or to read scripture is a useful practice. It would be easier for people to give up using oaths if they 'enter into fraternities and partnerships in this matter' and if they laid down rules and penalties for one another (*Hom. de Stat.* 9.1 and 11.15 (*PG* 49.103 and 126–8)).[42] The final method that Chrysostom used to try to maintain a more permanent Christian community was through his pastoral care outside his preaching. Although the details are unclear, he mentions that on certain occasions he visited Christians in their homes or met them privately to try to shore up their commitment.[43] When he was not able to do this, he asked them to imagine that he was standing by them as they ate their dinner 'dinning into you the things' he said to them in his preaching at church (*Hom. de Stat.* 5.23 (*PG* 49.80)).

It was not only through the spoken word that the Church sought to achieve a sense of community among Christians; it was also through the rituals. Michael Penn's recent study *Kissing Christians: Ritual and Community in the Late Ancient Church* has emphasized this. Penn shows how the ritual and bodily gesture of the kiss could aid in the construction of social boundaries and a sense of community among fourth-century Christians: it was a way to dispel strife among Christians and to 'unite and produce one body' of the Christian Church (*In Ep. ad 1 Cor. Hom.* 44.4 (*PG* 61.376)).[44] The kiss 'casts out all calculation . . . and [every] impulse for mean spirit, in order that neither the greater despise the lesser, nor the little envy the greater . . . [it] appeases and levels everything' (*In Ep. ad Rom. Hom.* 21.4 (*PG* 60.671)). Using Mary Douglas' notion of the human body as an image of society, Penn argues that the kiss on the mouth practised by Christians emphasized membership of a community.[45] Because Christians kissed each other at a bodily aperture, an entryway into their physical bodies, they were symbolizing the shared body of the Christian Church and thus of Christians. When they appropriated the gesture of the kiss, usually used by

---

[41] See also *Hom. de Stat.* 9.2–3, 20.23 (*PG* 49.103–4 and 210); *Catéchèse* 6.17 (SC 50.223–4)); *Hom. in Gen.* 6.22, 10.20, 35.1–3 and 10 (*PG* 53.61, 90, 321 and 325)) and also Guillaumin 1975: 171; Malingrey 1975: 213; Jackson 1990: 349; and Garret 1992: 218–21.
[42] See also *Hom. in Gen.* 6.22 (*PG* 53.61).
[43] *Hom. de Stat.* 6.19, 9.1 and 20.23 (*PG* 49.91–2, 103 and 210).
[44] Penn 2005: 26 and 45–6. [45] Penn 2005: 50.

family members, they also appropriated the feeling of familial bonds that went with it: 'the kiss is given . . . so that we may love each other as brothers [love] brothers, as children [love] parents' (*In Ep. ad 2 Cor. Hom.* 30.2 (*PG* 61.607)).

The most important rituals in the Christian Church were those of baptism and the mystery of the Eucharist.[46] It was during initiation in baptism that Christians were said to achieve their incorporation in the body of Christ as they were brought into the Christian community where, ideally, other social bonds and designations would be put aside. After the 'putting on of Christ' in baptism, 'there can neither be Jew nor Greek, there can be neither slave nor freeman, there can be neither male nor female, for you are all one in Christ' (*In Cap. ad. Galat. Comment.* 3.27 (*PG* 61.656) on Galatians 27 and 28).[47] Chrysostom clearly envisaged baptism as a ritual of social transition. He described it as a marriage to Christ;[48] as enlisting in an army;[49] and as gaining a new citizenship.[50] Just as with all these other life-changing experiences, the initiates were resocialized by their experience, but in this case from being non-Christian to being Christian. The ritual of baptism is typical of rituals of transition (or rites of passage), in which marking the changes of an individual's social status is a primary function.[51] By moving through phases of separation, transition and then incorporation the individual is removed from one social status (adolescent, prospective initiate, catechumen, etc), taken to a liminal state that exists outside time and space (where frightening rituals often took place), and then reintegrated into a new social grouping (adult male, initiate, Christian, etc.).[52]

The ritual of baptism first separated people from their state as a non-Christian, it then took them into the liminal state of the neophyte (where they had a special status and underwent a series of dramatic rituals) and then, finally, integrated them into their new Christian community. In his accounts of baptism Chrysostom shows the dramatic nature of the ritual. In the final days leading up to baptism the catechumens were sent to the exorcist every day after their instruction (*Catéchèse* 2.12 (SC 50.139)). They stood before the exorcist with bare feet, in only a short tunic and with outstretched hands or upturned hands, while the exorcist used 'the awesome formula and the invocation of the common master of all things' to

---

[46] Stock 1990: 153. [47] See also *Catéchèse* 2.13 and 3.17 (SC 50.140 and 161).
[48] *Catéchèse* 1.9 and 11–18 and 6.24–5 (SC 50.113 and 114–15 and 227–8).
[49] *Catéchèse* 1.1, 18, and 40, 2.1 and 8 (SC 50.108, 118 and 40, 133 and 137).
[50] *Catéchèse* 1.18, 2.9, 4.29 and 7.12 and 23 (SC 50.118, 138, 197 and 234–5 and 240–1).
[51] Van Gennep 1977: 1–3 and Turner 1995: 93–4 and 95.
[52] Van Gennep 1977: 11 and Turner 1995: 94. On the liminal state, see Turner 1995: 95–110.

drive out the devil (*Catéchèse* 2.14 (SC 50.141) and *Catéchèse* 1.7 and 2.6 (SC 366.125–6 and 366.189–93) = Harkins, *Baptismal Instruction* 9.11 and 10.14). The ritual of baptism itself took place on the night of Easter Saturday, as it turned into Easter Sunday. Leading up to this, on Good Friday or during the day on Easter Saturday, the renunciation of Satan and statement of adherence to Christ took place.[53] The initiate had to kneel on the floor, again with outstretched hands, and answer a series of questions in which they both made their statement of faith in Christ (which was also referred to as a contract) and renounced Satan and all his pomps. Chrysostom describes the anointment of the candidate directly before baptism. Unlike other descriptions of baptism that we have from the ancient world, this is a twofold anointment, once on the head and once on the whole body. First the priest anoints the candidates' foreheads with a cross in order to turn away the devil (*Catéchèse* 2.23 (SC 50.146–7) and *Catéchèse* 3.7 (SC 366.235–6) = Harkins, *Baptismal Instruction* 11.27). Then, in 'the full darkness of night' the candidate is stripped naked by the priest and anointed in holy oil so that all their 'limbs may be fortified and unconquered by the darts which the adversary aims at' them (*Catéchèse* 2.24 (SC 50.147) and *Catéchèse* 3.8 (SC 366.237–8) = Harkins, *Baptismal Instruction* 11.28). It is only after this double anointing that the actual baptism takes place. The priest makes the candidate 'go down into the sacred waters, burying the old man and putting on the new' (*Catéchèse* 2.25 (SC 50.147)). As in all baptismal rituals the candidate is immersed in the water three times 'in the name of the Father and of the Son and of the Holy Ghost' (*Catéchèse* 2.26 (SC 50.147–8)). After the baptism the candidate emerges from the water and 'all who are present embrace them, greet them and kiss them'. Finally they are led to the altar, the 'royal table' to 'taste of the Master's body and blood' (*Catéchèse* 2.27 (SC 50.148–9) and *Catéchèse* 3.10 (SC 366.241) = Harkins, *Baptismal Instruction* 11.32).

This Antiochene baptismal ritual shares much with other liminal and transitional ceremonies as described by van Gennep and Turner. The candidates took a passive posture throughout the stages of the ceremony. They had to kneel on the ground, raise their hands to heaven and present themselves naked or under-dressed.[54] Chrysostom interprets this as showing the candidate's submission to God but it also fits the universal pattern of such

---

[53] On the different days given by Chrysostom in two different series of catechetical sermons, see *Catéchèse* 2.17–21 (SC 50.143–5) and *Catéchèse* 3.4 (SC 366.227–8 = Harkins, *Baptismal Instruction* 11.19). See also, Harkins' note on this (1963: 221, note 37).

[54] On the tendency of initiands to be naked, see Turner 1969: 98–9: as 'transitional beings . . . they *have* nothing'. Nakedness can also be seen to represent the death and rebirth of the initiand.

rituals. The fact that initiates were put in this vulnerable and subordinate position was meant to make them more open to the impact of the experience they were undergoing.[55] This would have been heightened by certain parts of the ritual taking place in the darkness of night and by the disorientating effect of being dunked in the water. Finally, the associations of death and rebirth that were implicit in the whole ceremony show its similarity with other such rituals.[56] The initiate died in one social persona and was reborn in another. Of course, this also had specific Christian connotations (as Chrysostom described it) in that the candidate was said to experience the death and rebirth of Christ through baptism.[57] However, this particular interpretation only adds to the universal significance of the ritual.

Once Christians had been baptized, they were supposed to reaffirm their commitment to Christ and their oneness in the Christian community ritually through regularly taking the Eucharist. As it was exclusive to those who had been baptized, this was a ritual that was meant to reaffirm their shared identity gained at baptism.[58] The mysteries of the Eucharist were probably celebrated three or four times a week, giving Chrysostom's audience ample opportunity to attend, and took place at end of the liturgy after the daily lection, preaching and prayers, once all the non-baptized had been dismissed.[59] The experience of the Eucharist was less dramatic than that of baptism but it had great potential to embody in a physical experience the changed status of the Christian. Those who did remain to take part had to wash their hands ceremonially, give the kiss of peace and say the prayer of thanksgiving before ingesting the bread and wine that had been transformed into the body and blood of Christ by means of special words spoken by the priest or bishop. In this way the Eucharist ceremony did not simply tell Christians that they were part of the body of Christ – it enacted it as a bodily and physical expression of the Christian's community in Christ and connection with Christ the saviour.[60] By taking the Eucharist, Christians shared in Christ's death and sacrifice as well as

---

[55] On the submission of neophytes to their instructors, see Turner 1969: 99–100.
[56] Turner 1969: 96–7.
[57] *Catéchèse*, 2.11 (SC 50.139), *Catéchèse* 1.4 and 8 (SC 366.122–3 and 127) = Harkins, *Baptismal Instruction* 9.8 and 12), *Catéchèse* 2.3 and 4–5 (SC 366.175–6 and 183–7) = Harkins, *Baptismal Instruction* 10.5, 7 and 8–13, *Catéchèse* 3.8 (SC 366.239) = Harkins, *Baptismal Instruction* 11.29 and *Ad Illum. Catech.* 2.1 (*PG* 49.233) = Harkins, *Baptismal Instruction* 12.12.
[58] Hein 1975: 55 and 67. On baptism as a 'criteria by which members could be set apart from the "outsider" and recognized by all other members', see Hein 1975: 421.
[59] For the former see Harkins 1979: xxiv; also Chrysostom, *Adv. Jud.* 3.4.3 (*PG* 48.867). For the latter, see Jedin and Dolan 1980: 296–8.
[60] Hein 1975: 51. On the importance of the Eucharist ceremony in Chrysostom's understanding of the Church and the Christian community, see Christo 2006: 89–153.

his rebirth.⁶¹ At the same time, however, the Eucharist was supposed to encourage communal feelings between Christians themselves at both the local level, where it was supposed to transcend differences in wealth, and at the global level, where it was supposed to bind local Christian communities together.⁶² Chrysostom discusses the significance of the Eucharist, and its community-building features, in his exegesis of 1 Corinthians following his discussion of the problems of eating meat sacrificed to the idols. It is the eating of the body of Christ, in the form of the bread, that enables all Christians to become the body of Christ and so be united as one whole (*In Ep. ad 1 Cor. Hom.* 24.4 and 7–8 (*PG* 61.200–1 and 203–6)). The holy kiss that Christians engage in during the mysteries blends Christian souls as if they were in one body and binds Christians together (*Catéchèse* 3.10 (SC 366.241–2) = Harkins, *Baptismal Instruction* 11.32–4). Sharing in the body of Christ could even entail equality between the Christian priest and the laity: 'everything in the Eucharistic thanksgiving is shared in common' because both priest and laity share in the same 'one body' and the same 'one chalice' (*In Ep. ad 2 Cor. Hom.* 18.3 (*PG* 61.527)).

Chrysostom clearly wanted to transform the labelling of a group of people as Christian into a permanent and long-lasting form of social organization: a Christian community. He tried to develop a sense of communal feeling in them as well as encourage them to relate to one another *as Christians* in their lives away from church. In particular he promoted baptism and the Eucharist as ceremonies that brought Christians into a shared community or 'body' where all were equal, ideally at least. This construction of a sense of community for Christians was an essential part of constructing a Christian identity. It was only by uniting them with each other in this way that Chrysostom had any hope of making his imposition of a clear-cut Christian identity meaningful to his audiences. But it is not at all clear that the majority of people in Chrysostom's audience had undergone baptism. It is to this problem that I now turn.

UNBAPTIZED CHRISTIANS AND THE CHRISTIAN COMMUNITY

Chrysostom's teaching on the community-building aspects of baptism and the Eucharist could only be successful if large numbers of his audience had been baptized. On a number of occasions Chrysostom suggests that this was not the case. He refers to the 'uninitiated members of the congregation'

[61] Hein 1975: 53–4 and 56. [62] Hein 1975: 57–64 and 67–8.

among his ordinary audience, calls on them to be baptized and speaks of the laxity of those who put off baptism until their deathbed.[63] Compared to those who receive baptism in their prime, such people do not approach the ritual with the right state of mind. Rather than being joyful and with a clear mind, they are surrounded by the sadness of death and illness or might even be unconscious and therefore unable to make the proper responses during the ceremony (*Catéchèse* 1.4–11 (SC 366.121–35) = Harkins, *Baptismal Instruction* 9.5–19). In another sermon Chrysostom chides those who put off baptism until a time of crisis, because the 'throng of the unbaptized' enabled the Greeks to ridicule the power of Christian 'philosophy' (*Hom. in Act.* 23.4 (PG 60.23d–4a and 25a)). Many scholars have mentioned the extent of the phenomenon of baptism on death in the fourth century but few have followed through its implications.[64] It was only those who had been baptized who were supposed to take the name of Christian and of believer or faithful, and even the catechumenate were not included in this (*Catéchèse* 1.44 (SC 50.131)).[65] If only a minority of those attending church were actually baptized, then those truly bearing the name 'Christian' would be small in number. It is likely that many were bearing the name Christian even when they had not been baptized. Chrysostom refers to people who called themselves Christians 'many of them who are already baptized', implying that there were some who called themselves Christian who were not yet baptized (*Adv. Oppug.* 1.2 (PG 47.321)). There is also some evidence from Antioch that 'baptized Christians were required to carry signed letters from their bishops certifying their eligibility to participate in the entire church service', which suggests there were people who were trying to pass themselves off as baptized Christians.[66]

We are thus faced with the very strong likelihood that there were many in Chrysostom's audiences who had not undergone the ritual of baptism and did not regularly take the Eucharist.[67] This meant that they missed out on the dramatic transformative experience of these rituals and were far less likely to feel any common bond with fellow Christians who had undergone the experience. They would also have to leave the church after Chrysostom's

---

[63] For the former, see *Hom. in Gen.* 12.1 (PG 53.98). For the latter, see *Catéchèse* 1.3–6 (SC 366.119–25) = Harkins, *Baptismal Instruction,* 9.4–10); *In Ep. ad 2 Cor. Hom.* 2.6–8; and *In Ep. ad 1 Thess. Hom.* 9 (PG 62.447).
[64] On baptism at death as the norm, see Riley 1974: 212–13 and Jedin and Dolan 1980: 294.
[65] See also *Catéchèse* 3.3 (SC 366.221 and 225) = Harkins, *Baptismal Instruction* 11.11 and 15–16); *Catéchèse* 2.8 (SC 366.195–6) = Harkins, *Baptismal Instruction* 10.18); and *Adv. Jud.* 2.3.6 and 4.6.7 (PG 48.861 and 880).
[66] Maxwell forthcoming: 120–1 and *Constitutiones Apostolae* 2.58.1 and 2.57.21.
[67] On this problem, see Meyendorf 1974: 202.

preaching, before the Eucharist ceremony. As lessons on the Eucharist, including the notion of the embodiment in Christ, were reserved for the final stages of the mystagogic instruction that was given to those directly about to undergo baptism, they would not have been known by all members of Chrysostom's audiences. At times Chrysostom even acknowledged that he had to be careful in what he said about the significance of the Eucharist ceremony and about baptism because uninitiated people were listening (*In Ep. ad 1 Cor. Hom.* 40.2 (*PG* 61.348)). The uninitiated would thus not have fully understood the connection between the image of the Church as a body and the participation in the body of Christ that baptism and taking the Eucharist brought about.

Rather than assume that there was a single community of Christians unified by the rituals of baptism and the Eucharist we need to imagine that there were many different levels of allegiance to Christianity among Chrysostom's audience. At the outer level there could be Greeks who were interested in taking a step towards Christianity and who had 'goodwill' towards Christian teachings.[68] Those who had this goodwill might have gone to hear Chrysostom preaching occasionally – such as those who attended during the Riot of the Statues.[69] This group of interested Greeks would have been joined by those who thought of themselves as Christian but who were not yet ready to make a stronger commitment to Christianity by undergoing formal instruction. For these people it would have been relatively easy to associate themselves more or less closely with worship of Christ and the name Christian at different times. At the next level of adherence to the Christian religion we can suppose that there would have been those who were at the early stages of instruction into Christianity. These are the people whom Baur referred to as receiving 'remote' preparation for Baptism.[70] Those beginning this period of training would have attended ordinary preaching (although they would have been dismissed after the prayer for the catechumens and penitents)[71] as well as catechism classes, possibly in subjects such as Genesis, God and creation.[72] It is this group of people who should most properly be known as the catechumenate, rather than those at the later stage of instruction. We should imagine that those who formed the catechumenate made up the other large percentage of Chrysostom's

---

[68] *Adv. Oppug.* 2.2 (*PG* 47.333). See also Schatkin 1988: 31 and 134.
[69] Van der Paverd 1991: 18, 197 and 200.
[70] Baur 1959–60: vol. I, 81. See also Harkins 1963: 290 and 301–2.
[71] Van der Paverd 1991: 191 and 199.
[72] Van der Paverd 1991: 197 and Bradshaw 2002: 92. See also Augustine, *de Catechizandis Rudibus* (*On the Catechism of the Uneducated*), which describes instruction in Genesis as suitable for the catechumen.

audiences.⁷³ At one point Chrysostom suggests that the catechumenate might have been a self-conscious group in Antioch when he asks the rhetorical question, '"What then must we say about the catechumens?" you ask. "For if no one can say that Jesus is Lord but in the Holy Spirit, what must we say of them who do name His Name but are lacking the Spirit?"' (*In Ep. ad 1 Cor. Hom.* 29.3 (*PG* 61.242–3)).⁷⁴

In a passage devoted to the question of catechumens at the beginning of his preaching on 2 Corinthians Chrysostom describes 'Catechumens' as 'aliens, for they are not yet of the body of Christ, they have not yet partaken of the mysteries, but are divided from the spiritual flock' (*In Ep. ad 2 Cor. Hom.* 2.6 (*PG* 61.399)). He also relates how Paul referred to catechumens as 'veiled' because their 'eyes of understanding' were shut and because the Gospel was hidden from them (*In Ep. ad 2 Cor. Hom.* 2.7 (*PG* 61.399–400)). These definitions of the catechumenate do not sound too dissimilar from how Chrysostom spoke about Greeks.⁷⁵ In contrast to his treatment of the Greeks, however, Chrysostom looked on the catechumens much more favourably and states that despite their otherness they should not be 'disowned' (*In Ep. ad 2 Cor. Hom.* 2.6 (*PG* 61.399)). He exhorts the faithful to pray for the uninitiated and argues that God will listen to the prayers of catechumens as much as to those of the faithful (*In Ep. ad 2 Cor. Hom.* 2.6–7 (*PG* 61.399–400)). Elsewhere, in his catechetical sermons, Chrysostom gives another presentation of the status of the catechumens. Describing the reasoning behind the need for daily exorcism of the candidate about to undergo baptism, he explains that 'the catechumen is sheep without a brand, a deserted inn, a hostel without a door, which lies open to all without distinction' (*Catéchèse* 2.7 (SC 366.193) = Harkins, *Baptismal Instruction* 10.16).⁷⁶ Such images nicely capture the vulnerable and unbounded state of the catechumen who had yet to undergo baptism and had not yet received the final stages of catechetical and mystagogic instruction that were intended to make 'strong and secure the walls of the inn which were weak and unsound' (*Catéchèse* 2.7 (SC 366.193) = Harkins, *Baptismal Instruction* 10.16).

Those who did go on to receive this final instruction can be described, following Baur, as 'proximate' or 'direct' candidates for baptism.⁷⁷ This was

---

⁷³ Harkins 1963: 301–2.
⁷⁴ See also *Hom. in Gen.* 12.1 (*PG* 53.98), where Chrysostom urges 'the uninitiated' to be baptized, and *Adv. Jud.* 1.3.4 (*PG* 48.847) on the contrast between baptized and unbaptized Christians.
⁷⁵ See chapter 3 above.
⁷⁶ On the in-between status of catechumenate, see also *In Ep. ad 1 Cor. Hom.* 29.3 (*PG* 61.242) and *In Ep. ad 2 Cor. Hom.* 2.6–7 (*PG* 61.399–40).
⁷⁷ Baur 1959–60: vol. I, 81.

the group that went on to receive the intensive thirty-day period of training before baptism, given by the bishop, in this case Flavian, in the final days running up to Lent. It included special training in Christian morals and mystagogic instruction on the meaning of the mysteries as well as on the Creed and *Pater Noster*. Most of Chrysostom's catechetical sermons were delivered to those undergoing this final instruction as an extra part of their training. It was only at this stage that the catechumens were supposed to have understood what baptism and the Eucharist ceremony signified, although it was of course possible that they had gained informal knowledge of this from other sources. Because of the knowledge and experience they gained at this stage, this group of catechumens had a special status distinct from those at earlier stages of instruction. During the final stage, they were referred to as 'those about to be illumined' and 'those being illumined'.[78] During baptism, and for seven days afterwards while they received final mystagogic instruction from the bishop, they took the name of 'neophytes' (as exemplified in the catechetical sermons of Cyril of Jerusalem).[79] Five of Chrysostom's catechetical sermons also show the extra instruction that he as priest would have given to the neophytes and here we see that they were regarded as being in an especially pure state and in a particularly close relationship to God (*Catéchèse* 4–8 (SC 50.183–260)).[80] It is likely, however, that only a small group of more committed Christians, who did not want to put off baptism until death, underwent this final important stage of instruction.[81]

After the newly baptized, we finally come to the body of baptized Christians. It is difficult to judge the numbers of these; we should probably imagine that they were a reasonably large group but far from a majority among Chrysostom's audiences. These were the people who could truly bear the names of Christian and believer, who would have been able to stay after Chrysostom's preaching to receive the Eucharist and who would thus have truly been part of the 'body of Christ'. As a result these people should have been the heartland of Christianity, people who lived up to all Chrysostom's ideals of Christian identity and community, but even this group were often not the Christians that they were meant to be. Chrysostom himself says that even those who had been baptized sometimes did not stay to receive the Eucharist (*In Ep. ad 1 Thess. Hom.* 4 (*PG* 62.422.19–21 and 25–8).[82] They

---

[78] Harkins 1963: 301–2.   [79] On these, see Yarnold 1994: 67–98 and 165–250 and Riley 1974.
[80] Harkins 1963: 243.   [81] Jedin and Dolan 1980: 294–5.
[82] See also *In Ep. ad 2 Thess. Hom.* 3 (*PG* 62.484.32–59)) and *De Bapt. Christi* 1 (*PG* 49.363–4). See also Allen 1997: 3–21; Leyerle 2001: 60–7; and van der Paverd 1991: 180 and 186. This was despite the fact that the Synod of Antioch in 341 had passed a decree to excommunicate those who failed to stay until the end of the service to join in the prayers and the Eucharist ceremony (Hefel 1907: 715).

too, like many of the unbaptized, would thus not have been receiving the regular ritual reaffirmation of their oneness with the body of Christ and the Christian community as a whole. They also still often had a tendency to sin or act in unchristian ways. As Chrysostom states, the baptized underwent a change for ten or twenty days after their baptism but soon went back to the 'oldness' they 'had before' (*In Ep. ad Rom. Hom.* 10 (*PG* 60.480)).[83] For this reason, he could never cease from exhorting his audience to change their ways and to repent.[84] Repentance was crucial to what it meant to be a Christian. As Christo puts it, 'it is during repentance that the human being's baptismal seal . . . is continuously preserved and perpetuated' and repentance 'is necessary' for 'church membership.[85] Repentance could also be a means of 're-entry into the Christian flock' after sin.[86] Watkins has argued, in his *History of Penance*, that Chrysostom stood out in a period of strict, ordered penitential discipline in the fourth century in his willingness to allow people to repent.[87] Chrysostom preached to actual audiences and had to deal with the realities of being Christian in the fourth-century context. If he wanted there to be any Christians he had to be laxer about letting them repent than the very strict rules of penitential discipline allowed. As Watkins says, in the context of fourth-century Antioch 'it was not so much unlikely as impossible that a rigid system of penitential discipline could be imposed'.[88] Instead, Chrysostom allowed a variety of ways in which his audience might repent for sin and he accepted as normal that even the worst sins could be forgiven after baptism.[89] His most extreme punishment was to exclude people temporarily from the church and from participation in the communal service: they could not take the Eucharist and had to leave the service at the same time as the catechumens.[90] This would weaken their link to the Christian community for a while, but eventually they would be allowed back.

In fourth-century Antioch there were groups of people with very different levels of knowledge about Christian teachings and different levels of experience of Christian rituals and therefore with very different levels of commitment to the faith. Those who legitimately bore the name Christian

---

[83] See also *In Ep. ad 1 Cor. Hom.* 2.10 (*PG* 61.21–2).
[84] See Sandwell 2001: 187–90. For examples in Chrysostom, see *Hom. in Gen.* 21.18, 24.18–19, 24.22, 25.9, 37.10 (*PG* 53.182, 214–15, 217, 221, 346); *Hom. de Stat.* 3.19–20, 6.5, 12.2 (*PG* 49.57–8, 63 and 127); *In Ep. ad 1 Cor. Hom.* 7.5 (*PG* 61.57); and *In Ep. ad 2 Cor. Hom.* 4.6 (*PG* 61.425).
[85] Christo 1998: xiv and xviii.   [86] Christo 1998: xviii.
[87] Watkins 1961: 33. See also Jedin and Dolan 1980: 299.   [88] Watkins 1961: 33.
[89] For the list of ways in which Chrysostom allowed Christians to repent, see Watkins 1961: 330, 331 and 336. See *In Ep. ad 2 Cor. Hom.* 15.6 (*PG* 61.510), where adulterers are allowed to repent but are excluded from the Eucharist until they have done so.
[90] See *In Ep. ad 1 Thess. Hom.* 10 (*PG* 62.455) and *Adv. Jud.* 2.3.6 (*PG* 48.861), where Chrysostom outlines different punishments for catechumen Judaizers and for believer Judaizers.

because they were baptized were not the majority and it seems that many who had not been baptized also used the name of Christian. If one could 'become' Christian simply by adopting the name oneself and turning up at Church occasionally then the experience should not be seen as some great or sudden life change.[91] Even for the baptized, there were many opportunities for people to vacillate between different stages of being Christian and to sin and repent many times even after baptism. People could be a little bit Christian, not-quite Christian, or something between the two, and at any of these stages the individual could turn back to non-Christian, Greek ways. Ordinary Christians might simply have defined what it meant to be Christian in far less demanding terms than their leaders and in a way that made very little impact on their lives. For these reasons, we should be wary of assuming that the label 'Christian' relates to a distinct and unified Christian community: some Christians might have been tightly bonded to one another, others might have interacted much more widely with non-Christians. We shall now turn to these ideas.

CHOICE AND MULTIPLICITY OF SOCIAL ALLEGIANCE AMONG CHRISTIANS

I have now begun to challenge some of the assumptions that underlie the picture of a unified Christian community focused on Chrysostom's preaching, for example the idea that there was a shared sense of communal feeling among all who heard Chrysostom preach. In addition I have shown that there were several different levels of commitment to Christianity. Because there was not a unified Christian community it is much harder for us to talk of the relationship of Christians to Jews and Greeks in terms of simple dichotomies. As Boyarin has pointed out for the relationship between early Christianity and Judaism, there is often a 'gap between the explicit claims of certain texts that groups are different and separate and the actual situation "on the ground" in which there was much more fuzziness at the borders'.[92] This 'fuzziness' results from the range of social interactions available to Christians, from the variety of enactments of identity possible in the social sphere and from the different degrees to which Christians allowed their Christian identity to impact on their forms of social organization. In this section, we will explore a variety of social relationships that Chrysostom's audiences could have with those whom he labelled as non-Christians.

---

[91] As Nock once suggested for early Christian conversion (Nock 1998). See also Fredriksen 1986; North, 1992: 174–93; Goodman 1994; Liebeschuetz 1979: 306–7; and Beard, North and Price 1998: vol. 1, 313–63. On the state of conversion in the fourth century, see Jedin and Dolan 1980: 293–4.
[92] Boyarin 1999: 10.

Even within Christianity at Antioch there were a number of different communities with which people could choose to align themselves. As well as the congregation based in the Old Church and that based in the Great Church on the Island, there were Christians who attended the services of the alternative Nicene bishop from the Eustathian party, and those who followed the Arian (Anomoean) and Nicolatian Christian leaders in the city.[93] We know very little about where the congregations of these other Christian leaders were based but we do know that Chrysostom saw them as a threat and that all of them would have labelled themselves as Christian. The existence of these alternative Christian focuses of loyalty and community meant that some Christians might have had allegiance to more than one Christian congregation or might have moved between different congregations as it suited them.[94] This could be for theological reasons but might also depend on which congregation was on their route home and most convenient or on which preacher they preferred. In his five sermons addressed to the Anomoeans *On the Incomprehensibility of God*, Chrysostom suggests that certain Anomoeans had challenged him to address them, which implies that they were present in his audience.[95] Those who normally attended Chrysostom's preaching might also occasionally have attended the preaching of Arian priests and bishops. Chrysostom seemed to be aware that at certain times the Christian community in Antioch was more divided than he would have liked. He contrasts the early Christian community of the past, which he saw as united, with the one in the present, saying, 'not so, however, now, but altogether the reverse. Many and various are the contests between all, and we are worse than wild beasts in how we act towards our own members' (*In Ep. ad 1 Cor. Hom.* 24.4 (*PG* 61.201)). He also complains that the Arian–Nicene controversy divided families and friends and that those within the Nicene community could be divided 'in their dealings with each other' despite the fact that they agreed in doctrine (*In Ep. ad 2 Cor. Hom.* 30.1 (*PG* 61.605)).[96]

Normal Graeco-Roman social relations also provided alternative forms of social loyalties for people in Chrysostom's audiences, especially in the social

---

[93] Mayer 1998: 126 and Wilken 1983: 10–16. On the legal rights of Arians to assemble under Theodosius, granted in 386, the year when Chrysostom was ordained preacher, see Wilken 1983: 14 and *CTh* 16.1.4.
[94] Mayer 1998: 116. See also *In Ep. ad Ephes. Hom.* 12 (*PG* 62.87.28–88.28).
[95] Wilken 1983: 15 and Lim 1995: 172–3, although Lim claims that the Anomoeans Chrysostom was addressing were regular members of his audiences.
[96] See Wilken 1983: 15. As Lim has shown, debate about theological matters, both by those educated with Greek learning and by common people, was seen by Christian preachers to be dangerous and to upset Church hierarchy and community unity (Lim 1995: 24–30 and (on Chrysostom in particular) 171–7).

distinctions between the poor and the rich. Chrysostom's references to social status and wealth are problematic because of their rhetorical nature and we should not necessarily assume that by 'the poor' he meant the very poor, or by the 'rich', the educated upper classes only.[97] However, his constant complaints about 'rich' Christians do suggest that normal social hierarchies persisted among members of his audiences. On one occasion Chrysostom discusses a passage in which Paul accused the Corinthian Christians of assembling together at church to take the Eucharist, but of eating their meals separately (*In Ep. ad 1 Cor. Hom.* 27.4 (*PG* 61.227–8)). Chrysostom then turns to his own audience saying, 'let us all listen to these words, as many of us who approach with the poor to the holy table while in the church but when we go out do not even seem to have seen them, but are both drunken and pass by the destitute, the very thing of which the Corinthians were accused' (*In Ep. ad 1 Cor. Hom.* 27.7 (*PG* 61.230–1)).[98] The moment of taking the Eucharist could temporarily elide class differences but could not lead to a lasting sense of community between rich and poor Christians once they had left church. Chrysostom complains of the massive differences in wealth and lifestyle that existed between the richest and the poorest people in Antioch (*In Ep. ad 1 Cor. Hom.* 11.5 (*PG* 61.51).[99] Some people insisted on showing off differences in social status even inside the church.[100] The wealthy could put on ridiculous displays of their riches while at the same time ignoring the extreme poverty around them.[101] Chrysostom even suggests that the very poorest of the poor, the beggars and the homeless, did not come into the church but could only be found waiting outside (*In Ep. ad Coloss. Hom.* 7 (*PG* 63.3651) and *In Ep. ad 1 Thess. Hom.* 11 (*PG* 62.466)). Even though it is likely that Chrysostom's contrast between the rich and poor is exaggerated, there is perhaps some truth to the picture of social divisions continuing among Christians. Chrysostom's preaching lacked any real ability to provide a unified Christian community that transcended normal Graeco-Roman social hierarchies. It seems that once they left church, elite Christians became once again typical men of their class carrying out their normal jobs and engaging in their usual social practices and forms of social relations. Chrysostom complains of rich *curiales* who enjoyed spending their large fortunes on public banquets, spectacles

---

[97] Kyrtatas 1987: 102–7 and Mayer 1998: 123. [98] See also *Hom. in Matt.* 59.3 (*PG* 58.581).
[99] See also *In Genesin Sermo* 4 (*PG* 54.603).
[100] *In Ep. ad 2 Thess. Hom.* 3 (*PG* 63.511) and *In illud: Filius ex se nihil facit* (*PG* 56.241).
[101] *In Ep. ad 1 Tim. Hom.* 2 and 8 (*PG* 62.513 and 541); *In Ep. ad Coloss. Hom.* 10 (*PG* 62.371); *In Ep. ad Philip. Hom.* 10 (*PG* 62.260); and *In Ep. ad 1 Cor. Hom.* 9 (*PG* 61.80). See also Hartney 2004: 133–70.

and buildings or on their own private mansions (*Hom. in Gen.* 48.21 (*PG* 54.440).[102] He condemns the wish of such rich Christians to see their names 'inscribed on the baths and buildings of Antioch' (*Hom. in Gen.* 22 (*PG* 53.195). Elsewhere he condemns rich 'believers' who exploited a drought for financial gain, just as an 'unbeliever' would (*In Ep. ad 1 Cor. Hom.* 39.13–15 (*PG* 61.343)). As Natali has argued, the growth of Christianity and the 'conversion' of the elite to the new religion did not change the euergetical habits of these men.[103] Antioch gained a forum, a new wall, a prison, many halls and a public baths during the fourth century, and its Olympic games, chariot races and spectacles, for which someone must have paid, continued to be put on.[104] Many of the *curiales* and *honorati* were now Christian.[105] Libanius agrees with the view that elite Christians supported the city. He tells us that Modestus, the Christian *comes orientis* in AD 359, commissioned a Portico of Dionysus (*Ep.* B.68 (F.242)) and that the previous *comes* had, sometime before 355/6, built baths and a portico in the city (*Ep.* N.13.7 (F.441) and *Ep.* B.25.6 (F.435)).

As a result of such tendencies among rich Christians, Natali argues that they acted as if their membership of the Christian community should not change their role in the civic community of Antioch. When they left church after attending preaching and the rest of the liturgy, they felt themselves to become ordinary citizens of Antioch again.[106] Natali also emphasizes the solidarity of class, culture and family that united the upper classes across any religious differences.[107] Elite Christians might well have felt greater affinity with elite non-Christians than with poor Christians, and no amount of Chrysostom's preaching could change that or develop social relations that would transcend such differences. The rich were also guilty of letting their normal social pleasures prevent them from listening to preaching: they sometimes chose to have their normal afternoon siesta or to eat their evening meals rather than attend the extra daily services and preaching put on during Lent.[108] At times, Chrysostom complains that members of his audience did not attend these Lenten services because they had eaten their midday meal and so broken their Lenten fast (*Hom. de*

---

[102] *Conciones de Lazaro* 1 (*PG* 48.979); *Hom. in Matt.* 66 (*PG* 58.630); *Adv. Oppug.* 3 (*PG* 47.359); *Expositio in Psalmos* 48 (*PG* 55.240); *Hom. in Gen.* 20 (*PG* 53.173); and *In Ep. ad 2 Cor. Hom.* 12 (*PG* 61.488). See also Natali 1975: 45–6.
[103] Natali 1975: 52–3. See also Mayer forthcoming.
[104] Natali 1975: 43 and 52, with reference to P. Petit 1955: 315–18, and Downey 1939b: 428–38 and 1961: 441.
[105] Natali 1975: 44 and P. Petit 1955: 83 and 201. See also the evidence of Chrysostom, *Hom. de Stat.* 21.2 (*PG* 49.211–12).
[106] Natali 1975: 53. [107] Natali 1975: 57.
[108] Van der Paverd 1991: 180 on Chrysostom, *Hom. de Stat.* 10.1 (*PG* 49.111).

Stat. 9.1 (*PG* 49.104) and *Hom. in Gen.* 10.1–2 (*PG* 53.81–4).[109] That this was particularly a crime of the rich can be seen in a passage in which Chrysostom compares the rich who sleep, bathe and eat with the poor who are not able to do so (*In Ep. ad 1 Cor. Hom.* 11.5 (*PG* 61.51)). This notion of wealthy Christians still enjoying their normal social pleasures also fits with Libanius' complaints about the Christian office-holders in Antioch who put on 'fine parties, where there is plenty of iced water laid on and plenty of misconduct' (*Or.* 2.59 and 61 (F. 1.258)).

There were also traditional, civic social gatherings that could attract both non-elite and elite Christians.[110] Events such as the theatre and the races could distract Chrysostom's audiences from his preaching.[111] In one of his catechetical sermons Chrysostom complains that after Lent fewer neophytes came to hear him because most had rushed off to the racecourses (*Catéchèse* 6.1 (SC 50.214)). Similarly, in his *Homilies on Genesis*, also delivered at Lent, Chrysostom complains that members of his audience had 'put out of their minds' all his 'unremitting teaching' and 'daily exhortations' and 'rushed off' to the races (*Hom. in Gen.* 6.1 (*PG* 53.54)).[112] On other occasions he has to urge his audiences not to attend traditional civic festivals (*In Kal.* (*PG* 48.953–62) and *Hom. in Matt.* 7 (*PG* 57.39–82)). Even when attending Christian festivals his audiences sometimes treated them as if they were Graeco-Roman festivals, at least in Chrysostom's opinion. Martyr festivals could involve market days and feasting just as Graeco-Roman civic festivals did.[113] Chrysostom complains that his audiences often came to these Christian festivals in 'a random and frivolous manner', dressing up in their most lavish clothes and preparing extravagant meals (*Hom. de S. Phil.* (*PG* 48.755). Especially to be condemned were the large numbers who would rush off after the festival to nearby drinking establishments to drink and revel (*Hom. in Mart.* (*PG* 50.663–4)). Smaller-scale social events could also be occasions for his audiences to fall back on old social customs. In Chrysostom's sermons on Genesis, his discussion of the marriage of Isaac and Rebecca leads him to criticize current marriage ceremonies among members of his audiences; he berates the 'devilish rites' so often found at these traditional marriage celebrations in the form of 'cymbals, pipes and dances' (*Hom. in Gen.* 48.30 (*PG* 54.443)).[114] He argues that Christians should summon a (Christian) priest to their marriage 'to strengthen the harmony of the union by prayers and blessings', suggesting that this was not

---

[109] See van der Paverd 1991: 168–9. [110] Wilken 1983: 1–94 and Mayer 1998: 121.
[111] Pasquato 1976 and Mayer and Allen 1993: 265. [112] See also *Hom. in Gen.* 41.1 (*PG* 53.374–5).
[113] Leemans *et al.* 2003: 19 and 21 and also Basil of Caesarea, *Homily on Riches* (*PG* 31.281).
[114] For a similar description, see *Hom. in Gen.* 56.1 (*PG* 54.486).

yet common practice among Christians (*Hom. in Gen.* 48.30 (*PG* 54.433)). Many Christians were still working with traditional Graeco-Roman customs and norms for marriage and defended their music-filled marriage ceremonies by saying that they were legitimate practices (*Hom. in Gen.* 56.7 (*PG* 54.488)). Chrysostom answered these people by saying that even legal experts in his own time knew that the ancient marriage ceremony had arisen only from custom and that it was not legally binding in any sense. It could thus easily be replaced by God's laws and by a marriage union sanctified by God (*Hom. in Gen.* 56.7 (*PG* 54.487)). Chrysostom understood that replacing such ceremonies would be central to creating a completely Christian community, but his audience found it hard to leave behind traditional customs.[115]

At other times Jewish festivities and customs drew Chrysostom's audiences away. It was because there was so much interaction between Jews and (Judaizing) Christians in his audience that Chrysostom had had to make a special effort to distinguish Jews and Christians in his sermons *Against the Jews*. As Wilken points out, these Judaizers were regular members of Chrysostom's congregation, 'who thought they could remain members of the Church while observing Jewish rites and customs. They saw no contradiction between going to the synagogue on Saturday to hear the reading of the Law and coming to church on Sunday to participate in the Eucharist.'[116] In these sermons Chrysostom described how some of his congregation rushed off to partake in the Jewish festivals, such as the festival of the trumpets held on New Year's Day, or to take part in the rituals of Matrona.[117] Others took part in Jewish fasts and attended the synagogue or even went as far as to celebrate Easter according to the Jewish calendar and to treat Saturday as the Sabbath (*Adv. Jud.* 3.3.1 and 9 (*PG* 48.864 and 866)).[118] This meant that they separated themselves from the rest of their congregation at Lent and Easter, precisely when the bonds of the Christian community were, in other ways, tightening. Such different practices and different ways of marking the religious year would have been a very divisive force for Chrysostom's audiences, as Chrysostom himself realized (*Adv. Jud.* 2.3.3 and 6 and 3.2.1 (*PG* 48.860, 861 and 863)).[119] Such Christians were not totally committed either to Chrysostom's congregation

---

[115] On Christian use of traditional marriage and funeral ceremonies, see Maxwell forthcoming 157–61.
[116] Wilken 1983: 75.
[117] *Adv. Jud.* 1.1.5, 1.6.7 and 8.1.5 (*PG* 48.844, 852 and 856) (general); 1.5.7 (*PG* 48.851) (trumpets); 1.6.1 (*PG* 48.851) (Matrona); *Adv. Jud.* 1.3.4 (*PG* 48.847) (feast). See also Wilken 1983: 93.
[118] *Adv. Jud.* 1.4.6; 8.1.5 (fasts) (*PG* 48.849); 1.5.2 (*PG* 48.850) (synagogue); or 3.5.7 (*PG* 48.869) (celebrate Passover.), Wilken 1983: 76 (Easter) and 1983: 92–3 (Sabbath).
[119] Wilken 1983: 78 and 92–3.

or to Judaism, but wanted to have both 'fellowship with the Jews' and 'fellowship at the holy table sharing the precious blood' (*Adv. Jud.* 2.3.5 (*PG* 48.861).

The attendance of many in Chrysostom's audiences at Graeco-Roman social events and Jewish festivals and rituals showed that they still had social ties and social allegiances outside the Christian community. As Chrysostom puts it, 'Here is a Christian who has shared in our teaching and enjoyed the fruit of the awe-inspiring and ineffable mysteries, spending time with the Jews and the Greeks and enjoying the same things that they enjoy' (*Catéchèse* 6.15 (SC 50.190)). Interaction between Christian, Greek and Jew was, in fact, very common, even at the most simple level of holding conversations with one another. Chrysostom himself tells us how he 'once heard a Christian disputing in a ridiculous manner with a Greek' about Paul and Plato (*In Ep. ad 1 Cor. Hom.* 3.8 (*PG* 61.27).[120] To Chrysostom's horror, Greeks and Christians would also talk and laugh with each other in 'the market place' and 'in the doctor's offices' about attacks carried out against monks by other Christians (*Adv. Oppug.* 1.2 (*PG* 47.322)). When they should 'stand with [their] own brothers and hear the prophetic words' they instead 'loitered about in the agora and took part in meetings that were in no way profitable' (*Hom. de Stat.* 10.1 (*PG* 49.111)).[121] While Chrysostom was horrified by certain kinds of interaction between Christians and Greeks, he did realize that in a city in which Greek and Christian intermingled other kinds of interaction were unavoidable. As he says,

> I do not say that we should not mingle with the Gentiles (*tois ethnesin*), but that we should be constant to our own virtues and when socializing with them attract them to piety . . . For this reason the Lord common to everyone permitted evil and good people to mingle together, and the pious and the impious, so that evil might profit from good . . .[122] (*Hom. in Gen.* 40.17 (*PG* 53.374))

The Christian should care about those outside the Church just as much as those inside and should seek to bring them into the Christian fold.[123] Although the Greeks were outsiders and enemies of the Christians, all humans were God's people (*In Ep. ad 1 Cor. Hom.* 33.5 (*PG* 61.282)).[124] In the past God's message was confined to the Jewish race but since the time

---

[120] Schatkin agrees that it would have been (Schatkin 1988: 193).
[121] On this passage and the view that 'pagans' would have been involved in these meetings in the agora, see van der Paverd, 1991: 174 and 181.
[122] See also *In Ep. ad 1 Cor. Hom.* 16.1 (*PG* 61.129–30).
[123] *In Ep. ad 1 Cor. Hom.* 25.2 (*PG* 61.207). See also *In Ep. ad 1 Cor. Hom.* 3.9 (*PG* 61.27), 4.11 (*PG* 61.38); and *Hom. in Gen.* 7.10 (*PG* 53.65).
[124] See also *De S. Bab. Contra Jul. et Gent.* 6–7 (*PG* 50.535).

of Christ, the possibility of salvation had been opened up to all humanity. Thus, Chrysostom argues, God did not let the Jews mix with the Gentiles in marriage and made them physically distinct through circumcision, in case friendship with them 'proved an occasion for transgression' (*In Ep. ad 1 Cor Hom.* 33.5 (*PG* 61.282). Now, however, the opposite was true and while the Gentiles were welcomed in, the Jews were excluded (*In Ep. ad 1 Cor. Hom.* 33.5 (*PG* 61.282).[125] Chrysostom's views on the mixing of Christians with Greeks can be seen when he discusses marriage between Christians and unbelievers. He tackles this problem in various passages, but in each case the conclusions are very similar. The fullest discussion is in his commentary on Paul's argument that a Christian man or woman should not leave an unbelieving spouse, in 1 Corinthians 7.12. Chrysostom follows Paul's argument in stating that marriage was far better than living in danger of lust. Only adultery of the spouse was reason for divorce because being an unbeliever, although worse in the greater scheme of things, was less harmful to marriage. It is possible that Chrysostom's parents were mixed, his mother being Christian and his father not.[126] Thus, even within families there would have been difficulties in developing a sense of communal Christian family, let alone in larger social units.

Antioch was a cosmopolitan city that offered its inhabitants many different kinds of social interaction. The Nicene Church of Chrysostom was just one of these options. Despite Chrysostom's ideals, it was very difficult for him to ensure that his audience primarily mixed with other Christians and did not mix with non-Christians, which is something we need to bear in mind when we use the terms 'Christian' and Christian 'community'. There might have been moments of great social cohesion between Christians but this cohesion far from dominated their lives. To talk of a Christian community as some kind of permanent, constantly visible and unified social structure is thus inappropriate. We must recognize that Chrysostom's audiences would have been divided in a number of ways: in terms of where and how often they heard his preaching; in terms of the extent of their instruction and initiation into Christianity; and by their social status and by their numerous other social and religious commitments. Any Christian might be a member of many communities, Christian and non-Christian, religious and non-religious at any one time. Interaction between those of different faiths was normal in fourth-century Antioch, even to the extent that mixed marriages were common. Many of these points have been made before

---

[125] *Adv. Jud.* 1.2.1–2, 5.3.2 (*PG* 48.845, 886).
[126] See J. Kelly 1995: 5. It is probably a question that we can never answer for certain.

about fourth-century Antioch, but we need to remind ourselves of them when thinking about issues of social organization and communal feeling in relation to Chrysostom's preaching. We must challenge the assumption, so often made without thought of its implications, that we can talk of a Christian 'community' around Chrysostom. Instead, we need to accept that most who called themselves Christians probably practised much looser forms of social organization. We must, in turn, accept that these loose forms of social organization among Christians in Antioch also undermine the impact of Chrysostom's preaching about clear-cut identities.

CHAPTER 8

Libanius, religious allegiance and social structure

LIBANIUS' WRITINGS AND 'PAGAN PARTY' FOCUSED ON JULIAN

Paul Petit has argued that Libanius' writings reveal to us a 'confrérie' or 'société' based on religious allegiance in Antioch: 'le parti Païen'.[1] He suggests that various references in Libanius to 'good men (*agathoi*)', 'companions (*hetairoi*)' (F.1433) and 'literary clubs (*syllogoi*)' (*Or.* 14.42 (F.11.102)) enable us to construct a picture of a literary-religious group meeting under Constantius to recruit new followers and prepare for Julian to come to power.[2] Petit continues to track the existence of such a 'pagan party' after the accession of Julian, as it gained favour from imperial power. He lists six people who formed a gang or 'brains trust' around the emperor Julian: Maximus of Ephesus, Priscus 5, Himerius, Oribasus, Secundius Salutius and Anatolius 5/4.[3] After the death of Julian, Petit sees this party as continuing to exist into the reign of Valens and Valentinian, but only in 'semi-secrecy' and 'remembrance of past activities'.[4] The idea of the 'pagan party' was revisited more recently by Malosse, who suggests that we can identify certain friends and old students of Libanius as its members.[5] Malosse's list includes Entrechius, Helpidius 6, Seleucus 1, Fortunatianus and Celsus, as well as Ablabius, otherwise unknown (*Ep.* F.493). The focus for Malosse's pagan party, as for Petit's, is the emperor Julian. Malosse refers to the fact that in 353 Entrechius was looking forward to seeing the emperor in Bithynia (*Ep.* B.23 (F.13)) and that Libanius described Ablabius and Helpidius as

---

[1] P. Petit 1955: 204. Bouchery and Bowersock also support this view (Bouchery 1936: 39–43 and Bowersock 1978: 30).
[2] P. Petit 1955: 204–5. As evidence he uses: *Or.* 13.13–15 and 35 (F.11.67–8 and 75); *Or.* 14.41–2 (F.11.102); *Ep.* B.129 (F.697); *Ep.* B.170 (F.1336); and (*Ep.* B.253 (F.661).
[3] P. Petit 1955: 208.
[4] P. Petit 1955: 210–11. As evidence he uses: *Ep.* F.1256; *Ep.* F.1456; *Ep.* N.140 (F.1473); and N.142 (F.1508); N.142 (F.1508) in 365; and *Ep.* F.1526.
[5] Malosse 1995a: 252.

213

bringing letters from the emperor Julian (*Ep.* B.24 (F.493)[6] and (*Ep.* N.38 (F.35)).[7] The idea of a pagan group or association in Antioch has also recently been discussed by Soler. He argues that Libanius was involved in a 'reconstitution' of certain Neoplatonic *hetaireiai* that had been based in Daphne at the beginning of the fourth century. There is some evidence that Iamblichus of Apamea had spent some time in Daphne before his death in AD 330.[8] Soler describes how groups developed around Iamblichus of Apamea that were versions of Pythagorean and Neoplatonic *hetaireiai* and shared their cult of friendship.[9] He then claims direct continuity between these *hetaireiai* and the groups we supposedly see in Libanius' writings.

These arguments for a 'pagan group' in Antioch have largely been constructed by taking references to socio-religious groups at face value or by reading Libanius' references to religious allegiance in a simplistic way.[10] Whitmarsh has recently argued that to scan the literature of second-sophistic writers 'for the "beliefs", "attitudes" or "opinions"' of the author as if these were 'dimly visible through the opaque fug of literature' is mistaken.[11] The complex, self-reflexive and literary texts of this period simply did not aim to reveal what their authors believed in any straightforward way. Instead, such literature was a site in which these authors sought to create and construct a sense of self.[12] One aspect of self-creation is how an individual relates to others.[13] Steel, in her study of genre and performance in Cicero, has shown that Cicero used his writing to emphasize his social connections precisely because he lacked these as a *novus homo*: 'Cicero uses text to place himself in relation to others' both by emphasizing social links that did exist and by describing ones that did not.[14] In these ways, 'Cicero uses writing to construct community' for himself.[15] Representations of social organization and social links in rhetorical writings such as those of Libanius and Cicero were not disinterested. They could be made for strategic reasons in order for the author to achieve something or to represent himself in a particular way. Libanius' references to his socio-religious connections might not be descriptive of some social group that was already in existence but might themselves be involved in constructing this group. By writing to people

---

[6] Although it is unclear whether this letter refers to the emperor Julian or not; see Bradbury 2004: 53, in the introduction to his translation of this letter.
[7] For another reference in passing to the 'pagan party', see Criscuolo 1994: 9.
[8] Soler 1999: 86 and Malalas 12.47 (312).   [9] Soler 1999: 163–77. See also Soler 2004.
[10] Drinkwater 1983: 349.   [11] Whitmarsh 2001: 29.   [12] Whitmarsh 2001: 30–4.
[13] On the importance of relations with others and a sense of community in the construction of self-hood through letter writing, see Conybeare 2000:17.
[14] Steel 2005: 83–4.   [15] Steel 2005: 84, 88, 91, 93, 103 and 105–6.

Libanius, religious allegiance and social structure   215

about religious allegiance and by emphasizing his religious connections with them at certain times, Libanius was actively involved in creating and maintaining social links and relationships that might not otherwise exist. Rather than accept Libanius' representations of socio-religious organization and socio-religious links as descriptions of reality we need to explore their strategic and creative functions. As the scholarly notion of a 'pagan group' in Libanius' writings depends so much on loyalty to Julian and his religious policy, we must look at how Libanius depicts his relationship with this emperor. We need to understand that this too might be part of Libanius' self-representation and should be wary of accepting everything he says. As Heather and Moncur have argued for Themistius, scholars have too often fallen into the trap of 'taking Themistius' account of himself' and his relation to fourth-century emperors 'at face value' when in fact his writings present 'a cultivated image self-consciously created and sustained in speeches composed explicitly for public consumption'.[16] Themistius sought to present himself as a disinterested philosopher speaking his mind impartially to each emperor but he was much closer to the imperial regimes he served under and adjusted his views to suit changes in these regimes.[17] In a similar way, the persona and opinions that Libanius attributes to himself in relation to the fourth-century emperors should not be seen as simple expressions of how things were but as constructions he created.[18] Before understanding how and why Libanius represented socio-religious links as he did we need to understand how he represented his relationship with Julian.

In the next section of this chapter, I shall explore Libanius' representation of his attitude to and relationship with Julian and seek to criticize some of the assumptions that are made about this. In the third section of the chapter, I shall investigate whether we can really say there was a religious group that existed before the reign of Julian and continued to exist after his death. Finally, I shall consider the kind of social relations that we see in Libanius' letters. I shall suggest that the model of the network rather than the social group is better able to describe Libanius' social relations generally. We shall see that religion was a relatively unimportant factor in these social relations.

---

[16] Heather and Moncur 2001: xiii.   [17] Heather and Moncur 2001: xiv and 12.
[18] Pack and Norman have explored, for example, the extent to which Libanius' account in his *Oration* 1 *The Autobiography* of his first meeting with Julian in Antioch intentionally echoed Aristides and his relationship with Marcus Aurelius (Pack 1947: 17–20 and 1953: 173–4; and Norman, 1953: 239 and 1951: 20–3).

LIBANIUS' SELF-REPRESENTATION AND HIS RELATIONSHIP WITH JULIAN

Libanius' writings can give the impression that Julian's reign was the only time when he was truly happy, compared to his unpleasant experiences under other emperors. In a passage on his *Oration* 30, which was written in the 380s near the end of his career, Libanius leaves us a summary of this stereotypical view. He blames the Christian emperors before Julian for destroying the traditional cults. Constantine had stripped the temples of their wealth, but had otherwise 'made absolutely no alteration to the customs of worship' (*Or.* 30.6 (F.III.90)).[19] Constantius then went further by 'adopting the misguided policy' of banning sacrifice (*Or.* 30.7 (F.III.90)) and is later described as destroying temples *en masse* and giving his courtiers gifts of temples (*Or.* 30.38 (F.III.107–8)). Julian, in contrast, is praised for his restoration of the temples of the gods (*Or.* 30.7 and 40–1 (F.III.91 and 108–10)) but his reign was short lived and he was soon replaced by the 'the two imperial brothers', Valens and Valentinian, who again banned sacrifice (*Or.* 30.7 (F.III.91)).[20] Under Theodosius worship of the gods can be seen as under threat again, this time not from imperial legislation but from the actions of a minority of zealous Christian monks, who, under the orders of Bishop Flavianus, destroyed the temples around Antioch.[21] *Oration* 30 thus gives us a concise summary of the usually accepted picture of Libanius' feelings towards the various fourth-century emperors and their religious policies. Evidence to support this picture can then be found elsewhere in Libanius' writings.

On a number of occasions Libanius depicts Constantius as the villain of the piece. In orations written after Julian's death Libanius compares the short reign of Julian to Constantius' reign of forty years, describing Constantius as 'witless and little better than a painted image or a figure of clay' (*Or.* 17.8 (F.II.210)). In *Oration* 18 *The Funeral Oration on Julian*, Libanius also describes in detail the conflict between Julian and Constantius and makes the accusation that Constantius had tried to have Julian killed when they were young men (*Or.* 18.27 (F.II.248)). This depiction of Constantius echoes a view expressed in *Oration* 62 *Against the Critics of his Educational System*,[22] in which Libanius describes how Constantius

---

[19] See also *Or.* 30.37 (F.III.107). For Libanius on Constantine's religious policy, see Wiemer 1994: 520–3.
[20] Norman 1969–77: vol. II, 106–7, note e.
[21] On the monks, see *Or.* 30.8–9, 11, 21–3 and 31 (F.III.91–2, 93, 98–9 and 103). On Flavian, see *Or.* 30.46–9 (F.III.112–14). On Cynegius, see *Or.* 30.46–9 (F.III.112–14).
[22] For the dating of this oration, see Norman 2000: 87–8. Norman favours a date of 382 but the speech could have been delivered later.

'fanned into a mighty flame' the 'spark of evil' he had inherited from his father and so destroyed and robbed temples as well as disparaging oratory (*Or.* 62.8 (F.IV.350)).[23] In contrast, Libanius' Julianic orations support the picture that Julian's reign was a time of restoration.[24] Libanius expresses great happiness about Julian's accession to power and what appears to be almost unqualified support for Julian's 'restoration' of Graeco-Roman religion. He praises Julian's restoration of temples, his replacement of statues of the gods and the reinstitution of festivals and mourns their loss once Julian was dead.[25] As Libanius says, 'he cared about nothing before sacred affairs (*ta hiera*) . . . he built up temples, constructed altars, and made his fatherland accustomed to not fighting against good things, at a time when it was least supportive of the sacrificial smoke that was so advantageous to it' (*Or.* 12.69 (F.II.34)).

Passages such as these have caused scholars to accept the notion of a shared religious allegiance between Libanius and Julian. This view of Libanius' loyalty to Julian and his religious policy and his unhappiness at its loss is also supported in other later orations. A number of Libanius' works written just after Julian's death in the 360s speak of the grief shared by Libanius and others at the emperor's death.[26] In *Oration 17 Lament over Julian*, written between 363 and the autumn of 365,[27] Libanius mourns the victory that Julian's death handed to the Christians, bewailing the fact that,

> So then, a creed that was laughable before is now doing better, a creed which had started such violent, unending war against you. It has extinguished the sacred flame. It has put a stop to the sweet sacrifices. It has sent people to trample on and overturn the altars. It has closed the temples and sanctuaries, or demolished them, or given them to profane use, permitting whores to dwell in them. Having completely worn away your way of life, it has established the coffin of a corpse in place of your inheritance. (*Or.* 17.7 (F.II.210))

---

[23] On Libanius' writings as evidence for Constantius' religious policy, see Seiler 1998: 179–84.
[24] The Julianic Orations are: *Oration 13, The Address to Julian*, a speech of welcome for the new emperor soon after his arrival in Antioch in July 362; *Oration 14 In Defence of Aristophanes* delivered a little later in 362; *Oration 12 An Address to the Emperor Julian as Consul*, which was delivered on New Year's Day when Julian became consul and which had been requested by him; *Oration 15 The Embassy to Julian*, sent to Julian in Spring 363 after he had left Antioch; *Oration 16 To the Antiochenes: On the Emperor's Anger*, which was probably never published; *Oration 17 A Lament over Julian*, delivered in 363, immediately after Julian's death; *Oration 18 The Funeral Speech*, written a little later in 363; and, finally, *Oration 24 On Avenging Julian*, written in 379.
[25] P. Petit 1978: 77. See, for example, *Or.* 13.45–7 (F.II.79–80); *Or.* 17.1–9 (F.II.206–11); *Or.* 18.126, 287–8 and 298 (F.II.290, 362–3) and *Or.* 24.36 (F.II.530). See also letters written during the reign of Julian such as *Ep.* B.129.2–3 (F.697) and those just after his death such as *Ep.* N.129 (F.1187).
[26] *Ep.* F.1424.7; *Ep.* N.111 (F.1424); *Ep.* B.137 (F.1124); *Ep.* B.141 (F.1217); *Ep.* N.112.1 (F.1426); *Ep.* N.123 (F.1128); *Ep.* F.1326; and *Orations* 17, 18 and 24.
[27] On the dating, see Norman 1969–77: vol. I, xxxiv.

On two occasions Libanius even hints that Christians on the Roman side had been responsible for Julian's death (*Or.* 18.274 (F.II.356) and *Or.* 24.6 (F.II.517)).[28] These kinds of references are usually taken as evidence that Julian's most avid supporters were being persecuted at the time and that they were losing positions given to them by him. References to the religious situation in the reign of Julian also appear in a number of orations written in the late 370s to 380s and again support the same picture. In *Oration 1 The Autobiography*, Libanius describes both his happiness when Julian came to power (*Or.* 1.118–20 (F.1.140–1)) and his distress after Julian's death (*Or.* 1.135–6 (F.1.148–9)). In his *Oration 2 On Those Who Call Me Tiresome*, written in the early 380s, he responds to accusations that he was tiresome by listing all that was wrong with the current times, including the loss of Julian's religious restoration. He says that while 'in the past there were sacrifices in plenty: the temples used to be full of worshippers, there were festivities, music, songs, garlands and treasure' now no temples can be found in this good state (*Or.* 2.30 (F.1.248)). Libanius also mourns the influence of the monks and of the Christian *honorati* and courtiers – who held parties 'where not the gods but those responsible for our present woes receive hymns of praise' (*Or.* 2.32 and 59 (F.1.249 and 258)).

The picture that these orations leave in our minds is one of Libanius going through great lows and then great highs and then great lows again as the rule of the various emperors progressed. While they present Julian's reign as a time of great joy and of revival of the traditional cults, they depict the reigns of Constantius, Jovian and Valens and Valentianian as times of trials and troubles for those who supported the traditional cults and the emperor Julian. By the time of Theodosius they see all hope to be lost; scholars take the despairing tone of *Oration 2* as representative and as marking a permanent shift towards a more negative and defeatist attitude on Libanius' part. For a long time scholars accepted this picture. Despite some recognition of the problems in Libanius' relationship with Julian most scholars still tend to see Libanius as supporting the more traditional aspects of Julian's religious restoration and as preferring the reign of Julian to that of any other emperor.[29] Petit has reasserted this position in a recent work stating that the witness of Libanius on Julian and his reign is 'pratiquement toujours favorable' because so many things united them including: 'un grand amour pour l'hellénisme, teinté avantage de rhétorique chez Libanios et de philosophie chez Julien; des fortes convictions païennes,

---

[28] See also *Ep.* N.129 (F.1187) and *Or.* 1.133 (F.1.147) and Amm. Marc. 25.3.
[29] Swain 2004: 398; Malosse 1995b: 334; Festugière 1959; and P. Petit 1955.

malgré des differences sur lequelles nous reviendrons'.[30] As a friend and ex-teacher of Julian as well as an ardent worshipper of the traditional gods, Libanius appears as a natural supporter of the new emperor.[31] Looking back at Libanius' writings as a whole, we cannot but be affected by the image Libanius presents of himself in the years after Julian's death. The image that he seeks to leave the world of himself as a sincere supporter of Julian and his religious policy and as suffering at all other times becomes fixed in our minds and distorts how we see his life. In this way we are presented with a similar problem to one that Whitmarsh identifies in the case of the second-century orator Dio Chrysostom. Whitmarsh has shown that Dio's 'self-constructed narrative of his career can . . . be viewed as a barometer of the changing temper of the imperial household'.[32] According to this narrative, Dio prospered under Vespasian, was exiled under Domitian, and was recalled and prospered again under Trajan. However, as Whitmarsh points out, we have to remember that this perception of events has been 'artfully constructed' by Dio 'so as to tell a story' that emphasizes his own resistance to the tyrannical emperor. In so doing, he was able to highlight both his strength of character and the positive nature of Trajan's rule at a time when it was politic to do so.[33] Turning again to Libanius' presentation of his position during the fourth century, we can view the dominant picture that he seeks to leave of his loyalty to Julian and his religious policy and his suffering at other times as a self-constructed image that might have had little bearing on reality. This can give us a new starting point in understanding Libanius.

In his recent work on Libanius' life Wintjes has sought to correct some of the faults in the way that we have perceived Libanius' biography and career. Wintjes has shown that Libanius had great influence under Constantius because of the strong network of contacts that he had among court officials at this time.[34] In this period we see Libanius interacting with courtiers and high officials of Constantius' reign and freely asking for favours. During most of this time Libanius was not an outspoken critic of Constantius' reign and was certainly not oppressed or constrained in his actions. We can remind ourselves that Libanius wrote *Oration 59 In Praise of Constans and Constantius* at the request of the praetorian prefect Philippus at this time and delivered it before Philippus and other courtiers in Nicomedia.[35] In this oration Libanius was able to praise the two Christian rulers in the traditional form of the *basilikos logos*, touching on most positive aspects

[30] P. Petit 1978: 71.   [31] P. Petit 1978: 67–9; Malosse 1995a: 252–3; and Scholl 1994: 14–16.
[32] Whitmarsh 2001: 156.   [33] Whitmarsh 2001: 156 and 125–9.
[34] Wintjes 2005: 99–118.   [35] See Wiemer 1994: 513.

of their rule while ignoring any faults.[36] This shows Libanius active at the centre of power under Constantius and pandering, to some degree at least, to his religious policy.[37] While Libanius did not make any direct reference to Constantius' propagation of Christianity, he did make consistent use of the monotheistic conception of divinity in this speech (*Or.* 59.48, 50, 72, 125 and 143 (F.IV.232, 233, 243–4, 272–3 and 281–2)).[38] As Wiemer has noted, this does not happen anywhere else in Libanius' writings and makes Libanius' tone 'remarkably close to the neutral monotheistic theology to be found in courtly rhetoric'.[39] Wintjes has also shown that the importance of Julian's death to Libanius has been exaggerated because, despite his complaints of persecution, Libanius still had great influence under Jovian.[40] We can add to this the suggestion of Heather and Moncur that Themistius' *Oration 5*, delivered in Jovian's court and advocating tolerance on religious matters, reflected a policy of religious toleration that Jovian was already pursuing.[41] The idea of a persecution on religious grounds of those who had supported Julian, as Libanius' writings sometimes suggest, thus becomes less tenable. We do know that Libanius himself must have been under threat in the later years of the reign of Valens and Valentinian as he did not publish any of his letters from this time.[42] However, it seems that his fear was a result not of his religious allegiance but of Valens' fear of magic and treason.[43] In contrast, in the years of Theodosius' rule Libanius appeared to feel more at ease in expressing his views openly. There were some moments, such as in *Oration 2 On Those Who Call Me Tiresome*, when he presented himself as in great despair. However, we also see some of his most outspoken and positive orations from this period: *Oration 30 To Theodosius, In Defence of the Temples* presents Theodosius as the tolerant, benevolent emperor to whom Libanius can address himself freely. This very different picture of Libanius doing quite well under Constantius, Jovian and Theodosius (and doing badly under Valens and Valentinian for different reasons than we might at first imagine) can help us to build up an alternative picture to the one that Libanius paints in many of his letters and orations. We can see that he might not have had such a difficult time under Christian emperors as it first appears, that he found it easier to deal with their religious policies

---

[36] See Lieu and Montserrat 1996: 153–64. [37] See Wiemer 1994: 513.
[38] Wiemer 1994: 514. [39] Wiemer 1994: 514.
[40] Wintjes 2005: 151–62. See also Bradbury's introduction to his translation of *Ep.* B.168 on Libanius' continued political influence under Jovian.
[41] Heather and Moncur 2001: 154–8, introduction to *Oration 5*. [42] Wintjes 2005: 163–76.
[43] As Wintjes has noted, it was from the early 370s in the reign of Valens and Valentinian that Libanius really suffered a loss of influence (Wintjes 2005: 243). On the idea that worshippers of the gods might have suffered more from charges of magic at this time, see Sandwell 2005: 120 and 122.

than he himself suggests and that that he never suffered as a result of his religious allegiance being different from theirs.

Scholars now generally accept that Libanius' relationship with Julian was far from straightforward. The two men had been friends while Julian was a student at Nicomedia and Libanius was his teacher. Julian was not allowed to attend Libanius' lectures but had gained access to his orations and had some communication with him. One letter (if the addressee has been correctly identified) testifies to the warmth of this early relationship as it shows Libanius writing to Julian after he had left Nicomedia to express concern for his health (*Ep.* B.23 (F.23) of 353).[44] After this, there had been a long gap in the correspondence in which relations between the two men appear to have cooled or even dwindled to nothing.[45] Libanius' delay in visiting Julian when he became emperor in Constantinople and when he first came to Antioch can be seen as suggestive of problems in their relationship – Libanius had declined to be part of Antioch's embassy to Constantinople to congratulate the new emperor and did not rush to attend on Julian when he took up residence in Antioch (*Or.* 1.121 (F.1.141) and *Ep.* B.129 (F.697)). In fact, Libanius recorded that Julian did not even recognize him when the two first encountered each other in Antioch.[46] Wintjes suggests that a primary reason for these problems might have been the success of Libanius during the reign of Constantius and his very good connections with leading figures in Constantius' court.[47] It was only after this initial coldness between the two men had thawed that they appear to have properly established friendly relations; after the reconciliation Libanius began to write the Julianic orations (*Orations* 12–14) as well as a number of letters to the emperor. The friendship between the two men continued even after Julian fell out with the city of Antioch as a whole and left for his Persian campaign (Julian, *Ep.* 98). What is not clear is whether shared religious allegiance was the primary reason for their friendship. Some have suggested that the friendship was instead based on rhetoric, or that Libanius' usefulness to Julian as a friendly member of the otherwise hostile civic council

---

[44] With Bradbury's introduction to this letter (Bradbury 2004: 52). See also *Ep.* B.24 (F.493).
[45] The dating and extent of this period of coolness is debated. Malosse places it in 360–2 (sometime after Julian's arrival in Antioch; 1995a: 254). Wiemer has been the main proponent of the view that the period of hostility extended back into the 350s (1995a: 20). Wintjes has argued, however, that we have to be cautious about characterizing Libanius' and Julian's relationship in the 350s owing to lack of evidence (Wintjes 2005: 121–3). Drinkwater even argues that Libanius was not aware of Julian's apostasy from Christianity in this period (Drinkwater 1983: 353–4).
[46] Swain 2004: 395 and 398–400; Bradbury 2004: 10; and most recently Wintjes 2005: 126–9.
[47] Wintjes 2005: 124. Swain suggests that Julian's hostility towards Libanius' close friend Thalassius might have been another contributing factor to this enmity (Swain 2004: 397).

in Antioch was a more important factor.[48] In a recent article Malosse has argued that Libanius praises Julian's religious policy only with tepidity and out of obligation.[49] Similarly, Swain has suggested that Julian's uncompromising policy on religious matters meant that 'Libanius found it much easier to deal with Julian when he was dead' and that Libanius placed less emphasis on shared religious ideas as the basis for their friendship.[50] Scholl has focused on the religious differences between Libanius and Julian (in particular on Julian's monotheism and Libanius' favouring of rhetoric) and has concluded that we should not identify Libanius' religious ideas with those of Julian.[51] It is not at all clear that Julian would have provided the focus for religious loyalty for Libanius that some have imagined. Just as Libanius was happier under Constantius and other Christian emperors than people have often imagined, so he might have been less identified with Julian and his religious policy than many have previously thought. Rather than see Libanius' experience of the reigns of the various emperors as a series of peaks and troughs, we can see that it might have actually been more of a constant.

We saw in chapter 4 that part of the skill of 'playing' the fourth-century religious situation was to adjust the representation of one's religious allegiance without being seen as a flatterer. We saw that Libanius accused a number of people of flattery because of what he considered to be their insincere speech or actions in relation to religion. It seems, however, that Libanius himself might have fallen on the wrong side of the fine line that lay between tactful suppression of one's true religious allegiance and abject flattery of the religious allegiance of others. Eunapius' *Lives of the Sophists* shows us how Libanius was viewed as a flatterer during the fourth century. As Eunapius says: 'Those who pursued modes of life directly opposed to one another would applaud in him [Libanius] qualities that were directly opposed, and everyone without exception was convinced that it was his views that Libanius admired, so multiform was he, so completely all things to all men' (Eunapius, *VS* 496).[52] During the course of his life Libanius had been accused of flattery on a number of occasions. During the reign of Constantius some people appear to have viewed Libanius' *Oration 59 In Praise of Constans and Constantius* as flattery of a Christian emperor: it caused them to accuse Libanius of 'being acquainted with men whom

---

[48] On Eunapius' view of Julian and Libanius, see Swain 2004: 377 and Wintjes 2005: 128.
[49] Malosse 1995b: 333.   [50] Swain 2004: 395, 377 and 398.   [51] Scholl 1994: 99–100.
[52] See also Libanius, *Ep.* N.40.7 (F.19), in which Libanius answers a good-natured charge from a friend that he 'sings the praise of many people', by explaining what he does when he sets out to compose a eulogy or panegyric.

Apollo would reject' (*Or.* 1.74 (F.119–20)). Again, when Julian first came to power, Libanius had to justify to his friend, Seleucus 1 (a confidant of the emperor and eventually appointed as his high priest of Cilicia), why he had not acted as a legate to the new emperor in Constantinople on behalf of Antioch.[53] His excuse was that he had not wished to appear to be a flatterer of Julian. He states that when Julian came to power he had spoken celebratory words for him and his religious policy and words of hatred against Constantius but that he had 'not said them because he saw in them hope of recompense' (*Ep.* B.129 (F.697)). After Julian's death too Libanius had to answer charges of flattery. He was criticized for using his friendship with Julian in order to benefit himself and because he was not an ardent enough supporter of Julian and had been too friendly to Christians. In one letter of early 363 he had to rebut the accusations of Antipater 1 (who had been a priest during Julian's reign) that he had used Julian's rule to 'outdo his neighbours' in his 'private affairs' by arguing that he had not gained buildings or land from the emperor (*Ep.* N.97 (F.797)).[54] In another, to Julianus 14/8, written soon after the emperor Julian's death Libanius had to argue that he had gained neither influence nor money from Julian's reign and that on Julian's death he 'had not lost any flatterers' because he 'never had any' (*Ep.* N.124 (F.1154)).[55] That Libanius might well have seen 'flattery' of Julian as a useful technique can be seen in his approval of the way that a Christian relative, Bassianus, in 362, praised the emperor in traditional terminology as a way to regain his favour.[56] Others accused of Libanius of dropping his support for Julian too soon after Julian's death. Thus, we see that Nicocles, a grammarian and close associate of Julian, appears to have accused Libanius of being two-faced and of trying to find favour with Christians in the changed circumstances. Libanius feels the need to ask Nicocles to 'not think of me as a time server, or a Euripus [the strait between Attica and Euboea whose current reverses] or the wind's plaything because of the changes that have occurred' (*Ep.* B.161.2 (F.1196)).[57] He also denies that he is now criticizing Nicocles or praising those that

---

[53] On Seleucus 1, see Bradbury 2004: 265–6.
[54] On Libanius' influence under Julian, see Malosse 1995a: 259 and also *Ep.* B.96 (F.1360)).
[55] Julianus was member of a prominent family from Tarsus with whom Libanius had many connections. For the identification of Julianus as Christian, see P. Petit 1994: 142. For similar accusations against Libanius, see *Or.* 1.125 (F.1.142–3) of 374; *Or.* 2.8 (F.1.241) of 381–2; and *Or.* 51.30 (F.IV.145) of 388.
[56] *Ep.* N.79 (F.679)). See Norman 1992: vol. II, 89, note c.
[57] For a similar complaint against Libanius, see also *Or.*1.74 (F.1.119) and *Ep.* F.1195 to Eumolpius in 364. For Nicocles' relationship with Julian, see Athanassiadi 1992: 27–8 and Kaster 1988: 125, 202–4 and 214–15. It did seem that Nicocles, who had held great influence under Julian as his former teacher, suffered because of his loss of influence after the death of Julian, see Kaster 1988: 214–15 and also Libanius, *Ep.* B.81 (F.1266) and *Ep.* F.1492.2.

he had previously blamed. On another occasion Libanius has to answer the complaints of his friend Aristophanes, the subject of *Oration* 14, that he was 'keeping silent about the murder of our noble emperor' (*Ep.* N.133 (F.1264)); he does so by saying that open publication of his *Oration 17 Lament over Julian* would be dangerous and that to release it would make him a simpleton who was asking for trouble.[58] To some Libanius' friendship with Julian and support for his religious policy made him suspect; for others his friendship with Christians led to doubts about the depth of his support for Julian.

Once we place Libanius' letters and orations to or about Julian in this context we can begin to see why they might not be simple statements of true feeling. They could instead be part of the means by which he strategically mediated his relationship with Julian in order to ward off criticisms that he changed his religious allegiance with each emperor. During Julian's life Libanius wrote about him in the panegyric form in order to convince him that he had always been a loyal supporter: his success under Constantius had put this in question. He praised every aspect of Julian's religious policy and presented him in typical panegyric terms as having divinely ordained power. As P. Petit has shown, in orations written while Julian was still alive Libanius described scenes in terms that fitted with the emperor's own religious ideology.[59] Malosse has also shown that praising Julian's piety was one way in which Libanius fitted into the rhetorical tradition of praising the character of an emperor in the *basilikos logos*.[60] Such praise was not intended to be a true representation of Libanius' own feelings but was adjusted to present Julian in the light most acceptable to the emperor. In a similar way, playing up his loyalty to Julian in certain circles after Julian's death was useful to Libanius because his religious loyalty might be called into doubt. Doing so allowed Libanius to counterbalance both that he had made overt displays of support for Constantius, including praising him in the monotheistic terms popular at Constantius' court, and that on Julian's death he began courting the new regime and Christian officials again. Using this technique at the end of his life was again useful to Libanius; it enabled him to leave an image of himself as a loyal supporter of Julian and as

---

[58] See also *Ep.* F.1214 to Aristophanes in 364 and a letter to Themistius in which he justifies his silence after Julian's death and that he had not stopped the people of Antioch rejoicing on the news of Julian's death (*Ep.* N.116.3–4 (F.1430)). On such passages, see P. Petit 1955: 210–11.
[59] On the differences in Libanius' various representations of Julian's crowning, see P. Petit 1956: 479. For Libanius on Julian's divine status, see Nock 1957: 115–23 and Z. Stewart: 1972. On the proclamation of Julian as emperor, see also more recently Scholl 1994: 52–9, and on divine favour towards him, 70–4.
[60] Malosse 1995b: 320–1 and 332.

someone who suffered for this loyalty, so as to counteract the image that other people (such as Eunapius) were propagating of him as a flatterer. Far from describing the reality of the religious situation, Libanius' writings were part of the rhetorical cut and thrust of the fourth century. In them Libanius sought to present an image of himself that counteracted the picture created by his own actions (shape-shifting and surviving under emperors of different religious allegiance) and by the accusations made against him by others.

These conclusions mean that the notion that Libanius' loyalty to Julian's religious policy formed the basis for some kind of 'pagan group' needs to be re-examined.

REFERENCES TO RELIGIOUS ORGANIZATION IN JULIAN'S REIGN

If Libanius' representation of his relationship with Julian is not as straightforward as we first imagined this must also make us question his representation of a 'pagan group' focused on Julian. On a number of occasions Libanius appears to refer to the existence of certain religious groups focused on Julian during the reign of Constantius.[61] In a letter of 361 Libanius writes to Fortunatianus, an old friend and schoolmate, about the prospect of Julian coming to power (*Ep.* B.153 (F.661)) and expresses sorrow that Fortunatianus will be absent from the Bacchic revel in Antioch of that year as it means that Libanius will not have a chance to share his true feelings about Julian with him (*Ep.* B.153.3 (F.661)).[62] Instead, Libanius says that he will converse with Celsus, another close friend and ex-pupil. One interpretation of this reference is that the festival of Dionysus provided a religious context in which people could share their views about Constantius and Julian. In a description of the activities of Aristophanes of Corinth in his *Oration 14 In Defence of Aristophanes*, Libanius also appears to suggest that worshippers of the gods met at literary gatherings during the reign of Constantius:

> He [Aristophanes] caused not a few people to share with him in this prayer [for Julian to come to power] by making war against that regime [Constantius' regime] and leading them over to our side. In the (literary) gatherings (*tois syllogois*) he uttered words that were not without danger but pleasurable to him as he celebrated the feast of anticipation of things that would happen [once Julian came to power] . . . above all for the matters concerning the gods. (*Or.* 14.42 (F.11.102))

---

[61] On the question of the existence of a 'pagan underground' focused on Julian in the reign of Constantius, see Drinkwater 1983.
[62] The harvest festival for Dionysus, see Liebeschuetz 1972: 231, note 6.

Here Libanius describes Aristophanes as involved in converting people to the support of Julian and speaks of some kind of gatherings or assemblies at which Aristophanes could anticipate the benefits of Julian's coming to power (with emphasis on the religious, although Libanius also lists benefits to all other aspects of society (*Or.* 14.42–3 (F.II.102–3)). Another example from later in the 360s after Julian's death again suggests that the festival of Bacchus was a focus of some kind of assembly or meeting place for like-minded members of the elite. In 365 Libanius writes to Gerontius, who had probably been Julian's prefect of Egypt 361–2, to describe how he and some friends had read aloud a letter from him at a festival in the temple of Dionysus. Libanius describes Gerontius as his 'companion'. He tells Gerontius how he and his friends read the letter 'when the festival was started and the bacchantes were in motion' (*Ep.* F.1480.5). Here we see again the combination of men gathering together to share a literary experience in a way that might suggest some kind of formal social organization.

Taken at face value these passages could be seen as evidence for a religious group meeting under Constantius. The problem is that in each case we can see that Libanius had something to gain from representing these as religious forms of social organization. The purpose of his *Oration* 14 was to convince Julian that Aristophanes was a worthy person who should be recalled from exile. Libanius' presentation of Aristophanes as taking part in a publicly visible and socially organized form of 'pagan' resistance could thus have been designed largely to impress Julian with Aristophanes' consistent loyalty to Julian even under Constantius. Similar points can be made about the references in the letters mentioned above. Because letters were public documents, they might be circulated by the receiver, so they were a good medium for Libanius' promotion of an image of himself. At the very end of Constantius' reign it suited Libanius, Fortunatianus and Celsus to play up their religious links with each other because they thought it likely that Julian might come to power in the near future (*Ep.* B.153 (F.661)). We have seen that Libanius was successful under Constantius and that it suited him as Julian's accession became imminent to display his social links with other worshippers of the gods. Similarly, the suggestion that Libanius was involved in some kind of meeting of those who worshipped the gods could be useful in 365 in counteracting claims that Libanius was being a traitor to Julian's cause. Just as Libanius sought to present himself as being in close social relations with worshippers of the gods after Julian's death, he also sought, at times, to distance himself from social relations with Christians. In the years after Julian's death Libanius had to defend himself from the accusation that because he lived in Antioch he too was responsible for the way the city had turned against the emperor. In a letter to Nicocles Libanius suggests that it was just one individual – probably the bishop of Antioch at the time, the Arian Euzoius – who was acting against those who worshipped the gods, and not the city as a whole. Libanius says that Nicocles should not 'make the wickedness of one man a reason for an accusation against the city as a whole but should know how to distinguish the impious (*ton dussebon*) from those who are not like that' (*Ep.* N.122.3 (F.1119)). In another letter from the same period he defends himself against the charge that he was too friendly with Christians by portraying himself and the rest of the 'pious' minority as separate from the population of Antioch as a whole (*Ep.* B.161 (F.1196)). In a third letter written at the same time (363), this time to Scylacius, Libanius describes his feelings of shame that Antioch had joined in celebrations at Julian's death. He represents these people as 'bad men (*kakoi*)' and says that 'this is the sort of crowd (*toioutoi ochloi*) among whom I live my life, enemies of the gods and of him about whom you have the right opinion by listing him in the chorus of the gods' (*Ep.* N.120.3 (F. *Ep.* 1220)). Libanius' writings cannot be taken as straightforward descriptive evidence of actual religious groups. Rather they sought either to emphasize or to play down his social relations with particular groups of people at particular times.

In a number of letters Libanius built up religious links with associates of Julian by making explicit reference to religious practices. In one letter to Maximus of Ephesus Libanius describes how the 'noble Pythiodorus' brought 'the worship of the gods to its prime, sprinkled every altar with blood' and encouraged even 'laggards' to sacrifice by bringing news to Antioch that Julian had come to power (*Ep.* N. 80.7 (F.694)). In this letter Libanius is implying that Pythiodorus and large numbers of people in Antioch, including himself, had made the correct religious response to Julian's coming to power and so should be looked on favourably by Maximus. Libanius then goes on to include his friend Fortunatianus in this religious networking. He tells Maximus that he had commissioned Fortunatianus to take this letter to him by hand because Fortunatianus 'resembled' Pythiodorus (*Ep.* N.80.7 (F.694)).[63] Libanius uses a similar technique on another occasion when he excuses his absence from Julian's sacrifice in Antioch to Anatolius 5/4, another close confidant of Julian's. Libanius states that his friend Olympius 3 will be present at the sacrifices instead (*Ep.* B.43 (F.739) of 362).[64] In so doing, Libanius both links Olympius closer to Anatolius 5/4 and to Julian and manages to maintain a connection to the event through

---

[63] See also *Ep.* F.1361 and *Ep.* F.1118.3.   [64] See Amm. Marc. 22.14.4.

his close friendship with Olympius. On other occasions Libanius forms and strengthens religious links between people by emphasizing their closeness to Julian and his religious activity. In letters to his friends Seleucus 1 (high priest of Cilicia for Julian in 362) and Celsus he records their role in Julian's religious restoration (*Ep.* N.92 (F.770) and *Ep.* N.88.3 (F.736) of 362)). In the letter to Celsus he creates another link by stating how his friend Olympius was present at the religious event in which Celsus took part and reported it back to Libanius (*Ep.* N.88.3 (F.736)).

Recording and publicizing the activities of his friends in promoting Julian's religious restoration could be used to create links between Libanius and his friends and those at the heart of Julian's religious restoration. Libanius praises Bacchius of Tarsus for his restoration of a festival in honour of Artemis in 362 and says that he had been told about the festival by the carrier of the letter from Bacchius (*Ep.* N.83.1 (F.710)). He then gives further publicity to the event by recounting the details of the festival, as he had heard it, including the sacrifices, the processions, the feasting and a speech delivered by Demetrius 2/1 (*Ep.* N.83.2–3 (F.710)). In this way news of such activities could spread and become the focus of contact between people. In another letter Libanius informs Bacchius that he had also told Julianus, *comes orientis* and uncle of the emperor Julian, about Bacchius' restoration of the festival and about all the details of the festival, adding that Julianus was going to 'mention to the emperor himself what had been done' (*Ep.* B.181.1 (F.712)).[65] Through his letters and conversations with officials Libanius was able to create and strengthen ties of religious unity by recording the religious activities of his friends and by disseminating knowledge of these activities to others.

In other cases sending artwork and literary compositions could be a way of making religious links. In the reign of Julian Libanius writes to his friend Theodorus 3, then governor of Bithynia, about some pictures of Aelius Aristides that Theodorus and another friend Italicianus had sent to him (*Ep.* N.143 (F.1534)). Libanius describes how he had put the portraits up in the temple of Zeus Olympius in order to replace what had been removed by 'the people who intimidate us' (*Ep.* N.143.4 (F.1534)). The sending of the painting and of the letters about the painting were precisely what built up the religious link and the relationship between Libanius, Theodorus and Italicianus. Similarly, in the reign of Julian the restoration of the shrine of Asclepius at Aegae in Cilicia led to an exchange of speeches on the shrine

---

[65] See also *Ep.* F.1361.3, where Libanius describes how his friend Theodorus came back from Seleucia and reported on the good state of the religious revival (including sacrifices) there.

between Libanius, Demetrius 2 and Acacius 7 of Tarsus.[66] Thus, in one letter Libanius requested that Demetrius send him his two speeches on the shrine, which he had heard about from an acquaintance (*Ep.* B.146.3 (F.727) of summer 362). Libanius also described his own health problems and asked Demetrius to consult Asclepius for an 'oracle' that would cure these problems, just as Demetrius himself had received an oracle from the god telling him to compose his orations (*Ep.* B.146.2 (F.727)).[67] Then in two other letters of the same year Libanius praised a speech that Acacius had written on the shrine and that Acacius' son, Titianus (Libanius' student) had brought to class for Libanius (*Ep.* B.147 (F.695) and *Ep.* B.148 (F.1342)). Acacius too had used the shrine to cure his own illness (*Ep.* N.138.4 (F.1301)): his oration described the cures carried out by the god, the temple itself and its destruction by Christians (*Ep.* B.147.2 (F.695) and *Ep.* B.148.2 (F.1342)). Finally, we also know that Libanius sent a copy of his own *Oration 60* the *Monody on the Burning of the Shrine of Apollo at Daphne* to Demetrius (*Ep.* N.96.2 (F.785)). Rather than dismiss these references as 'ironic' or 'only literary' or take them as sincere statements about religious 'belief', we can more usefully see them as attempts to construct relationships based on religion.

Libanius continued to reaffirm religious links with people after Julian's death. As he and others sought to ward off accusations of flattery and religious opportunism through dropping allegiance to Julian too swiftly, it was again useful to maintain links with people based on worship of the gods and to continue to assert their loyalty to Julian and his religious policies.[68] The social aspect of this is made clear by Libanius as in one letter in which he defends himself from a charge of flattery: he states that after the death of Julian 'my earlier friends are my friends now' (*Ep.* N.24 (F.1154)). Through writing letters to each other expressing the shared grief and troubles that they faced after the death of Julian, Libanius and his correspondents could strengthen and maintain the bonds that had developed between them under Julian and could present themselves as consistent in their religious loyalties. In one letter of 363/4 to Caesarius 1/4 of Tarsus, *comes rei privatae* at Jovian's court, Libanius recommended that Caesarius offer Acacius 8/1 an office. Acacius had held several important posts under Julian but had trouble in finding an appointment after Julian's death. According to Libanius, offering

---

[66] On the destruction of this shrine under Constantine or Constantius and its restoration under Julian see Eusebius, *VC* 3.56 and Zonaras, *Epitome* 13.12.30–4.
[67] On Libanius' use of the shrine of Asclepius at Aegae, see *Epp.* F.707–8.
[68] As at *Ep.* F.1424.7; *Ep.* N.111 (F.1424); *Ep.* B.137 (F.1124); *Ep.* B.141 (F.1217)); *Ep.* N.112.1 (F.1426); (*Ep.* N.123 (F.1128); *Ep.* F.615; and *Ep.* F.1326.

him a post would put a stop to the 'backbiters' who were 'having a laugh' at the supporters of Julian (*Ep.* B.46.2 (F.1449)). Libanius was thus suggesting that Acacius was someone who was in the pro-Julian camp and that helping him could further the goals shared by Caesarius and Libanius.[69] The post that Caesarius eventually offered to Acacius was *comes domorum per Cappadociam* for 363–5 and later, in 365, we see Libanius writing to Acacius in Cappadocia to recommend the Athenian priest Lemmatius to him. Libanius recommended Lemmatius by describing how he, like Acacius, had come under attack after Julian's death and by suggesting that the same man was responsible for both attacks (*Ep.* B.159.1 and 3 (F.1458)).[70] Libanius emphasized Lemmatius' loyalty to Julian and the religious activity that Lemmatius had been involved in in Athens even before Julian came to power. During his period of study in Athens, Libanius had seen Lemmatius 'steeped in sacred rites and concourse with the gods'. When the two met again in the 360s, Lemmatius was grieving for the death of Julian, as was the whole of his hometown, Athens (*Ep.* B.159.2 (F.1458)). Libanius recommended him to Acacius through his loyalty to Julian and traditional religion in order to create a bond between the two men through their persecution by the same Christian man after Julian's death. Just as Libanius had recommended Acacius 8/1 to Caesarius 1/4 after Julian's death, he recommended Lemmatius to Acacius in turn to help with the same difficult circumstances. We also see Libanius writing a number of letters to Scylacius, a lawyer from Berytus and ardent supporter of Julian, convincing Scylacius of the loyalty of himself and other people to Julian. In two letters he expresses his own grief at Julian's death and speaks of sharing this with Scylacius (*Ep.* N.114 (F.1431) and *Ep.* N.120 (F.1220)). In another letter Libanius recommends Evanthius to Scylacius on the basis that he 'never ceases to praise the other (Julian)' even though 'he [Evanthius] is held in honour by those who now have come to power' (*Ep.* B.170.2 (F.1336) of 365). Evanthius had apparently held some position under Julian but appears to have been dismissed by him and was back in favour only under Valens and Valentinian, which was why he needed a recommendation based on his religious allegiance and loyalty to Julian.[71]

Descriptions of religious groups and religious links in a writer such as Libanius were never going to be straightforward representations of reality. The rhetorical nature of his letters and orations and their role in the construction of Libanius' public image meant that they were always going

---

[69] See also *Ep.* F.1432.   [70] See Bradbury 2004: 197–8, introduction to *Epistle* 159 and note 66.
[71] See Bradbury's interpretation (Bradbury 2004: 207, introduction to *Ep.* B.170).

to have functions other than telling us how things were. Libanius used representation of his socio-religious relations in his writings in order to strengthen his position before, during and after the reign of Julian. It was because Libanius was not part of Julian's inner religious circle and was in fact close to the centres of Constantius' power that he felt the need to present himself in this way. This self-presentation enabled him to maintain his importance under Julian, to make clear his religious loyalties in a public way and to build up religious links with people who would be useful to him. This being the case, can we say anything about how Libanius' religious allegiance related to social organization?

SOCIAL NETWORKS AND RELIGIOUS ALLEGIANCE

Libanius was very concerned with social relationships. It mattered to him that he was well-connected and that he managed to maintain contact with all the right people. In order to maintain social relationships with significant individuals whom he did not see regularly, such as friends, ex-pupils and officials, he used the medium of letter writing. Libanius has left almost two thousand letters that act as a map of his diverse and wide-ranging social connections and reflect his concern to maintain these social connections. What is interesting about letter writing as a medium is that the act of sending and receiving the letters created the links between people: a large part of the social relationship was in the connection made by the letter itself.[72] Libanius formulated explicitly the idea that letters themselves equated to social relations. He often speaks of letters standing in for individuals and replacing *actual* social gatherings. In a letter to a father of one of his pupils Libanius suggests that the pupil acted as a very good stand-in for direct association with the father and that because the father was recalling the pupil, the father's letter would now have to serve this function instead (*Ep.* N.28.1–2 (F.359)). On other occasions Libanius writes that a letter from an ex-pupil could make up for Libanius' being unable to attend his wedding feast (*Ep.* N.31.1 (F.370)); that not receiving letters and orations from a correspondent was like being 'excluded from ... a feast' (*Ep.* N.102.3 (F.818)); and that his letters could be 'introduced' to a correspondent's 'guests at dinner' instead of Libanius himself (*Ep.* N.104.2 (F.1351)).[73] Letters could also be used to create and develop new friendships where they did not exist before and between individuals who had not even met (*Ep.* 151 (F. 867) and

---

[72] On the importance of letter writing for creating and maintaining social connections, in reference to Paulinus' of Nola's epistolary activity, see Trout 1999: 199 and Conybeare 2000: 35 and 131.
[73] See also *Ep.* 148.5 (F.846) and *Ep.* N.112.1 and 6 (F.1426).

Ep. 186 (F.1057)); they could redevelop friendships that had fallen by the wayside (*Ep.* 187 (F.1058)). As was typical of the ancient world the language and conventions of friendship played a large role in the connections that Libanius made with his correspondents.[74] He often referred to emotional connections between himself and those to whom he wrote – for example, to sadness at their absence or when they are facing hard times, or to the longstanding nature of his friendships with them or with mutual acquaintances.[75] We also see the characteristic features of a desire for frankness (*Ep.* N.47.1 (F.81)), teasing of one another and humour (*Ep.* N.4.7 (F.391)) and of outspoken advice (*Ep.* N.11.2 (F.430)). This use of the language and features of friendship is because many of Libanius' correspondents were people with whom he had a personal relationship: family members, ex-pupils and those he had studied and worked with during his years in Athens, Constantinople and Nicomedia.[76]

Through good development and manipulation of these personal ties Libanius actively created for himself a strong social network in which he had a central position. When cousins, ex-pupils and old friends went on to hold positions in the imperial bureaucracy, in the court or senate of Constantinople or in civic government, these personal relationships tied Libanius into the centres of power of the late Roman empire. His connections with people in letters often went beyond simple friendship to have a more practical function.[77] Personal friendship could be the basis for getting things done: the personal was political in a very real sense for Libanius.[78] References to longstanding friendship could be used as justification for asking a favour of a friend who was also an official or as the reason for recommending someone whom Libanius was trying to promote (*Ep.* N.157.1–2 (F.907) and *Ep.* N.158.1 (F.908)).[79] The language of friendship, or at least of courteous relations, could also ease the way when Libanius had to ask a favour of someone with whom he did not have good relations, as was the case in some of his letters to Datianus (*Ep.* N.7 (F.409) and *Ep.* N.13 (F.441)). The personal relationships developed in letter writing were thus essential to remaining well connected in fourth-century imperial

---

[74] Stowers 1986: 29–31 and Trapp 2003: 40–2.
[75] For the former, see *Ep.* N.4.12 (F.391); *Ep.* N.6 (F.405); *Ep.* N.72 (F.263); and *Ep.* N.142.1 (F.1508). For the latter, see *Ep.* N.9 (F.427); *Ep.* N.11.12 (F.430); *Ep.* N.22.10 (F.552); *Ep.* N.23 (F.557); *Ep.* N.43 (F. 70); *Ep.* N.46.2 (F.80); *Ep.* N.53.2 (F.97); *Ep.* N.151.1 (F.867); *Ep.* N.153.3 (F.901); and *Ep.* N.157 (F.907).
[76] On Libanius' networks based on family connections, see Wintjes 2005: 43–62.
[77] Matthews 1974: 64.
[78] On the ambiguous private/public nature of letters, see Conybeare 2000: 12 and 21.
[79] See also *Ep.* N.46.2 (F.80).

social life. Through them Libanius could maintain significant friendships but he could also exercise his role as patron for ex-pupils and friends and show his influence by exerting it with contacts he had in court circles.

The importance of social relationships to Libanius, and of the role of letter writing in maintaining these, can be seen on occasions where connections falter or fail. When Libanius wrote to someone and received no reply or when someone did not maintain regular contact with him, he could show great anxiety.[80] On numerous occasions he associates not receiving a letter with the end of a friendship asking, for example, 'are you still a friend?' of one correspondent who had not written to him for a while (*Ep.* N.119.4 (F.1459)).[81] He also often writes to complain to correspondents that others had received a letter from them when he had not.[82] The great fear of social isolation that lies behind such complaints can be seen in references he makes to friends' surprise and curiosity when he does not receive letters from certain individuals: such queries make Libanius 'blush' and struggle to find a suitable explanation for the absence of a letter (*Ep.* N.165.2 (F.938)).[83] Most seriously, not receiving a reply to his letters could mean the loss of influence and the loss of contact with those in power, which, Libanius tells us, could make him look bad (*Ep.* N.119.4 (F.1459)).[84] If someone did not reply to Libanius, it meant the ending of a social relationship, a weakening of Libanius' social position, and a marginalization of his person.

This brief overview of social relations as revealed in Libanius' letters suggests that it is mistaken to think in terms of social groups, associations or communities (if we use the technical sense as defined by theorists of social organization as I suggest we should). A group requires that the social relationships between individuals take some kind of visible and more permanent presence, usually in the form of regular meetings in a specially designated place.[85] What we see in Libanius' social relations is a much more elusive and less solid situation because often his connections were with people in other cities and provinces and often the only contact he had with them was by letter. Throughout his letters the absence of friends and family members is stated as a cause for writing.[86] For this reason the

---

[80] Complaints about not receiving a letter from someone were to some degree part of social and epistolary convention (as Libanius himself notes at *Ep.* N.133.1 (F.1264)). But, many of Libanius' complaints do reveal some real anxiety.

[81] See also *Ep.* N. 20.3 (F.509) and *Ep.* N.102.1–4 (F.818).

[82] *Ep.* N. 20.1–2 (F.509); *Ep.* 22.2 (F.552); *Ep.* N.86.1–2 (F.725); and *Ep.* 102.3 (F.818).

[83] See also *Ep.* 146.2 (F.840).   [84] See also *Ep.* N.146 (F.840); and *Ep.* N.165 (F.938).

[85] Eriksen 1993: 42–3.

[86] *Ep.* N.4.7 and 12 (F.391); *Ep.* N.11.8–10 (F.430); *Ep.* N.19.1 (F.501); *Ep.* N.27.1 (F.345); *Ep.* N.146.5 (F.840); and *Ep.* N.151.1 (F.867).

model or the metaphor of the network is more useful than that of the group for describing his social relations.[87] Libanius can be seen as part of a complex, and geographically extended, web of social relationships that had to be continually constructed and maintained through the sending and receiving of letters. He could maintain links with friends and relations in other cities, ask favours of officials based in Constantinople or in other provinces and maintain a web of connections that stretched from Rome to the Euphrates and from Egypt to Illyricum. In this way he was very successful at enmeshing himself in interlocking circles of social connection that provided him with support throughout the changing circumstances of the fourth century. He could then use this network to enable the 'flow of resources' between network members.[88] Late-antique men did not maintain relationships through letters purely for the sake of it, whatever their rhetoric of friendship might suggest, but in order to manipulate, to produce results.[89] Libanius used his extensive social network to gain promotions, jobs and favours for friends and ex-pupils as well as to bring cultural capital to himself simply through the influence he wielded by having so many connections.

When considering the role of religion in Libanius' social networks, I shall not try to identify which of his friends shared his religious allegiance and then posit this as the basis for his connection to them. Rather, I shall take a more subjective approach and explore the points where Libanius himself made religion a reason for a connection with someone. What soon becomes clear is how small a role religion played in his social relationships. Even among his closest friends references to religion are the exception rather than the rule and are far from being the primary reason for these relationships. The greatest density of references to religion appears in Libanius' nineteen letters to or about Secundius Salutius. Even here just seven have some direct reference to the gods, and often these are the briefest kind of references of the nature of: 'by Zeus' or 'oh gods'.[90] There is also one reference to grief at Julian's death, which might imply sorrow at the failure of Julian's religious policy, although religion is not mentioned specifically in the letter (*Ep.* N.112 (F.1426)). A lower density of references to religion is, however, more normal. Out of thirty-seven letters written to or concerning his close

---

[87] The model of the network is now increasingly being used to describe Libanius' social and political relationships with other elite men of the time (Wintjes 2005: 242; Bradbury 2004: 1–2; and Malosse 1995a: 252).
[88] Handelman 1977: 196; Eriksen 1993: 42; and Wellman 2003: 40.   [89] Matthews 1974: 64.
[90] *Ep.* N.89 (F.740); *Ep.* B.154 (F.1425); *Ep.* N.136 (F.1298); *Ep.* B.168 (1124); *Ep.* B.169 (F.1251); *Ep.* F.1467; and *Ep.* F.1474.

friend Aristaenetus 1, only one letter directly makes a clear and unambiguous reference to the importance of religious allegiance (*Ep.* N.24 (F.571)), while two others have very brief references to the god or the divine (*Ep.* F.537 and *Ep.* F.550). Similarly, out of forty-eight letters written to or about Libanius' friend and ex-pupil Celsus only four have explicit reference to religious practice (*Ep.* N.88 (F.736); *Ep.* B.153 (F.661); *Ep.* F.717; and *Ep* F.1480) and two others have very brief references to Zeus or 'the god' (*Ep.* F.76 and *Ep.* 1190). Often Libanius does not emphasize religious concerns even where we might expect to see them playing a major role. In Libanius' letters to Symmachus, often seen as the leader of the 'pagan party' in Rome at this time, there are no explicit mentions of their possible shared religious goals other than brief references to fortune, the gods of eloquence and to prayer (*Ep.* N.177.4, 5 and 8 (F.1004)). Taking this more subjective approach and looking at the points where Libanius himself makes religion the reason for a connection, we can see how untrue is the view that religion was regularly a primary element in Libanius' social networks. Ties of family and shared culture and education were much more common.

The ties that Libanius did have with those who shared his religious allegiance were just as widespread geographically as his other social connections. Those who supported Julian and those who supported the old gods were dispersed throughout the empire in posts in the provinces, in their hometowns, at court (wherever it was stationed at the time), and in the senate at Constantinople. Libanius made religious connections with the young philosopher Iamblichus from Apamea while he was in Greece, with members of the family with whom he had ties in Tarsus, with friends he had made in Nicomedia (such as Entrechius) and with priests in Egypt. Even though these men were unable to meet or to have any more solid form of social organization they maintained links with one another through letter writing.[91] In the two examples of people meeting at the festival of Bacchus (discussed above), it was precisely the absence of Fortunatianus and Gerontius from the festival that Libanius focused on (*Ep.* B.153 (F.661) and *Ep.* F.1480). When we look at the evidence, the *lack* of a regular meeting place and *lack* of shared social occasions can be seen to be one of the characteristic features of those that might be imagined to be in a 'pagan society' with Libanius.

When Libanius did emphasize religion as a reason for a connection between people, he could express this in terms of the personal, friendship

---

[91] On Paulinus of Nola's letters and this characteristic in Christian social relations, see Trout 1999: 199–200 and 209 and Conybeare 2000: 35 and 131.

language that is so common to letters. In the 380s and 390s he developed a relationship with the military man Richomer, who was *magister militum* until 383, consul sometime before 384 and close to the emperor Theodosius in the 390s. In his letters to Richomer Libanius constantly refers to their shared religious allegiance and their friendship simultaneously. On one occasion he states that out of all the 'blessings [he has] received from the gods, the greatest is [Richomer's friendship]' (*Ep.* N.172.1 (F.972)). On another occasion he describes how happy he was when Richomer came to spend the New Year festival of 392 in Antioch and talks of how he will pray to the gods for him (*Ep.* N.180.3 (F.1024)).[92] Elsewhere, in his *Oration* 1 *The Autobiography* Libanius describes Richomer as 'a man inclined to sacred things (*hierois*) and to the gods (*theois*)' and says that this was part of the reason why the two men became such strong friends when Richomer first came to Antioch in 383 (*Or.* 1.219 (F.1.180)). Here shared religious allegiance was the basis for a personal tie but not for some more public and visible form of social organization. This kind of religious connection made in letters was also more private than if Libanius had set up some kind of 'pagan' group based in Antioch. He was able to express personal religious feelings less visibly and more privately in letters in a world where it could be dangerous to express such feelings publicly and communally. The private nature of letters can, however, be deceptive. They could be read aloud by others or passed on to people in written form and so become very public. At the same time letters could often have 'political' functions in that they could be used to get things done and to achieve specific goals. This must remind us that even when Libanius makes religion the reason for a connection between himself and another we should be a little wary of taking this at face value as a 'true' expression of religious feeling as opposed to publicly expressed false views.

Just as Libanius could make connections with those who shared his religious allegiance, he could also make connections with those who did not. We could try to ascertain which of his correspondents were Christians and to construct an 'objective' picture of his social relations with Christians, but it can be very hard to identify which of those he wrote to were Christian, especially when there is no external evidence on the matter or when Libanius does not tell us himself. Libanius must have been connected to, and must have written to, a number of family members, officials and ex-pupils who were Christians without this being seen as a problem or, very often, even worth mentioning. His family connections provide just one example of this, though we should remember that not all the identifications of family

---

[92] See also *Ep.* F.1007.2 and 5.

members as Christian are certain.⁹³ The descendants of Libanius' uncle Panolbius 1 all appear to have been Christians, including Panolbius' sons (Libanius' cousins) Spectatus and Thalassius 1, and Thalassius 1's children Bassianus 2 and Thalassius 2 as well as an unnamed daughter. Bassianus 2 then married Prisca the daughter of Helpidius 4, the Christian praetorian prefect of the orient in 360–1 (it is interesting to note that the sister of Bassianus 2 and Thalassius 2, and so probably Christian, was at one point engaged to be married to Libanius' friend Italicianus, who was very much a worshipper of the gods). These family relations show how intermixed people of different religious allegiances could be. For the rest of this chapter, however, I shall take a subjective approach and look at examples where Libanius mentions the religious difference of Christians to whom he writes. I shall consider examples of letters addressed to senior figures in the Christian and Jewish communities because they show just how far Libanius' social connections could range across boundaries of religious difference.

On at least two occasions we see Libanius writing to, or about, Christian bishops. Amphilochius of Iconium had been his student in the 350s (as well as being a cousin of Gregory of Nazianzus) and then trained as a lawyer before retiring to the Cappadocian countryside to look after his father.⁹⁴ Libanius praises the fact that in 373/4 Amphilochius has been 'seized' by the Christians to hold the 'chair' of the bishopric of Iconium in Cappadocia (*Ep.* N.144.2 (F.1543)). This is a clear reference to Amphilochius' Christianity, but what pleased Libanius about this situation was that it meant that Amphilochius would be practising his eloquence again – even if in the form of preaching. Although Libanius refers to Amphilochius' Christianity, he emphasizes the love of eloquence that he and Amphilochius share as the reason for the connection between the two men.⁹⁵ In another letter, of 358–9, Libanius writes to his friend Modestus to ask for help for George, bishop of Alexandria. Libanius praises the actions of Bishop George in trying to have a fine remitted that had been imposed on the Alexandrian people for rioting between Arian and Nicene Christians. He also asks Modestus, who was *comes orientis* at the time, for his help in this matter (*Ep.* N.70 (F.205)), exhorting Modestus do this in order to oblige 'yourself, him [George], me and the gods of Egypt' (*Ep.* N.70.2 (F.205)). By this reference to the gods of Egypt Libanius could gloss over the fact that he was helping a Christian bishop, of whom elsewhere he vehemently

---

⁹³ P. Petit 1955: 405.
⁹⁴ For a useful discussion of Amphilochius and his relationship to Libanius, see Maxwell forthcoming: 36–9.
⁹⁵ See also Libanius' letter to the Christian Firminus 3/2 when he retired from office to become a sophist (*Ep.* F.1048).

disapproved (*Or.* 14.65 (F.II.110)). It is odd that he does this in a letter addressed to Modestus, who, according to Libanius, was at this time 'not acknowledging' his admiration of the gods (*Ep.* B.74.5 (F.804)). We can perhaps add Libanius' correspondence with Basil of Caesarea (*Ep.* F.647 if it is authentic), which again did not refer to the religious differences between the two men.[96]

We have also seen that Libanius had a number of connections with leaders of Jewish communities. We saw that in 364 he wrote a letter on behalf of the Jewish community in Antioch ('our Jews') again to his friend Priscianus as governor of Palestine (*Ep.* N.131 (F.1251)). This shows us that Libanius was at least on speaking terms with some senior members of the Jewish community at Antioch and that these Jews saw him as someone they could ask to speak for them at a moment of crisis. The situation referred to in this letter concerned the Jewish council of elders in Antioch. A certain 'wicked old man' had been expelled from the council because he had not governed well but was now seeking to have himself reinstated. As this decision lay with the Jewish authorities in Palestine, this old man had apparently turned to Priscianus to help influence the decision in his favour. In response, the Jews of Antioch had asked Libanius to represent their views to Priscianus and to deter him from helping their enemy.[97] Later, in the late 380s to early 390s, we see that Libanius was also on very friendly terms with the Jewish patriarch in Palestine.[98] We have eight of the letters that Libanius wrote to this patriarch and the tone of each is friendly if not deferential.[99] The two men clearly shared an upbringing in classical culture and education and the patriarch even intended to send his son to Libanius' school (*Ep.* F.917).[100] As the highest Jewish authority in Palestine, the patriarch had as much influence as the governor of the province (*Ep.* F.974.2) and could thus be a very useful connection to Libanius. We see Libanius writing letters of recommendation to him for his friends and ex-pupils just as he would to any governor (*Ep.* F.973; *Ep.* F.974; *Ep.* F.1084; and *Ep.* F.1105).

Libanius' religious connections with people again suggest that the network model is more appropriate than that of the social group. Using the former, we can understand that Libanius' social relations maintained through letter writing resemble the diverse and extensive social relations that exist in the modern world as a result of telephones and email. Networks built up through these media have little visible or public presence in society because they are created through one-to-one contact carried out in the virtual space

---

[96] See Rousseau 1994: 16, 57–60 and 70–1.   [97] For these events, see Wilken 1983: 60–1.
[98] The identity of this patriarch has been debated (Wilken 1983: 58 and Meeks and Wilken 1978: 59.
[99] Wilken 1983: 59.   [100] Wilken 1983: 58–9 on their shared culture.

of the internet or the phone line, and across wide geographical distances, but they are still incredibly potent. The connections that Libanius established through letter writing were often 'virtual' too, because they existed primarily through the medium of letter writing itself. They took the form of personal bonds spread over a wide geographical area with the minimum of actual physical contact. Religion could be one reason for making the connection, when this was useful, but it was often not the primary reason. The loose nature of the social bonds between those who shared Libanius' religious allegiance meant that it was very easy for Libanius also to have links with those of different religious allegiances. This is because networks are much more flexible than groups and can create ties that cut across other groupings or networks.[101]

Once we view Libanius' letters as creating and constructing religious networks rather than describing religious groups that were already in existence we can allow ourselves a much more complex view of the religious situation of the fourth century. We do not see, and should not look for, interaction between closed, well-organized and publicly visible groups with clear-cut identities. Rather, we should see that on the ground social relations were much more mutable than this, especially among worshippers of the gods, who could belong to loose religious networks that had a barely visible impact on their lives but could at times build up more closely connected groupings when it suited them. At other times, however, they could have links with those who were involved in more permanent and well-organized social groups – such as Christian bishops and the leaders of the Jewish community and the Christian Church. Having an understanding of the different levels of social organization, from simple categorization through to network, enables us to see that an individual might move through different levels of organization 'depending on the context and scale of interaction'.[102] Seeing the fourth-century religious situation as represented by Libanius in terms of networks allows us to 'move further away from ... group to non-group, from a "cookie-cutter" concept of culture to a finer understanding of the ephemerality and inconsistency of social relations'.[103] This much looser model of social organization also fits better with Libanius' attitude to religious allegiance as something fluid that could be changed at will, emphasized or played down as necessary. It might also be more representative of how those in Chrysostom's audiences acted.

---

[101] See Wellman 2003: 21.   [102] S. Jones 1997: 75 and also Eriksen 1993: 43.   [103] Vincent 1974: 376.

PART V

Assessing the impact of constructions of identity

INTRODUCTION

In part III we explored the relationship between Libanius' and Chrysostom's understandings of religious identity/allegiance and social organization. This was a question of how far constructions of identity could be seen to translate into social organization but at the same time was also a question of the relationship between text and social practice. We saw in chapter 7 that Chrysostom sought to construct a sense of community for his audience through his preaching and the Christian ritual of baptism and that it is possible to suggest that a 'textual community' could have grown up around his preaching. However, we also saw that there was little basis for such a textual community: it was impossible to associate one consistent audience with Chrysostom's preaching, and his audiences did not appear to have formed any permanent social organization based on their Christianity. Instead, a more 'fuzzy' model of Christianity in Antioch was suggested, in which individuals had varying degrees of commitment and could interact socially with non-Christians. In chapter 8 we saw that the notion that Libanius' writings give any real evidence of a 'pagan faction' or 'group' should also be questioned. It was argued that loyalty to the emperor Julian and his religious policy should not be taken as the basis for a 'pagan faction' around Libanius, because Libanius had goals other than representing his relationship with Julian 'as it really was'. It was suggested that his representation of his socio-religious links with others should not always be taken at face value, because it too could be a strategic device for playing up his loyalty to Julian as and when it suited him. We saw that Libanius' letters give a picture of his social relations as a whole as a diffuse and widespread network, rather than a tight-knit group. References to socio-religious links with others were far from prominent in these networks and had only a relatively minor role. Libanius had constantly to maintain his network of social contact through writing letters; the inclusion of references to religion was just one means amongst many that he used to do this. Because of the more diffuse nature of Libanius' social relations and because religious allegiance was not a crucial factor in them, he was able to maintain social contacts with Jews and Christians as well as with those who shared his religious allegiance.

Chrysostom and Libanius were using notions of social organization in different ways in their writings. While Chrysostom was trying to construct a clear sense of community and of social bonds between Christians, Libanius utilized a more flexible network-based approach to social relations in order to promote his own goals. What is even more interesting in the comparison of these two chapters, however, is that they may begin to show a slight convergence between the social behaviour of Chrysostom's audience and the picture we see arising from Libanius' writings. We saw that Chrysostom's attempts to instil a sense of community do not appear to have been successful since his audiences continued to partake of a number of other competing forms of social relations. Many Christians seem to have seen Christianity as something that had the minimum impact on how they lived their social lives and would on different occasions position themselves within different forms of social organization *as it suited them*. At times their Christianity was something that bound them in social bonds to other Christians but at other times it was irrelevant and they were able to mix socially with non-Christians at festivals, wedding days and in work life. They were also quite able to mix with Jews and to take part in Jewish social events. In this loose and flexible approach to socio-religious relations Chrysostom's audiences had something in common with the picture presented to us by Libanius. He too could interact socially with people across religious boundaries and could prioritize certain socio-religious relations or push them into the background when it was necessary to do so.

Once we begin to understand how texts relate to social reality, the contrast between Chrysostom's and Libanius' representations of the religious situation starts to collapse. The notion of the existence of distinct 'pagan' and 'Christian' groups becomes less tenable and Chrysostom's attempts to represent Christians as distinct from others no longer stand up. In this concluding section, part V, I shall take these ideas a step further by continuing to explore how representative Chrysostom's and Libanius' approaches to religious identity and religious allegiance were and how they related to what people were actually doing. In chapter 9 I shall look at how Libanius' and Chrysostom's views of religious identity/allegiance can be seen to map onto religious practice among fourth-century individuals. I have already spoken of the practical and strategic use of religion in Libanius' writings, which involves understanding how notions of religious identity become more flexible when put into practice in the rough and tumble of daily life.

This can be thought of as a contrast between an ideal of religious identity that emanates from Christian circles and the way in which that ideal is put into practice by people acting from the unspoken dispositions of how to deal with questions of religious difference and religious allegiance. In chapter 9 I shall also explore the practice of religion from the slightly different angle of the rituals and behaviours that people exhibit in the religious field. While these two concepts of practice can be seen to be distinct, they can also be seen to have some features in common because there is not a straightforward relationship between claiming a particular religious identity and carrying out certain religious practices. Just as the practical and strategic use of religious allegiance will transform an ideal identity into something less binding, so, when a religious identity is enacted or performed in religious practice, it can appear much less clear-cut. Religious practices can be shared in common across supposed religious boundaries and are, sometimes at least, carried out automatically as the taken-for-granted right thing to do without speculation whether or not they fit with a prescribed religious identity. By examining practice, we might thus be able to gain some sense of the 'undifferentiated background' and 'the threads of continuity' that lie behind textual constructions of identity and difference. Throughout this chapter I shall try, as far as is possible, to paint a picture of what Antiochene individuals were *doing* religiously and to ascertain whether this correlates better with Chrysostom's firm constructions of religious identity or with Libanius' less clearly defined notions of religious allegiance. We shall have to consider how far religious practice could be utilized in Christian discourse as a marker of religious identity and whether Libanius ever made use of reference to religious practice in discourses about religious allegiance.

In chapter 10 I shall summarize the findings and try to judge the comparative merits of Chrysostom's and Libanius' representations of the religious situation. I shall come to some conclusions as to whether we should talk in terms of interaction between well-defined religious identities, or in terms of the interaction of shifting religious allegiances that were often far from the central means by which people defined themselves.

CHAPTER 9

Religious identity, religious practice and personal religious power

DEFINING RELIGIOUS *PRACTICE* AND DEFINING *RELIGIOUS* PRACTICE

Constructions of identity are largely textual and linguistic in nature. They take place in the sphere of language, in what people say and write and how they think about themselves and others. In the sphere of practice, however, they are far less visible. As Barth noted long ago, practice and behaviour are often shared across the boundaries of ethnic difference that human discourses seek to construct. Practice, and religious practice in particular, will often be the site of syncretism: the normal mixed and undifferentiated state that exists prior to attempts to create pure traditions and identities.[1] As Lieu has shown for the religious situation of the early empire, however strongly Christian leaders and authoritative texts sought to create clearcut religious identities, these were often undermined in actual life and practice. Jews, Christians and even sometimes adherents of Graeco-Roman religions acted in the same ways, 'observed common practices' and felt affinity towards each other.[2] As other recent studies have shown, the *theos hupsistos* inscriptions from second- and third-century Asia Minor and cultic lamps from fourth-century Corinth give little indication of the religious allegiance of the users and show little concern with defining distinct religious identities.[3] Religious practices do not have to be *totally* antithetical to identity construction and could potentially be particularly good markers of identity because of their public and visible nature – by doing something that everyone can see, you can clearly show your allegiance to one religious identity rather than another. The essential point to remember, however,

---

[1] Stewart and Shaw 1994: 5–9.
[2] Lieu 2004: 147–77, especially pages 176–7. See also Rothaus 1996: 303 and 307. For prayer as a practice shared across religious boundaries, see Lieu 2004: 161.
[3] For the former see Lieu 2004: 176 and 155 and S. Mitchell 1993: 11–51 and 1999. For the latter see Rothaus 1996: 301–4: 'If we apply definitions based on practice, we gain a very different . . . image of late antique religion.'

is that no practice *automatically* or *essentially* defines identity; it has to be selected and chosen to do so. Only through explicit articulation in textual and linguistic forms can practice be made a marker of identity. As Lieu has shown for the early imperial period there was no one single marker of Jewish, Christian or Graeco-Roman identity; rather, Jewish and Christian leaders singled out different practices at different times to mark the differences between religions.[4] For fourth-century Antioch, Wilken has argued that the choice between religious identities is expressed most pressingly in a choice of religious practice.[5] He argues that attending a Jewish festival or a Jewish festival *in itself* constituted a statement about religious identity. In fact, it was only Chrysostom's *interpretation* of attendance at a Jewish synagogue or festival that made it a defining feature of a firm Jewish identity and therefore incompatible with being Christian. Religious *practice* is not the natural site of identity formation without textual elaboration.

The reasoning behind the practices, actions and behaviours of individuals is also different from that seen in textual and linguistic modes of expression because the former tend to be less clearly defined and less explicitly formulated. People tend to do what they have always done because it is engrained in their bodies and thought world as what feels right. Practice is just the way things are done, the unconscious answer to problems that might not even have been explicitly posed. Just as you automatically know how to drive when you get in a car or which tap is the hot tap when you wash your hands in your own sink, without the intervention of any conscious thought process, so you know the appropriate behaviour that is expected of you or that will solve a particular problem. Thus, in the field of religion individuals might automatically know which religious behaviour was expected of them or which kind of religious rite should be used to cure an illness or bring back the favour of the gods.

The opposition between textual representations and practice has particular resonance in debates about religion: religions based on text and belief can be contrasted with those based on practice and ritual.[6] For anthropologists who work with a wide range of cultures and societies it is clear that Christianity's focus on texts and dogma is not the norm and that religious practice is the core of many religions.[7] While the importance of ritual is usually accepted, how to interpret it is not. Some anthropologists argue that ritual and religious practice behave like language in being a form of

---

[4] Lieu 2004: 112–15.   [5] Wilken 1983: 77–8.   [6] Brooten 1994: 471–9 and Needham 1972.
[7] Kunin 2003: 186–93 and 152; Bowie 2000: 151–89; Rappaport 1999 and Wallace 1966: 102, to name just a few.

symbolic communication that can be interpreted to gain a meaning. Others suggest that this approach is misguided because it always entails the external observer's imposing his or her own meaning onto a ritual: when anthropologists ask their informants what a particular ritual 'means', the informant is often unable to answer or even to understand what is being asked.[8] For this reason, they suggest instead that we should focus on the performative and practical aspects of the ritual.[9] As Scheid states of Roman religion, '"understanding" a rite in Rome meant knowing how to perform it, and from this perspective the meaning or sense of the activity becomes an extremely problematic concept'.[10] The ultimate significance of ritual is often based, partially at least, outside human language in the biological or psychological sphere.[11] Rituals focus on the body, in the form of repetitive bodily actions, inducing certain bodily postures and dispositions, or in the form of submitting the body to extreme or transformative experiences.[12] For this reason, rituals are a particularly good medium for facilitating 'the succession of a culture's most deeply held values from one generation to another' and so for reinforcing already deeply held values. Religious *practices* provide a site of religious expression that can be particularly resistant to verbal and linguistic attempts to co-opt them as new expressions of religious identity.

What, though, are we to take as distinctively '*religious* practice'? Defining religion or what counts as the religious in any general way is notoriously difficult. As Talal Asad has shown, religion is not just differently constructed in each society and in each historical context; 'religion' constituted as a separate sphere is itself a historically situated social construct that will only occur in some societies and not others.[13] The difficulty with defining religion also has a direct bearing on the issue of distinguishing *religious* practice from other kinds of practice.[14] Ritual behaviour can be found in all kinds of situations that we (as western scholars) would not define as religious.[15] Typical definitions of ritual say that it is 'prescribed formal behaviour for occasions *not given over to technical routine*' or 'that which is *not seen as pragmatic when viewed by the anthropologist*' in contrast to

---

[8] Bowie 2000: 155–6; Kunin 2003 187; Asad 1993: 57 and 61; and Sperber 1975.
[9] Bowie 2000: 155–6 and Kunin 2003: 187–8.   [10] Scheid 2003: 116.
[11] Some of these theories are based on the connection between ritual and primordial violence (Girard, 1992 and Burkert 1983) and Freudian theories of the development of mankind (Bowie 2000: 176–8 and Spiro 1968: 115). Others take a more moderate view and simply emphasize the importance of the body within in cultural interpretations of ritual (Bloch 1992: 4, who argues that rituals are related to the fundamental psycho-biological human categories of life and death, and Rappaport 1968: 241–2, who argues that rituals can be a characteristic of animal as well as human life).
[12] Kunin 2003: 188 and Whitehouse 1996: 710.   [13] Asad 2002: 114–32, especially 116.
[14] Bowie 2000: 154.   [15] Rappaport 1999: 24–6.

'those actions that serve a spiritual or religious' purpose.[16] In this approach it is the anthropologist who decides whether a specific practice is pragmatic and technical or not and it is the anthropologist who reads a meaning into those practices defined as symbolic. As Bell has pointed out, those using the practices might not have made this distinction between actions that are pragmatic or instrumental and those that are seen as symbolic and therefore religious.[17] Instead, she argues, we need to explore the processes of ritualization by which the people themselves in the society being studied distinguish religious practices from everyday actions.[18] For Asad there is a problem with prioritizing the symbolic as the distinctively religious just as there is a problem with defining religion prima facie as a sphere separate from the rest of society as a whole.[19] Any attempt to single out certain practices involving the supernatural and claim that they are not 'religious' but 'social' is going to come up against this problem; it always means taking for granted that there is a distinct and easily definable field of 'religion' that can be separated out from the sphere of the 'social' so allowing the latter to be privileged as the significant field of interpretation. Such approaches rely on an unspoken definition of what religion is (that is, not the 'social'). They take for granted that the 'social' is an objective category when in fact it is just as constructed as the 'religious'.[20] It is not easy to distinguish the social from the religious sphere in any simple way. Religious rituals can have a pragmatic purpose, just as social practices can have symbolic meaning, and religion can be bound up in the social sphere rather than be distinct from it. As Bowie has argued, Quakers stress the 'sacrament of the every day', and many other Christian traditions also seek to turn all actions into 'religious acts through conscious intent by directing or dedicating them to god'.[21] We have also seen Chrysostom exhorting his audience to do everything, including going to the market place or putting on a sandal, in a way that was pleasing to God; the Latin and Greek terms *religio* and *eusebia* could cover a much wider range of activities than we would consider normal for religion.

Another problem with using the instrumental/pragmatic versus symbolic distinction to mark off religious practices is that it brings us into the debate about the distinction between magic and religion. One of the stereotypical ways by which 'religion' has, in the past, been distinguished from 'magic' is through the notion that magic is instrumental. As Versnel has shown, the instrumental view of magic grew out of Frazer's characterization

---

[16] Turner 1982: 79 and Kunin 2003: 160 summarizing Spiro 1968: 98.   [17] Bell 1992: 70.
[18] Bell 1992: 74 and Penn 2005: 16–17.   [19] Asad 1993: 55.
[20] See, for example, Hennessy 1993: 14–15.   [21] Bowie 2000: 154–5.

of magic as 'bad science', in which it is seen to offer 'operational knowledge which can be exploited to attain control over the environment and to achieve concrete goals'.[22] Magic is seen as manipulative, controlling and having the purpose of achieving concrete goals, while religion is seen to be 'not primarily purpose-motivated' and as entailing an 'attitude of submission and supplication' in humans.[23] This distinction between 'magic' and 'religion' is, however, far from applicable to all societies.[24] In mainstream Graeco-Roman religion, for example, animal sacrifice was often carried out with the explicit intention of gaining something in return from the God to whom the offering was made. Sacrifice would often be accompanied by a prayer that specified what those sacrificing desired in return, or a vow might be made to a particular divinity promising sacrifices if that divinity granted a particular outcome.[25] Religion can also be distinguished from magic according to the types of practices used. Thus prayer, sacrifice and divination carried out in public, as well as the Eucharist ceremony, to name just a few, are usually seen as 'religious' practices. Spells, the use of amulets, incantations, curse-tablets and certain divinatory techniques including astrology, on the other hand, are usually placed in the camp of magic. But still there is no definition that is agreed upon by all. Phillips has shown that while ancient people did have a sense that there could be unsanctioned religious activity, they had no single definition of what practices were characteristic of this activity. Rather they could construct religion and magic differently at different times depending on the circumstances and could use the term 'magic' to outlaw almost any practice if they decided they objected to it.[26] In fact the rituals used in practices defined as magical were almost indistinguishable from those used in religious rites, as has recently been shown for prayers and spells.[27] 'Magic' has also often been distinguished from 'religion' because it is seen to be carried out in private for the individual practitioner alone. Since Durkheim, religion has been valued as the communal, the social and the institutional and opposed to magic as the private and the individual.[28] Some have taken as a defining feature of religious practices, as of religion, that they are 'cultural actions rather than those created by the individual'.[29] For this reason, the use of the label 'magic' will often include a denigration of private practices.[30] This is

---

[22] Versnel 1991: 178. [23] Versnel 1991: 178. See also Leach 1964.
[24] Versnel 1991: 179. [25] S. R. F. Price 1999: 33 and 37–8 and Scheid 2003: 193–4.
[26] Phillips 1991: 260–1. See Janowitz 2001: 9–26. For example, for the way that practices outlawed by legislation shifted over time, see Rives 2003 and Sandwell 2005.
[27] Graf 1991 and Versnel 1991: 180. [28] Kunin 2003: 159–60.
[29] Kunin 2003: 160 summarizing Spiro 1968: 98. [30] Kippenberg 1997: 151–2 and 163.

as true for use of the term by ancient people as by modern scholars. However, this too cannot be taken as an essential or universally defining feature of 'magic' because there are a number of non-institutionalized actions that can also be considered religious.[31] Certainly in the ancient world, there was a recognized 'private' sphere of religion that related to the family and to privately funded cult (Festus, *De Significatione Verborum* 245).[32]

No practice can be said to be 'social, 'religious' or 'magical' in and of itself, just as very few practices can be said to be essential markers of particular religious identities in and of themselves: it was the actors involved who defined these functions, uses and significances of practice. It is thus impossible for us as external observers to decide prima facie that some practices count as religious and some do not. Instead, I shall start with as broad a definition of religion as possible, so as not inadvertently to exclude any practices that ancient people might have included in this sphere of activity. This broad definition will be: 'beliefs in mystical (or non-empirical) beings or powers regarded as the first and final causes of all effects'.[33] As a universal definition of religion this is not valid, because Buddhism challenges the notion that all religions must have supernatural beings as their defining feature. When talking about the ancient world, however, this definition is much less problematic as ancient people readily accepted a range of divine beings and demonic powers.[34] Our modern word 'religion' does not really capture this more inclusive way of thinking about supernatural powers because we tend to associate it with institutional religions. In this chapter I shall consider a range of religious practices open to individuals at Antioch that called on divine and supernatural powers or brought individuals into some relationship with them. This will include mainstream religious practices such as taking the Eucharist and attending church, any ritual that seeks to call on or make use of the demonic world, and bodily practices, control of self and desires in asceticism.

I shall then explore how the inhabitants of fourth-century Antioch might have defined and understood these practices as religious, social, or magical or as indicative of a particular religious identity. I shall consider how Chrysostom used references to religious practice to help to construct identities and how Libanius referred to religious practice as part of his self-representation and part of his strategic use of religion. We cannot use

---

[31] Bowie 2000: 154–5.
[32] See Bakker 1994: 3–4. See also Rives 1995: 173–94 and Beard, North and Price 1998: vol. I, 48–54.
[33] Goody 1961: 144; Turner 1982: 79; C. Stewart 1991: 8; Bell 1992: 74; and Alexander 1997: 139
[34] On the inclusion of demonic powers in this, see Brink 1986. On the continued importance of a wide range of supernatural powers in late antiquity, see Trzcionka 2004: 16, 41, 178 and 211–14 and Greenfield 1988.

the rhetorical writings of these two figures as straightforward 'evidence' of actual religious practice and, unlike anthropologists, we cannot go back to observe behaviour outside these representations. However, once we have recognized the importance of the rhetorical and discursive writings about religious practice in helping to create the range of meanings that a practice might have, this is less of a problem.[35] If we want to understand how different practices were defined as religious rather than magical or social, or as Greek rather than Christian, we have to pay attention to these discourses. We can also attend 'to what is implicit, un-remarked or rejected' in the writings of Chrysostom and Libanius and 'in these ways' 'catch partial, but only partial, glimpses of a wider range of social experience than that directly represented by the texts'.[36] By comparing what these forms of analysis reveal with the little we do know about fourth-century religious practice from material other than the writings of Chrysostom and Libanius, we can hope to gain some understanding of how far religious identities were, or were not, marked out in religious practice in fourth-century Antioch. We shall be able to see that Chrysostom's audience did not simply follow his guidelines for proper religious practice, because they had their own ideas about what it involved.[37]

RELIGIOUS PRACTICE AND RELIGIOUS IDENTITY

Chrysostom understood that religious practice could be a marker of Christian identity. He continually exhorted his audiences to display their Christianity to make clear their difference from Greeks and Jews. In so doing, he was utilizing the great potential that religious practices had to enact and display differences publicly. The rituals of baptism and taking the Eucharist could, for example, be very powerful experiences that allowed the initiate's change of status to be physically embodied. Being immersed semi-naked in water and adopting a pose of submission before the priest or bishop might be remembered by the initiate for a long time afterwards. Similarly, Chrysostom held up animal sacrifice as the defining marker of Greekness because it was a public and communal ritual with very distinctive and visible features – altars stained with blood, for example.[38] Chrysostom constructed these religious practices as markers of religious identity and used them to display the differences between the two religions. Libanius, in contrast, tended to avoid overt displays of religious allegiance and saw them either as tasteless display or as a form of flattery. He thus placed little emphasis

[35] Penn 2005: 52–5. [36] Lieu 2004: 9. [37] C. Stewart 1991: 10–11. [38] S. R. F. Price 1999: 33.

on blood sacrifice as a marker of his religious allegiance at least outside the reign of Julian. In this distrust of overt displays of religious allegiance Libanius might have had something in common with others in Antioch. Ammianus recorded that one of the reasons why the people of Antioch disapproved of the emperor Julian was that 'for the sake of display (*ostentationis gratia*)' 'he improperly took pleasure in carrying the sacred emblems in the place of the priests' (Amm. Marc. 22.14.3). There were many people in fourth-century society who wanted to move away from public displays of religious difference in order to ease religious tension.

I shall now show in greater detail how these different attitudes to religious practice and display of religious difference worked out in relation to four examples: ascetic behaviour, prayer, divination and the use of amulets and incantations.

Asceticism/monasticism. Control of bodily needs and the monastic life are often singled out as two of the most important features of late-antique Christianity. This is true of Antioch as elsewhere.[39] From the reign of Valens, at least, monks began to be prominent in the life of the Antiochene region.[40] Theodoret speaks of a number of holy men who were active in and around Antioch and who entered the city or served its inhabitants on a number of occasions (*H.Rel.* 4.14 and 24, 5.9, 8.13 and 9.5–7 and 13). Both Chrysostom and Libanius also refer to the activities of the monks in the region (Chrysostom, *Hom. de Stat.* 17 (*PG* 49.172–3); *Catéchèse* 8.1–6 (SC 50.247–50) and Libanius *Or.* 30.31 and 48 (F.II.103 and 114) and *Or.* 45.26 (F.IV.371–2)).[41] Scholars often characterize this Antiochene monasticism as taking an extreme form. They describe the monks as living solitary lives outside the city in the wilds of the mountain and contrast their way of life with that of the supposedly more city-based and communal monasticism of Constantinople.[42] They also compare Antiochene monasticism with the striking behaviour of Syrian Holy men, who are presented in ancient texts as engaging in a range of ascetic and abstemious practices. Theodoret describes these men as abstaining from sexual intercourse, eating very little, living alone and wearing only the most basic of clothing (Theodoret, *H.Rel.* Prologue 7, 3.2, 6.1, 13.3, 17.6, 18.2, 24.4, 26.9 and 27.1).[43] Similarly, Chrysostom refers to the shabby clothing of the monks, their lack of worldly goods and the fact that they lived alone and outside the city (*In Ep. ad 1 Tim. Hom.* 14 (*PG* 62.574–8) and the numerous references

[39] Rousseau, 1978 and Brown 1982b: 103–52 and 1988. [40] Liebeschuetz 1972: 234.
[41] See also Chrysostom, *Against Those Who Oppose Monasticism*.
[42] On this stereotypical contrast, see Mayer 1999. [43] Brown 1971: 98.

in *Against the Opponents of Monasticism*). In one passage he describes how they ate only bread and water and wore rough clothing made from animal hair (*Hom. in Matt.* 69.2–3 (*PG* 58.650–3)). The monks and their practices and behaviour functioned as the ideal symbol of Christian difference.[44] As Chrysostom says, 'everything with them has been made different from what we have: clothing and food, houses and shoes, and the way they speak [they spoke Syrian and not Greek]' (*Hom. in Matt.* 69.4 (*PG* 58.654)). He thus wanted his audience to look towards the monastic ideal as a model for their behaviour (Chrysostom, *De Virginitate*).[45] Libanius too saw the behaviour of the monks as one of the most distinctive features of those who did not worship the gods. He consistently vilified the monks, and his hatred for them resulted largely from their extreme behaviour and the marked differences in their physical appearance.[46] Their black robes and pale faces, their lack of sociability and the way they lived in caves disgusted him.[47] Libanius refers to the unusual diets and extreme sexual abstinence of the monks, but he inverts the Christian ideal so that they become greedy and lustful instead of frugal and chaste (*Or.* 30.21 (F.III.98–9) and *Or.* 17.7 (F.II.210)). He could also associate the external display of religiosity exhibited by the monks with a lack of inner religiosity: the monks were only virtuous externally, in the way they dressed (*Or.* 30.46 (F.III.113–14), and *Or.* 2.32 (F.II.249)). This view was also shared by Eunapius, who describes the monks as impious and uncivilized and who again seems to single them out from other Christians (Eunapius, *VP* 472).

For non-Christians such as Libanius and Eunapius, as for Chrysostom, the extreme behaviour of monks and ascetics could be a marker of religious difference. Because the monks were the only Christians who so visibly displayed their Christianity, it was they who drew the anger of Libanius and Eunapius, who could be far more forgiving of other less 'showy' Christians.[48] At the same time Libanius and Eunapius, like Chrysostom and Theodoret, also leave the impression that there were large numbers of Christians engaged in these very visible and distinctive practices. If this picture was representative of fourth-century Antioch, then we could say that ascetic practices were a very successful defining feature of Christianity. Not only were they noticed and accepted by non-Christians as well as Christians, they also had the potential to transform those involved

---

[44] Mayer 1999.
[45] Maxwell forthcoming: 130; Hartney 2004: 11 and 27–9; and Festugière 1959: 330 and 344–6.
[46] As Maxwell has also noted (Maxwell forthcoming: 129–30).
[47] *Or.* 30.8 (F.III.91–2); *Or.* 62.10 (F.IV.351–2); *Or.* 45.26 (F.III.371–2); and *Ep.* 120.5 (F. *Ep.* 1220).
[48] On the spectacular nature of asceticism, see Leyerle 2001: 75.

in them. The physically demanding practices of abstinence from food and sexual intercourse and the wearing of rough clothes could transform the individual's self-understanding and enact their allegiance to, and relationship with, the Christian God in bodily form. If all Christians were involved in such practices they would indeed appear entirely different and separate.

Hagiographic texts such as those of Theodoret and Chrysostom are, however, problematic as our main source for the actions of these monks and ascetics.[49] The texts had a vested interest in presenting this behaviour in its most extreme and most Christianized form. As Brown states, in his reappraisal of his earlier work on holy men, it is easy to 'collude' with 'the hagiographic texts . . . that presented the holy man in dramatic, epic terms' and as a result to assume that he was 'starkly different from everyone else'.[50] The writings of men such as Eunapius and Libanius are just as problematic because they too benefited from depicting the monks' behaviour as the antithesis of Graeco-Roman social life. The depictions given in these literary texts might not be representative of the nature and diversity of ascetic and monastic behaviour that actually took place in Antioch. A number of recent studies have sought to give more subtlety and nuance to the stereotypical picture of monks and holy men in Antioch and Syria. Peter Brown has recently suggested that we turn our attention to the mundane nature of the life of the holy man and to the 'collective representations' that he shared 'with the average believer'.[51] Urbainczyk has also shown that Theodoret was critical of holy men who advocated complete withdrawal from ordinary life: instead, he favoured those who lived a more communal life and deferred to the authority of the Church.[52] In fact, to talk of just one kind of monasticism as characteristic of Antioch or Syria flattens the diversity of forms that ascetic behaviour could take. Antiochene monks might not live solitary existences in the mountains, but could be well integrated into communal and civic life.[53] John Chrysostom's own bishop, Flavian, lived an ascetic life within the city, as did other members of the clergy who might have run an *asketerion* in Antioch itself.[54] There were also large numbers of ascetic virgins and widows who might have 'continued to dress and behave in ways that made them indistinguishable' from other women rather than display their asceticism in the poverty of their dress and lack of concern for their personal appearance.[55] These more civic forms of ascetic behaviour

---

[49] On this problem, see Rousseau 1990: 116.   [50] Brown 1998: 370 and 368.
[51] Brown 1998: 373–4.   [52] Urbainczyk 2002: 68, 80 and 84.   [53] Mayer 1999: 281–2.
[54] Mayer 1999: 282–3 and Hartney 2004: 88–9.   [55] Mayer 1999: 285.

existed alongside that of the monks who lived in the mountains around Antioch, the Syrian-speaking monks who once a year came into the city to consult with the bishop (Chrysostom, *Catéchèse* 8.1–6 (SC 50.247–50) and Theodoret, *HE* 13.7).[56]

This diversity of ascetic practice meant that even when people adopted the ascetic life it was not always in a form acceptable to Chrysostom. In a series of sermons he shows his disapproval of male and female ascetics living together because it brought their claims to high morals and holiness into disrepute.[57] Chrysostom's greatest concern seems to have been about how this practice would appear to outsiders (*Adv. Eos.* 7 (*PG* 47.506)). The lack of restraint of male ascetics in displaying their associations with ascetic women would make people question the ascetics' chastity and serve as justification for the accusation that they were 'gluttons, flatterers and slaves of women' (*Adv. Eos.* 1 and 10 (*PG* 47.496 and 509)). These ascetics thus devalued what was supposed to be one of the defining features of Christian superiority and difference: their attitude to sexual relations. They lived as any other man subject to lust for women and so no longer stood out 'within the urban community as being obviously Christian'.[58] Chrysostom's primary concern that ascetic behaviour should mark Christian difference is revealed here, but the behaviour of actual ascetics could challenge this ideal. Even when individuals did adopt ascetic behaviour, it might not serve to mark out their Christian identity in the right way.[59]

In one passage Chrysostom describes different levels of Christian achievement among his audiences. Some Christians 'shone' and were more celebrated and of greater repute than others and so, for Chrysostom, were the ideal model of Christian behaviour that his audiences should imitate (*In Ep. ad 1 Cor. Hom.* 31.6–7 (*PG* 61.262–4)). Many ordinary Christians, however, thought that these high achievers had attained such levels of holiness that it was impossible to imitate them, complaining that they 'were not monks' (*Hom. in Gen.* 21.6 (*PG* 53.183) and *Adv. Jud.* 8.4 (*PG* 48.932)).[60] Others 'trembled and turned pale' at the sight of those displaying Christian

---

[56] Mayer 1999: 283.
[57] *Adversus Eos qui apud se habent subintroductas virgines* and *Quod Regulares Feminae Viris Cohabitare non Debeant*. It is unclear whether Chrysostom's works on the cohabitation of ascetics were delivered at Antioch, but what Chrysostom says in these works reveals his attitude to asceticism more generally. On the provenance of these works, see Adkin 1992 and Leyerle 2001: 75–99. See also: E. A. Clarke 1977; Mayer 1999: 282–3; and Hartney 2004: 88–9.
[58] Hartney 2004: 91 and 93.
[59] See Leyerle 2001 on Chrysostom's disapproval of this kind of ascetic behaviour more generally.
[60] Maxwell forthcoming: 129–30; Brown 1988: 311; and Jedin and Dolan 1980: 322.

excellence (*In Ep. ad 1 Cor. Hom.* 31.7 (*PG* 61.262)). Chrysostom argues that these criticisms and complaints simply reveal 'envy' of those who 'shine' and berates his audiences for trying to bring these high achievers down to their own level (*In Ep. ad 1 Cor. Hom.* 31.6–7 (*PG* 61.262–4)). His treatise *Against the Opponents of Monasticism* shows Christian parents, as well as non-Christian ones, objecting to their sons' adoption of the monastic life. These Christian parents disapproved of the fact that the monastic lifestyle meant giving up a life of wealth and comfort for one of poverty. Chrysostom thus had to tackle their fears that their son would dress in shabby clothes, live alone and lose his social and political contacts. One baptized Christian even stated that 'he would withdraw from the faith and sacrifice to demons because he was choked with rage to see persons who are free, well born and able to live in luxury being led to this harsh life' (*Adv. Oppug.* 1.2 (*PG* 47.321)). In these attitudes Chrysostom's audiences did not differ much from Libanius, who would have shared the social background of many of these elite Christians and, like them, found the monks' overt displays of poverty and denial distasteful and incomprehensible. Such elite Christians were happy to be Christian as long as this did not entail differentiating themselves too much from elite society. Like Libanius, they had profound distrust of the lack of sociability and tactlessness of extreme displays of religious difference shown by the monks.

Prayer. Prayer had always been a central part of Graeco-Roman religion, accompanying sacrifice in order to specify to which gods the sacrifice was offered and making clear what humans wanted in return.[61] Whether in the context of public religion or of more personal requests, prayers very often took the form of asking the gods to grant a favour to humans.[62] They might ask for help in winning a war, bringing prosperity to a city or curing an illness. The contractual nature of Graeco-Roman prayers was most clear when a sacrifice or an offering was promised in return for a request being granted.[63] In Roman state religion there were often set formulas for prayers that accompanied sacrifices and they had to be repeated correctly word-for-word in order to be successful. Prayer could also be ritual available to individuals to express the strength of feeling of the person praying or their special relationship with the divine.[64] In certain branches

---

[61] S. R. F. Price 1999: 34 and Scheid 2003: 97–8.
[62] Ogilvie 2000: 29–37, although Ogilvie overemphasizes the difference between prayers and spells.
[63] Ogilvie 2000: 37–40. On prayers as part of a reciprocal relationship of exchange between gods and men in the Greek tradition, see Pulleyn 1997: 56–69.
[64] Ovid, *Tr.* 1.1.27–30 and Juvenal, *Sat.* 6.539–41. See also van der Horst 1998: 295 and 301 and Versnel 1981: 30.

of Neoplatonic thought prayer was seen as a superior way to have contact with the divine: it was one of the 'spiritual' sacrifices, such as pure thoughts and hymns that were contrasted to 'material' sacrifices' of meat, incense, fruit and barley.[65] Early Christians also adopted prayer because of its centrality in Jewish practice.[66] From references in the Gospels and Paul's writings prayer entered into the Christian liturgy and became one of the most regular features of Christian worship. Most assemblies of Christians included prayer, and a special Eucharistic prayer was read during the taking of the Eucharist.[67] Prayer was also supposed to accompany Christian meals and to be spoken regularly throughout the day by Christians.[68] These Christian prayers were usually addressed to God (rather than Christ) and included a glorification of God and a list of his achievements through the person of Christ, the giving of thanks to God, confession of sins and a request for forgiveness.[69] This model for prayer was taken into the fourth century and prayer continued to be a central part of liturgy and worship in this period too. Prayer would end the meeting of the normal congregation (with a prayer for the catechumenate and the whole world) but would also be a part of the Eucharistic ritual for the baptized Christians who stayed behind.

Chrysostom prescribed prayer for his audiences and tried to impress on them the importance of it as a form of Christian spirituality: it was a 'conversation with God' in which they should readily engage (*Hom. in Gen.* 30.5 and 16–19 (*PG* 53.275 and 280–2)).[70] He wanted his audiences to 'make a serious effort to come [to church] before dawn to offer prayers and confessions to the God of all things' (*Catéchèse* 8.17 (SC 50.256–7)). Prayers, however, did not have to be said in church, so they provided a particularly flexible religious practice. They were a way in which Chrysostom's audiences could keep their 'mind purified', and 'call on God' whether they were 'in the market place, at home, on a journey, appearing at court, at sea . . .' (*Hom. in Gen.* 30.16–19 (*PG* 53.280–2)).[71] Prayer was a way of bringing God into every aspect of people's lives and of putting Christian values into action and so should mark out the true Christian. Chrysostom was thus careful

---

[65] On this, see Bradbury 1995: 332–41. On prayer as a form of sacrifice, see also Versnel 1981: 51–2.
[66] *EEC*, 'Prayer': 744.
[67] Tertullian, *Apol.* 39; Hippolytus, *The Apostolic Tradition* 35 and 10; and Justin Martyr, *1 Apol.* 65 and 67.
[68] Tertullian, *Apol.* 36.16–18; Hippolytus, *The Apostolic Tradition* 25–7; and *The Didache* 8.2–3.
[69] *EEC*, 'Prayer': 746.
[70] On the importance of prayer, see also *Hom. in Gen.* 34.13 (*PG* 53.318) and *Catéchèse* 1.46 (SC 50.132) and 7.24–5 (SC 50.241–2) 8.4 (SC 50.249–50)).
[71] On prayer before and after mealtime, see *Catéchèse* 7.30 (SC 50.244–5).

to outline the correct kind of communication and relationship with God that should be expressed in prayer. His audiences should not use prayers to make requests for themselves whether this was to seek their own gain, to cure illness or to avenge enemies (*In Ep. ad 2 Cor. Hom.* 5.4 (*PG* 61.432) and *De Poenitentia* 4.18 (*PG* 49.305)). Instead they should pray in supplication to God and simply ask that he should forgive their sins (*De Poenitentia* 4.19 (*PG* 49.305)). The supplication and submission to God that was expressed in prayer could also be physically embodied in the posture adopted during prayer. In his catechetical sermons Chrysostom describes how candidates for baptism should kneel with their hands outstretched or upturned to heaven while addressing God (*Catéchèse* 3.18 (SC 50.161–2) and *Catéchèse* 2.6 (SC 366.125–6) = Harkins, *Baptismal Instruction* 10.14).[72] Prayer was very much a bodily practice and a physical experience as well as simply a way of communicating with God.

Libanius also refers to prayer as a common practice for himself and those he knew. Prayer, especially silent prayer, was a ritual that accompanied or replaced sacrifice and other public acts when these were no longer possible ((*Ep.* F.1183 and *Ep.* B.161.4 (F.1196), *Or.* 14.41 (F.II.102) *Or.* 18.112–16 (F.II.283–4)).[73] As such, prayer was part of a turn to less 'ostentatious' religious practices that would have been less noticed by, and less offensive to, Christian authorities. The one occasion where Libanius quotes a prayer in full appears in a letter of 360 written to Modestus, Constantius' *comes orientis*, in order to gain Modestus' help on behalf of Calliopus 2 (*Ep.* B.71).[74] This letter includes the words of a short prayer or invocation as part of Libanius' plea that Modestus be kindly towards Calliopus, 'Zeus Meilichius [Zeus the Mild], father to men in the most gentle way, make the well-born Modestus kindly to Calliopus, and make him resemble you!' (*Ep.* B.71.3–4 (F.220)). The letter containing this prayer was written during Constantius' reign when, according to a later letter of Libanius, Modestus was not 'acknowledging' his 'admiration of the gods' (*Ep.* B.74 (F.804)). As a result, it would be possible to argue that this prayer was a way for Libanius and Modestus to revel in their shared, if hidden, allegiance to the Graeco-Roman gods, but this seems unlikely. In a world where private letters could very easily become public documents a reference to prayer as a marker of religious difference would negate Modestus' attempt to downplay his

---

[72] This can be compared with Canon 20 of the Council of Nicaea, which forbade kneeling in prayer on Sundays.
[73] Van der Horst 1998: 293–306 and Versnel 1981: 28–31; also Homer *Il.* 7.191–6.
[74] Calliopus had once been an assistant teacher of Libanius', but was now facing charges over his actions while employed in the imperial chancery (*Ep.* B.71 (F.220)).

allegiance to the traditional gods. It is more likely that prayer was seen by Libanius, Modestus and others as a neutral, shared practice that was considered acceptable to all and not as something that aligned the individual with one religious identity rather than another.[75] Even the reference to Zeus can be seen in this light because Zeus Meilichius, the kindly Zeus, could easily appeal to Christian notions of forgiveness. Libanius' presentation of prayer as an act used at times of trouble and anguish, which should be accompanied by depth of feeling, also shows overlap with Christian conceptions. During the plague and famine of AD 385 Libanius states that he spent his time 'joylessly, in prayer to the gods to grant us food and health' (*Or.* 1.233 (F.I.185)). During the Riot of the Statues in AD 387 he describes how humans 'in times of dire trouble' 'call on the gods and beg them to help us' (*Or.* 22.5 (F.II.73)).[76] He also mentions the prayers and laments that he made to the gods on the occasions of the death of Julian and the exile of his friend Seleucus (*Ep.* N.129.3 (F.1187) and (*Ep.* N.142.1 (F.1508)). He suggests that prayer can be connected to one's moral state: he helped the bakers during the grain shortage so as not to feel unworthy to address the gods when praying (*Or.* 29.18 (F.III.72)).[77] Libanius, like Chrysostom, depicts prayer as something that can be quite spontaneous in nature and as being unconstrained by requirements of place (*Or.* 18.112–16 (F.II.283–4) and *Or.* 1.201 (F.I.173–4)).[78] On one occasion, Libanius mentions that he 'addressed the temple (of Calliope) from afar as I stood in the colonnade' (*Or.* 1.103 (F.I.133)) and, on another, that at the baths he addressed Saturn and Aphrodite in thanks for the pleasure of bathing (*Or.* 6.17 (F.I.361)). There is also some evidence that he particularly practised daily prayer in the morning and evening just as Chrysostom prescribed prayer at dawn for his audiences (*Ep.* N.129.3 (F.1187)).[79]

Libanius, like Chrysostom, did criticize people for using prayer for the wrong purposes: wealth was not something people should pray for (*Or.* 52.29 (F.IV.39) and (*Or.* 4.28 (F.I. 296)).[80] However, unlike Chrysostom, he did think it acceptable that people should pray to the gods to gain other individual benefits: prayers for health and family were appropriate and Libanius himself often used prayers to help him with his own health

---

[75] See also *Ep.* B.36 (F.510); *Ep.* B.39.1.2 and 6 (F.61) to Florentius; *Ep.* B.66.4 (F.251) to Honoratus; *Ep.* N.18.1 (F.497) to Strategius Musonianus; and *Ep.* N.13 (F.441) to Datianus.
[76] See also *Or.* 2.74 (F.II.261) and *Or.* 29.5 (F.III.65).
[77] See also *Ep.* N.53.1 (F.97); *Ep.* N.53.1 (F.97); *Or.* 29.18 (F.III.72); *Or.* 20.48 (F.II.443); *Ep.* N.129.3 (F.*Ep.* 1187)); and (*Ep.* N.142.1 (F. *Ep.* 1508).
[78] Misson 1914: 119.   [79] *Ep.* F.1183.1–2; *Or.* 4.28 (F.I.295–6); and *Or.* 52.29 (F.IV.39).
[80] See also *Or.* 64.78 (F.IV.470); *Ep.* B.155 (F.734); and *Ep.* B.64.5 (F.362).

problems (*Or.* 1.142 (F.I.151)).[81] In this he showed some commonality with what Chrysostom's audiences were *actually* doing in prayer, when they were not following to the letter the guidelines Chrysostom had laid down for them. The fact that Chrysostom had to persuade his audiences not to pray for their own health and well-being suggests that many of his audience were doing precisely that (*In Ep. ad 2 Cor. Hom.* 5.4 (*PG* 61.432) and *De Poenitentia* 4.18 (*PG* 49.305)). If this was the case, then the only feature that would distinguish their prayers from those that Libanius described is that they addressed the Christian God rather than Graeco-Roman ones. The fact that prayer was not dependent on attendance at a religious building also leaves room for ambiguity about how distinct their prayers were from non-Christian forms of prayer. Libanius, like Chrysostom, presented prayer as an activity that could take place anywhere and anytime but perhaps especially in the morning and evening (Libanius *Or.* 1.103 (F.I.133); *Or.* 6.17 (F.I.361)) and *Ep.* 129.3 (F. *Ep.* 1187)).[82] We also know that the posture Chrysostom recommended for prayer during baptism was the same posture that Romans sometimes used in prayer (Horace, *Carm.* 3.23.1).[83] As a result, there might be little to distinguish a Christian at prayer from a non-Christian. There was no obvious way of knowing which gods were being addressed in prayer, or whether they were being addressed in supplication, as Chrysostom wanted, or simply being asked for favours. As Libanius says of peasants forcibly converted to Christianity in the countryside around Antioch, they can adopt 'the outward posture of prayer' but still call on the gods (*Or.* 30.28 (F.III.102)). This reveals the ambiguity in defining the religious allegiance of those engaged in prayer. The *Miracles of Saints Kosmas and Damian* support this picture by telling us of an individual who went to the shrine of these martyrs but invoked Castor and Pollux instead (*Miracles of Saints Kosmas and Damian* 113–17).[84] Prayer did not function well as a marker of religious difference in the fourth century, despite Chrysostom's efforts. It is a typical example of a practice tending towards syncretism and lack of definition because its personal nature made it hard for Church authorities to prescribe how people experienced it. Once prayers by adherents of Graeco-Roman religion could be spoken without other accompanying rituals, such as blood sacrifice, it became hard to tell which gods were being addressed or what was the religious allegiance of the user. Prayers could thus provide a common ground to both religions and could be used by men like Libanius when he wanted to play down religious differences.

[81] See also *Or.* 1.243–4 (F.I.188–9) and *Ep.* 171.2 (F. *Ep.* 964).
[82] *Ep.* F.1183.1–2; *Or.* 4.28 (F.I.295–6); and *Or.* 52.29 (F.IV.39).
[83] Harkins 1963: 309, note 52.   [84] Trombley 1994: vol. I, 166.

Divination. Divinatory and prophetic techniques had always been an essential part of Graeco-Roman religion, from the augury and haruspicy of Roman state religion and the great Oracles of Zeus and Apollo of Greek religion to the more personal use of soothsayers and interpretation of omens.[85] This continued to be the case throughout the imperial period and there is some evidence that there was an increased interest in divination and prophetic rituals in the second to third centuries AD.[86] As Veyne has argued, in this period humans moved from negotiating with the gods through sacrifice to seeking guidance from them about what the future had in store.[87] Less has been written about the place of divination and prophecy in the fourth century, and discussion of divination at least has often been subsumed under discussion of 'magic'. Official forms of divinatory activity continued to function in the earlier fourth century. In 329 Constantine issued a piece of legislation commanding that *haruspices* of Rome could still be consulted about publicly significant omens such as lightning striking the palace (*CTh* 16.10.1).[88] Official sites of public oracles and dream-incubation also continued to be popular until they were closed to the public. Ammianus describes the large-scale consultation of the Oracle of Bes in Egypt in the reign of Constantius, and Libanius' writings often refer to the use of the shrine of Asclepius at Aegae.[89] Individuals were involved in more personal forms of divinatory and prophetic activity in the fourth century. The restrictions placed by imperial legislation on *haruspices* entering private houses suggest that these figures offered contact with the divine for individuals as well as the state (*CTh* 9.16.1 issued by Constantine in 320).[90] Ammianus' long and detailed descriptions of the magical trials under Constantius and Valens give the impression that large numbers of people were using soothsayers and reading omens (Amm. Marc. 19.12.1–19 and 29.1.5–10).[91] There are problems with taking his words as straightforward evidence for the extent of the use of divination: he might have exaggerated his accounts of the

---

[85] On state divination, see Ogilvie 2000: 53–69; Scheid 2003: 111–28; and S. R. F. Price 1999: 28, 73–6, 81, 131 and 137. On personal use of a soothsayer, see Dickie 2001: 61–74.
[86] Veyne 1986: 254 and 269–71 and Lane-Fox 1986: 168–261. On oracles, see Veyne 1986: 269–71. On dreams and omens, see Veyne 1986: 269–72.
[87] See Veyne 1986: 254–61 and also Festugière 1960: 27. For similar ideas, see Davies 2004: 238–42 and Young 1979: 19–21.
[88] Although he did forbid private use of *haruspices*.
[89] For the former, see Amm. Marc. 19.12.8. For the latter, see Libanius *Or.* 1.143 (F.1.151–2); *Ep.* N.137 (*Ep.* F.1300); *Ep.* F.1483.5; *Epp.* F.706–8; *Or.* 1.143 (F.1.151–2); *Ep.* N.138.4 (F.1301); *Ep.* B.147.2 (F.695); *Ep.* B.148.2 (F.1342); and *Ep.* B.146.2 (F.727).
[90] See also Augustine, *Conf.* 4.2; Paulinus, *Life of Ambrose* 20 (*PL* 14.36); and Amm. Marc. 28.1.19–20. For these examples, see Dickie 2001: 284–7.
[91] See Downey 1961: 401–2.

magical trials, in which we find references to divination, in order to portray the tyrannical nature of the reigns of Constantius, and Valens and Valentinian.[92] However, one can set aside the labelling of divination as magical while still accepting that personal divination is popular in this period.

Ammianus suggests that Constantius carried out his trials against those charged with using the Egyptian Oracle of Bes at Scythopolis because Antiochenes figured particularly prominently among their number (Amm. Marc. 19.12.8). The regularity of references to divinatory techniques in the writings of Libanius and Chrysostom can support this picture of the popularity of divination at Antioch. Even if we do not accept all of Libanius' descriptions of his own use of divination as the straightforward truth, their frequency suggests that this practice was important to him. In his *Oration 1 The Autobiography* (written in the late 370s (up to *Or.* 1.155) and throughout the period of 380–93 (from *Or.* 1.155 onwards)), he presents himself as someone who had constant recourse to soothsayers, either to cure his illness or to give predictions to himself or his family members (*Or.* 1.3, 1.244 and 268 (F.I.1.80–1, 189 and 197)). In this work Libanius also describes how dreams and waking visions could cure his illnesses, reassure his anxiety or warn him of danger ((*Or.* 1.67, 141, 143 and 245 (F.I.115, 150, 151–2 and 189)).[93] He also presents himself as reading events small and large in the world around him as predictive omens (*Or.* 1.134 and 283–4 (F.I.147–8 and 205–6)).[94] Elsewhere he also describes his consultation of the shrine of Asclepius at Aegae to receive dream cures. During Julian's reign, he consulted the god by proxy through his brother (*Epp.* F.706–8).[95] In the early years of Valens' reign, a slave and a friend travelled to the shrine on his behalf (*Or.* 1.143 (F.I.151–2)) and *Ep.* 137 (*Ep.* F.1300 of 364))).[96] Although disparaging of some astrologers and their predictions (*Or.* 37.18 and 21 (F.III.247 and 249)), Libanius clearly accepted the validity of the art of astrology as a whole (*Or.* 1.281 (F.I.204)). He also represented others as using these divinatory practices. During Valens' trials against illicit divination the accused people had an innocent 'desire to learn something from heaven of (their) own fortunes' (*Or.* 1.171 (F.I.964)).[97] On other occasions members of the senate at Constantinople were affected by dreams and visions (*Or.* 1.239 (F.I.187)) and others used astrology as a means to achieving success (*Ep.* N.95.3 (F.758)). Chrysostom often berates his audiences for using various

---

[92] Funke 1967: 145–75; von Haehling 1978: 74–101; and Trzcionka 2004: 98 and 117–21.
[93] On Libanius and dreams and waking visions, see Misson 1914: 109–12.
[94] Compare the former with other portents of Julian's death as at *Or.* 17.30 (F.II.218)).
[95] See also *Ep.* B.146.2 (F.727); *Ep.* N.138.4 (F.1301); *Ep.* B.147.2 (F.695); and *Ep.* B.148.2 (F.1342).
[96] See also *Ep.* F.1483.5 to Modestus in 365. [97] See also *Or.* 14.16 (F.II.93–4).

techniques of divination. They read events in their daily lives as if they had prognostic powers, followed the observance of days and nativities (*In Ep. ad Ephes. Hom.* 12 (*PG* 62.92) and *In Kal.* 2 (*PG* 48.954)).[98] They also used soothsayers for curing sickness, finding out whether a child would survive, or for assistance in finding lost property or money (*In Ep. ad 1 Tim. Hom.* 10 (*PG* 61.552)).[99] Some in Chrysostom's audience also still had a propensity to use incubation at the Jewish shrine of the Cave of Matrona in Daphne (*Adv. Jud.* 1 (*PG* 48.852)). From the admittedly difficult literary sources, it appears that divinatory techniques were popular among both Christians and non-Christians in Antioch and the surrounding region.

Chrysostom labelled divination as a practice of the Greeks and sought to present it in the most negative light possible (*In Cap. ad. Galat. Comment.* 1 (*PG* 61.623)).[100] He belittled his audiences for taking the smallest sign as an omen, such as a cock crowing or a man sneezing, or for being willing to believe the whole year would turn out well if the Kalends of January was a lucky day (*In Ep. ad Ephes. Hom.* 12 (*PG* 62.92) and *In Kal.* 2 (*PG* 48.954)).[101] Such popular, 'Greek' divinatory practices could further be dismissed by labelling their practitioners as soothsayers (*manteis*) and oracle-mongers (*chrēsmologoi*) in contrast to true Christian prophecy (*prophēteia*) (*In Ep. ad 1 Cor. Hom.* 29.2 (*PG* 61.241) and *In Ep. ad 2 Tim. Hom.* 8 (*PG* 62.543–4)). Chrysostom also associated divinatory practices with demonic powers, arguing that diviners gained their power from demons and that using them made people subject to the devil (*In Ep. ad 2 Tim. Hom.* 8 (*PG* 62.648–50) and *In Ep. ad 1 Thess. Hom.* 3 (*PG* 62.412–13)).[102] He compares Christian prophets in New Testament times, who 'declared the truth' and spoke 'with understanding and entire freedom', with Greek soothsayers, who were compelled by demonic powers, spoke like madmen and were characterized by a 'darkening of their minds' (*In Ep. ad 1 Cor. Hom.* 29.2 (*PG* 61.241) quoting Plato, *Apology of Socrates* c7). Soothsayers spoke in incomprehensible riddles, similar to the oracles delivered by the Pythia, and were ineffective because they were unable to find the property

---

[98] *Ad Illum. Catech.* 2.5 (*PG* 49.239–40) = Harkins, *Baptismal Instruction* 12.53–4; *In Ep. ad Ephes. Hom.* 12 (*PG* 62.92); *Catéchèse* 3.6 (SC 366.233) = Harkins, *Baptismal Instruction* 11.25; *In Ep. ad 1 Tim. Hom.* 10 (*PG* 62.552); and *In Ep. ad 1 Cor. Hom.* 4.11 (*PG* 61.38). See also Dickie 1995: 28–9.

[99] *In Ep. ad 1 Thess. Hom.* 3 (*PG* 62.412–3); *In Ep. ad Coloss. Hom.* 8 (*PG* 62.357–8); and *In Ep. ad 2 Tim. Hom.* 8 (*PG* 62.650).

[100] See also *Catéchèse* 1.39 (SC 50.129); *In Ep. ad Ephes. Hom.* 12 (*PG* 62.91–2); *In Ep. ad 1 Cor. Hom.* 4.11 and 12.13–14 (*PG* 61.38 and 106).

[101] See also *Ad Illum. Catech.* 2.5 (*PG* 49.239–40) = Harkins, *Baptismal Instruction* 12.53–54 and *In Ep. ad Ephes. Hom.* 12 (*PG* 62.92). See also Eusebius of Alexandria, *Sermo 7, De Neomeniis et Sabbatis et de non observandis avium vocibus* and Dickie 1995: 28–9.

[102] Compare with Augustine, *De Civ. Dei* 7.10, 8.15 and 9.20–2.

belonging to the temples of the gods (*In Ep. ad 2 Tim. Hom.* 8 (*PG* 62.543–4)). Similarly, demons tricked adherents of Graeco-Roman religion into thinking that statues of deities could deliver oracles in order to convince people that they were not just dumb idols (*In Ep. ad 1 Cor. Hom.* 29.2 (*PG* 61.241–2)). In his two major apologetic works, *The Discourse on Blessed Babylas* and *The Demonstration against the Pagans*, Chrysostom sought to demonstrate the fulfilment of Christian prophecy in history and its superiority to Graeco-Roman prophecy (*De S. Bab. Contra Jul. et Gent.* 9 (*PG* 48.536)).[103] The fact that the oracle of Apollo at Daphne had stopped functioning in the recent past gave support to his argument about the inferiority of traditional Greek oracles (*De S. Bab. Contra Jul. et Gent.* 73 and 127 (*PG* 50.553 and 570–1)). Because Chrysostom made no distinction between popular divinatory practices and mainstream Graeco-Roman religion he could describe the emperor Julian as surrounded by 'sorcerers, soothsayers, augurs and mendicant priests' (*De S. Bab. Contra Jul. et Gent.* 77 (*PG* 48.554)). What we thus see is a twofold process: in order to discredit traditional Graeco-Roman prophecy Chrysostom associated it with the disreputable practices of soothsayers but he also associated the use of soothsayers with mainstream Graeco-Roman prophecy to reinforce his notion that it was Greek and incompatible with being Christian.

Libanius too could at times associate divination with mainstream Graeco-Roman religion. In his Julianic orations and letters he praises Julian for making possible again the use of divination for all as part of his religious restoration (*Ep.* N.108.1 (*Ep.* F.1400)).[104] He suggests that divination was part of the package that makes up Graeco-Roman religion and that must be restored along with sacrifices, temples and festivals. Outside Julian's reign, however, Libanius was forced to keep state religion and divination separate. As Ammianus states, when describing a portent that was recorded at Antioch during Constantius' reign, 'portents ... often see the light, as indications of various affairs' but now they tend to 'pass by unheard of and unknown' because they are 'no longer expiated by public rites' (Amm. Marc. 19.12.19–20). As a result, Ammianus was left to give his own interpretation of this portent: 'that the state was turning into a deformed condition' under the brutality of Constantius as signified by the trials at Scythopolis (Amm. Marc. 19.12.20).[105] After Julian's death Libanius too refers to the way that 'oracles (*ta manteia*)' were now 'silent' and people had to rely on 'human calculation (*anthrōpinos logismos*)' (*Or.* 24.2 (F.11.515)).

---

[103] Schatkin and Harkins's introduction to the translation of these treatises (1983: 17–23 and 169–86).
[104] *Or.* 1.119 (F.1.140).   [105] Davies 2004: 238–41 and 284. See also Amm. Marc. 19.12.14–15.

When public divination was no longer possible under Christian emperors, men such as Libanius and Ammianus were able to envisage this practice in terms of personal or 'human' calculations.

By the late 370s and 380s, when Libanius was writing his *Oration* 1 *The Autobiography*, this way of thinking about divination had become dominant. One of the goals of the oration was to present the intervention of the divine in his own life:[106] Libanius read his life as if it were a text full of messages from the divine that had to be interpreted, whether the bolting of a horse, a dream, or the actions of Fortune.[107] It is in this context that many of Libanius' references to his own use of divination, as recorded above, were found. Using divination was one of his responses to the vicissitudes of his life. At times his references to the use of soothsayers are embedded in his descriptions of magical trials and how he was caught up in these.[108] When this is the case, Libanius does not present it in terms of Christian emperors persecuting non-Christians and does not accept the label of 'magic' for his actions – magic for him was characterized by the use of body parts and dead animals and by the desire to do harm.[109] For Libanius divination was not about being Greek, as opposed to being Christian, and was certainly not magical. Rather, it was simply about having personal contact with the divine in order to cure his own illnesses and to predict the outcome of events in his life. Throughout his writings Libanius emphasizes his own ability to make prophetic calculations about the future.[110] The use of the language of divination in these examples often borders on the metaphorical and seems to be a means for Libanius to suggest that he is good at judging current affairs (as at *Ep.* B.51.5 (F.1259): 'and everyone called ... me a prophet although I had not been believed when I gave my prediction. I foretold that I would persuade you ...'). But, it also shows Libanius 'ritualizing' the ability he had to work out the future course of events in order to emphasize his personal religious power: this was the 'human calculation that people had to resort to once the public oracles no longer functioned.[111]

There were in fact a number of trends in the fourth century that privileged personal and individual contact with the divine in this way. In one

---

[106] On the dating, see P. Petit 1951.   [107] Misch 1950: 561 and 556.
[108] *Or.* 1.39 and 43 (F.1.103 and 104); *Or.* 1.173 and 177 (F.1.164 and 165); *Or.* 14.15–19 (F.II.93–4); *Or.* 20.15 (F.II.427–8); *Or.* 1.239 (F.1.187); *Or.* 42.12 (F.III.313), 54.40 (F.IV.88); *Or.* 36.15 (F.III.234–5); and *Ep.* N.49 (F.37).
[109] See Sandwell 2005: 111–13.
[110] *Or.* 15.6 (F.II.122); *Ep.* B.33.1, 3 and 6 (F.604); *Ep.* B.39.1 (F.61); *Ep.* B.51.5 (F.1259); *Ep.* B.55.2 (F.438); *Ep.* B. 56.4 (F.512); *Ep.* B.104.2 (F.1223); *Ep.* B.179.5 (F.704); *Ep.* N.97.3 (F.797); *Ep.* N.168 (F.957); *Ep.* N.177 (F.1004); *Ep.* N.178.1 (F.1021); and *Ep.* N.191 (F.1075).
[111] Bell 1992: 74 and Penn 2005 16–17.

of his best-known digressions Ammianus describes how 'a spirit pervading all elements' makes 'us also share in the gifts of divination' (Amm. Marc. 21.1.8). Similarly, the Platonist Synesius of Cyrene, who later converted to Christianity, argued that there was no need of specialist dream interpreters 'because every man and woman was capable of interpreting his or her own dreams'.[112] These ideas about the special status of personal divination were reinforced by the place that divinatory practices had in Neoplatonism and theurgy. For men such as Iamblichus divination and possession were avenues by which they could experience the divine and work towards mystical union.[113] They thus placed less emphasis on finding out about future events or gaining information from the gods and instead focused on the contact with the divine that divination made possible.[114] The privileged position given to divination by theurgists would have increased the standing of divination in society as a whole and contributed to it being a popular practice more generally even if in more mundane forms. The impact of such ways of thinking can be seen in some of Libanius' descriptions of Julian. Libanius did not primarily refer to divination as part of Julian's restoration of state religion but instead as an aspect of Julian's special relationship with the divine: Julian's prophetic skill enabled him to have direct, personal access to the will of the gods (*Or.* 12.60 (F.11.31) and *Ep.* N.100.5 (*Ep.* F.811)).

It can be suggested that for Libanius and many others the practice of divination was not thought of in terms of constructing religious identities at all. Rather it was about personal power gained through individuals access to the divine. This was why fourth-century emperors were so concerned with the use of divination and oracles by the elite and why, despite their own adherence to Christianity, they accused Christians of magic as often as non-Christians. As Ammianus shows, the Christians Bassianus 2, Libanius' cousin, and Eusebius 40/2 and Hypatius, who were brothers of Constantius' wife Eusebia and consuls in 359 (Amm. Marc.29.2.5 and Amm. Marc. 29.2.9–13), were all accused under the magical trials in the reigns of Constantius and Valens.[115] Clearly, what angered the emperors was not the religious allegiance of the individuals involved but that they were gaining unauthorized access to the divine for their own benefit. Christians too liked the idea of having personal contact with the divine and there is no reason to assume that they all shared Chrysostom's view that the use of soothsayers and other divinatory techniques was Greek and unacceptable. Klingshirn

---

[112] As le Goff points out (1988: 201). [113] Athanassiadi 1993a: 120.
[114] Trzcionka 2004: 276–7. For a recent summary of modern works on theurgic divination, see Trzcionka 2004: 272–7.
[115] On Eusebius' friendship with Libanius, see *Ep.* F.417; *Ep.* F.457; and *Epp.* B.113–14 (F.458–9).

has shown the popularity of certain Christian forms of divination from religious texts.[116] Theodoret of Cyrrhus gives evidence of Christians around Antioch using such Christianized forms of divination: a Christian monk used the practice to identify a murderer (Theodoret, *H.Rel.* 7.2). Thus it should not surprise us that Libanius could use the language of divination in letters to those who can probably be identified as Christians just as much as to those who appear to have shared his religious allegiance.[117] It is likely that many in the fourth century saw divination in terms of personal access to the divine rather than in terms of debates about religious identity.

The use of amulets. The use of amulets and incantations was widespread in late antiquity. J. B. Russell has shown that people in the small Christianized town of Anemurium in Turkey used objects such as amulets, phylacteries, rings and bells to ward off the evil eye and demonic powers throughout their daily lives.[118] Ammianus also gives evidence of the widespread use of amulets: people wore them 'against any kind of complaint' and used 'old wives' incantations and unbecoming love potions' (Amm. Marc. 19.12.12, 19.12.19, 29.2.3 and 29.2.26). Even Christian leaders were not immune to the use of such practices. Canon 36 of the Synod of Laodicea forbade priests from being 'magicians, enchanters . . . and astrologers' and from making and wearing amulets, which suggests that they were doing precisely these things.[119] The popularity of amulets and incantations can be seen at Antioch as elsewhere. Heinz has published from the city a silver phylactery (a flattened piece of silver that would have been rolled up inside a tube and worn around the neck) that bears a Greek inscription seeking protection for the 'soul and body' of a man named Thomas.[120] Libanius and Chrysostom also give evidence of the popularity of such practices in Antioch. Libanius refers to both himself and others using amulets and incantations and tying coins around their bodies as a lucky charm.[121] Chrysostom often chastises his audiences for bringing into their houses old women sorcerers or 'people skilled in witchcraft' to sell them amulets and incantations.[122] They placed

---

[116] Klingshirn 2002.
[117] *Or.* 15.6 (F.11.122); *Ep.* B.33.1, 3 and 6 (F.604); *Ep.* B.39.1 (F.61); *Ep.* B.51.5 (F.1259); *Ep.* B.55.2 (F.438); *Ep.* B.56.4 (F.512); *Ep.* B.104.2 (F.1223); *Ep.* B.179.5 (F.704); *Ep.* N.97.3 (F.797); *Ep.* N.168 (F.957); *Ep.* N.177 (F.1004); *Ep.* N.178.1 (F.1021); and *Ep.* N. 191 (F.1075).
[118] J. B. Russell 1982: 540–6.
[119] Trzcionka's PhD dissertation brought this example to my attention (Trzcionka 2004: 190–1).
[120] Heintz 1996 and 2000: 166.
[121] *Ep.* N.39.1 (*Ep.* F.388); F. *Ep.* 1483; *Or.* 1.201 (F.1.173); and *Or.* 25.67 (F.11.570).
[122] *Adv. Jud.* 8.7.5 (*PG* 48.938); *Ad Illum. Catech.* 2.5 (*PG* 49.240) = Harkins, *Baptismal Instruction* 12.58–9; *In Ep. ad Coloss.* 8 (*PG* 62.357–8); *Adv. Jud.* 8.6.5–6 (*PG* 48.936); and *In Ep. ad Thess. Hom.* 3 (*PG* 62.412).

mud, soot or salt on children's foreheads as apotropaic devices against the evil eye and made people 'amulets and bells' and 'tablets inscribed with impious inscriptions' to protect them from illness.[123] They also used coins with heads of Alexander the Great or the names of rivers inscribed on them (*Ad Illum. Catech.* 2.5 (*PG* 49.240) = Harkins, *Baptismal Instruction* 12.57, *In Ep. ad Coloss. Hom.* 8 (*PG* 62.357–8) and *In Ep. ad 1 Cor. Hom.* 12.7 (*PG* 61.106)). At times the amulets and incantations used in Antioch could take more Christianized forms. Chrysostom, like Jerome and Augustine, describes how his audiences tied phylacteries containing passages from the Bible around their necks.[124] Similarly, Theodoret of Cyrrhus refers to the Christian use of amulets by the Antiochene holy man Maësymas while 'imprecating a curse' against a wealthy landlord (Theodoret, *H.Rel.* 14.4) and to the monk Aphrahat, based in Antioch from AD 360/1, who released a woman's husband from bewitchment (Theodoret, *H.Rel.* 8.13).[125]

Literary sources will often tell us whether a person using amulets and incantations was a Christian or an adherent of Graeco-Roman religion. However, if we look instead at material finds of amulets and incantations from the ancient world, such distinctions are much less clear. These material finds reveal a world that was inherently syncretic, in which people called on a range of divinities without discrimination.[126] They could call on Graeco-Roman and Judaeo-Christian divinities in combination, for example Alexander alongside Jesus or God and Kronos;[127] the figures depicted could be given either a Judaeo-Christian or a Graeco-Roman interpretation, depending on who was viewing them – a figure on horseback spearing a demon could be interpreted either as Solomon or as Alexander the Great.[128] Even when the Christian God might also be called upon, it did not necessarily 'Christianize' these practices. As Greenfield shows in his study of Byzantine demonology, when people used amulets that called on Christian figures 'they cannot really be said to refer to the God and angels of Orthodox

---

[123] *In Ep. ad 1 Cor. Hom.* 12.13 (*PG* 61.106); *In Ep. ad Coloss. Hom.* 8 (*PG* 62.357–8); and *In Cap. ad Galat. Comment.* 1 (*PG* 61.623).
[124] Chrysostom, *In Matt. Hom.* 72 (*PG* 62.669); Jerome, *Hom. in Matt.* 23.5–7 (*PL* 26.175); and Augustine, *Tractatus in Joannis Evangelium* 7.12 (*PL* 35.1443). On this, see also Leclerque 1907: 1788 and Maguire 1995b: 65.
[125] Trzcionka's PhD dissertation brought these important examples to my attention.
[126] For Christian divinities on amulets, see J. B. Russell 1995: 39–40. On Solomon, see Bagatti 1971 and 1972; Vikan 1984; Maguire 1997: 1038; Kotansky 1991a pl. 1; Betz 1986: 253–4; *ACM* nos. 4, 10, 14 and 15; and *PGM* 1.56–8.
[127] Leclercq 1907: 1790; Maguire 1997: 1040 and 1995b: 61; Fulgham 2001: 144–6; Gager 1992: 12 and 209 no. 111; Kotansky 1995: 263, 268 and 271; Barb 1963: 104 and 123; Vikan 1984: 86–7; and Greenfield 1988: 165.
[128] Fulgham 2001: 144–7 and Maguire 1995b: 57. See also Fulgham 2001: 141, note 8.

belief'. Rather, the Christian divinities 'are reduced to virtually the same level as the demons' and the 'practitioner can appear to be actually commanding or conjuring God'.[129] People using amulets and incantations were little concerned to categorize divine powers as being Christian, Greek or Jewish but called on whichever divinities could best answer their needs. We might even imagine that the power of these symbols lay precisely in their ambiguity and in their ability to be associated with a number of powerful figures simultaneously: this gave them the greatest chance of an effective outcome.

In such a context it is not surprising that Chrysostom and his audiences disagreed on how to interpret the use of amulets and incantations. For Chrysostom such practices were clear markers of Greek identity, and so of religious difference. He labelled the use of amulets and incantations as Greek, idolatrous or Jewish (*In Cap. ad. Galat. Comment.* 1 (*PG* 61.623) and *Adv. Jud.* 8.6–8 (*PG* 48.935–42));[130] this included the supposed Christianized alternatives of phylacteries containing passages of the Bible, which he labelled as Jewish (*Hom. in Matt.* 72 (*PG* 62.669)).[131] For Chrysostom's audiences, however, 'there is no idolatry' in these practices but 'a simple incantation' (*In Ep. ad Coloss. Hom.* 8 (*PG* 62.358)).[132] They could thus happily accept that experts in making and using amulets were Christians who called on God (*Ad Illum. Catech.* 2.5 (*PG* 49.240) = Harkins, *Baptismal Instruction* 12.59). While Chrysostom saw the use of amulets as exclusively Greek, his audiences had a more inclusive understanding of them as practices that could be part of the repertoire of Christian behaviour.

Questions of religious identity were not, however, the only area of disagreement between Chrysostom and his audiences over the use of amulets.[133] Some people in his audiences saw the use of amulets as evidence for the continued efficacy of Christian miracles in the present day and this too was a query that he had to answer: 'are there not now those who raise the dead and perform cures?' (*In Ep. ad Coloss. Hom.* 8 (*PG* 62.358)). Chrysostom strongly objected to the view that the 'miracle' cures provided by amulets could take place: people should not 'serve God for hire' or 'cling to these signs' of the present life but should be ready for death. Christian miraculous healers were confined to apostolic times and were only given

---

[129] Greenfield 1988: 273. See also *CTh* 16.10.7.
[130] See also *In Ep. ad Coloss. Hom.* 8 (*PG.* 62.358); *Catéchèse* 1.39 (SC 50.129); *In Ep. ad Ephes. Hom* 12 (*PG* 62.91–2); and *In Ep. ad 1 Cor. Hom.* 4.11 and 12.13–14 (*PG* 61.38 and 106).
[131] Maguire 1995b: 65 and compare with Jerome, *Hom. in Matt.* 23.5–7 (*PL* 26.175).
[132] *Ad Illum. Catech.* 2.5 (*PG* 49.240) = Harkins, *Baptismal Instruction* 12.59.
[133] On the identification of areas of disagreement between Chrysostom and his audiences, see Maxwell forthcoming.

by God then because 'man's nature was weak'. In Chrysostom's day such measures were no longer needed. Two passages in the sermons against the Judaizers also place the use of amulets within a debate about miracles in the present day; here Chrysostom does accept the possibility that prophets could arise in the fourth century who might be able to cure sickness, but does not see these as true miracles.

> Then suppose the man who said this could cure the blind man and could bring to life a corpse, God said that you must not be persuaded by him. Why? Because God only permitted that man to have this power because he is testing you... Even if those who try their hardest to drag us away from God show us corpses brought back to life, those of us who truly love God will not be separated from him because of this. (*Adv. Jud.* 8.5.8 (*PG* 48.935))[134]

On a number of occasions Chrysostom argues that performing miracles was not the most valid form of Christian behaviour and that in the current day many miracles were fake anyway (*Hom. in Matt.* 32.8 and 46.3 (*PG* 58.57.387–8 and 474–5) and *De Incomp. Dei Nat.* 1.6 (SC 28.96–9)).[135] When he does accept that miracles could happen in the present day, he is always referring to those carried out by famous martyrs (*In S. Rom. Mart.* 1.4 (*PG* 50.612)).[136] In his *Demonstration against the Jews and Gentiles* Chrysostom uses the technique of fulfilled prophecy to prove the truth of Christianity to Gentiles, but he uses only the prophecies of Jewish holy books and of Jesus and the Apostles. He makes no mention of later prophetic activity in the Church, so he seems to exclude it from acceptable Christian activity. That these debates about the role of Christian miracles often occur in discussion of the use of amulets and incantations by his audiences suggests that the way these practices gave ordinary Christians access to potent forms of divine power was just as problematic as their supposed 'Greek' nature.

Chrysostom's audience still wanted access to the personal contact with the divine that miracle workers provided for them but Chrysostom argued that the age of Christian miracle working had now passed and that access to the divine had to be mediated by the Church. In this way Chrysostom supported a routinized and institutionalized model of Christianity that was typical of the post-apostolic period. By the fourth century the Church had gained an established position that did not allow for charismatic and personal forms of religious authority. It was no longer acceptable for individuals to have control and contact with the divine for their own

---

[134] See also *Adv. Jud.* 1 (*PG* 48.854–5), quoting *Deuteronomy* (13.2–4.70).
[135] See Maxwell forthcoming: 127.
[136] See also *De S. Bab. Contra Jul. et Gent.* 22, 73 and 75 (*PG* 48.539, 553 and 554).

ends (rather than the prescribed ends of the Church), even if they were calling on Christian divinities. For this reason, miracle-cures and attempts to foretell events by ordinary individuals and by personal means had to be excluded, as we saw Chrysostom was trying to do. However, this contrasted with the needs and desires of Chrysostom's audiences, who wanted religious practices that would answer their own everyday concerns and that they could use for themselves. In this Chrysostom's audience had much in common with Libanius, who also used amulets for his personal needs, to cure his own illnesses or those of close relatives (*Ep.* N.39.1 (*Ep.* F.388); F. *Ep.* 1483; *Or.* 1.201 (F.1.173); and *Or.* 25.67 (F.11.570)). They, like him, found it natural and appropriate to turn to personal religious practices, such as amulets, incantations and divination, when faced with illness, theft or business troubles.

DEMONIC FORCES AND PERSONAL RELIGIOUS POWER

In this chapter I have begun to suggest that Libanius, other adherents of Graeco-Roman religion and Chrysostom's audiences regarded individual and personal access to the divine as more important to them than adhering to well-defined religious identities. They all wanted to use prayer, personal divination and amulets to cure illnesses, help their careers and find lost objects. Libanius and Chrysostom's audiences lived in a world permeated by divine and demonic powers that they saw to be just as valid and powerful as either the Christian God or the pantheon of Graeco-Roman divinities. They, like other late-antique individuals, felt the presence of these powers everywhere and saw the marks of their activities in all areas of life, whatever their religious allegiance. As Trzcionka has recently shown, these demonic powers were thought to cause and cure illness, to induce love and to be able to help individuals see their future or find lost objects.[137] Ammianus saw the ever-present nature of divine and demonic powers as responsible for the predictive powers of omens and portents; a god could 'reveal impending events' by directing the flight of the birds or the entrails of an animal (Amm. Marc. 21.1.9–10). Libanius also clearly accepted the existence of demons and, as was typical of the ancient world, did not see a clear distinction between them and other divine powers. He used the term *daimōn* interchangeably with *theoi* and did not see it to have exclusively negative connotations in any sense.[138] Throughout his *Autobiography* Libanius described daemonic

---

[137] Trzcionka 2004: 41; Miller 1994: 51; and also Brink 1986 and Greenfield 1988: 166.
[138] See also *Or.* 5.33 (F.1.314); *Or.* 1.204 (F.1.174); *Or.* 11.69 (F.1.459); *Or.* 12.79–80 and 88–9 (F.11.37–8 and 40–1); *Or.* 13.20, 41 and 47 (F.11.70, 77 and 80); *Or.* 14.7 and 65 (F.11.90 and 110); *Or.* 15.29

powers as having a direct impact on his life and on the lives of others.[139] He also often referred to the actions of daemons in Julian's life and was able to blame evil demonic powers for causing the Riot of the Statues in 387 (*Or.* 12.79 and 89 (F.11.37 and 41) and *Or.* 19.7 and 29 (F.11.387 and 398)).[140] Chrysostom's audiences also appear to have put faith in demonic powers to a large degree. Chrysostom had to combat their views that demonic powers controlled their lives (in his three sermons *That Demons Do Not Govern the World* (*PG* 49.243–76)), or could cause the functioning of the evil eye and the success of divination.[141] Belief in demonic powers was often connected to a belief in fate since both had the ability to control or dictate the actions of men. On a number of occasions Libanius used the figure of Fate/Fortune and of the *daimōn* interchangeably.[142] He placed great emphasis on the power of Fate/Fortune and demonic powers to control, and to have an impact on, the lives of himself and others.[143] Chrysostom too saw demonic powers and a belief in fate to be associated (*De Fato et Providentia* 1 (*PG* 50.749–50)). He complained that people used fate as an excuse for their actions in much the same terms as he criticized those who believed demonic powers to control all their actions (*De Diab. Tent. Hom.* 3.1 and 3 (*PG* 49.265 and 268) and *In Kal.* 2 (*PG* 48.955)).[144] He spoke of the way that his audiences allowed themselves to be placed 'under the false domination of fate' through their use of omens, observance of days, nativities and divination just as they placed themselves under the control of demonic powers (*In Cap. ad Galat. Comment.* 1. (*PG* 61.623) and *In Ep. ad Ephes. Hom.* 12 (*PG* 62.92)). A belief in the power of Fate and Fortune was the absolute norm in the ancient world. It led men to believe that that their lives were planned in advance and so could be foretold in prophecy and other kinds of signs (Amm. Marc. 21.1.8).[145]

---

and 75 (F.130 and 150); *Or.* 16.7 (F.11.163); *Or.*17.12, 23 and 38 (F.11.211, 215–16 and 221); *Or.* 18.308 (F.11.370–1); *Or.* 20.28 (F.11.434); *Or.* 24.1 and 36 (F.11.514 and 530); *Or.* 30.3 (F.111.89); and *Or.* 50.16 (F.111.478).

[139] See also *Or.* 17.12, 14, 20, 23 and 38 (F.11.211, 212, 214, 215 and 221).

[140] *In Cap. ad Galat. Comment.* 3 (*PG.* 61.648); *Homiliae in Iohannem* 4 (*PG.* 59.52); *In Ep. ad 1 Cor. Hom.* 31.7 (*PG* 61.262–4); and *In Ep. ad 2 Cor. Hom.* 24.4 (*PG* 61.568).

[142] *Or.* 1.13, 24, 45, 126, 133, 137, 146, 165, 178 and 195 (F.1.87–8, 94, 106, 143, 147, 149, 153, 160, 165 and 171); *Or.* 6.2 (F.1.354–5); *Or.* 12.38 and 52 (F.11.21 and 28).

[143] *Oration 6 On Dissatisfaction*; *Or.* 25.7–8 (F.11.540–1); *Or.* 18.298 (F.11.366); *Ep.* F.1266; *Or.* 12.38 and 52 (F.11.21–2 and 28). See also *Or.* 21.17 (F.11.458); *Or.* 34.17 (F.11.521–2); *Ep.* 187.2 (F.1058); and *Or.* 37.21 (F.111.249).

[144] *De Diab. Tent. Hom.* 3.3 (*PG* 49.268); *De Fato et Providentia* 1, 3 and 5 (*PG* 50.749–50, 757–60 and 765–70) and *Oratio adhortatoria ad Stagirium ascetam a Daemonio vexatum.* 1.2 (*PG* 47.427). See also Schatkin 1988: 129–31; Barton 1994: 159; Halton 1964; and Cioffari 1935: 9.

[145] Cioffari 1935.

Divine and demonic powers could have even greater impact on humans in the ancient world because individuals could manipulate and control these powers for their own ends. Late-antique, Graeco-Roman society was a highly competitive world that was dominated by the notion of limited good (the idea that one man's gain was another man's loss).[146] Libanius refers to the problem of envy in relation to rivalry from other teachers who begrudged him his success (*Ep.* 4.10 (F.391), *Or.* 1.44 (F.I.105), *Or.* 6.8 (F.I.357) and *Or.* 16.7 (F.II.163)).[147] He also cites envy or an envious demon as responsible for the Riot of the Statues, the anger of Theodosius towards Antioch after the riot, Julian's anger towards the city, Julian's death, and earthquakes and famines.[148] Chrysostom too describes envy of wealth and success as a pervasive problem among his audiences (*In Ep. ad 2 Cor. Hom.* 27.3–4 (*PG* 61.586–8) and *In Ep. ad 1 Cor. Hom.* 31.7 (*PG* 61.262–4)).[149] In such societies the casting of the evil eye is a common response to the success of others, as are practices to protect people from it.[150] The mosaics from a villa just outside Antioch include a depiction of the evil eye with many apotropaic symbols to ward off the power of envy and demonic powers.[151] Libanius and Chrysostom both refer to the evil eye and the demonic powers behind it (Libanius, *Ep.* F.1403 and Chrysostom, *In Ep. ad 1 Cor. Hom.* 12.13 (*PG* 61.106) and *In Ep. ad Coloss. Hom.* 8 (*PG* 62.357–6)).

Belief in an envious force, fate and the pervasive power of demons cut across religious boundaries and was shared by all in late-antique society, so it is not surprising that individuals, whatever their stated religious allegiance, felt the need to turn to the personal forms of religious power that the use of amulets and divination provided. When divine and demonic powers are thought to be everywhere, it is quite natural to want to have personal control over and access to them through small-scale practices that can be performed on a daily basis.[152] As Russell states, 'the measures taken to cope with the unseen menace of demons constituted a domestic necessity as familiar as cooking, working, playing games or bringing up children'.[153]

This tendency was problematic from the point of view of the established Church. Belief in demonic powers, and the practices that interacted with

---

[146] Trzcionka 2004: 41, 47–8, 92, 94, 115, 122–3 and 182–5.
[147] Trzcionka 2004: 107–8, 115, 122 and 157–8 and Sandwell 2001: 312–13.
[148] *Or.* 19.7, 29, 31 and 34 (F.II.387, 398, 399–400 and 401); *Or.* 22.10 (F.II.476); *Or.* 1.126 and 252 (F.I.143–4 and 192); *Or.* 62.18 (F.IV.355); *Or.* 16. 7, 15 and 45 (F.II.163, 166 and 178); *Or.*18.2 (F.II.237); and *Or.* 31.42 (F.III.144).
[149] See also *In Ep. ad 2 Cor. Hom.* 15.2 (*PG* 61.503–4) and 24.4 (*PG* 61.568); *In Ep. ad Philip. Hom.* 14 (*PG* 62.286–8); and *In Ep. ad 1 Tim. Hom.* 3 (*PG* 518–20).
[150] Trzcionka 2004: 155–70 and Dundes 1981.   [151] See Levi 1941: 220–32.
[152] Trzcionka 2004: 92 and 170 and Miller 1994: 51.
[153] J. B. Russell 1995: 50. See also Vikan 1984: 71.

them, provided a realm of religious power that it could not easily control. It was for this reason that Chrysostom devoted three sermons to playing down the power of demons to govern human action and sought instead to emphasize consistently the power of God or the role of human failing (*Daemones non Gubernare Mundum* 1 and *De Diab. Tent. Hom.* 2 and *De Diab. Tent. Hom.* 3 (*PG* 49.243–76) and *In Cap. ad Galat. Comment.* 3 (*PG* 61.648) and *Homiliae in Iohannem* 4 (*PG* 59.52)).[154] It was only in this way that God's ultimate authority and the notion of human freewill could be maintained. The problem for Chrysostom and other Church leaders was that people in the ancient world were not accustomed to the influence of demonic powers being excluded in this way. Before the fourth century, accusations of *superstitio* or *deisidaimonia* could be made against those who were deemed somehow to have an excessive belief in divine powers. However, these accusations were usually used to outlaw particular religious groups rather than as universal definitions. Usually, Greeks and Romans made no straightforward distinction between the practices directed at the gods and those directed at demonic powers. The Church's attempt to assert unified control over the religious beliefs of all its members was a phenomenon that was new to the ancient world, as was its attempt to present God and Christ as the one ultimate source of religious power across the whole Roman empire.[155] In the fourth century, when the Church had the resources to impose this vision on society to a much greater degree, this caused a clash of worldviews. Recent works of anthropologists have explored the consequences of imposing a monotheistic institutional religion on native African polytheistic religions.[156] One of these consequences is that native peoples find it alienating to direct all their loyalties to one all-powerful God. Because they are used to addressing a number of local divinities with specific, 'this worldly' functions, they find it hard to adjust suddenly to seeing one single, distant God as the force to whom they should turn in all circumstances.[157] As a result, while accepting the Christian God, they give great prominence to powers labelled as demonic by the proselytizing Christian authorities and often favour independent African forms of Christianity, because these

---

[154] For example, in *In Ep. ad 1 Cor. Hom.* 31.7 (*PG* 61.262–4) envious men can be compared to demons because it is in the nature of demons to be envious and in *In Ep. ad 2 Cor. Hom.* 24.4 (*PG* 61.568) the person who is envious 'invites an evil demon against his own soul'. Compare with Augustine, *Div. Daem.* 6.10 and *De Civ. Dei.* 9.18–22

[155] Imperial cult had never sought to replace worship of local divinities and in fact often fitted into local traditions.

[156] Horton 1971 and 1975 and B. Meyer 1994.

[157] Horton 1971: 88, 96–7, 101–3 and 106–7 and B. Meyer 1994: 51–7. See also C. Stewart 1991 on the distinction between the 'great and the little tradition' in Christian thinking.

provided smaller-scale and more accessible religious options.[158] This process is, paradoxically, aided by the fact that Christian leaders often keep alive the demonic powers whose authority they are trying to restrict. Through their labelling of local gods as demonic and through the baptismal exorcism ritual that involves the expulsion of demonic forces, bishops and priests reinforce the existence of these powers.[159] This has the unintended effect of giving increased importance to practices such as the use of amulets, incantations and the like as people seek to call on these smaller-scale demonic powers. The attempt to impose worship of one single all-powerful divinity on Graeco-Roman society as a whole and to create an institutional religion that spanned the empire might well have had a similar impact on a people who were also used to dealing with local divinities.[160] They too might have reacted by showing an increased desire for personal access to the divine through private religious practices.

In a similar way, the position and goals of the Church in the fourth century contributed to a turn to private conceptions of religion and more personal forms of religious power: it was often the outlawing of public forms of religion that encouraged Libanius, Ammianus and others like them to find satisfaction in practices such as the use of amulets and personal divination. They could compensate for the loss of their public religion by valuing personal contact with divine powers and their ability, as individuals, to have divine prescience. At the same time, the increase in the number of people claiming to be Christians in the fourth century, together with the fact that people of different religious allegiances increasingly lived side-by-side, again led men like Libanius to play down tactless displays of religious difference that would make social interaction difficult. It is thus ironic that just as the Christian Church, or whichever form of it was dominant at the time, was seeking to institutionalize religious worship, it was also creating the conditions in which many people were likely to favour non-institutional forms of religion. This tension made it impossible for the Church to avoid Christian forms of local religious worship, as represented by the cult of the martyrs and the services offered by Christian holy men. However, Christian leaders still held to the ideal that the official Church

---

[158] B. Meyer 1994: 58–64 and Horton 1971 and 1975.
[159] For this in the African context, see B. Meyer 1994. For the Graeco-Roman context see Greenfield 1988: 165–6 and 270; Trzcionka 2004: 242; and Kalleres 2002. For Chrysostom's views on demonic powers at baptism see *Catéchèse* 2.12 (SC 50.140); *Catéchèse* 2.14 (SC 50.141); and *Ad Illum.* 2.2 (*PG* 49.233–4) = Harkins, *Baptismal Instruction* 12.14–15. See also the *Euchologion*, Harkins 1963: 219.
[160] MacMullen 1997: 121: 'the concerns of the little people were little' and 'not comfortably filled by the Power preached from the urban pulpits'. Almey also explores similar ideas in her MA dissertation (2005).

should mediate all contact with the divine and that the one God was always the ultimate source of divine power.

Libanius and some people in Chrysostom's audiences shared a distaste of excessive and tactless displays of religiosity and religious identity, as seen in the behaviour of the monks. They also shared an interest in private practices that gave to individuals personal forms of religious power and some personal control over the demonic world. This favouring of more private and less visibly distinctive practices by people, whatever God or gods they worshipped, in turn contributed to religious practice being a poor marker of religious identity at this time: private practices by their very nature are less able to be constitutive of religious difference and religious identity. Thus, while some members of Chrysostom's audience were strongly marked as Christian through their religious practices (such as asceticism and regularly taking the Eucharist) others distinguished themselves less clearly from those who did not take the name Christian (at least on occasions where they were not actually attending Church). In making these arguments, I am not suggesting that late-antique individuals saw no distinction at all between using divination, amulets and omens and taking the Eucharist or attending Church. I am also not saying that the lack of religious differentiation in the sphere of religious practice meant that individuals did not believe in the Christian God or that they did not have some allegiance to Christianity. All I am suggesting is that while Chrysostom's audiences might well have thought they were still being 'Christian', this was not in the sense that Chrysostom meant (and that modern scholars mean) of a constantly visible, fixed identity. However hard Chrysostom sought to mark out religious identities in what people did as well as what they said, the distinction between Christian, Greek, and Jew was far less marked in practice than it was in texts and preaching.

CHAPTER 10

Conclusion

Chrysostom stood at the end of a long line of Christian leaders in antiquity who had sought to lay down rules and guidelines about what it meant to be Christian, Jewish and Greek and so to construct Christian identity. Like these earlier Christian leaders, Chrysostom wanted to define clearly what it meant to be Christian to ensure that this was something that transformed individuals permanently. In the context of the late fourth century this meant preaching the message of Christian identity and Greek and Jewish difference to his large civic audiences at every possible opportunity. He continually exhorted these audiences to display their Christianity in visible and recognizable ways and in every aspect of their lives: being Christian should permeate everything they said and did and they should always work to distinguish themselves from adherents of other religions. Chrysostom's ideal was that this should lead Christians to have their primary social relations with other Christians in a distinct community based on Christian values, beliefs and texts. This Christian community was then supposed to encompass and replace all other social allegiances, whether cultural, civic or even, to some degree at least, political: being Christian was supposed to be all there was. If one did not accept this all-encompassing Christian identity, one was not only labelled as Greek or Jewish, but could also be considered demonic.

Libanius, in contrast, shows us a very different perspective on the situation. Writing in the mid to late fourth century, he could not help but be aware of the different religious options available to people or of the significance of statements about religious allegiance. However, this did not mean that he accepted the notion of Christian leaders that constructions of religious identities were rules that should be strictly observed. He did not feel that he had to define himself and those he knew as either Greek or Christian at every moment. Rather, he acted out his awareness of choice and difference in religious labels and religious allegiance according to an unspoken sense of what was appropriate and useful in imperial society. This entailed emphasizing religious allegiance at certain moments, but letting it fall into the background at others. For this reason, Libanius did not make shared religious allegiance the grounds for a well-organized or tight-knit social group but instead had more personal and more tenuous links with others who worshipped the gods as well as with adherents of other religions. He also allowed religious allegiance to be disengaged from political, civic and cultural loyalties and affiliations when it was useful to do so. Libanius' response to the threats posed by the aggression of certain Christian groups was not to follow the approach of Christian leaders or of the emperor Julian of constructing a firm Graeco-Roman religious identity. Rather, it was to sidestep the whole religious issue by playing down the importance of religion to other areas of life.

The approaches of Chrysostom and Libanius to issues of religious identity and religious allegiance thus present us with a stark contrast. On the one hand, we have Chrysostom's approach in which religious identity was to be displayed publicly at all times. Chrysostom focused on visibly identifiable markers of what it was to be Christian, Greek or Jewish and exhorted people to display their religious allegiance in every aspect of their behaviour. The individual's internal state of belief in Christ and God was supposed to be exhibited in external forms that all could see. For this reason, the ascetic practices of the monks were Chrysostom's ideal model for Christianity, just as blood sacrifice became his symbolic marker for all that was Greek and even Jewish. Chrysostom also wanted all Christian practices to be those associated with, and approved of by, the established Christian Church (or at least, the Nicene branch of it that he represented) and allowed little room for practices that gave people access to personal religious power. Libanius, on the other hand, found overt displays of religious difference abhorrent due to their lack of tact and subtlety. Instead, the notion of the private sphere was central to how he dealt with the fourth-century religious situation. He could favour the use of private religious practices as a way to avoid religious persecution and to replace public rituals that were no longer possible. He could also value the private sphere as the space where true religious feeling existed, whatever the outward appearance might be, and could make shared religious allegiance the reason for personal bonds of friendship. Finally, Libanius' own involvement with religious practices such as personal divination and the use of amulets suggests that he was most concerned with his own access to religious power rather than with institutional religion.

That Chrysostom and Libanius saw issues of religious identity and religious allegiance in such different ways also meant that they conceived of religious interaction differently. Chrysostom wanted religious interaction to be between different, clear-cut religious identities. He could envisage that people might move from one identity to another but insisted that they would always belong to one or other of the religious options open to them: there were to be no areas of ambiguity where people could exist between religions. The corollary of this was that one's religious identity would always be a factor in social interaction; in fact, social interaction would always be religious interaction. For Chrysostom religious allegiance was supposed to matter at all times and in all social relationships and there was no space in which it could be put aside or made less significant. Libanius, on the other hand, presents us with a very different model of religious interaction. He did not envisage religious allegiance in terms of distinct religious identities that defined people at all times but instead accepted that people could play down religious allegiance at certain moments in order to aid smooth social relations. This means that Libanius did not see religious interaction as the definitive form of social interaction in the first place. Rather, interactions based on religion were subsumed under social relations more generally and were just one factor in these relations that could be activated when needed.

The different approaches to religious identity and religious interaction that we see exemplified in the writings of Libanius and Chrysostom were both options that were available to and chosen by individuals in the fourth century. Both approaches thus need to be taken seriously by scholars. As a result, I would like to posit a model of the fourth-century religious situation as one in which there were competing ways of understanding the place and role of religion: on the one hand, clear-cut notions of religious identity, as proposed by Chrysostom, and, on the other hand, more strategic and practical uses of religious allegiance, as represented by Libanius. The former approach was accompanied by an understanding of social interaction in which religious factors were central, the latter by one in which they were marginal. On the one hand, there were Christian leaders and men such as John Chrysostom and the emperor Julian who sought to impose their ideas about religious identity in the rule-bound form of a prescriptive ideology. On the other hand, there were men such as Libanius and ordinary adherents of Graeco-Roman religion and Christianity who were acting out religious allegiance in practice. The way in which these two groups interacted was always going to involve the former group preaching to, badgering and coercing the latter group, often with little success. For most people, who had to live alongside one another despite differences of religious allegiance, it simply was not practical to be constantly asserting a strong religious identity. We can be certain that being able to put aside religious difference would have been useful and even essential to them, whatever their social class, whether they were working in the imperial bureaucracy, serving on the civic council, buying and selling in the shops of Antioch or attending the baths, the races and the theatre. During the time of Christianity's presence in the empire, but particularly in the fourth century, people had developed a set of unspoken but deeply held dispositions about the correct ways to express their religious allegiance. To put it in Bourdieu's words, they had developed a good 'practical knowledge . . . based on the continuous decoding of the perceived – but not consciously noticed – indices of the welcome given to' how they acted in regard to religion 'to ensure the adjustment of [religious] practices and expressions to the reactions and expectations of other agents'.[1] It was this practical knowledge that determined how, when and where people expressed their Christianity or their adherence to the Graeco-Roman gods, not the explicitly formulated rules laid down by Chrysostom's preaching.

Whether they adopted 'Christ . . . as the guardian' of their city or favoured 'Zeus, Apollo and Calliope', ordinary individuals understood both the inexplicit expectation that controlled the expressions of these religious identities, and the value of personal and private religious practices in such a context (Julian, *Mis.* 357c)). As a result, talking of Antioch in terms of a change from loyalty to the Graeco-Roman gods to loyalty to Christ, as the emperor Julian does, is to miss the point. What is important is that individuals often continued to work with the same habitual expectations about when it was appropriate to express religious allegiance and when not, even after they had decided to worship the Christian God. The difference between those who 'loved' Christ and those who 'loved' Zeus, Apollo and Calliope might well have been less than that between those who sought to impose ideas about clear-cut religious identities on their world and those who continued to work with a practical sense of what was appropriate in regard to these matters. If we accept this, we can conclude that Chrysostom's ideological, rule-bound constructions of exclusive religious identities made little permanent impact on people. Fourth-century individuals could associate themselves primarily with the worship of one god, or sets of gods, rather than another. They could also understand that statements about religious allegiance mattered and could be important. But, none of this means that they accepted that religious identities constituted what could 'be seen heard, spoken, thought, believed and valued – in other words what

---

[1] Bourdieu 1977a: 10.

count[ed] as the socially made reality' for them.[2] Their attitude to religious allegiance and religious interaction was far subtler than this.

It might be easier for us, as external observers, to divide the fourth-century world into pagans and Christians, to assume that these categories can always be used to explain the behaviour of those we study and to try to measure how far society or individual members of it were truly Christianized. But, taking this approach runs the risk of showing the same 'untimeliness' that the emperor Julian showed when he thought it was appropriate to ask litigants in court which gods they worshipped. It makes blatantly clear our lack of understanding of the implicit sense of the 'feel for the [religious] game' in fourth-century society, and it risks making an oversimplification of the religious situation. It is much harder to try to gain an understanding of this implicit sense of what was appropriate, and to write accounts of the fourth century based on it, but the effort is worth while for the more subtle picture that it gives. We, unlike Julian or Chrysostom, should not make religious identity an issue on occasions when it is inappropriate to do so.

[2] Hennessy 1993: 75.

Bibliography

The titles of journals are abbreviated according to the conventions of *L'Année Philologique*.

TEXTS AND TRANSLATIONS

Ammianus Marcellinus
Rolfe, J. C. (ed.) (1939) *Ammianus Marcellinus: Histories*, text with translation. Loeb Classical Library. Cambridge, MA and London.

Cyril of Jerusalem
Gifford, E. H. (ed. and trans.) (1893) *Cyril of Jerusalem: the Catechetical Lectures of S. Cyril Archbishop of Jerusalem*, in *Nicene and Post-Nicene Fathers*, first series 5.7. Grand Rapids, MI: 1–184.

Eusebius
Heikel, I. A. (ed.) (1902) *Über das Leben Constantins: Constantins Rede an die heilige versammlung, Trincennatsrede an Constantin*, text and editorial comment. Die griechischen Christlichen Schriftsteller der ersten Jahrhunderte, Bd. 1. Leipzig.
Cameron, A. and Hall, S. G. (eds. and trans.) (1999) *Eusebius: Life of Constantine*, translation and commentary. Oxford.

John Chrysostom
Brändle, R. and Jegher-Bucher, V. (eds. and trans.) (1995) *Johannes Chrysostomus: Acht Reden gegen Juden*, translation and commentary, Bibliothek des griechischen Literatur. Stuttgart.
Christo, G. G. (ed. and trans.) (1998) *On Repentance and Almsgiving*, The Fathers of the Church 96. Washington.
Daniélou, J., Malingrey, A.-M. and Flacelière, R. (eds. and trans.) (1970) *Jean Chrysostome: Sur l'incompréhensibilité de dieu Homélies 1–5*, text and translation, Sources chrétiennes 28. Paris.
Gillet, B. (ed. and trans.) (1968) *Jean Chrysostome: A une jeune veuve sur le mariage unique*, text and translation, Sources chrétiennes 138. Paris.

Harkins, P. W. (ed. and trans.) (1963) *John Chrysostom: Baptismal Instructions*, Ancient Christian Writers 31. London.
    (ed. and trans.) (1979) *John Chrysostom: Discourse against Judaizing Christians*, The Fathers of the Church 68. Washington.
Hill, R. C. (ed. and trans.) (1986, 1990 and 1992) *Saint John Chrysostom: Homilies on Genesis*, The Fathers of the Church 74, 82 and 87. Washington.
Hunter, D. G. (ed. and trans.) (1988) *John Chrysostom: A Comparison between a King and a Monk and Against the Opponents of Monastic Life*, Studies in the Bible and Early Christianity 13. Lewiston, New York.
Malingrey, A.-M. (ed. and trans.) (1972) *Jean Chrysostome: Sur la vaine gloire et l'éducation des enfants*, text and translation, Sources chrétiennes 188. Paris.
    (ed. and trans.) (1980) *Jean Chrysostome: Sur le sacerdoce (Dialogue et Homélie)*, text and translation, Sources chrétiennes 272. Paris
    (ed. and trans.) (1994) *Jean Chrysostome: Sur l'égalité du Père et du Fils: contre les anoméens homélies 7–12*, text and translation, Sources chrétiennes 396. Paris.
Migne, J. P. (ed.) (1862) *Patrologia Graeca 47–64*, John Chrysostom. Paris.
Piédagnel, A. (ed. and trans.) (1990) *Jean Chrysostome: Trois catéchèses baptismales*, text and translation, Sources chrétiennes 366. Paris
Schaff, P. (ed. and trans) (1889) *St John Chrysostom, Nicene and Post-Nicene Fathers*, second series 9–14. Grand Rapids, MI.
Schatkin, M. and Harkins, P. W. (eds. and trans.) (1983) *Saint John Chrysostom as Apologist (Discourse on Blessed Babylas and Against the Greeks and Demonstration against the Pagans that Christ Is God)*, Fathers of the Church 73. Washington.
Wenger, A. (ed. and trans.) (1957) *Jean Chrysostome: Huit catéchèses baptismales inédites*, text and translation, Sources chrétiennes 50. Paris.

John Malalas
Jeffreys, E., Jeffreys, M. and Scott, R. (eds. and trans.) (1986) *The Chronicle of John Malalas*, Byzantina Australiensa 4. Melbourne.

Julian
Bidez, J. (ed. and trans.) (1924) *L'empereur Julien, œuvres completes*, vol. I.2 (letters and fragments), text and translation, Collection des Universités de France, publiée sous le patronage de l'Association Guillaume Budé. Paris.
Wright, W. C. (ed. and trans.) (1938) *The Works of the Emperor Julian*, vol. II, Loeb Classical Library. Cambridge, MA and London

Libanius
Bradbury, S. (ed. and trans.) (2004) *Selected Letters of Libanius From the Age of Constantius and Julian*, translation and commentary, Translated Texts for Historians 41. Liverpool.
Cabouret, B. (ed. and trans.) (2000) *Libanius, Lettres aux homes de son temps*. Paris.
Fatouros, G. and Krischer, T. (ed. and trans.) (1980) *Libanios: Briefe*. Munich.

Foerster, R. (ed.) (1903–22) *Opera*, vols. I–XII, text and edition. Liepzig.
Gálvaz, A. G. (ed. and trans.) (2005) *Libanio, Cartas. Libros I–V*. Introduccíon y traduccíon y notas a cargo. Madrid.
Martin, P. (ed. and trans.) (1978 and 1988) *Libanios: Discours*, vols. I–II, Collection des Universités de France, text and translation. Paris.
Norman, A. F. (ed. and trans.) (1969–77) *Libanius: Selected Works*, vols. I–II, text and translation, The Loeb Classical Library. Cambridge, MA and London.
  (ed. and trans.) (1992) *Libanius: Autobiography and Selected Letters*, vols. I–II, text and translation, The Loeb Classical Library. Cambridge, MA and London.
  Orations 3–9, translation. Unpublished.
  (ed. and trans.) (2000) *Antioch as a Center for Hellenic Culture*, translation (includes translations of *Orations* 11, 31, 62, 43, 36, 34, 42, 58 and 3), Translated Texts for Historians 34. Liverpool.
Russell, D. A. (ed. and trans.) (1996) *Libanius: Imaginary Speeches: a Selection of Declamations*. London.
Schouler, B. (ed. and trans.) (1973) *Discours moraux, De l'insatisfaction (discours 6), La richesse mal acquise est un malheur pire que la pauvreté (discours 7), De la pauvreté ou des amis (discours 8), De l'esclavage (discours 25)*, text and translation. Paris.

Porphyry
Clark, E. G (trans.) (2000) *Porphyry, On Abstinence from Killing Animals*. London.

Socrates
Hansen, G. C. (ed.) (1995) *Socrates: Kirchengeschichte, Die Griechischen Christlichen Schriftsteller der ersten Jahrhundert*, text and edition. Berlin.
Zenos, A. C. (ed. and trans.) (1904) *The History of the Church*, in *The Greek Ecclesiastical Historians of the First Six Centuries AD, Nicene and Post-Nicene Fathers*, second series 2. Grand Rapids, MI: 1–178.

Tertullian
Dekkers, E. (ed.) (1954) *Tertulliani Opera*, text and editorial comment. Corpus Christianorum Series Latina 1 and 2. Brepols.

Theodoret
Canivet, P. (ed. and trans.) (1958) *Théodoret of Cyrrhus, Thérapeutique des maladies hellénique*, text and translation, Sources chrétiennes 57. Paris.
Canivet, P. and Leroy-Molinghen, A. (ed. and trans.) (1977 and 1979) *Théodoret of Cyrrhus, Histoire des moines de Syrie*, text and translation, Sources chrétiennes 234 and 257. Paris.

MODERN WORKS

Adkin, N. (1992) 'The date of St John Chrysostom's treatises on *subintroductae*', *RBen* 102: 255–66.

Alexander, B. C. (1997) 'Ritual and current studies of ritual: overview', in *Anthropology of Religion: a Handbook*, ed. S. D. Glazier. Westport, CT: 139–60.
Allen, P. (1991) 'Homilies as a source for social history', *Studia Patristica* 24: 1–4.
  (1994) 'Chrysostom and the preaching of homilies in series', *Orientalia Christiana Periodica* 60: 21–39.
  (1997) 'John Chrysostom's Homilies on 1 and 2 Thessalonians: the preacher and his audience', *Studia Patristica* 31: 3–21.
Almey, L. (2005) 'An exploration of Christian attitudes to divination in late antiquity', Unpublished MA dissertation. Bristol.
Ameringer, T. E. (1921) *The Stylistic Influence of the Second Sophistic on the Panegyrical Sermons of St. John Chrysostom: a Study in Greek Rhetoric*. Washington.
Amirav, H. (2003) *Rhetoric and Tradition: John Chrysostom on Noah on the Flood*. Leuven.
Ando, G. (1996) 'Pagan apologetic and Christian intolerance in the ages of Themistius and Augustine', *JECS* 4.2: 171–207.
Andres, P. (1935) *Der Missionsdanke in den Schriften des Joh. Chrysostomus*. Hunfield.
Asad, T. (1993) *Genealogies of Religion: Discipline and Reasons of Power in Christianity and Islam*. Baltimore and London.
  (2002) 'The construction of religion as an anthropological category', in *A Reader in the Anthropology of Religion*, ed. M. Lambek. Malden: 114–32.
Atchley, E. G. (1909) *A History of the Use of Incense in Divine Worship*. London.
Athanassiadi, P. (1992) *Julian: an Intellectual Biography*. London.
  (1993a) 'Dreams, theurgy and freelance divination: the testimony of Iamblichus', *JRS* 83: 115–30.
  (1993b) 'Persecution and response in late paganism: the evidence of Damascius', *JHS* 113: 1–29.
Athanassiadi, P. and Frede, M. (1999) *Pagan Monotheism in Late Antiquity*. Oxford.
Atkins, E. M. and Dodaro, R. J. (eds.) (2001) *Augustine Political Writings*. Cambridge.
Aubin, P. (1963) *Le problème de la 'conversion': étude sur un terme commun à l'hellénisme et au christianisme des trois premiers siècles*. Paris.
Auerbach. E. (1965) *Literary Language and its Public in Late Antiquity and the Middle Ages*. New York.
Babcock, S. (1990) *Paul and the Legacies of Paul*. Dallas.
Bagatti, B. (1971) 'Altre medaglie di Salomone cavaliere e loro origine', *RAC* 47: 331–42.
  (1972) 'I Giudeo-Cristiani e l'anello di Salomone', *RecSR* 60: 151–60.
Bakker, J. T. (1994) *Living and Working with the Gods: Studies for the Evidence of Private Religion and its Material Environment in the City of Ostia (100–500 AD)*. Amsterdam.
Baldovin, J. F. (1987) *The Urban Character of Christian Worship: the Origins, Development and Meaning of Stational Liturgy*. Orientalia Christiana Analecta 228. Rome.
Banchich, T. M. (1985) 'Libanius' refusal of a prefecture', *Phoenix* 39: 384–6.

Barb, A. A. B. (1963) 'The survival of magical arts', in *The Conflict of Paganism and Christianity in the Fourth Century AD*, ed. A. Momigliano. Oxford: 100–25.
Barnes, T. D. (1981) *Constantine and Eusebius*. Cambridge, MA.
    (1984) 'Constantine's prohibition of pagan sacrifice', *AJPh* 105: 69–72.
    (1998) *Ammianus Marcellinus and the Representation of Reality*. Ithaca, NY and London.
Barth, F. (1969) *Ethnic Groups and Boundaries: the Social Organization of Cultural Difference*. Oslo, Boston, MA and London.
    (1981) *Process and Form in Social Life: Selected Essays of Frederick Barth: Selected Essays of Fredrik Barth*, vol. I. London and Boston, MA.
    (1983) *Sohar, Culture and Society in an Omani Town*. Baltimore.
Barton, T. (1994) 'Astrology and the state in Imperial Rome', in *Shamanism, History and the State*, ed. C. Humphreys and N. Thomas. Ann Arbor: 146–63.
Baur, J. C. (1959–60) *John Chrysostom and his Times*, vols. I and II. London and Glasgow [*Der heilige Johannes Chrysostomus und seine zeit*, 1929–30].
Beard, M. (1987) 'A complex of times: no more sheep on Romulus' birthday', *PCPhS* 213/33: 1–5.
Beard, M., North, J. and Price, S. (1998) *Religions of Rome*, vols. I and II. Cambridge.
Beatrice, P. F. (1990) *L'intolleranza cristiana nei confronti dei pagani*. Bologna.
Bell, C. (1992) *Ritual Theory, Ritual Practice*. Oxford and New York.
Benin, S. D. (1983) 'Sacrifice as education in Augustine and Chrysostom', *Church History* 52: 7–20.
Betz, H. D. (1986) *The Greek Magical Papyri in Translation*. Chicago.
Bickerman, E. J. (1949) 'The name of Christians', *HThR* 42: 109–24.
Binns, J. W. (ed.) (1974) *Latin Literature of the Fourth Century*. London and Boston, MA.
Bloch, M. (1977) 'The past and present in the present', *Man* 12: 278–92.
    (1986) *From Blessing to Violence. History, Violence and Ideology in the Circumcision Ritual of the Merina of Madagascar*. Cambridge and New York.
    (1991) 'Language, anthropology and cognitive science', *Man* 26: 183–98.
    (1992) *Prey into Hunter. The Politics of Religious Experience*. Cambridge and New York.
Blumenthal, H. J. and Markus, R. A. (eds.) (1981) *Neoplatonism and Early Christian Thought: Essays in Honour of A. H. Armstrong*. London.
Boismard, M.-É. and Lamouille, A. (1993). *Un évangile pré-johannique, I Jean Chrysostome 1.1–2.12*. Études bibliques N.S. 17–18, vols. I–II. Paris.
Bonner, C. (1932) 'Witchcraft in the lecture room of Libanius', *TAPhA* 63: 32–44.
    (1950) *Studies in Magical Amulets, Chiefly Greco-Roman*. Ann Arbor.
Bouchery, H. F. (1936) *Themistius in Libanius' Brieven*. Antwerp.
Bourdieu, P. (1977a) *Outline of a Theory of Practice*. Cambridge [*Esquisse d'une théorie de la pratique, précédé de trois études d'ethnologie kabyle*, 1972].
    (1977b) 'Marriage strategies as strategies of social reproduction', in *Family and Society: Selections from the Annales*, ed. R. Foster and O. Ranum. Baltimore: 117–44 ['Les stratégies matrimonials dans le système des strategies de reproduction', *Annales* 4–5 (1972), 1105–27].

(1990a) *The Logic of Practice*. Stanford, CA [*Le sens pratique*, 1980].
(1990b) *In Other Words: Essays towards a Reflexive Sociology*. Stanford, CA (translation of selected works of P. Bourdieu, *Leçon sur la leçon*, 1982 and *Choses dites*, 1987).
(1991) *Language and Symbolic Power*. Cambridge [*L'économie des échanges linguistiques*, 1982].
(1992) 'Thinking about limits', *Theory, Culture and Society* 9: 37–49.
Bourdillon, M. F. C. (1978) 'Knowing the world or hiding it: a response to Maurice Bloch', *Man* 13: 591–9.
Bowersock, G. W. (1969) *Greek Sophists in the Roman Empire*. Oxford.
(1978) *Julian the Apostate*. London.
(1990a) *Hellenism in Late Antiquity*. Cambridge.
(1990b) 'Review of J. Matthews, *The Roman empire of Ammianus*', *JRS* 80: 244–50.
Bowersock, G. W., Brown P. and Graber, O. (1999) *Late Antiquity: a Guide to the Post Classical World*. Cambridge, MA and London.
Bowie, F. (2000) *The Anthropology of Religion*. Oxford.
Bowman, A. K. and Wolf, G. (1994) 'Literacy and power in the ancient world', in *Literacy and Power in the Ancient World*, ed. A. K. Bowman and G. Wolf. Cambridge: 1–16.
Boyarin, D. (1999) *Dying for the God: Martyrdom and the Making of Christianity and Judaism*. Stanford, CA.
(2004) *Border Lines: the Partition of Judaeo-Christianity*. Philadelphia.
Bradbury, S. (1994) 'Constantine and the problem of anti-pagan legislation in the fourth century', *AJPh* 89: 120–39.
(1995) 'Julian's pagan revival and the decline of blood sacrifice', *Phoenix* 49: 331–56.
(2000) 'A Sophistic prefect: Anatolius of Berytus in the letters of Libanius', *CPh* 95: 155–77.
Bradshaw, P. F. (2002) *The Search for the Origins of Christian Worship: Sources and Methods for the Study of Early Liturgy*, 2nd edn. Oxford.
Brink, F. E. (1986) 'In the light of the moon: demonology in the early imperial period', *ANRW* II.16.3: 2068–145.
Brinkerhoff, D. M. (1970) *A Collection of Sculpture in Classical and Early Christian Antioch*. New York.
Brooten, B. J. (1994) 'Is belief the centre of religion?', in *Religious Propaganda and Missionary Competition in the New Testament World*, ed. L. Bornemann, K. del Tredici and A. Standhartinger. Leiden: 471–9.
(2000) 'The Jews of Antioch', in *Antioch: the Lost Ancient City*, ed. C. Kondoleon. Princeton: 29–37.
Brottier, L. (2004) 'Jean Chrysostome un Pasteur face à des demi-chrétiens', in *Antioch de Syrie. Histoire, images et traces de la ville antique*, ed. B. Cabouret, P.-L. Gaiter, and C. Saliou. Paris: 439–57.
Brown, P. R. L. (1970) 'Sorcery, demons and the rise of Christianity from Late Antiquity into the middle ages', in *Witchcraft Confessions and Accusations*, ed.

M. Douglas. Association of Anthropologists Monographs 9. London: 17–34. Reprinted in P. R. L. Brown, *Religion and Society in the Age of Augustine*. London, 1972: 119–46.
  (1971) *The World of Late Antiquity from Marcus Aurelius to Muhammed*. London.
  (1972) *Religion and Society in the Age of Augustine*. London.
  (1981) *The Cult of the Saints: its Rise and Function in Latin Christianity*. London.
  (1982a) *Society and the Holy in Late Antiquity*. London.
  (1982b) 'The rise and function of the holy man in Late Antiquity', in *Society and the Holy in Late Antiquity*, P. R. L. Brown. London: 103–52.
  (1988) *The Body and Society: Men, Women and Sexual Renunciation in Early Christianity*. New York.
  (1992) *Power and Persuasion: Towards a Christian Empire*. Madison, WI.
  (1995a) *Authority and the Sacred: Aspects of the Christianisation of the Roman World*. Cambridge.
  (1995b) *The Rise of Western Christendom: Triumph and Diversity AD 200–1000*. Cambridge, MA and Oxford.
  (1998) 'The rise and function of the holy man in Late Antiquity 1971–1997', *JECS* 6.3: 353–76.
  (2001) 'Charmed lives' (review of C. Kondoleon (ed.), *Antioch: the Lost Ancient City* and accompanying exhibition), in *The New York Review of Books* 48, 12 April 2001.
Browning, R. (1952) 'The riot of AD 387 in Antioch: the role of the theatrical claques in the later empire', *JRS* 42: 13–20.
Bruggisser. P. (1990) 'Libanios, Symmaque et son père Arianus: culture littéraire dans les cercles païens tardifs', *Anc Soc* 21: 17–31.
Bruit Zaidman, L. and Schmitt-Pantel, P. (1992) *Religion in the Ancient City*. Cambridge [*La religion grecque: dans la cité grecque à l'époque classique*, 1991].
Buell, D. K. (2001) 'Rethinking the relevance of race for early Christian self-definition', *HThR* 94: 449–76.
Burkert, W. (1983) *Homo Necans: the Anthropology of Ancient Greek Sacrificial Ritual and Myth*. Berkeley.
Burns, M. A. (1930) *St John Chrysostom's Homilies on the Statues: a Study of Rhetorical Qualities and Form*. Washington.
Burns, T. S. and Eadie, J. W. (2001) *Urban Centres and Rural Contexts in Late Antiquity*. Michigan.
Burr, E. (1996) 'Pluralism and universalism in the world of Libanius'. Harvard. Unpublished PhD dissertation.
Cabrol, F. *et al.* (eds.) (1907–53) *Dictionnaire d'archéologie chrétienne et de liturgie*. Paris.
Cabouret, B. (2004) 'Pouvoir municipal, pouvoir impérial au IVe siècle', in *Antioch de Syrie. Histoire, images et traces de la ville antique*, ed. B. Cabouret, P.-L. Gaiter and C. Saliou. Paris: 117–42.
Cabouret, B., Gaiter, P-L. and Saliou, C. (eds.) (2004) *Antioch de Syrie. Histoire, images et traces de la ville antique*. Colloque organisé par B. Cabouret, P.-L.

Gaiter and C. Saliou, Lyon, Maison de l'Orient et de la Méditerraneé, 4–6 octobre 2001, Topoi supplément 5. Paris.

Cameron, A. and Garnsey, P. (1998) *The Cambridge Ancient History*, vol. XIII: *The Later Roman Empire AD 337–425*. Cambridge.

Cameron, Av. (1991) *Christianity and the Rhetoric of Empire: the Development of Christian Discourse*. Berkeley, Los Angeles and London.

Carrie, J-M. (1976) 'Patronage et propriété militaire au IVe siècle. Objet rhétorique et objet réel du discours sur les patronages de Libanoios', *BCH* 100: 159–76.

Carter, R. E. (1958) 'Saint John Chrysostom's rhetorical use of the Socratic distinction between kingship and tyranny', *Traditio* 14: 370–3.

(1970) 'The future of Chrysostom studies: theology and Nachleben', *Text und Untersuchungen* 107: 14–211.

Casana, J. (2004) 'The archaeological landscape of late Roman Antioch', in *Culture and Society in Later Roman Antioch*, ed. I. Sandwell and J. Huskinson. Oxford: 102–25.

Caseau, B. (1999) 'Sacred landscapes' in *Late Antiquity: a Guide to the Post Classical World*, ed. G. W. Bowersock *et al.* Cambridge, MA and London: 21–59.

Christo, G. G. (1997) *Martyrdom according to John Chrysostom: 'To Live Is Christ, To Die Is Gain'*. Lewiston.

(2006) *The Church's Identity Established through Images according to John Chrysostom*. Rollinsford, NH.

Chuvin, P. (1990) *A Chronicle of the Last Pagans*. Cambridge, MA.

Cioffari, V. (1935) *Fortune and Fate from Democritus to Thomas Aquinas*. New York.

Clark, E. A. (1977) 'John Chrysostom and the *Subintroductae*', *Church History* 46: 171–85.

Clark, E. G. (2001) 'Pastoral care: town and country in late-antique preaching', in *Urban Centres and Rural Contexts in Late Antiquity*, ed. T. S. Burns and J. W. Eadie. Michigan: 265–84.

(2004) *Christianity and Roman Society*. Cambridge.

Cohen, A. P. (1985) *The Symbolic Construction of Community*. Chichester and London.

Coleman-Norton P. R. (1930) 'St Chrysostom and the Greek philosophers', *CPh* 25: 305–17.

(1932) 'St Chrysostom's use of the Greek poets', *CPh* 27: 213–21.

Comaroff, J. and Comaroff, J. (1992) *Ethnography and the Historical Imagination*. Boulder, CO and Oxford.

Conybeare, C. (2000) *Paulinus Noster: Self and Symbols in the Letters of Paulinus of Nola*. Oxford.

Cracco Ruggini, L. (1996) 'Libanio e il camaleonte: politica e magia ad Antiochia sul finire del IV secolo', in *Italia sul Baetis*, ed. E. Gabba *et al.* Torino: 159–66.

Criscuolo, U. (1994) *Libanio Sulla Vendetta di Giuliano (Or. 24), testo, introduzione, traduzione, commentario e appendice*. Naples.

(1995) 'Aspetti della resistenza ellenica dell' ultimo Libanio', *Pagani e cristiani da Giuliano l'Apostat al sacco di Roma. Atti del convegno internazionale di studi.* Messina.
Cunningham, M. (1990) 'Preaching and the community', in *Church and People in Byzantium*, ed. R. Morris. Birmingham: 29–47.
Cunningham, M. and Allen, P. (1998) *Preacher and Audience: Studies in Early Christian and Byzantine Homiletic.* Leiden.
Daley, B. E. (1999) 'Building a new city: the Cappadocian Fathers and the rhetoric of philanthropy', *JECS* 7.3: 431–61.
Daly, L. J. (1971) 'Themistius' plea for religious toleration', *GRBS* 12: 65–79.
  (1980) 'In a borderland: Themistius' ambivalence towards Julian', *ByzZ* 73: 1–11.
Daly, R. J. (1978) *Christian sacrifice: the Judaeo-Christian background before Origen.* Washington DC.
Daniélou, J. (1956) *Bible and Liturgy.* Notre Dame.
Davies, J. (2004) *Rome's Religious History.* Cambridge.
Detienne, M. and Vernant, J.-P. (eds.) (1989) *The Cuisine of Sacrifice among the Greeks.* Chicago and London.
Dickie, M. W. (1995) 'The Fathers of the Church and the evil eye', in *Byzantine Magic*, ed. H. Maguire. Washington DC: 9–34.
  (2001) *Magic and Magicians in the Greco-Roman World.* London and New York.
Dorcey, P. F. (1992) *The Cult of Silvanus: a Study in Roman Folk Religion.* Leiden.
Dossey, L. (2001) 'Judicial violence and the Ecclesiastical courts in late antique north Africa', in *Law, Society and Authority in Late Antiquity*, ed. R. W. Mathisen. Oxford: 98–114.
Doukellis, P. N. (1995) *Libanios et la terre: discours et idéologie politique.* Beyrouth.
Downey, G. (1938) 'The Shrines of St Babylas at Antioch and Daphne', *Antioch-on-the-Orontes*, vol. II: *The Excavations of 1933–36*, ed. R. Stillwell. Princeton: 45–8.
  (1939a) 'Julian the apostate at Antioch', *Church History* 8: 305–15.
  (1939b) 'The Olympic Games of Antioch in the fourth century', *TAPhA* 70: 428–38.
  (1940) 'Representations of abstract ideas in the Antioch mosaics', *JHI* 1: 112–13.
  (1959) 'Libanius' *Oration in Praise of Antioch*: translation, introduction and commentary', *PAPhS* 103: 652–86.
  (1961) *A History of Antioch in Syria from Seleucus to the Arab Conquest*, (including translations of *Orations* 5 and 10). Princeton.
  (1962) *Antioch in the Age of Theodosius the Great*, Oklahoma.
  (1963) *Ancient Antioch.* Princeton.
  (1966a) 'Libanius' *Oration in Praise of Antioch*', *PAPhS* 103: 652–86.
  (1966b) 'Polis and civitas in Libanius and St Augustine', *Bulletin de la classe des lettres et des sciences morales et politiques* (*Académie Royale de Belgique*) 52: 356–66.
Drake, H. A. (1982) 'Review of Barnes, *Constantine and Eusebius*', *AJPh* 103: 462–66.
  (1996) 'Lambs into lions: explaining early Christian intolerance', *P&P* 153: 3–36.

(2000) *Constantine and the Bishops: the Politics of Intolerance*. Baltimore and London.
Drinkwater, J. F. (1983) 'The "pagan underground", Constantius II's "secret service" and the survival and usurpation of Julian the Apostate', in *Studies in Latin Literature*, vol. III, ed. C. Deroux. Brussels: 348–87.
Duijzings, G. (2000) *Religion and the Politics of Identity in Kosovo*. London.
Dujarier, M. (1979) *A History of the Catechumenate: the First Six Centuries*. New York.
Dundes, A. (ed.) (1981) *The Evil Eye: a Case Book*. Wisconsin.
Durliat, J. (1990) *De la ville antique à la ville byzantine: le problème des subsistances*. Rome.
Dvornik, F. (1966) *Early Christian and Byzantine Political Philosophy: Origins and Background*, vol. II, Dumbarton Oaks Centre for Byzantine Studies. Harvard University, Washington and Columbia.
Edmunds, L. (ed.) (1990) *Approaches to Greek Myth*. Baltimore and London.
Edwards, M., Goodman M. and Price, S. (1999) *Apologetics in the Roman Empire: Pagans, Jews and Christians*. Oxford.
Eltester, W. (1937) 'Die Kirchen Antiochias im IV Jahrhundert', *ZNTW*, 36: 251–86.
Eriksen, T. H. (1993) *Ethnicity and Nationalism: Anthropological Perspectives*. London.
Errington, R. M. (1988) 'Constantine and the pagans', *GRBS* 29: 309–18.
Faraone, C. A. (1991) 'The agonistic context of Greek binding spells', in *Magika Hiera: Ancient Greek Magic and Religion*, ed. C. Faraone and D. Obbink. New York and Oxford: 3–32.
 (1993) 'Molten wax, spilt wine and mutilated animals: sympathetic magic in near eastern and early Greek oath ceremonies', *JHS* 113: 60–80.
Fatouros, G. (1996) 'Julian und Christus: Gegenapologetik bei Libanios?', *Historia* 45: 114–22.
Fatouros, G. and Krischer, T. (eds.) (1983) *Libanios*. Darmstadt.
Feeney, D. (1988) *Literature and Religion at Rome: Cultures, Contexts and Beliefs*. Cambridge.
Ferguson, E. (1980) 'Spiritual sacrifice in early Christianity and its environment', *ANRW* II.23.2: 1151–89.
Ferguson, J. (1984) *Demonology in the Early Christian World*. New York.
Festugière, A. J. (1959) *Antioche païenne et chrétienne, Libanius, Chrysostome et les moines de Syrie*. Paris.
 (1960) *Personal Religion among the Greeks*. Berkeley.
Finn, T. M. (1992) *Early Christian Baptism and the Catechumenate: West and East Syria*. Collegeville, MN.
Fogen, M. T. (1995) 'Balsamon on magic', in *Byzantine Magic*, ed. H. Maguire. Washington DC: 99–115.
Folemer, L. D (1946) 'A study of the catechumenate', *Church History* 15: 286–307.
Fornara, C. W. (1992) 'Studies in Ammianus Marcellinus. I. The letters of Libanius and Ammianus' connection with Antioch', *Historia* 42: 329–44.

Fortin, E. L. (1981) 'Christianity and Hellenism in Basil the Great's address *Ad Adulescentes*', in *Neoplatonism and Early Christian Thought: Essays in Honour of A. H. Armstrong*, ed. H. J. Blumenthal and R. A. Markus. London: 189–203.
Foucault, M. (1984a) *The History of Sexuality*, vol. II: *The Use of Pleasure*, translated from the French by R. Hurley. London.
  (1984b) *The History of Sexuality*, vol. III: *The Care of Self*, translated from the French by R. Hurley. London.
Fowden, G. (1991) 'Constantine's porphyry column: the earliest literary allusions', *JRS* 81: 119–31.
  (1993) *Empire to Commonwealth: Consequences of Monotheism in Late Antiquity*. Princeton.
  (1998) 'Polytheist religion and philosophy', in *Cambridge Ancient History*, vol. XIII: *The Late Empire AD 337–425*. Cambridge: 538–60.
Francesio, M. (2004) *L'idea di città in Libanio*, Geographica Historica 18. Stuttgart.
Fredrikson, P. (1986) 'Paul and Augustine: conversion narratives, orthodox traditions and the retrospective self', *JThS* 37: 3–34.
French, D. R. (1998) 'Rhetoric and the rebellion of AD 387 in Antioch', *Historia* 47: 469–84.
Fulgham, M. M. (2001), 'Coins used as amulets in late antiquity', in *Between Magic and Religion: Interdisciplinary Studies in Ancient Mediterranean Religion and Society*, ed. S. Asirvatham, C. O. Pache and J. Watrous. New York and Oxford: 139–203.
Funke, H. (1967) 'Majestäts und Magieprozesse bei Ammianus Marcellinus', *JbAC* 10: 145–75.
Furnival, J. S. (1948) *Colonial Policy and Practice: a Comparative Study of Burma and Netherlands India*. New York.
Gager, J. (1992) *Curse Tablets and Binding Spells*. New York and Oxford.
Gamble, H. Y. (1995) *Books and Readers in the Early Church*. London and New Haven.
Garnsey, P. (1984) 'Religious toleration in classical antiquity', in *Persecution and Toleration*, ed. W. J. Sheils. Studies in Church History 21. Oxford: 1–21.
Garret, D. A. (1992) *An Analysis of the Hermeneutics of John Chrysostom's Commentary on Isaiah 1–8 with an English Translation*. Lewiston.
Geffcken, J, (1978) *The Last Days of Graeco-Roman Paganism*. Amsterdam [*Der Ausgang des griechisch-römischen Heidentums*, 1920].
Gignac, F. (1998) 'Evidence for deliberate scribal revision in Chrysostom's homilies on the Acts of the Apostles', in *Nova et Vetera Patristic Studies in Honour of Thomas Patrick Halton*, ed. J. Petruccione. Washington DC: 209–25.
Girard, R. (1992) *Violence and the Sacred*. Baltimore.
Gleason, M. W. (1986) 'Festive satire: Julian's *Misopogon* and the New Year at Antioch', *JRS* 76: 106–19.
Gonosová, A. (2000) 'City and people', in *Antioch: the Lost Ancient City*, ed. C. Kondoleon. Princeton: 115–44.
Goodall, B. (1979) *The Homilies of St John Chrysostom on the Letters of Paul to Titus and Philemon*. Berkeley and London.

Goodman, M. (1994) *Mission and Conversion: Proselytizing in the Religious History of the Roman Empire*. Oxford.
Goody, J (1961) 'Religion and ritual: the definitional problem', *British Journal of Sociology* 12: 142–64.
Gorday, P. (1983) *Principals of Patristic Exegesis: Romans 9–11 in Origen, John Chrysostom and Augustine*. New York.
Graf, F. (1991) 'Prayer in magical and religious ritual', in *Magika Hiera: Ancient Greek Magic and Religion*, ed. C. Faraone and D. Obbink. New York and Oxford: 188–213.
 (1997) *Magic in the Ancient World*. Cambridge, MA and London.
Greenfield, R. P. M. (1988) *Traditions of Belief in Late Byzantine Demonology*. Amsterdam.
Griffiths, P. J. (2001) *Problems of Religious Diversity*. Oxford.
Gruen, E. S. (2001) 'Jewish perspectives on Greek culture and ethnicity', in *Ancient Perspectives of Greek Ethnicity*, ed. I. Malkin. Cambridge MA and London: 347–73.
Guignebert, C. (1923) 'Les demi-chrétiens et leur place dans l'église antique', *RHR* 2: 65–102.
Guillaumin, M-L. (1975) 'Bible et liturgie dans la prédication de Jean Chrysostome', in *Jean Chrysostome et Augustine: Actes du colloque de Chantilly*, ed. C. Kannengiesser. Paris: 161–74.
Guinot, J.-N. (2004) 'L'histoire du siège d'Antioche relu par Jean Chrysostome: idéalisation ou déformation intentionnelle?', in *Antioch de Syrie. Histoire, images et traces de la ville antique*, ed. B. Cabouret, P.-L. Gaiter and C. Saliou. Paris: 459–79.
Haaland, G. (1969) 'Economic determinants in ethnic processes', in *Ethnic Groups and Boundaries: the Social Organization of Cultural Difference*, ed. F. Barth. Oslo, Boston, MA and London: 58–74.
Haddad, G. (1949) *Aspects of Social Life in Antioch in the Hellenistic-Roman Period*. New York.
Haehling, R. von (1978) 'Ammianus Marcellinus und der Prozess von Skythopolis', *JbAC* 21: 74–101.
Hall, J. M. (1997) *Ethnic Identity in Greek Antiquity*. Cambridge.
 (2002) *Hellenicity: Between Ethnicity and Culture*. Chicago.
Halton, Th. P. (1964) 'St John Chrysostom, *De Fato et Providentia*: a study of its authenticity', *Traditio* 20: 1–25.
Handelman, D. (1977) 'The Organization of ethnicity', *Ethnic Groups* 1: 187–200.
Harl, M. (1981) 'La dénonciation des festivités profanes dans le discours épiscopal et monastique en Orient chrétien à la fin du IVe siècle', in *La fête pratique et discours d'Alexandrie hellénistique à la Mission de Besançon*. Paris: 123–47.
Harries, J. D (2001) 'Resolving disputes: the frontier of Roman law in Late Antiquity', in *Law, Society and Authority in Late Antiquity*, ed. R. W. Mathisen. Oxford: 68–82.
Hartney, A. (2004) *John Chrysostom and the Transformation of the City*. London.

Haubold, J. and Miles, R. (2004) 'Communality and theatre in Libanius' oration 64 *In Defence of the Pantomimes*', in *Culture and Society in Later Roman Antioch*, ed. I. Sandwell and J. Huskinson. Oxford: 24–34.
Heather, P. and Moncur, D. (2001) *Philosophy, Politics and Empire in the Fourth Century: Select Orations of Themistius* (including translations of *Orations* 1, 3, 5 and 6). Liverpool.
Hefel, C. J. (1907) *Histoire des conciles*, vol. 1.2, Paris.
Hein, K. (1975) *Eucharist and Excommunication in Early Christian Doctrine and Discipline*. Bern.
Heintz, F. (1996) 'A Greek silver phylactery in the MacDaniel collection', *ZPE* 112: 295–300.
   (2000) 'Magic tablets and the games at Antioch', in *Antioch: the Lost Ancient City*, ed. C. Kondoleon. Princeton: 163–8.
Hennessy, R. (1993) *Materialist Feminism and the Politics of Discourse*. New York.
Honneth, A., Kocyba, H. and Schwibs, B. (1986) 'The struggle for symbolic order: an interview with Pierre Bourdieu', *Theory, Culture and Society* 3: 35–51.
Horst, P. W. van der (1994) 'Silent prayer in antiquity', *Numen* 41: 1–25. Reprinted in van der Horst (ed.), *Hellenism–Judaism–Christianity: Essays in their Interaction*. Leuven, 1998: 293–316.
   (1998) *Hellenism–Judaism–Christianity: Essays in their Interaction*. Leuven.
Horton, R. (1971) 'African conversion', *Africa* 41.2: 85–108.
   (1975) 'On the rationality of conversion', *Africa* 45.3: 220–35.
Hubbel, H. M. (1924) 'Chrysostom and rhetoric', *CPh* 19: 261–76.
Humphreys, C. and Thomas, N. (eds.) (1994) *Shamanism, History and the State*. Ann Arbor.
Hunt, D. (1993) 'Christianisation of the Roman empire and the evidence of the Code', in *The Theodosian Code: Studies in the Imperial Law of Late Antiquity*, ed. J. Harries and I. Wood. London: 143–58.
Hunter, D. G. (1989) 'Preaching and propaganda in fourth-century Antioch: John Chrysostom's Homilies on the Statues', in *Preaching in the Patristic Age: Studies in Honour of W. J. Burghardt*, ed. D. G. Hunter. New York: 117–36.
Huskinson, J. (2004) 'Surveying the scene: Antioch mosaic pavements as a source of historical evidence' in *Culture and Society in Later Roman Antioch*, ed. I. Sandwell and J. Huskinson. Oxford: 134–52.
Jackson, P. (1990) 'John Chrysostom's use of scripture in initiatory preaching', *Greek Orthodox Theological Review* 35: 345–66.
Jaeger, W. W. (1961) *Early Christianity and Greek Paideia*. Cambridge, MA.
Janowitz, N. (2001) *Magic in the Roman World: Pagans, Jews and Christians*. London.
Jedin, H. and Dolan, P. A. (1980) *History of the Church*, vol. II: *The Imperial Church from Constantine to the Middle Ages*. London.
Jenkins, R, (2002) *Pierre Bourdieu*, 2nd edn. London and New York.
   (2003) *Social Identity*, 2nd edn. London and New York.
Jones, A. H. M. (1953) 'St John Chrysostom's parentage and education', *HThR* 46: 171–3.

(1964) *The Later Roman Empire* AD *284–602: A Social and Economic Survey*. Oxford.
Jones, S. (1997) *The Archaeology of Ethnicity: Constructing Identities in Past and Present*. London.
Jungman, J. A. (1959) *The Early Liturgy to the Time of Gregory the Great*. London.
Kalleres, D. (2002) 'Exorcising the Devil to silence Christ's enemies: ritualized speech practices in late antique Christianity'. Providence, RI. Unpublished PhD dissertation.
Kannengieser, C. (ed.) (1975) *Jean Chrysostome et Augustine: Actes du colloque de Chantilly*. Paris.
Kaster, R. A. (1983) 'The salaries of Libanius', *Chiron* 13: 13–37.
  (1988) *The Guardians of Language: the Grammarian and Society in Late Antiquity*. Berkeley.
Kelly, H. A. (1985) *The Devil at Baptism: Ritual Theology and Drama*. Ithaca, NY.
Kelly, J. (1995) *Golden Mouth: the Story of John Chrysostom – Ascetic, Preacher and Bishop*. London.
Kennedy, G. (1980) *Classical Rhetoric and its Christian and Secular Tradition from Ancient to Modern Times*. London.
  (1983) *Greek Rhetoric under the Christian Emperors*. Chapel Hill, NC.
Kippenberg, H. G. (1997) 'Magic in civil discourse: why rituals could be illegal', in *Envisioning Magic: a Princeton Seminar and Symposium*, ed. P. Schäfer and H. G. Kippenberg. Leiden and New York: 137–63.
Kleinberg, A. (1987) '*De Agone Christiano*: the preacher and his audience', *JThS* 38: 16–33.
Klingshirn, W. E. (2002) 'Defining the *sortes sanctorum*: Gibbon, De Cange and early Christian lot divination', *JECS* 10.1: 77–130.
Kondoleon, C. (ed.) (2000a) *Antioch: the Lost Ancient City*. Princeton.
  (2000b) 'Mosaics of Antioch' in *Antioch: The Lost Ancient City*, ed. C. Kondoleon. Princeton: 63–78.
Kotansky, R. (1991a) 'Incantations and prayers for salvation on inscribed Greek amulets', in *Magika Hiera: Ancient Greek Magic and Religion* ed. C. Faraone and D. Obbink. New York and Oxford: 107–37.
  (1991b) 'Magic in the court of a governor of Arabia', *ZPE* 88: 41–60.
  (1995) 'Greek exorcist amulets', in *Ancient Magic and Ritual Power*, ed. M. Meyer. Leiden and New York: 243–78.
Kraeling, C. H. (1932) 'The Jewish community at Antioch', *JBL* 51: 130–60.
Kunin, S. D. (2003) *Religion: the Modern Theories*. Edinburgh.
Kyrtatas, D. (1987) *The Social Structure of Early Christian Communities*. London.
  (1988) 'Prophets and priests in early Christianity: production and transmission of religious knowledge from Jesus to John Chrysostom', *International Sociology* 3: 365–83.
Laistner, M. L. W. (1951) *Christianity and Pagan Culture in the Later Roman Empire* (contains a translation of Chrysostom's, *On Vainglory and the Right Way to Bring up Children*). Ithaca, NY and London.
Lane-Fox, R. (1986) *Pagans and Christians*. Harmondsworth.

(1990) 'Literacy and power in early Christianity', in *Literacy and Power in the Ancient World*, ed. A. K. Bowman and G. Wolf. Cambridge: 126–48.

Lassus, J. (1938) 'L'église cruciforme', *Antioch-on-the Orontes*, vol. II: *The Excavations of 1933–36*, ed. R. Stillwell. Princeton: 5–44.

(1947) *Sanctuaires chrétiennes de Syrie: essai sur la génèse, la forme et l'usage des édifices du culte chrétien en Syrie du IIIe siècle à la conquête musulmane*. Paris.

Leach, E. (1964) 'Magic', in *Dictionary of the Social Sciences*, ed. J. Gould and W. L. Kolb. New York.

Leclercq, H. (1907) 'Amulettes', in *Dictionnaire d'archéologie chrétienne et de liturgie, publié par du Rme dom Fernand Cabrol et du R. P. dom Henri Leclercq; avec le concours d'un grand nombre de collaborateurs*. Paris: 1784–859.

Leemans, J., Mayer, W., Allen, P. and Dehandschutter, B. (eds.) (2003) *'Let Us Die that We May Live': Greek Homilies on Christian Martyrs from Asia Minor, Palestine and Syria (c. AD 350–450)*. London.

Le Goff, J. (1967) 'Culture cléricale et traditions folkloriques dans la civilisation mérovingienne', *Annales* 22: 780–91.

(1988) *The Medieval Imagination*. Chicago and London [*L'imaginaire médiéval*, 1985].

Lenski, N. (2001) 'Evidence for the *Audientia episcopalis* in the new letters of Augustine', in *Law, Society and Authority in Late Antiquity*, ed. R. W. Mathisen. Oxford: 83–97.

Levi, D. (1941) 'The evil eye and the lucky hunchback', in *Antioch-on-the-Orontes*, vol. III: *Excavation of 1937–9*, ed. R. Stillwell. Princeton and London: 220–32.

(1947) *Antioch Mosaic Pavements*. Princeton and London.

Leyerle, B. (1994) 'John Chryostom on almsgiving and the use of money', *HThR* 87: 29–47.

(2001) *Theatrical Shows and Ascetic Lives: John Chrysostom's attack on Spiritual Marriage*. Berkeley, CA and London.

Liebeschuetz, J. H. W. G. (1959) 'The Syriarch in the fourth century', *Historia* 8: 113–26.

(1972) *Antioch: City and Imperial Administration in the Later Roman Empire*. Oxford.

(1979) *Continuity and Change in Roman Religion*. Oxford.

(1988) 'Ammianus, Julian and divination', in *Roma Renascens, Beiträge zur Spätantike und Rezeptionsgeschichte Ilona Opelt geuridmet*, ed. M. Wissemann. Frankfurt: 198–213. Reprinted in J. H. W. G. Liebeschuetz (ed.), *From Diocletian to the Arab Conquest*. Northampton, 1990.

(1992) 'The end of the ancient city', in *The City in Late Antiquity*, ed. J. Rich. London and New York: 1–49.

(1995) 'Pagan mythology in the Christian empire', *IJCT* 2: 193–208.

(2004) 'Malalas on Antioch', in *Antioch de Syrie. Histoire, images et traces de la ville antique*, ed. B. Cabouret, P.-L. Gaiter and C. Saliou. Paris: 143–53.

Lieu, J. (2004) *Christian Identity in the Jewish and Graeco-Roman World*. Oxford.

Lieu, J., North, J. A. and Rajak, T. (1992) *The Jews among the Pagans and Christians in the Roman Empire*. London and New York.

Lieu, S. and Montserrat, D. (1996) *From Constantine to Julian: Pagan and Byzantine Views, A Source History* (for a translation of *Oration* 59). London and New York.
Lim, R. (1995) *Public Disputations and Social Order in Late Antiquity*. Berkeley.
Loy, R. van (1933) 'Le *Pro Templis* de Libanius', *Byzantion* 8: 7–39.
Maas, M. (2000) 'People and identity in Roman Antioch', in *Antioch: the Lost Ancient City*, ed. C. Kondoleon. Princeton: 13–22.
Maat, W. A. (1944) *A Rhetorical Study of St John Chrysostom's De Sacerdotio*. Washington DC.
MacMullen, R. (1966) 'A note on *Sermo Humilis*', *JThS* 17: 108–12.
  (1981) *Paganism in the Roman Empire*, New Haven.
  (1983) 'Two types of conversion to early Christianity', *VC* 37: 174–92.
  (1984) *Christianising the Roman Empire AD 100–400*. New Haven.
  (1986) 'What difference did Christianity make?', *Historia* 35: 322–43.
  (1989) 'The preacher's audience AD 350–400', *JThS* 40: 503–11.
  (1997) *Christianity and Paganism in the Fourth to Eighth Centuries*. London.
Magoulias, H. J. (1967) 'The lives of the saints as sources of data for the history of magic in the sixth and seventh centuries AD: sorcery, relics and icons', *Byzantion* 37: 228–69.
Maguire, H., Dauterman-Maguire, E. and Duncan-Flowers, M. J. (1989) *Art and Holy Powers in the Early Christian House*. Illinois.
Maguire, H. (1995a) *Byzantine Magic*. Washington DC.
  (1995b) 'Magic and the Christian image', in *Byzantine Magic*, ed. H. Maguire. Washington DC: 51–71.
  (1997) 'Magic and money in the early Middle Ages', *Speculum* 72: 1037–54.
Malina, B. J. (1995) 'Early Christian groups. Using small group formation theory to explain Christian organization', in *Modelling Early Christianity: Social-scientific Studies of the New Testament in its Context*, ed. P. F. Esler. London and New York: 96–113.
Malingrey, A. M. (1975) 'Les sentences des sages dans la prédication de Jean Chrysostome', in *Jean Chrysostome et Augustine: Actes du colloque de Chantilly*, ed. C. Kannengiesser. Paris: 199–220.
Malkin, I. (ed.) (2001) *Ancient Perceptions of Greek Ethnicity*. Washington.
Malosse, P.-L. (1995a) 'Les Alternances de l'amitié: Julien et Libanios (249–263 et au-delà)', *RPh* 69: 249–62.
  (1995b) 'Rhétorique et psychologie antiques: éloge des vertus et critiques obliques dans le portrait de l'Empereur Julien par Libanios', *Ktema. Civilisations de l'Orient, de la Grèce et de Rome Antiques* 20: 319–38.
  (1997) 'Libanius on Constantine again', *CQ* 47: 519–24.
  (2000/1) 'Libanios, ses "témoins oculaires" Eusèbe et Praxagoras: le travail préparatoire du sophiste et la question des sources dans L'*Éloge de Constance et de Constant*', *REG* 113: 172–87.
  (2004) Antioche et le Kappa', in *Antioch de Syrie. Histoire, images et traces de la ville antique*, ed. B. Cabouret, P.-L. Gaiter and C. Saliou. Paris: 77–96.
Mann, M. (1986) *The Sources of Social Power*. Cambridge and New York.

Markus, R. A. (1970) *Saeculum: History and Society in the Theology of Saint Augustine.* Cambridge.
  (1990) *The End of Ancient Christianity.* Cambridge.
  (1994) *Sacred and Secular: Studies on Augustine and Latin Christianity.* Aldershot.
Marrou, H. I. (1963) 'Antioche et l'hellénisme chrétien: à propos d'un livre récent', *REG* 76: 430–6.
Mathisen, R. W. (ed.) (2001) *Law, Society and Authority in Late Antiquity.* Oxford.
  (2003) *People, Personal Expression and Social Relations in Late Antiquity*, vol. I. Michigan.
Matroye, F. (1930) 'La répression de la magie et le culte des gentils au IVe siècle', *Revue historique du droit francais et etranger* 9: 669–701.
Matthews, J. (1974) 'The letters of Symmachus', in *Latin Literature of the Fourth Century*, ed. J. W. Binns. London and Boston, MA: 58–99.
  (1989) *The Roman Empire of Ammianus.* London.
  (1994) 'The origin of Ammianus', *CQ* 44: 252–69.
  (2000) *Laying down the Law: a Study of the Theodosian Code.* New Haven.
Maurice, J. (1925) 'La terreur de la magie au IVe siècle', *REG* 4: 108–22.
Mauss, M. (1966) 'Les techniques du corps', in *Sociologie et anthropologie, Précédé d'une Introduction à l'œuvre de Marcel Mauss, par Claude Lévi-Strauss*, 3rd edn. Paris: 365–86.
Maxwell, J. L. (forthcoming) *Christianization and Communication in Late Antiquity.* Cambridge.
Mayer, W. (1995a) 'Chrysostom and the preaching of homilies in series: a reexamination of the fifteen homilies *In epistulam ad Philippenses* (CPG 4432)', *VC* 49: 27–89.
  (1995b) 'The thirty-four homilies on Hebrews: the last series delivered by Chrysostom in Constantinople?', *Byzantion* 65: 309–48.
  (1997) 'John Chrysostom and his audiences: distinguishing different congregations at Antioch and Constantinople', *Studia Patristica* 31: 70–5.
  (1998) 'John Chrysostom: extraordinary preacher, ordinary audience', in *Preacher and Audience: Studies in Early Christian and Byzantine Homiletic*, ed. M. B. Cunningham and P. Allen. Leiden: 103–37.
  (1999) 'Monasticism at Antioch and Constantinople in the late fourth century: a case of exclusivity or diversity', in *Prayer and Spirituality in the Early Church*, ed. P. Allen, W. Mayer and L. Cross. Everton Park, Queensland: 275–88.
  (2000) 'Who came to hear John Chrysostom preach? Recovering a late fourth-century preacher's audience', *EThL* 76: 73–87.
  (2001a) 'At Constantinople, how often did Chrysostom preach? Addressing assumptions about the workload of a Bishop', *SEJG* 40: 83–105.
  (2001b) 'The homily as historical document: some problems in relation to John Chrysostom', *Lutheran Theological Journey* 35: 17–22.
  (2005) *The Homilies of St John Chrysostom – Provenance, Reshaping the Foundations.* Orientalia Christiana Analecta 273. Rome.
  (forthcoming) 'Poverty and generosity towards the poor in the time of John Chrysostom', in *Wealth and Poverty in Early Christianity*, Grand Rapids, MI.

Mayer, W. and Allen, P. (1993) 'Computer and homily: accessing the everyday life of early Christians', *VC* 47: 260–80.
　(1994) 'Chrysostom and the preaching of homilies in series: a new approach to the twelve homilies *In epistulam ad Colossenses* (CPG 4433)', *OCP* 60: 21–39.
　(2000) *John Chrysostom* (including selected sermons). London and New York.
Meeks, W. A. and Wilken, R. L. (1978) *Jews and Christians in Antioch in the First Four Centuries CE.* Missoula, MT.
　(1993) *The Origins of Christian Morality: the First Two Centuries.* New Haven and London.
Meslin, M. (1970) *La fête des Kalendes de Janvier dans l'empire romain.* Brussels.
Meyendorf, J. (1974) *Byzantine Theology: Historical Trends and Doctrinal Themes.* New York.
Meyer, B. (1994) 'Beyond syncretism: translation and diabolization in the appropriation of Protestantism in Africa', in *Syncretism/Anti-Syncretism: the Politics of Religious Synthesis*, ed. C. Stewart and R. Shaw. London and New York: 45–68.
Meyer, M. (ed.) (1995) *Ancient Magic and Ritual Power.* Leiden and New York.
Miles, R. (ed.) (1999) *Constructing Identities in Late Antiquity.* London and New York.
Miller, P. C. (1994) *Dreams in Late Antiquity: Studies in the Imagination of a Culture.* Princeton: 184–204.
Misch, G. (1950) *A History of Autobiography in Antiquity.* London.
Misson, J. (1914) *Recherches sur le paganisme de Libanius.* Louvain.
Mitchell, M. (1998), 'A variable and many sorted man: John Chrysostom's treatment of Pauline inconsistency', *JECS* 6.1: 93–111.
　(2000) *The Heavenly Trumpet: John Chrysostom and the Art of Pauline Interpretation.* Tübingen.
Mitchell, S. (1993) *Anatolia. Land, Men and God in Asia Minor*, vol. II: *The Rise of the Church.* Oxford.
　(1990) 'Festivals, games and civic life in Roman Asia Minor', *JRS* 80: 191–3.
　(1999) 'The cult of Hypsistos between pagans, Jews and Christians', in *Pagan Monotheism in Late Antiquity*, ed. P. Athanassiadi and M. Frede. Oxford: 81–148.
Mitchell, S. and Greatrex, G. (eds.) (2000) *Ethnicity and Culture in Late Antiquity.* London.
Moffat, A. (1972) 'The occasion of St Basil's Address to young men', *Antichthon* 6: 74–86.
Molley, M. E. (1996) *Libanius and the Dancers* (including text and translation of *Oration* 64). New York.
Momigliano, A. (1963) *The Conflict of Paganism and Christianity in the Fourth Century AD.* Oxford.
　(1971) 'Popular religious beliefs and the late Roman historians', *Studies in Church History* 8: 1–18.
　(1977) 'The lonely historian Ammianus Marcellinus', in *Essays in Ancient and Modern Historiography*, ed. A. Momigliano. Oxford: 127–40.

Morris, R. (1990) *Church and People in Byzantium*. Birmingham.
Naegele, A. (1908) 'Chrysostomos und Libanios', *CRYSOSTOMIKA: Studi e ricerche intorno a S. Giovanna Crisostomo*. Rome: 81–214.
Natali, A. (1975) 'Christianisme et cité à Antioche à la fin du IVe siècle d'après Jean Chrysostome', in *Jean Chrysostome et Augustine: Actes du colloque de Chantilly*, ed. C. Kannengiesser. Paris: 41–60.
 (1985) 'Tradition ludique et sociabilité dans la pratique religious à Antioche d'après Jean Chrysostome', *Studia Patristica* 16: 463–70.
Needham, R. (1972) *Belief, Language and Experience*. Chicago.
Nicholson, O. (1994), 'The 'pagan churches' of Maximinus Daia and Julian the Apostate', *JEH* 45: 1–15.
Nock, A. D. (1954) 'The praises of Antioch' (a translation of *Oration* 11), *JEA* 40: 76–82.
 (1957) 'Deification and Julian', *JRS* 47: 115–23. Reprinted in Z. Stewart, *Essays on Religion in the Ancient World. Arthur Darby Nock; selected and edited, with an introduction, bibliography of Nock's writings, and indexes*. 2nd edn. Oxford, 1986: 833–46.
 (1998) *Conversion: the Old and the New in Religion from Alexander the Great to Augustine of Hippo*, 2nd edn. Oxford.
Norman, A. F. (1951) 'Philostratus and Libanius', *CPh* 48: 20–3.
 (1953) 'Julian and Libanius again', *CPh* 48: 239.
 (1960) 'The book trade in fourth century Antioch', *JHS* 80: 122–6.
 (1964) 'The library of Libanius', *RhM* 107: 158–75.
 (1983) 'Libanius: the teacher in the age of violence' in *Libanios*, ed. G. Fatouros and T. Krischer. Darmstadt: 150–69.
Norris, F. W. (1982) 'Isis, Sarapis and Demeter in Antioch in Syria', *HThR* 75: 189–207.
 (1990) 'Antioch as a religious centre I', *ANRW* 11.18.4: 2322–79.
North, J. A. (1976) 'Conservatism and change in Roman religion', *PBSR* 44: 1–12.
 (1979) 'Religious toleration in republican Rome', *PCPhS* 205: 85–103.
 (1992) 'The development of religious pluralism', in *The Jews among the Pagans and Christians in the Roman Empire*, ed. J. Lieu, J. A. North and T. Rajak, London and New York: 174–93.
 (1994) 'Religion in republican Rome', in *Cambridge Ancient History*, vol. IX: *The Last Age of the Roman Republic*, ed. J. A. Crook, A. Lintott and E. Rawson. Cambridge.
 (1998) *Religions of Rome* vol. I: *A History* and vol. II: *A Sourcebook*. Cambridge.
 (2000) *Roman Religion*. Greece and Rome: New Surveys in the Classics 30. Oxford.
 (2005) 'Pagans, polytheists and the pendulum', in *The Spread of Christianity in the First Four Centuries AD: Essays in Explanation*, ed. W. V. Harris. Leiden and Boston: 125–43.
O'Daly, G. (1999) *Augustine's City of God: a Reader's Guide*. Oxford.
O'Donnell, J. J. (1977) '*Paganus*: evolution and use', *Classical Folia* 31: 163–9.

Ogilvie, R. M. (2000) *The Romans and their Gods*, 2nd edn. London.
Orr, D. G. (1978) 'Roman domestic religion: the evidence of household shrines', *ANRW* III.16.2: 1557–91.
Pack, R. A. (1935) *Studies in Libanius and Antiochene Society under Theodosius*. Menasha, WI.
  (1947) 'Two sophists and two emperors', *CPh* 42: 17–20.
  (1951) 'Curiales in the correspondence of Libanius', *TAPhA* 82: 176–92.
  (1953) 'Julian, Libanius and others: a reply', *CPh* 48: 173–4.
Parkin, D. (1974) 'Congregational and interpersonal ideologies in political ethnicity', in *Urban Ethnicity*, ed. A. Cohen. London and New York: 126–7.
Pasquato, O. (1976) *Gli Spettacoli in S. Giovani Crisostimo: Paganesimo e Christianismo ad Antiochia e Constantinople nel IV seclo*. Orientalia Christiana Analecta 201. Rome.
Paverd, F. van der (1991) *St John Chrysostom: the Homilies on the Statues*, Orientalia Christiana Analecta 239. Rome.
Penn, M. P. (2005) *Kissing Christians: Rituals and Community in the Late Ancient Church*. Philadelphia.
Perkins, J. (1995), *The Suffering Self: Pain and Narrative Representation in the Early Christian Era*. London and New York.
Pernot, L. (1993), *La rhétorique de l'éloge dans le monde gréco-romain*. Paris.
Petit, L. (1866) *Essai sur la vie et la correspondance de Libanius*. Paris.
Petit, P. (1950) 'Libanius et la *Vita Constantina*', *Historia* 1: 562–82.
  (1951) 'Sur la date du *Pro Templis* de Libanios', *Byzantion* 21: 285–310.
  (1955) *Libanius et la vie municipale à Antioche au IVe siècle après J.C*. Paris.
  (1956) 'Recherches sur la publication et la diffusion des discours de Libanius', *Historia* 5: 476–509.
  (1957a) *Les étudiants de Libanius*. Paris.
  (1957b) 'Les sénateurs de Constantinople dans l'œuvre de Libanios', *AC* 26: 347–82.
  (1978) 'L'empereur Julien vu par le sophiste Libanios', in *L'Empereur Julien de l'histoire à la légende*, vols. II–II (actes d'un colloque). Paris: 67–87.
  (1983) 'Zur Datierung des 'Antiochikos' (*Or.* 11) des Libanios', in *Libanios*, ed. G. Fatouros and T. Krischer. Darmstadt: 129–49.
  (1994) *Les fonctionnaires dans l'œuvre de Libanius: analyse prosopographique*. Paris.
Phillips, C. R. (1991) '*Nullum Crimen sine Lege*: socio-religious sanctions on magic', in *Magika Hiera: Ancient Greek Magic and Religion*, ed. C. Faraone and D. Obbink. New York and Oxford: 260–76.
Porter, S. E. (1997) *Handbook of Classical Rhetoric in the Hellenistic Period, 330 BC–AD 400*. Leiden, New York and Cologne.
Praet, D. (1992–3) 'Explaining the Christianization of the Roman empire: older theories and recent developments', *Sacris Eruditi* 33: 1–119.
Price, R. M (1989) 'Pluralism and religious tolerance in the empire of the fourth century', *Studia Patristica* 22: 187–8.
Price, S. R. F. (1984) *Rituals and Power: the Roman Imperial Cult in Asia Minor*. Cambridge.

(1986) 'The future of dreams: from Freud to Artemidorus', *P&P* 113: 3–39. Reprinted in R. Osbourne (ed.) *Studies in Ancient Greek and Roman Society*. Cambridge, 2004: 226–59.

(1999) *Religions of the Ancient Greeks*. Cambridge.

Pulleyn, S. (1997) *Prayer in Greek Religion*. Oxford.

Quiroga Puertas, A. J. (2006) 'Relación retórica-historia-mitología en los discursos 19–23 de Libanio de Antioquía'. Granada. Unpublished PhD dissertation.

R. A. Rappaport (1968) *Pigs for the Ancestors*. New Haven.

(1999) *Ritual and Religion in the Making of Humanity*. Cambridge.

Rich, J. (1992) *The City in Late Antiquity*. London and New York.

Rike, R. L. (1987) *Apex Omnium: Religion in the Res Gestae of Ammianus*. California.

Riley, M. M. (1974) *Christian Initiation: a Comparative Study of the Interpretation of the Baptismal Liturgy in the Mystagogical Writings of Cyril of Jerusalem, John Chrysostom, Theodore of Mopsuestia and Ambrose of Milan*. Washington.

Ritter, A. M. (1990) 'John Chrysostom as an interpreter of Pauline social ethos', in *Paul and the Legacies of Paul*, ed. S. Babcock. Dallas: 183–99.

Rives, J. (1995) *Religion and Authority in Roman Carthage from Augustus to Constantine*. Oxford.

(2003) 'Magic in Roman law: the reconstruction of a crime', *CA* 22: 313–39.

Robert, L. (1968) 'Trois oracles de la 'Théosophie'', in *Compte-rendus des Séances. Académie des inscriptions et Belles-Lettres*. Paris.

Rogers, G. (1991) *The Sacred Identity of Ephesos: Foundation Myths of a Roman City*. London.

Rothaus, R. (1996) 'Christianization and de-paganization: the late antique creation of a conceptual frontier', in *Shifting Frontiers in Late Antiquity*, ed. R. Mathisen and H. Siven. Aldershot and Brookfield: 299–308.

Rother, C. (1915) *De Libanii arte rhetorica quaestiones selectae*. Breslau.

Roueché, C. (1984) 'Acclamations in the later Roman empire: new evidence from Aphrodisias', *JRS* 74: 181–8.

Rousseau, P. (1978) *Ascetics, Authority and the Church*. Oxford.

(1990) 'Christian asceticism and the early monks', in *Early Christianity: Origins and Evolution to AD 600 in Honour of W. H. C. Frend*. London: 112–22.

(1994) *Basil of Caesarea*. Berkeley.

(2002) 'The preacher's audience: a more optimistic view', in *Ancient History in a Modern University*, vol. II: *Early Christianity, Late Antiquity and Beyond*, ed. T. W. Hillard, R. A. Kearsley, C. E. V. Nixon and A. M. Nobbs. Grand Rapids, MI: 391–400.

(2002) *The Early Christian Centuries*. London.

Russell, J. B. (1982) 'The evil eye in early Byzantine society', XVI Internationaler, Byzantinisten Kongress, Akten II.3, *JÖByz* 32: 539–48.

(1995) 'The archaeological context of magic in the early Christian period', in *Byzantine Magic* ed. H. Maguire. Washington DC: 35–50.

Said, S. (2001) 'The discourse of identity in Greek rhetoric from Isocrates to Aristides', in *Ancient Perceptions of Greek Ethnicity*, ed. I. Malkin. Washington DC: 275–99.

Salzman, M. (1987) '"*Superstitio*" in the *Codex Theodosianus* and the persecution of the pagans', *VC* 41: 172–88.
Sandwell, I. (2001) 'Religious interaction between pagans and Christians in Antioch in the late fourth century'. London. Unpublished PhD dissertation.
  (2004) 'Christian self-definition in the fourth century AD: John Chrysostom on Christianity, imperial rule and the city', in *Culture and Society in Later Roman Antioch*, ed. I. Sandwell and J. Huskinson. Oxford: 35–58.
  (2005) 'Outlawing "magic" or outlawing "religion"? Libanius and the *Theodosian Code* as evidence for legislation against "pagan" practices', in *Understanding the Spread of Christianity in the First Four Centuries: Essays in Explanation*, ed. W. V. Harris. Leiden and Boston, MA: 87–124.
Sandwell, I. and Huskinson, J. (eds.) (2004) *Culture and Society in Later Roman Antioch*. Oxford.
Schatkin, M. (1988) *John Chrysostom as Apologist. With Special Reference to De incomprehensibili, Quod laeditur, Ad eos qui scandalizati sunt and Adversus oppugnatores vitae monasticae.* Thessaloniki.
Scheid, J. (2003) *An Introduction to Roman Religion*. Edinburgh.
Scholl, R. (1994) *Historische Beiträge zu den Julianischer Reden des Libanios*, Stuttgart.
Schouler, B. (1984) *La tradition hellénique chez Libanios*, vols. I–II. Lille.
  (1985) 'Hommages de Libanios aux femmes de son temps', *Pallas* 32: 123–48.
  (1986) 'Le déguisement de l'intention dans la rhétorique grecque', *Ktema. Civilisations de l'Orient, de la Grèce et de Rome Antiques* 11: 257–72.
  (1991) 'Hellénisme et humanisme chez Libanios', in *Hellenismos: quelques jalos pour une histoire de l'identité greque: actes du Colloque de Strasbourg, 25–27 Octobre 1989* (ed. S. Said). Leiden: 267–85.
Schouler, B. and Million, C. (1988) 'Les jeux olympiques d'Antioche', *Pallas* 34: 61–76.
Schwartz, S. (2001) *Imperialism and Jewish Society 200 B.C.E. to 640 C.E.* Princeton and Oxford.
Seeck, O. (1920) 'Libanius gegen Lucianus', *RhM* 73: 84–101.
Seiler, E.-M. (1998) *Konstantios II bei Libanios. Eine kritische Untersuchung des überlieferten Herrscherbildes.* Frankfurt, Bern and Paris.
Siegert, F. (1997) 'Homily and panegyrical sermon', in *The Handbook of Classical Rhetoric in the Hellenistic Period 330 BC to AD 400*, ed. S. E. Porter. Leiden, New York and Cologne: 421–43.
Sievers, G. R. (1969) *Das Leben des Libanius*, 2nd edn. Amsterdam.
Simon, M. (1964) *Versus Israel. Étude sur les relations entre chrétiens et juifs dans L'empire romain (135–425)*. Paris.
Smith, J. Z. (1995) 'Trading places', in *Ancient Magic and Ritual Power*, ed. M. Meyer and P. Mirecki. Leiden and New York: 20–7.
  (1978) 'The temple and the magician', in *Map Is Not Territory: Studies in the History of Religion*. Leiden: 172–89.
Smith, R. (1995) *Julian's Gods: Religion and Philosophy in the Thought and Action of Julian the Apostate.* New York.

Soler, E. (1999) 'Le sacré et la salut à Antioche au IVe siècle après J.-C.: pratiques festives et comportements religieux dans le processus de christianisation de la cite'. Rouen. Unpublished PhD dissertation.

(2004) 'D'Apollonius de Tyane à l'empereur Julien, l'importance d'Antioche comme lieu de pèlerinage et centre philosophique grecs', in *Antioch de Syrie. Histoire, images et traces de la ville antique*, ed. B. Cabouret, P.-L. Gaiter and C. Saliou. Paris: 381–99.

Sperber, D. (1975) *Rethinking Symbolism*. Cambridge.

Spiro, M. (1968) 'Religion: problems of definition and explanation', in *Anthropological Approaches to the Study of Religion*, ed. M. Banton. London: 85–126.

Steel, C. (2005) *Reading Cicero: Genre and Performance in Late Republican Rome*. London.

Stephens, J. (2001) 'Ecclesiastical and imperial authority in the writings of John Chrysostom: a reinterpretation of his political philosophy'. Santa Barbara. Unpublished PhD dissertation.

Stewart, C. (1991) *Demons and the Devil: Moral Imagination in Modern Greece*. Princeton.

(2001) 'Secularism as an impediment to anthropological research', *Journal of Social Anthropology* 9: 325–8.

Stewart C. and Shaw, R. (1994) *Syncretism/Anti-Syncretism: the Politics of Religious Synthesis*. London and New York.

Stewart, Z. (1972) *Essays on Religion and the Ancient World*. Oxford.

Stock, B. (1983) *The Implications of Literacy: Written Language and Models of Interpretation in the Eleventh and Twelfth Centuries*. Princeton.

(1990) *Listening for the Text: On the Use of the Past*. Baltimore.

Stowers, S. K. (1986) *Letter Writing in Graeco-Roman Antiquity*. Philadelphia.

Straub, J. (1962) 'Die Himmelfahrt des Julianus Apostata', *Gymnasium* 69: 310–26.

Swain, S. (2004) 'Sophists and emperors: the case of Libanius', in *Approaching Late Antiquity: the Transformation from Early to Late Empire*, ed. S. Swain and M. Edwards: 355–400.

Takács, S. A. (2000) 'Pagan cults at Antioch', in *Antioch: The Lost Ancient City* ed. C. Kondoleon. Princeton: 198–200.

Taylor, J. (1994) 'Why were the disciples first called "Christians" at Antioch? (Acts 11.26)', *RBi* 101: 75–94.

Taylor, H. N. (1995) 'The social nature of conversion in the early Christian world', in *Modelling Early Christianity: Social-scientific Studies of the New Testament in its Context*, ed. P. F. Esler. London and New York: 128–36.

Theodorou, E. (1997) 'S. Jean Chrysostome et la fête de Noël', *Lex Orandi* 40: 195–210.

Thiessen, G. (1982) 'The strong and the weak in Corinth: a sociological study of a theological problem', in *The Social Setting of Pauline Christianity: Essays on Corinth*, ed. G. Thiessen. Edinburgh: 121–43.

Trapp, M. (2003) *Greek and Latin Letters: an Anthology with Translation*. Cambridge and New York.

Treloar, A. (1973) 'Libanius and unrest among the pupils', *Prudentia* 5: 51–67.

Trombley, F. (1985) 'Paganism in the Greek world at the end of antiquity: the case of rural Anatolia and Greece', *HThR* 78: 327–52.
  (1994) *Hellenic Religion and Christianisation AD 370–529*, vols. I and II. Leiden.
  (2004) 'Christian demography in the *territorium* of Antioch (4th–5th c.): observations on the epigraphy', in *Culture and Society in Later Roman Antioch*, ed. I. Sandwell and J. Huskinson. Oxford: 59–85.
Trout, D. E. (1999) *Paulinus of Nola: Life, Letters and Poems*. Berkeley, Los Angeles and London.
Trzcionka, Silke (2004) 'Relating to the supernatural: a case study of fourth century Syria and Palestine'. Adelaide. Unpublished PhD dissertation.
Turner, V. W. (1969) *The Ritual Process: Structure and Anti-Structure*. London.
  (1982) *From Ritual to Theatre and Back: the Human Seriousness of Play*. New York.
  (1995) *Ritual Process: Structure and Anti-Structure*, 2nd edn. New York.
Urbainczyk, T. (2002) *Theodoret of Cyrrhus: the Bishop and the Holy Man*. Michigan.
Valevicius, M. (2000), 'Les 24 homélies *De Statuis* de Jean Chrysostome. Recherches nouvelles', *Revue des Études Augustiniennes* 46: 83–91.
Van Gennep (1977) *The Rites of Passage*. London [*Les rites de passages*, 1909].
Vandenburgh, B. H. (1955) 'Saint Jean Chrysostome et les spectacles', *ZRGG* 7: 36–41.
Versnel, H. S. (1981) 'Religious mentality in ancient prayer', in *Faith, Hope and Worship: Aspects of Religious Mentality in the Ancient World*, ed. H. S. Versnel. Leiden: 1–64.
  (1990) 'What's sauce for the goose is sauce for the gander: myth and ritual, old and new', in *Approaches to Greek Myth*, ed. L. Edmunds. Baltimore and London: 25–90. Revised in H. S. Versnel, *Transition and Reversal in Myth and Ritual*, 1993. Leiden: 15–88.
  (1991) 'Some reflections on the relationship magic-religion', *Numen* 38: 177–97.
Veyne, P. (1986) 'Une évolution du paganisme gréco-romain: injustice et piété des dieux. Leurs ordres ou "oracles"', *Latomus* 45: 259–83.
Vikan, G. (1984) 'Art, medicine and magic in early Byzantium', *Symposium on Byzantine Medicine*, ed. J. Scarborough, Dumbarton Oaks Papers 38. Washington DC: 65–86.
Vincent, J. (1974) 'The structuring of ethnicity', *Human Organization* 33.4: 375–9.
Vinson, M. (1994) 'Gregory Nazianzen's Homily 15 and the genesis of the Christian cult of the Maccabean martyrs', *Byzantion* 64: 166–92.
Voicu, S. (1996) 'Pseudo-Giovanni Crisostomo: I confine del corpus', *JbAC* 18: 105–15.
  (1997) 'Johannes Chrysostomus II (Pseudo-Chrysostomica)', *Reallexikon für Antike und Christentum* 19: 503–15.
  (2005) 'La volontà e il caso: la tipologia dei primi spuri di Crisostomo', in *Giovanni Crisostomo: Oriente e Occidente tra IV e V seclo*, 23 Incontro di Studiosi dell' Antichità Cristiana, Augustinianum 6–8 maggio 2004, Roma (Studia Ephemeridis Augustinianum 93). Rome: 101–18.

Vorderstrasse, T. (2004) 'The Romanization and the Christianization of the Antiochene region: the material evidence from three sites', in *Culture and Society in Later Roman Antioch*, ed. I. Sandwell and J. Huskinson. Oxford: 86–101.
Vos, G. de (1982) 'Ethnic pluralism: conflict and accommodation', in *Ethnic Identity: Cultural Continuities and Change*, ed. G. A. de Vos and L. Romanucci-Ross, 2nd edn. Palo Alto, CA: 349–79.
Walcott, R. (1978) *Envy and the Greeks: a Study in Human Behaviour*. Warminster.
Wallace, A. F. C. (1966) *Religion: an Anthropological View*. New York.
Wallace-Hadrill, D. S. (1982) *Christian Antioch: a Study of Early Christian Thought in the East*. Cambridge.
Ward-Perkins, B. (1998) 'The Cities', *Cambridge Ancient History*, vol. XIII: *The Late Empire AD 337–425*. Cambridge: 371–410.
Watkins, O. D. (1961) *A History of Penance: Being a Study of the Authorities*. New York.
Wellman, B. (2003) 'Structural analysis from method and metaphor to theory and substance', in *Social Structures: a Network Approach*, ed. B. Wellman and S. D. Berkowitz, 2nd edn. Toronto: 19–61.
Wellman, B. and Berkowitz, S. D. (eds.) (2003) *Social Structures: a Network Approach*, 2nd edn. Toronto.
Wellman, B., Carrington, P. J. and Hall, A. (2003) 'Networks as personal communities', in *Social Structures: a Network Approach*, ed. B. Wellman and S. D. Berkowitz, 2nd edn. Toronto: 130–84.
West, M. L. (1999) 'Towards monotheism', in *Pagan Monotheism in Late Antiquity*, ed. P. Athanassiadi and M. Frede. Oxford: 21–40.
Whitehouse, (1996) 'Rites of terror: emotion, metaphor, and memory in Melanesian initiation cults', in *Journal of the Royal Anthropological Institute* 2.4: 703–15.
Whitmarsh, T. (2001) *Greek Literature and the Roman Empire: the Politics of Imitation*. Oxford.
Wiemer H-U. (1994) 'Libanius on Constantine', *CQ* 44: 511–24.
    (1995a) *Libanios und Julian – Studien zum Verhältnis von Rhetorik und Politk im vierten Jarhundert n. Chr*. Munich.
    (1995b) 'Die Rangstellung des Sophisten Libanios unter den Kaisern Julian, Valens und Theodosius: mit einem Anhang über Abfassung und Verbreitung von Libanios' Rede für die Tempel (*Or*. 30)', *Chiron* 25: 89–130.
    (1996) 'Der sophist Libanios und die Bäcker von Antiocheia', *Athenaeum* 84: 527–48.
Wilken, R. L. (1983) *John Chrysostom and the Jews: Rhetoric and Reality in the Late Fourth Century*. California.
Wintjes, J. (2005) *Das Leben des Libanius*, Historische Studien der Universität Würzburg, Band 2. Rahden.
Wöhrle, G. (1995) 'Libanios' Religion', *Études Classiques* (Luxembourg) 7: 71–89.
Woodward, K. (1997) 'Concepts of identity and difference', in *Identity and Difference*, ed. K. Woodward. London: 15–29.

Wylie, A. L. B, (1992) 'John Chrysostom and his Homilies on the Acts of the Apostles: Reclaiming Ancestral Models for the Christian People'. Princeton. Unpublished PhD dissertation.

Yalçin-Heckmann, L. (2001) 'Secularism and anthropological practice', *Journal Social Anthropology* 9: 33–6.

Yarnold, E. (1972) 'Baptism and pagan mysteries in the fourth century', *The Heythrope Journal* 13: 247–67.

(1994) *The Awe Inspiring Rites of Initiation: the Origins of the RCIA*, 2nd edn. Edinburgh.

Young, F. M. (1979) *The Use of Sacrificial Ideas in Greek Christian Writers from the New Testament to John Chrysostom*. Cambridge.

Zetterholm, M. (2003) *The Formation of Christianity in Antioch: a Social-Scientific Approach to the Separation between Judaism and Christianity*. London and New York.

Index

Acacius 7 of Tarsus, 165, 229
Acacius 8/1, 229–30
Alexander 5/3, 106, 159
allegiance, religious, 6–8, 9, 91–2, 99–100
    strategic approaches to, 9, 26–7, 61–2, 100–11, 114–19, 163, 277–8
Ammianus Marcellinus, 19, 40, 97, 252, 261–2, 264
amulets, 4, 87, 267–9
    Chrysostom's view of, 267–8, 269
    Libanius' view of, 267
Anatolius 3/1, 100–4, 116
Anatolius 5/4, 227
Anatolius 9/6, 99
Antioch, 30
    archaeology of, 39–40
    Christian city, 34–5, 37–8, 43–6
    Greek city, 35, 40
    imperial city, 34–9
    literary sources for, 40
    religious context of, 39–47
    sacred identity of, 41
    saints and martyrs of, 133–7, 142–3
    see also Julian, Antioch and
Apollo, 40
    Temple of, at Daphne, 164, 165
Aristaenetus 1/1, 103, 235
Aristophanes of Corinth, 104–6, 225–6
asceticism, 252, 253–4
    female, 254, 255
    see also monks
audiences
    of letters, 25–6
    of orations, 25–6, 49, 52–3
    of preaching, 5, 9, 14–15, 29–30, 51–2, 54–5, 188–90, 255–6, 260; social status of, 192, 205–8; use of Greek practices, 262–3, 267–8, 269, 272

Babylas, Saint, 128, 133, 134–5
baptism and catechism, 66–8, 195–7, 198–203, 251
Bassianus 2, 112, 223, 237
believers, *see* faithful, the
Bourdieu, Pierre, 17–18, 20, 27, 28, 187

Caesarius 1/4 of Tarsus, 229–30
Caesarius 6/7, 58
Celsus 3/1, 170, 213, 225, 226, 228, 235
Christianity, 5, 18
    Antiochene, 126, 146
    disputes within, 45–6, 204–5
    Libanius' view of, 93, 95–6, 98–9
    relationship with state; Chrysostom's view of, 125–31; Libanius' view of, 154–5
    textuality of, 12, 27, 28
Christianization, 4, 10, 29
Christians
    Arian, 45–6, 88, 205
    in Chrysostom's writings, 3, 4
    in Libanius' classroom, 53
    in Libanius' writings, 111–13, 159–60, 165–6, 169, 174–6, 217–18, 236–7
    name of, 34, 133
    numbers in Antioch, 44
    terminology, 8, 11, 63, 92–3, 199, 202, 204
Chrysostom, John, 4, 48
    writings, 50–2, 56–8
    writing about religion, 11–12, 58–9
churches in Antioch, 17, 38, 39, 44–5, 188
city
    Christianization of, 132–43
    Chrysostom's views of, 132–43, 144–8
classical culture, 35, 151–2, 176
    religion and, 21–2, 108, 177–9
community, 32, 185
    Christian, 182, 183, 185–90, 194–8
    civic, 169–76
    textual, 14, 32, 184, 185–6, 190

Constantine, emperor, 19, 35, 38, 44, 115–16
  religious policy of, 216
Constantius, emperor, 26, 35–6, 100, 104, 154, 156, 158
  Libanius and, 219–20
  religious policy of, 170, 216–17
conversion, 118, 159–60
councils
  Church, 38
  civic, Christians among, 207, 208
Cynegius 3, 38, 156

Datianus 1, 100–3, 232
Demetrius 2/1 of Tarsus, 165, 228, 229
demons, 271, 273–5
  Chrysostom's view of, 88–90, 144, 147, 263, 264
  envy and, 273
  Fate and, 272
  Libanius' view of, 271–2
discourse
  Christian, 13, 15, 17, 27
  theories of, 13, 16
divination, 158, 261–2, 265–7
  Chrysostom's view of, 263–4
  Libanius' view of, 262, 264–5

Eucharist, 96, 197–8, 200, 202, 251
Eunapius, 222, 253
Eusebius of Caesarea
  political philosophy of, 125–32
Eusebius 17/21, 112, 159
Eusebius 40/2, 266
exegesis
  biblical, 11, 12, 77–80, 186
exorcism, 68, 195

faithful, the
  fideles, 5
  pistoi, 63
festivals
  Christian, 44, 135–7, 189–90, 208
  Graeco-Roman, 42, 166–8, 172–3, 208–9
  Jewish, 209–10
  secularization of, 167, 172–3
flattery, 117
  accusations of, 101, 102, 117–18, 222–4
Flavian, bishop of Antioch, 46, 129, 155, 254
Fortunatianus 1/1, 107–8, 213, 225, 226

Gallus, Caesar, 25, 36, 38
Gentiles
  nationes, 5
  ta ethnē, 64, 148

Greeks,
  Chrysostom's view of, 3, 4, 200
  Libanius' view of, 177–9

habitus, the, 17, 20, 28, 30
Helios, 71, 74
Hellenism, *see* classical culture

Iamblichus of Apamea, 177, 214
Iamblichus 2, 103–4
identity
  Christian, 4–6, 11–12, 64–5, 66–75, 80–1, 82–3, 90, 126, 147, 198, 276, 277
  civic, 31, 122, 132–43, 144–8, 160–9
  cultural, 149, 151, 176–80
  ethnic, 31, 123, 148–53
  Greek, 64–5, 66–75, 148–53, 176, 177
  Jewish, 64–5, 82–3
  political, 31, 123, 125–32, 154–60
  practice and, 245–6, 251–71, 276
  religious, 3–11, 28–9, 30, 61–2, 152, 251–71
  social, 122–3, 180
  textuality of, 11, 13
ideology, 17, 19, 27–8, 30
interaction, religious, 3–4, 8, 9–10, 23, 210–11, 279–80

Jews, 5, 143
  in Antioch, 46–7
  Libanius' view of, 113–14, 179, 238
  terminology, 11, 64, 93
Jovian, emperor, 36
  Libanius and, 220
  religious policy of, 220
Judaism, in Antioch, 5, 18, 131–43
  Chrysostom's view of, 85–6
Judaizers, 64, 82–4, 191
Julian, emperor, 19, 36, 104–8, 154
  Antioch and, 169–73
  Libanius and, 97–8, 163–5, 213, 216–31
  religious policy of, 9, 22, 97, 98–9, 154, 159, 222
  temple of Jerusalem and, 88, 142

knowledge, practical, 18, 26–7, 28

law
  Christian: Chrysostom's view of, 127, 130; Libanius' view of, 155–6
  Jewish; Chrysostom's view of, 131–2
  secular: Chrysostom's views of, 129–31; Graeco-Roman religion, against, 37–8, 44, 155, 157; Libanius' views of, 155–6
letters, 8, 48, 49
  social relations and, 231–4

Libanius, 6, 47–8, 49
  religion of, 21–3
  teacher and orator, 52–3
  writings, 48–50, 55–6, 57–8
  writings on religion, 20–3, 49–50, 58–9, 91–2

magic, 248–50
  Libanius' view of, 265
Maximus of Ephesus, 106, 213, 227
miracles, 15
  Chrysostom's view of, 269–71
Modestus 2, 6–7, 258–9
monks, 252
  Chrysostom's view of, 138–40, 252–3, 254–5
  Libanius' view of, 96, 155, 253
  ordinary Christians and, 255–6
  Syrian, 252, 254–5
monotheism, 93–4, 274

Neoplatonism, 42, 98, 214
networks, social, 183, 231–9
  role of religion in, 234–9
Nicocles, grammarian, 223–4

Optatus 1/2, 109–10
oratory, 55
Orion of Bostra, 112, 113, 159

paganism, 5
  see also religion, Graeco-Roman; and pagans, terminology
pagans
  faction, group or party, 22, 32, 182, 225–31
  terminology, 7, 8, 10–11, 63–4, 92, 93, 148–9, 179
  see also Greeks
Paul, Saint, Chrysostom's use of, 77–80, 84, 130–1, 190, 191, 192
Philippus, 107–8
poverty, Chrysostom on, 140
power
  of the Church, 17, 38
  political, 123
practice, religious, 5, 15, 17, 32–3, 158–9, 246–51
  Christian, 5, 73–4, 192–3, 252–3, 255–6, 257
prayer, 256–7, 260
  Chrysostom's view of, 257–8, 259–60
  Libanius' view of, 258–60
preaching, 11, 13, 14–15, 187–8

religion
  civic, 40, 41–3, 132, 160, 161–4
  definition of, 250
  Graeco-Roman, 10, 11, 18, 40–1; Chrysostom's view of, 71–3, 75–7, 88–9; Libanius' view of, 93–5, 96–8, 109, 154, 264; literature and, 23–5; see also paganism
  institutional, 273–5
  private, 32, 41, 118–19, 153, 156–60, 168, 171, 271, 273, 275–6, 278
  writing and, 11
repentance, 203
rhetoric, 26, 55–7
Riot of the Statues, 129, 137–9, 173–6
ritual, see practice, religious

sacrifice
  blood/animal: Christian views of, 68, 74, 76, 77–81, 251, 252; Libanius' view of, 94–5, 96–8, 106–7, 167
  Christian, 81, 86
  Jewish, 85–6
Secundius Salutius 3, 107–8, 213, 234
Seleucus 1, 213, 223, 228
sermons, 50–1
  provenance of, 50
social organization, 31–2
Spectatus 1, 111–12, 237
Symmachus, 235
synagogues, in Antioch, 47, 131

tact, 19, 115, 116
temples in Antioch, 40, 42–3
  destruction of, 155, 163, 164–5, 170
  secularization of, 41, 166
Tertullian, 5
Thalassius 2/2, 112, 237
Thalassius 4, 109
Themistius, 9, 115–16
Theodulus, 112
Theodoret of Cyrrhus, 40, 252, 254, 267, 268
Theodosius, emperor, 36, 109–11, 129, 154, 155–6
  Libanius and, 218, 220
  religious policy of, 216
toleration, religious, 123, 148, 153, 154, 159, 180
Tyche, of Antioch, 40, 41

Valens, emperor, 36, 37
Valentinian, emperor, 36
  Libanius and, 220
  religious policy of, 216

Zeus, 40, 169, 258, 259

For EU product safety concerns, contact us at Calle de José Abascal, 56–1°, 28003 Madrid, Spain or eugpsr@cambridge.org.

www.ingramcontent.com/pod-product-compliance
Ingram Content Group UK Ltd.
Pitfield, Milton Keynes, MK11 3LW, UK
UKHW022115130426
469895UK00017B/225